ANALECTA BIBLICA
INVESTIGATIONES SCIENTIFICAE IN RES BIBLICAS

—————————— 129 ——————————

TIMOTHY A. LENCHAK

"CHOOSE LIFE!"

A Rhetorical-Critical Investigation of Deuteronomy 28,69 – 30,20

EDITRICE PONTIFICIO ISTITUTO BIBLICO – ROMA 1993

IMPRIMI POTEST

Romae, die 24 Februarii 1993

R.P. Klemens STOCK, S.J.

Rector Pontificii Instituti Biblici

ISBN 88-7653-129-7

EDITRICE PONTIFICIO ISTITUTO BIBLICO
Piazza della Pilotta, 35 - 00187 Roma

TABLE OF CONTENTS

ACKNOWLEDGMENTS

This work is a revised edition of a doctoral dissertation defended at the Pontifical Gregorian University in January, 1992. I would like to acknowledge a debt of thanks to a number of people who have contributed to it.

Thanks first of all to my superiors and confreres in the Society of the Divine Word (S.V.D.), who have encouraged and supported my efforts and made this study possible financially.

Thanks as well to those whose guidance and encouragement have helped me considerably: Carroll Stuhlmueller, C.P., of Catholic Theological Union in Chicago, who during my seminary years taught me to love Scripture; Wilhelm Wuellner of Pacific School of Religion in Berkeley, California, who introduced me to rhetorical criticism; and Charles Conroy, M.S.C., the director of my doctoral dissertation.

And finally thanks to Albert Vanhoye, S.J., the editor of Analecta Biblica, who graciously accepted this work for publication in this series.

INTRODUCTION

In Exod 4,10 Moses claims that he is no orator (...לא איש דברים אנכי
כי כבד־פה וכבד לשׁן אנכי) and thus God promises to teach him what to
say and to send him a spokesman. Moses seems to have learned his
lessons well, for the Book of Deuteronomy cites a number of diverse
discourses which Moses gives just before his death. One of these, the
Third Address, is a magnificent appeal to choose the observance of
Yahweh's covenant over the worship of other gods. Moses draws upon
both rational arguments and emotional appeals in his attempt to
convince his audience to make the right choice. Not a bad job at all for
someone slow in speech and tongue!

In the past thirty years there has been a resurgence of interest in
rhetoric, both ancient and modern. This interest has been evident even in
biblical studies, especially New Testament studies. It seems worthwhile
then to examine the oratory of Moses as it is "recorded" in the Book of
Deuteronomy. Basing itself on ancient rhetoric and on the work of
Chaim Perelman and Lucie Olbrechts-Tyteca, this work attempts to
discover a rhetorical-critical methodology which can be applied to the
Third Discourse of Moses.

Chapter one provides the background and context of the Third
Discourse. It does not seek to examine every aspect of Deuteronomy but
rather limits itself to the suggestion that this book is a prime candidate
for rhetorical criticism. Chapter two gives a brief description and critique
of rhetorical criticism as practiced to date in Old Testament studies. It
also reviews some fundamental concepts of rhetoric and opts for a
methodology which follows the ancient divisions of rhetoric (*inventio,
dispositio,* and *elocutio*) while adapting itself to the New Rhetoric of
Perelman and Olbrechts-Tyteca.

Chapter three examines the audience and the rhetorical situation of
the Third Discourse of Moses. Chapter four investigates *inventio,* the
finding of arguments (whether those of ethos, pathos, or logos). Chapter
five briefly determines the rhetorical unit and the literary structure of our
text. Then it examines the *dispositio* or rhetorical arrangement of Dt
28,69 – 30,20. Chapter six looks at *elocutio* or style. Finally chapter seven
summarizes and concludes this investigation by drawing out some of the
theological aspects of the Third Discourse of Moses.

CHAPTER 1

THE RHETORICAL NATURE OF DEUTERONOMY

1.1 Introduction

The Book of Deuteronomy (henceforth Dt) is a unique combination of old and new, laws and exhortations, history and cult. More than any other book of the Pentateuch, it seems to embody in itself exactly what *t-orah* ("instruction," "directions," "law") means — a term it calls itself.[1] "This book of the *torah*" (29,20; 30,10; 31,26; cf. 28,61) is an exposition of faith and of ancient Hebrew life — in other words, a theology.[2] Dt is a work which seeks to *communicate* a specific message.

The Book of Dt presents itself as the story of the last moments in the life of Moses. More precisely, Moses gives his "valedictory address"[3] or farewell speech to the people of Israel gathered together on the plains of Moab. This valedictory address is actually a series of three prose speeches followed by two poems (a "Song" and a "Blessing").[4] After these comes a short description of Moses' death. Other prominent figures in the Bible (e.g., Joshua, David, Samuel) also present valedictory addresses, but this

---

[1] A. LEMAIRE, *Les écoles et la formation de la Bible dans l'Ancien Israël* (OBO 39; Fribourg/Göttingen 1981) 77; S.D. McBRIDE, "Polity of the Covenant People: The Book of Deuteronomy," *Int* 61 (1987) 231-232; E.W. NICHOLSON, *Preaching to the Exiles: A Study of the Prose Tradition in the Book of Jeremiah* (Oxford 1970) 124, n. 2; G. VON RAD, *Theologie des alten Testaments,* 4th ed., I, *Die Theologie der geschichtlichen Überlieferungen Israels* (München 1962) 234-235; cf. G. LIEDKE and C. PETERSEN, "תּוֹרָה," *THAT* II, 1041.

[2] G.E. WRIGHT, *Deuteronomy* (*IB* II; New York 1953) 313.

[3] M. WEINFELD, "Deuteronomy — The Present State of Inquiry," *JBL* 86 (1967) 255-256, especially n. 36; *Deuteronomy and the Deuteronomic School* (Oxford 1972) 10-11.

[4] N. LOHFINK prefers to divide Moses' oration into four separate addresses, based on the superscriptions found in 1,1; 4,44; 28,69; and 33,1. For all practical purposes this does not alter the traditional division of Deuteronomy, since there remain three orations plus an appendix; but it connects the third address with the "Song" of Moses. *Das Hauptgebot: Eine Untersuchung literarischer Einleitungsfragen zu Dtn. 5-11* (AnBib 20; Rome 1963) 3; "Der Bundesschluß im Land Moab: Redaktionsgeschichtliches zu Dt 28,69-32,47," *BZ,* N.F. 6 (1962) 32-35. Cf. also G. SEITZ, *Redaktionsgeschichtliche Studien zum Deuteronomium* (BWANT 93; Stuttgart 1971) 23-44, especially 24-35. WEINFELD, *Deuteronomy and the Deuteronomic School,* 32, 37, 45, points out that within the main speeches of Moses occur other speeches, such as military orations (Dt 1,29-33; 2,24-25.31; 3,21-22; 7,17-24; 9,1-6; 11,22-25; 31,1-6) and prayers (3,23-25; 21,8; 26,3b-10a.15).

is certainly the longest. The individual speeches of Moses' address are themselves not of the same length or tone: the first speech (1,1 – 4,43) is largely historical, the second (4,44-28,68) contains the lion's share of Dt and consists of both laws and parenesis, while the third speech (28,69 – 30,20) is a kind of peroration or conclusion. Within these speeches and poems can be found a wide variety of laws, historical recollections, instructions, and exhortations.

The Hebrew name of Dt is אלה הדברים ("these are the words"), a title which comes from the opening words of the book. This name describes succinctly but accurately the contents of Dt, for it supposedly cites the words of Moses to Israel immediately prior to this people's entrance into the promised land. Thus Dt purports to record the last *words* or speeches addressed by Moses to his fellow Israelites.[5]

These words spoken by Moses in Dt have been the subject of great interest and intense research, particularly in the past two centuries. Modern research on Dt began with De Wette's 1805 dissertation. In it he questioned the assumption that Dt was written by Moses and proposed that it was linked to the reform of King Josiah in 621 B.C.E..[6] Modern scholars have not always agreed on the origin and evolution of the Book of Dt, but few today hold that the work actually originates in the time of Moses. The "words" ascribed to Moses, then, are not quotations. Rather, they are a kind of fiction placed in the mouth of Israel's founder and lawmaker.

This valedictory address to the people of Israel is notable for its particular style and its peculiar characteristics. Many scholars have described Dt as a sermon or a series of sermons.[7] A comparison of Dt's

---

[5] P. CRAIGIE, *The Book of Deuteronomy* (The New International Commentary on the Old Testament; Grand Rapids 1976) 17.

[6] W.M.L. DE WETTE, *Dissertatio critico-exegetica qua Deuteronomium a prioribus Pentateuchi libris diversum, alius cuiusdam recentioris auctoris opus esse monstratur* (Jena 1805); see especially the note on pp. 13-14. Cf also S. LOERSCH, *Das Deuteronomium und seine Deutungen: Ein forschungsgeschichtlicher Überblick* (Stuttgarter Bibelstudien 22; Stuttgart 1967) 18-20. It is to be noted that DE WETTE was not the first to make these proposals, but his work sparked off the modern discussion on the origin and meaning of Dt.

[7] G. VON RAD, *Deuteronomium-Studien*, 2nd ed. (FRLANT 58; Göttingen 1948) 11, calls it "gepredigtes Gesetz." In "Die levitische Predigt in den Büchern der Chronik," *Gesammelte Studien zum Alten Testament* I (TBü 8; München 1965) 248, he says that L. KÖHLER first raised the question of the form-critical categories of the exhortations in Dt. KÖHLER concluded that the style of Dt was that of a preacher. Cf. G. VON RAD, "Deuteronomy," *IDB I, 834-835; Das fünfte Buch Mose: Deuteronomium*, 3rd ed. (ATD [Neues Göttinger Bibelwerk] 8; Göttingen 1978) 13. See also P. BUIS, *Le Deutéronome* (Verbum Salutis, Ancien Testament 4; Paris 1969) 9; P. BUIS and P. LECLERCQ, *Le Deutéronome* (Sources Bibliques; Paris 1963) 6; R.E. CLEMENTS, *Deuteronomy* (Old Testament Guides; Sheffield 1989) 18-19, 34-35; M. LACONI, *Deuteronomio* (Roma 1981), 21; R. MASON, "Some Echoes of the Preaching in the Second Temple? Tradition Elements

laws with those of the Book of the Covenant (Exod 20,22 – 23,33) reveals how much more like a sermon is the material in Dt.[8] Breit even calls Dt the first sermon that we still possess.[9] Whether or not such "sermons" were ever delivered in a public liturgy, whether or not they were purely literary compositions, they have a tone and a style which seem adaptable for public occasions.[10]

The authors of Dt were concerned with driving home a message. That message is presented with a sense of urgency, not as a calm reporting of the facts. Its appeal is to the conscience of each individual, to his or her mind and heart. Dt is no mere promulgation of laws. Instead it aims to bring each member of its audience into a proper relationship with God.[11] The message then is a personal one, and it involves every individual who hears it. Dt's style is intended to awaken faith and inspire obedience, and its message has been called a "kerygmatic theology".[12]

So Dt pleads, exhorts, promises, threatens, curses, commands, excites, and uses words effectively — in other words, the Deuteronomist can be described not merely as a preacher, but as an orator.[13]

---

in Zechariah 1-8," *ZAW* 96 (1984) 221-235; E. W. NICHOLSON, *Deuteronomy and Tradition* (Oxford 1967) 46; *Preaching to the Exiles*, 7; R. TOURNAY, *Voir et entendre Dieu avec les Psaumes; ou la liturgie prophétique du Second Temple à Jérusalem* (Cahiers de la revue biblique 24; Paris 1988) 20; WEINFELD, "The Present State of Inquiry," 262. The concept of levitical sermons is criticized by D. MATHIAS, " 'Levitische Predigt' und Deuteronomismus," *ZAW* 96 (1984) 23-49; and by W. CLABURN, "Deuteronomy and Collective Behavior" (Diss. Princeton Univ., 1968) 10, who claims that it reflects Protestant values.

[8] VON RAD, *Deuteronomium-Studien*, 10.

[9] H. BREIT, *Die Predigt des Deuteronomisten* (München 1933) 29-30.

[10] C. BREKELMANS, "Wisdom Influence in Deuteronomy," *La Sagesse de l'Ancien Testament* (BETL 51; ed. M. GILBERT) (Leuven 1979) 30.

[11] VON RAD, *Das fünfte Buch Mose*, 76-77; E. BLAIR, "An Appeal to Remembrance: The Memory Motif in Deuteronomy," *Int* 15 (1961) 42-43; BUIS and LECLERCQ, *Le Deutéronome*, 19; J. MYERS, "The Requisites for Response: On the Theology of Deuteronomy," *Int* 15 (1961) 29; J. A. THOMPSON, *Deuteronomy: An Introduction and Commentary* (The Tyndale Old Testament Commentaries; Leicester/Downers Grove 1974) 12.

[12] J. WATTS, "The Deuteronomic Theology," *RevExp* 74 (1977) 322-323.

[13] J. MALFROY, "Sagesse et loi dans le Deutéronome," *VT* 15 (1965) 58. He also quotes J. NOUGAYROL from *Les Sagesses du Proche-Orient ancien* (ed. J. LECLANT; Paris 1964) 48. N. LOHFINK, "Die Bundesurkunde des Königs Josias (Eine Frage an die Deuteronomiumsforschung)," *Bib* 44 (1963) 495, prefers to avoid the term "sermon" and to use instead "rhetorical style." Cf. R. MOULTON, *The Literary Study of the Bible: An Account of the Leading Forms of Literature Represented in the Sacred Writings Intended for English Readers* (London 1896) 445.

The author of Deuteronomy has endowed the book with the typical features of an oration. The rhetorical technique is here fully developed. As is expected of a good orator the author directs his message to the heart and emotions of his audience, enlivening and variegating the ancient traditions by retelling them in such a manner as to capture and maintain the interest of his listeners.[14]

Rhetoric was not something foreign to the authors of Dt. They may not have theorized about their discourses, but they certainly knew what they were doing when they wrote this work.[15] This chapter will review some of the more important features of Dt which reveal its nature as rhetorical. These features have already been eamined by numerous exegetes, even if they have seldom used the term "rhetoric" when describing them.

1.2 Style and Pedagogy of Deuteronomy

1.2.1 Language

"Le style du Deutéronome est un des plus originaux de la Bible".[16] Dt's literary style has been consistently described as characteristic, homogeneous, and easy to recognize. It contrasts sharply with that of the rest of the Pentateuch, and it pervades all Dt except for the poetic passages in chapters 32 and 33. One of the difficulties faced by those engaged in source criticism or *Literarkritik* in Dt has been this homogeneity or similarity of style and language.[17]

This deuteronomic style is marked by a continual repetition of certain words and set phrases.[18] These idioms and expressions were not necessarily created by the authors of Dt, since many can be found in earlier works. But they do represent a specific jargon reflecting the

---

[14] WEINFELD, *Deuteronomy and the Deuteronomic School*, 3, 171-172. See also S. R. DRIVER, *A Critical Commentary on Deuteronomy*, 3rd ed. (ICC; Edinburgh 1895), lxxxvi-lxxxvii; H. FOWLER, *A History of the Literature of Ancient Israel* (New York 1927) 184-189.

[15] CLEMENTS, *Deuteronomy*, 35; LOHFINK, *Das Hauptgebot*, 191; D. MCCARTHY, *Treaty and Covenant*, 2nd ed. (AnBib 21A; Rome 1981) 204-205.

[16] BUIS, *Le Deutéronome*, 29. Cf. DRIVER, *Deuteronomy*, lxxvii, lxxxvi; N. HABEL, *Literary Criticism of the Old Testament* (Philadelphia 1971) 12; WEINFELD, "The Present State of Inquiry," 250-251; *Deuteronomy and the Deuteronomic School*, 1.

[17] NICHOLSON, *Deuteronomy and Tradition*, 26; G. ORMANN, "Die Stilmittel im Deuteronomium," *Festschrift für Leo Baeck* (Berlin 1938) 39; A. PENNA, *Deuteronomio* (La Sacra Bibbia; Torino 1976) 4, 10; J. A. SOGGIN, *Introduzione all'Antico Testamento: Dalle origini alla chiusura del Canone alessandrino*, 4th ed. (Biblioteca di cultura religiosa 14; Brescia 1987) 154; THOMPSON, *Deuteronomy*, 30; WRIGHT, *Deuteronomy*, 318.

[18] Examples are given in DRIVER, *Deuteronomy*, lxxviii-lxxxiv; WEINFELD, *Deuteronomy and the Deuteronomic School*, 320-365; and WRIGHT, *Deuteronomy*, 318-319.

religious upheaval of its time.[19] The repetition of these expressions gives a certain rhythm to the book, a rhythm characterized by rolling periods, expansion and contraction, a certain redundancy, even a feeling of warmth and color. Although the tone is urgent, that doesn't prevent it from relaxing at times to explain, qualify, or refine. Despite its repetitiveness Dt strikes one as simple, fluid, and lucid. It has been compared with music and with a flowing tide on a beach.[20] The style has also been termed "baroque."[21] Although it may at times appear monotonous to the modern reader, it actually exhibits a remarkable variety: freedom in the order of words, a moderate use of the waw-consecutive, absence of coordination comparable to poetry, frequent use of participial phrases and absolute infinitives, the use of "full" forms (e.g., אנכי instead of אני, לבב instead of לב), and repetition of vocabulary in varying combinations.[22]

1.2.2 Parenesis

A good part of Dt, especially those sections known as the "framework to the deuteronomic law" (chaps. 4-11 and 29-30),[23] could be

---

[19] WEINFELD, *Deuteronomy and the Deuteronomic School*, 1. There has been a good amount of discussion on the language in Dt and its origin. Obviously it did not suddenly appear out of the blue, and often it is related to similar language in Hosea and E. Cf. H. L. GINSBERG, *The Israelian Heritage of Judaism* (Texts and Studies of the Jewish Theological Seminary of America 24; New York 1982) 19-24; D. GREENWOOD, "The Origins of the Deuteronomic Literature," *Proceedings of the Sixth World Congress of Jewish Studies,* I (ed. A. SHINAN; Jerusalem 1977) 194-195; H. PREUSS, *Deuteronomium* (Erträge der Forschung 164; Darmstadt 1982) 175; WEINFELD, *Deuteronomy and the Deuteronomic School,* 366-370; "The Emergence of the Deuteronomic Movement: The Historical Antecedents," *Das Deuteronomium: Entstehung, Gestalt, und Botschaft* (BETL 68; ed. N. LOHFINK) (Leuven 1985) 83-89. The style and language of Dt was continued and expanded by the so-called Deuteronomic/Deuteronomistic School (LOHFINK, *Das Hauptgebot,* 51), and can be found even in prophetic and psalmodic literature (WEINFELD, "The Present State of Inquiry," 250-251). Outside of the Deuteronomistic History this language can be found especially in the book of Jeremiah: J.P. HYATT, "Jeremiah and Deuteronomy," *JNES* 1 (1942) 164-165; WRIGHT, *Deuteronomy,* 319. CLABURN, "Deuteronomy and Collective Behavior," suggests that this language and style reflects the propaganda of a mass movement in a time of social upheaval.

[20] G. A. SMITH, *The Legacy of Israel* (ed. E. BEVAN and C. SINGER: Oxford 1927) 17. See also N. LOHFINK, "Die deuteronomistische Darstellung des Übergangs der Führung Israels von Moses auf Josue: Ein Beitrag zur alttestamentlichen Theologie des Amtes," *Scholastik* 37 (1962) 32; J. FICHMAN, *'Arugot* (Jerusalem 1954), 248-251.

[21] LOERSCH, *Das Deuteronomium und seine Deutungen,* 11; C.J. LABUSCHAGNE, "Divine Speech in Deuteronomy," *Das Deuteronomium: Entstehung, Gestalt und Botschaft* (ed. N. LOHFINK) 120.

[22] BUIS and LECLERCQ, *Le Deutéronome,* 11-12.

[23] C. LEVIN, *Die Verheißung des neuen Bundes in ihrem theologiegeschichtlichen Zusammenhang* (FRLANT 137; Göttingen 1985) 83; R. SMEND, *Die Entstehung des Alten Testaments* (Stuttgart 1978) 73-74.

termed "parenetic." In general this does not mean so much a particular literary genre as an attitude or tone which arises from the text and influences its form.[24] *Parenesis* may be described by words and expressions such as "exhortation", "encouragement," "incitement," "inducement," perhaps even "pleading," "a sense of urgency," or "a call to action." Parenesis may promote social order or question it; in any case it reflects social conditions and didactic aims.[25]

This parenetic element is the most characteristic and perhaps also the most important feature of the book, for through it Dt's authors are stressing certain fundamental religious and moral principles. The "sermons" of Dt are concerned to stir up the right spirit, to appeal to the emotions and conscience of each individual in Israel, and to drive home the message of obedience to Yahweh, who is to be loved with one's whole heart and soul.

Although largely located within the "framework," some parenesis can be found even within the legal code of Dt. The authors are obviously not satisfied with simply collecting or announcing a series of laws. They also provide motives for observing those laws.[26] This style of exhortation is certainly leisurely and quiet in comparison with that of some of the prophets. Yet Dt also expresses a strong sense of urgency.[27] This sense of urgency shows that the authors wrote with a keen sense of the dangers of their day.[28]

1.2.3 Appeal to the Individual

This parenesis of Dt appeals to the heart,[29] to the individual's inner disposition. Obedience is not merely a matter of legalism, that is, of

---

[24] LOHFINK, *Das Hauptgebot*, 271; VON RAD, *Theologie des Alten Testaments* I, 233.

[25] E. W. NICHOLSON, "Deuteronomy's Vision of Israel," *Storia e tradizioni di Israele: Scritti in onore di J. Alberto Soggin* (ed. D. GARRONE and F. ISRAEL; Brescia 1991) 200; L. PERDUE, "The Social Character of Paraenesis and Paraenetic Literature," *Paraenesis: Act and Form, Semeia* 50 (1990) 5-39; L. STACHOWIAK, "Auf den Spuren der Paränese im Alten Testament," *ColT* 46 (1976) 59-80, especially 79-80; WEINFELD, *Deuteronomy and the Deuteronomic School*, 3.

[26] DRIVER, *Deuteronomy*, ii-iii. Actually Dt is not the only Old Testament book which provides motives for obeying the law. See B. GEMSER, "The Importance of the Motive Clause in Old Testament Law," *VTS* 1 (1953) 50-66.

[27] FOWLER, *A History of the Literature of Ancient Israel*, 184-189. Cf. BUIS and LECLERCQ, *Le Deutéronome*, 19; MALFROY, "Sagesse et loi," 56-57; NICHOLSON, *Deuteronomy and Tradition*, 46; THOMPSON, *Deuteronomy*, 12; VON RAD, *Das fünfte Buch Mose*, 13.

[28] CLEMENTS, *Deuteronomy*, 34, 55; VON RAD, *Theologie des Alten Testaments* I, 236.

[29] It's no accident that "heart" appears frequently in Dt: 4X as לב (Dt 4,11; 28,65; 29,3.18) and 47X as לבב (1,28; 2,30; 4,9.29.39; 5,26; 6,5.6; 7,17; 8,2.5.14.17; 9,4.5; 10,12.16; 11,13.16.18; 13,4; 15,7.9.10; 17,17.20; 18,21; 19,6; 20,3.8[2X]; 26,16; 28,28.47.67; 29,17.18;

outwardly conforming to the law. Dt expects and demands an inner acceptance of the covenant regulations, a personal moral decision, a response of love. The peculiar urgent tone of Dt thus appeals to the individual, who is free to choose and is not forced to obey.[30] In Dt the individual feels personally called and involved, for every reader or listener is addressed in warm and even passionate language, language which is not only rational but also emotional. Belonging to the people of Yahweh is no longer a guarantee of welfare or salvation: each individual must respond to God's call and avoid the folly of sin (cf. 29,18-20). This interest in the individual also occurs in other works of the Old Testament (e.g., Ezek 14,12-20; 18,4-5; Jer 31,29-31).[31]

So the aim is to persuade and not merely to command, to encourage rather than to force. This appeal to the individual is made through such techniques as the use of the first person by the speaker, the direct form of address, references to a common history, and the use of verbs which might indicate the right attitude toward the law (hear, learn, keep, observe, do, etc.).[32] Expressions such as "your eyes see" or "you have

---

30,1.2.6[3X].10.14.17; 32,10.46. Cf. MALFROY, "Sagesse et loi," 54; F. STOLZ, "לֵב," THAT I, 861. One favorite deuteronomic/deuteronomistic expression is בכל לבב ובכל נפש (ובכל מאד) "with all the heart and all the soul (and all the might)": Dt 4,29; 6,5; 10,12; 11,13; 13,4; 26,16; 30,2.6.10; Josh 22,5; 23,4; 1 Kgs 2,4; 8,48; 2 Kgs 23,3.25; Jer 32,41. Cf. WEINFELD, Deuteronomy and the Deuteronomic School, 334. For the ancient Hebrews the heart was the seat of the mind and the will as well as of certain emotions. The heart therefore was a kind of symbol for the inner life of a human being. Cf. R. LE DÉAUT, "Le thème de la circoncision du coeur (Dt XXX 6; Jér IV 4) dans les versions anciennes (LXX et Targum) et à Qumran," VTS 32 (1981) 179-180; MALFROY, "Sagesse et loi," 60; STOLZ, "לֵב," 862-863; VON RAD, Theologie des Alten Testaments I, 238-239; H. W. WOLFF, Anthropologie des Alten Testaments (München 1973) 68-95; WRIGHT, Deuteronomy, 374.

[30] G. BRAULIK, Die Mittel deuteronomischer Rhetorik (AnBib 68; Rome 1978) 142; BREIT, Die Predigt, 216; CLEMENTS, Deuteronomy, 8; W. EICHRODT, Theologie des Alten Testaments. Teil I: Gott und Volk. 7th ed. (Stuttgart/Göttingen 1962) 49; J. GOLDINGAY, Theological Diversity and the Authority of the Old Testament (Grand Rapids 1987) 147; LACONI, Deuteronomio, 22; B. LINDARS, "Torah in Deuteronomy," Words and Meanings (FS. D.W. Thomas; ed P.R. ACKROYD and B. LINDARS) (Cambridge 1968) 129; LOHFINK, Das Hauptgebot, 279; McCARTHY, Treaty and Covenant, 187; STACHOWIAK, "Auf den Spuren der Paränese," 69-70; THOMPSON, Deuteronomy, 76.

[31] The exile and the last years of the monarchy appear to have been a period of growing awareness of one's individuality both in Israel and throughout the Near East. See BUIS, Le Deutéronome, 138, 213-214; CLABURN, "Deuteronomy and Collective Behavior," 105; R. LIWAK, "Literary Individuality as a Problem of Hermeneutics in the Hebrew Bible," Creative Biblical Exegesis: Christian and Jewish Hermeneutics through the Centuries (ed. B. UFFENHEIMER and H. G. REVENTLOW; JSOTSS 59) (Sheffield 1988) 91-92; L. PERLITT, "'Ein einzig Volk von Brüdern': Zur deuteronomischen Herkunft der biblischen Bezeichnung 'Bruder,'" Kirche: Festschrift für Günther Bornkamm (ed. D. LÜHRMANN and G. STRECKER; Tübingen 1980) 51; VON RAD, Theologie des Alten Testaments I, 405-409.

seen" (e.g., 11,7; 29,1) give the listeners the feeling that they themselves
have participated in important communal experiences. Repetition and
rhetorical questions reinforce such feelings.[33]

1.2.4 Didacticism

Dt is a strongly didactic work motivated by a desire to instruct
which is perhaps greater than that of any other book in the Old Testament.[34] Weinfeld even claims that the use of writing for didactic purposes
originates with Dt.[35] Parenesis is a didactic technique reminiscent of the
wisdom tradition, and the style of Dt has been called not only that of the
preacher but also that of the teacher.[36] Dt could be understood as a kind
of instruction manual or teaching instrument, one which is at the same
time an exposition of the faith.[37]

This didacticism can be seen in the vocabulary used by Dt. The verb
למד (qal: "learn"; piel: "teach") doesn't even occur in the Pentateuch
outside Dt, which uses it frequently.[38] Also appearing in Dt are יסר

---

[32] G. Braulik, *Deuteronomio: Il testamento di Mosè* (Bibbia per tutti; Assisi 1987) 6;
A. D. H. Mayes, *Deuteronomy* (New Century Bible Commentary; Grand Rapids 1979),
58; Penna, *Deuteronomio*, 33.

[33] Weinfeld, *Deuteronomy and the Deuteronomic School*, 173.

[34] E. Achtemeier, "Plumbing the Riches: Deuteronomy for the Preacher," *Int* 61
(1987) 276; Claburn, "Deuteronomy and Collective Behavior," 58-59; Clements,
Deuteronomy, 17, 49; N. Lohfink, "Der Glaube und die nächste Generation: Das
Gottesvolk der Bibel als Lerngemeinschaft," *Das Jüdische am Christentum: Die verlorene
Dimension* (Freiburg 1987) 144-166; "Glauben lernen in Israel," *Katechetische Blätter* 108
(1983) 84-99; "Wie stellt sich das Problem Individuum-Gemeinschaft in Deuteronomium
1,6-3,29?" *Scholastik* 35 (1960) 406; P. Miller, "'Moses My Servant,': The Deuteronomic
Portrait of Moses," *Int* 61 (1987) 246-248; Penna, *Deuteronomio*, 30-31; Driver,
Deuteronomy, xvii; Thompson, *Deuteronomy*, 12; Von Rad, *Das fünfte Buch Mose*, 65;
"Die levitische Predigt," 248.

[35] Weinfeld, *Deuteronomy and the Deuteronomic School, 164.*

[36] Driver, *Deuteronomy*, xvii; Greenwood, "Origins," 192; Lindars, "Torah in
Deuteronomy," 129. It is not always possible to establish an absolute distinction between
preaching and teaching, since teaching may contain proclamation or other "homiletic"
qualities, while the sermon often conveys information. Among Christians preaching is
usually considered prior to teaching, since the teaching ministry developed largely as a
response to the needs of those converted by preaching. Cf. D. Ferguson, *Biblical
Hermeneutics: An Introduction* (London 1987) 120.

[37] G. Braulik, *Deuteronomium 1-16,17* (Die Neue Echter Bibel; Würzburg 1986)
14-15; R. Merendino, "La via della vita (Dt 30,15-20)," *ParSpV* 5 (1982) 38, 51;
Thompson, *Deuteronomy*, 12-13; Von Rad, *Das fünfte Buch Mose*, 21. Cf. A. Lemaire, *Les
écoles et la formation de la Bible*, 76.

[38] Breit, *Die Predigt*, 164; Lohfink, *Das Hauptgebot*, 194; Weinfeld, *Deuteronomy
and the Deuteronomic School*, 303; "The Present State of Inquiry," 256. Of the 94
occurrences of the root, 17 are in Dt: 7 times in *qal*: 4,10; 5,1; 14,23; 17,19; 18,9; 31,12.13;
and 10 times in *piel*: 4,1.5.10.14; 5,28; 6,1; 11,19; 20,18; 31,19. 31,19.22. Cf. E. Jenni,
"למד" *THAT* I, 872.

("chastise," "discipline," "teach") and its derivative מוסר (4,36; 8,5; 11,2 מוסר; 21,18; 22,18). Weinfeld calls the use of the vocative, the imperative (שמע ישראל), and characteristic forms such as ועתה "standard rhetorical terms which give the book the style of a didactic speech."[39]

But there is other evidence of Dt's didacticism as well. Like the Book of Proverbs, Dt mentions not only fatherly discipline (13,1; 19,18; 29,17) but also divine discipline (8,5).[40] In Dt the ark seems to have little more than a didactic function, since its only purpose is to house the tables of the covenant (10,1-5).[41] The doctrine that obedience and virtue are rewarded while disobedience and vice are punished is an important pedagogical principle emphasized in Dt.[42] The frequent repetitions can also be seen as a pedagogical method to impress the listener and to help him or her to remember the book's message.[43]

In fact Dt often has a command to "remember" (5,15; 6,12; 7,18; 8,2.18; 9,7; 16,3; 24,9; cf. 8,11.18-19, which orders the people not to forget). The exhortations of Dt generally attempt to help Israel recall what Yahweh has done for it.[44] Even certain laws in this book call upon Israel to remember, giving them a strongly didactic tone. One motive of the law of the release of slaves (15,12-18), for example, is the memory that Israel too is a redeemed slave. Such didactic calls to remembrance can also be seen in the laws of the feasts of Passover (16,3) and of Weeks (16,12), laws on kindness to the sojourner (24,18.22), and the confession on the discharge of the tithe (26,13-15).[45] By remembering, the past is

---

[39] WEINFELD, Deuteronomy and the Deuteronomic School, 176.

[40] Ibid., 303.

[41] Ibid., 208.

[42] DRIVER, Deuteronomy, xxxii-xxxiii.

[43] J. G. McCONVILLE, Law and Theology in Deuteronomy (JSOTSS 33; Sheffield 1984) 64.

[44] BLAIR, "An Appeal to Remembrance," 44; H. EISING, "זָכַר," TWAT I, 575; J. NTAGWARARA, "Alliance d'Israël au pays de Moab (Dt 28,69-30,20): Analyse exégétique, histoire rédactionnelle et théologie," (Diss. Univ. de Sciences Humaines de Strasbourg, 1983) 221; SMEND, Die Entstehung des Alten Testaments, 73. BLAIR, "An Appeal to Remembrance," 45, lists the following as the objects of remembrance in Dt:

1. The fact of servitude in Egypt (16,12; 24,22).
2. The deliverance from Egyptian servitude (often with some reference to the wonders and judgments of God) (5,15; 6,12; 7,18f.; 8,14; 15,15; 16,3; 24,18).
3. The giving of the covenant at Horeb (4,9-13.23).
4. Yahweh himself — his unity, his commandments (4,39-40; 6,6; 8,11.14.18.19; 11,18; 26,13).
5. The experiences in the wilderness — Israel's rebelliousness, God's providence and discipline (8,2.14-16; 9,7; 24,9).
6. What Amalek did (25,17-19).
7. The days of old (32,7).

[45] McCONVILLE, Law and Theology in Deuteronomy, 84-85. The root זכר may have been originally a cultic term. Cf. W. SCHOTTROFF, "זכר," THAT I, 509.

brought into contact with the present for the purpose of evoking some action. Thus an individual or a family is made conscious of belonging to a specific people, and through this sense of belonging one feels the necessity of obedience. Remembering is essential for cultural and religious continuity.[46]

To ensure the remembrance of Israel's history, religious traditions, and laws, Dt insists on the instruction of children. The audience is repeatedly charged to teach all these things to its offspring (4,9.10.14; 5,30-31; 6,1.7-9.20-21; 8,5; 11,19; 31,19.22). In 6,20 this instruction is prompted by questions supposedly initiated by the children themselves, the so-called *Kinderfrage*.[47] In fact Dt frequently includes questions of various sorts; some of these are rhetorical questions, while others are part of question-and-answer schemes (4,32-34; 7,17; 9,2; 12,30; 18,21; 29,23; 31,17).

1.3 Direct Address

1.3.1 First and Second Persons

Since Dt purports to be a farewell speech, it is only natural and logical that it is written in the first and second persons, that is, a speaker ("I" or "we") addresses an audience ("you" singular or plural). Only about 56 verses in the entire book are "reporting speech," as Polzin calls it — these are the narrator's direct utterances.[48] The rest of the book is "reported speech," a series of direct quotations of Moses — although the situation is actually more complex than it may at first appear. Moses

---

[46] BLAIR, "An Appeal to Remembrance," 42, 44; B. CHILDS, *Memory and Tradition in Israel* (SBT 37; London 1962) 50-51, 74-75, 78-79; EISING, "זכר," 575; M. FISHBANE, *Text and Texture: Close Readings of Selected Biblical Texts* (New York 1979), 79; H. GROSS, "Zur Wurzel *zkr*," *BZ*, N.F. 4 (1960) 236-237; SCHOTTROFF, "זכר," 517.

[47] Other examples: Exod 12,26-27; 13,14-16; Josh 4,6-7.21-24. See J.A. SOGGIN, "Kultätiologische Sagen und Katechese im Hexateuch," *VT* 10 (1960) 341-347. See also LOHFINK, *Das Hauptgebot*, 116; J. LOZA, "Les catéchèses étiologiques dans l'Ancien Testament," *RB* 78 (1971) 481-500; J. MYERS, "The Requisites for Response," 23. BUIS, *Le Deutéronome*, 460-461, calls 6,10-25 a catechetical "schéma de proclamation des comandements" which follows the example of Exod 12,25-27. It should also be noted that children/offspring or future generations are mentioned frequently in Dt: 1,39; 4,9-10.25.40; 5,14; 6,2.7.20-21; 7,3-4; 8,5; 11,2.19.21; 12,12.18.25.28; 14,2; 16,11.14; 18,10; 21,16-17.18-20; 24,16; 25,5.6; 28,32.41.46.53-57; 29,21; 30,2.6.9.19; 31,12-13.21; 32,5.19-20.46; 34,4. VON RAD, *Theologie des Alten Testaments* I, 238, indicates that this appeal to children and future generations was evidence of a dangerous weakening of the faith, for later generations were no longer familiar with the experiences of their ancestors.

[48] R. POLZIN, *Moses and the Deuteronomist: A Literary Study of the Deuteronomic History*; Part One: *Deuteronomy, Joshua, Judges* (New York 1980) 29. The reporting speech includes 1,1-5; 2,10-12.20-23; 3,9.11.13b-14; 4,41-5,1a; 10,6-7.9; 27,1a.9a.11; 28,69; 29,1a; 31,1.7a.9-10a.14a.14c-16a.22-23a.24-25.30; 32,44-45.48; 33,1; 34,1-4a.5-12.

often quotes others, so there are quotes within quotes. If one takes into account that every literary work speaks through a narrator (who gives the "reporting speech"), then one can describe such quotations as "an utterance (of the person quoted by Moses) within an utterance (of Moses) within an utterance (of the narrator)."[49] In 1,28 the narrator quotes Moses quoting Israel quoting its reconnaissance team. In 2,4-5; 32,26.40-42 the narrator quotes Moses who is quoting himself.

In a number of places in Dt the distinction between Moses, Yahweh, and the narrator tends to blur, and the listener or reader is not quite sure whose voice is being heard.[50] Unlike the other books of the Pentateuch, in Dt it is usually Moses who issues the laws. In fact, Moses is the normal speaker in this work, and he speaks with a voice of authority, an authority closely associated with that of God. In Dt 5,6-21 Moses quotes Yahweh proclaiming the Ten Commandments. But he also carefully explains his own commission to listen to and report God's other laws and regulations (4,10-14; 5,1-5.22-31). Polzin observes that in the Second Address Moses both reports and interprets God's words in such a way that it is sometimes impossible to distinguish between what belongs to Moses and what belongs to God.[51]

The use of the direct address is suitable for Dt's urgent appeal to the individual and to its parenetic style. It makes the exhortation more effective by directing it to those who are being addressed. The author is attempting to get his audience to identify with Israel on the plains of Moab. The fictitious words of Moses in direct address to an imaginary group of ancestors force themselves upon all those later generations

---

[49] Ibid., 25.

[50] Examples of places where Moses' and Yahweh's voices become confused or indistinguishable are 7,4; 11,13-15; 17,3; 28,20; 29,4-5. Cf. H. CAZELLES, "Pentateuch: Deutéronome," *SDB* VII, 814; LOHFINK, *Das Hauptgebot*, 61, n. 7; "Kerygmata des deuteronomistischen Geschichtswerks," *Die Botschaft und die Boten* (FS. Hans Walter Wolff; ed. J. JEREMIAS and L. PERLITT) (Neukirchen/Vluyn 1981) 90.

[51] POLZIN, *Moses and the Deuteronomist,* 55, 57; cf. LOHFINK, *Das Hauptgebot,* 61-62. POLZIN believes that the Deuteronomist, his term for the final redactor of the entire Deuteronomistic History, is carefully eliminating the distinction between the authority of Moses and that of the (Deuteronomist) narrator: "So that the supreme blurring of the words of God and of Moses in the lawcode serves the same purpose as the other devices of the Deuteronomist we have seen that overtly exalted the unique status of Moses: it contributes toward a subtle but powerful exaltation of the authority of the narrator's words to such an extent that when the narrator is ready to speak in his own voice so as to make the distinction between his words and Moses' practically irrelevant (Josh - 2 Kgs), the reader will have been already prepared for this by the hypostasis of the divine-Mosaic words of the lawcode" (57). L. ESLINGER, *Into the Hands of the Living God* (JSOTSS 84; BLS 24; Sheffield 1989) 123-124, n. 1, disagrees with POLZIN that there is a blending of voices in Dt.

listening to Dt. These ancestors become present to all those who listen to these words, and the audience has a sense of communion with them.[52]

The use of the first person singular, at least when it is phrased as a self-identification of Yahweh (e.g., Dt 5,6; 29,5), is considered to have originated in a liturgical context.[53] In Dt, however, the use of the first (and second) person fits in well with its form as a valedictory oration or farewell address. One expects Moses to address his people in the second person and to use the first person for himself. A sermon or an oration is not a mere recitaton or report. It engages both speaker and audience, and it is natural and appropriate to use the first and second persons.[54]

In Dt Moses occasionally uses the first person plural, thus identifying himself with his fellow Israelites. The phrases "God of *our* fathers" and "*our* God" appear 25 times in Dt, but it is used only once in the lawcode, which normally prefers "your God" or similar phrases.[55] Polzin concludes that Moses in chapter five leaves off speaking to his audience sometimes as a fellow Israelite and from this point on speaks only in his role as teacher.[56]

1.3.2 Singular and Plural Forms of Address

The use of the second person in Dt poses a problem, however, for Moses addresses Israel in both the singular and the plural. Often one form is mixed with the other. Why does Moses sometimes address the people in the singular and at other times in the plural? Why does he

---

[52] Imaginary direct speech often increases a sense of presence in an oration. Traditional rhetorical devices which use some form of imaginary direct speech include *prosopopoeia* (an imaginary or absent person is represented as speaking or acting), *sermocinatio* (fictitious attribution of words to a person), *dialogism* (fictitious attribution of words to a group of persons engaged in a dialogue), and *apostrophe* (breaking off discourse to address directly some person or thing either present or absent).

[53] BUIS, *Le Deutéronome*, 117; LOHFINK, *Das Hauptgebot*, 61-62; McCARTHY, *Treaty and Covenant*, 219; J. REITER, "Der Bundesschluß im Land Moab: Eine exegetische Studie zu Deuteronomium 29,1-20" (Diss. Universität Wien 1984) 38; VON RAD, *Das fünfte Buch Mose*, 40. The self-revelation formula is found frequently in the Holiness Code (e.g., Lev 18,2.4.5). Cf. MAYES, *Deuteronomy*, 166.

[54] BUIS and LECLERCQ, *Le Deutéronome*, 9.

[55] אלהיו appears 24 times in Dt: 1,6.19.20.25.41; 2,29.33.36.37; 3,3; 4,7; 5,2.24.25.27[2X]; 6,4.20.24.25; 29,14.17.28; 32,3. אלהי אבותינו appears only once, in 26,7. Cf. N. LOHFINK, "Zum 'Numeruswechsel' in Dtn 3,21f.," *BN* 49 (1989) 48.

[56] POLZIN, *Moses and the Deuteronomist*, 49. POLZIN's conclusion appears to be a good insight into the *ethos* of Moses and of Dt's author. However, his statistics do leave something to be desired. He comments that the phrases "God of *our* fathers" and "*our* God" appear "at least twenty-three times in the book." The references in n. 55 come to 25. Again POLZIN claims that Moses uses the "our" form eleven times in the First Address but only twice in the Second. His count in the First Address is accurate, but I find 10 occurrences of the "our" form in the Second Address.

sometimes change abruptly from one to the other? Every change of number is a new form of address, a new assault on the listener. The singular is considered to have been the standard form by which the cult community was addressed: Israel was viewed as one person before Yahweh in worship. In the plural then the community is no longer addressed as an entity but as a collection of individuals. Thus in the plural form the individual Israelite is emphasized and the approach is more personal.[57]

Steuernagel and Staerk first suggested that the differences in the second person singular and plural passages could serve as a criterion to separate layers of a text, that is, to discover what was the original text and what were later editorial additions.[58] It is believed that changes in the form of address in a text are signs of different origins and authors. Those who advocate this distinction between singular and plural forms as a literary criterion usually promote one of two theories concerning the formation of Dt. One theory sees in the present Dt the product of a combination of two or more originally separate editions of the work, one using the singular and the other using the plural forms. The second theory is a kind of supplementary hypothesis, for it holds that an original book grew through various additions and expansions until it became what we have today. Only this second theory is still accepted by modern scholars.[59]

---

[57] R. BEE, "A Study of Deuteronomy Based on Statistical Properties of the Text," *VT* 29 (1979) 5; C. BEGG, "The Literary Criticism of Deut 4,1-40: Contributions to a Continuing Discussion," *ETL* 56 (1980) 12-13; BUIS, *Le Deutéronome,* 31; BUIS and LECLERCQ, *Le Deutéronome,* 9; H. CAZELLES, "Passages in the Singular within Discourse in the Plural of Dt 1-4," *CBQ* 29 (1967) 219; MAYES, *Deuteronomy,* 36; "Deuteronomy 4 and the Literary Criticism of Deuteronomy," *JBL* 100 (1981) 29; W.L. MORAN, review of *Israel und die Völker: Eine Studie zum Deuteronomium,* by OTTO BÄCHLI, in *Bib* 44 (1963) 375. There is one or the other scholar, however, who seems to take exception to this view of the singular and plural. BREIT, *Die Predigt,* 102, might be indicating this with an isolated statement which he does not explain: "wobei die 'Du'form keineswegs immer dem Volk gilt." D. KNAPP, *Deuteronomium 4: Literarische Analyse und theologische Interpretation* (Göttingen 1987), 37, points out that 4,19 is in the singular but is meant for the individual Israelite, while on p. 71 he hints that the plural is used when it concerns all Israel. THOMPSON, *Deuteronomy,* 288, claims that the singular forms in Dt 30,19 refer to the individual. It is quite possible that the original distinction between singular and plural was not valid for later passages.

[58] SOGGIN, *Introduzione all'Antico Testamento,* 158; LOERSCH, *Das Deuteronomium und seine Deutungen,* 38-41; NICHOLSON, *Deuteronomy and Tradition,* 22, points out that in 1891 C.H. CORNILL first tried to demonstrate that some laws were secondary on account of their use of the plural instead of the singular.

[59] BRAULIK, *Deuteronomium 1-16,17,* 9; CLEMENTS, *Deuteronomy,* 17; MAYES, *Deuteronomy,* 37-38; NICHOLSON, *Deuteronomy and Traditon,* 23; PREUSS, *Deuteronomium,* 42-43.

The singular forms are generally considered to be earlier or more original (although there are exceptions), while the plural sections are usually held to be later additions.[60] Minette de Tillesse attempted to demonstrate that most of the plural passages in chapters 5-26 were added later by the Deuteronomistic historian to a Dt which was mostly singular. Minette de Tillesse also claims that the plural sections are no mere secondary accretions but the sign of a redaction of the text by this editor.[61]

But the use of singular and plural forms of address as a criterion to find original and later segments of Dt has been questioned and challenged by many scholars.[62] It has been doubted, for example, that such forms can be used to distinguish editorial work in a text: how could a redactor manage to grasp and develop his source's theology and yet fail to understand and follow the forms of a pronoun? Why couldn't an editor conform to the grammar of the text before him?[63] Even if the singular/plural criterion is valid, it would have to be used cautiously and only in conjunction with other criteria. Many feel it is questionable whether it is possible to remove the plural passages from Dt without damaging the sense. Some passages which are generally acknowledged to be late and by the same author, such as 4,1-40, also show this variation in singular and plural forms of address.[64] Apparently one cannot use the

---

[60] BEE, "Statistical Properties," 4-5; MAYES, *Deuteronomy*, 36-37; *The Story of Israel between Settlement and Exile: A Redactional Study of the Deuteronomistic History* (London 1983) 29; H.G. MITCHELL, "The Use of the Second Person in Deuteronomy," *JBL* 18 (1899) 61-109; W.L. MORAN, "Deuteronomy," *A New Catholic Commentary on Sacred Scripture* (ed. R. FULLER, L. JOHNSTON, and C. KEARNS; London 1969) 257; POLZIN, *Moses and the Deuteronomist*, 14.

[61] G. MINETTE DE TILLESSE, "Sections 'tu' et sections 'vous' dans le Deutéronome," *VT* 12 (1962) 29-87; "Martin Noth et la Redaktionsgeschichte des livres historiques," *Aux grands carrefours de la révélation et de l'exégèse de l'Ancien Testament* (RechBib 8; ed. CH. HAURET) (Louvain 1967) 67-68. See also BUIS and LECLERCQ, *Le Deutéronome*, 10; NICHOLSON, *Deuteronomy and Tradition*, 26-31.

[62] L. ALONSO SCHÖKEL, "Of Methods and Models," *VTS* 36 (1983), 11; G. BRAULIK, "Literarkritik und archäologische Stratigraphie zu S. Mittmanns Analyse von Deuteronomium 4,1-40," *Bib* 59 (1978) 354-355; LOHFINK, *Das Hauptgebot*, 240; W.L. MORAN, review of *Das Bundesformular*, by KLAUS BALTZER, in *Bib* 43 (1962) 103; NICHOLSON, *Deuteronomy and Tradition*, 33; ORMANN, "Die Stilmittel," 40; PENNA, *Deuteronomio*, 17; POLZIN, *Moses and the Deuteronomist*, 14; J. VERMEYLEN, "Les sections narratives de Deut 5-11 et leur relation à Ex 19-34," *Das Deuteronomium: Entstehung, Gestalt und Botschaft* (ed. N. LOHFINK), 194, n. 49. A. BERTHOLET, review of *Das Deuteronomium*, by Carl STEUERNAGEL, in *TLZ* 24 (1899) 482-486, especially 483, already questioned the idea in 1899.

[63] McCARTHY, *Treaty and Covenant*, 189, n. 1; MAYES, *Story of Israel*, 29; "Deuteronomy 4," 27-28.

[64] BEGG, "Literary Criticism of Deut 4,1-40," especially 19, 46; BRAULIK, *Die Mittel*, 149; N. LOHFINK, "Verkündigung des Hauptgebots in der jüngsten Schicht des Deuteronomiums (Dt 4,1-40)," *BibLeb* 5 (1964) 253; P. KEARNEY, "The Role of the

criterion here to distinguish what is late and what is early, since all of it is late!

The phenomenon of both singular and plural forms of address mixed together is also found outside Dt. Exod 21-23 (the Code of the Covenant) and Lev 19 (within the Holiness Code) also alternate the second person singular and plural, but not with the frequency of Dt.[65] A similar phenomenon occurs in the New Testament[66] and in *Oedipus Rex*, Xenophon, and the *Iliad*.[67] It has also been observed in ancient Near Eastern treaties, especially those contracted between the Hittite Empire and various Syrian states.[68] The fact that the Versions often disagree with MT on singular and plural variations also complicates the issue.[69]

Other suggestions have been made for understanding this phenomenon of second person singular and plural variation. Some scholars have indicated that sudden changes in number may be due to citations/quotations or the use of technical terms which normally are associated only with a singular or plural form.[70] Lohfink has suggested (although he disclaims any absolute rules) that the plural forms point to

---

Gibeonites in the Deuteronomic History," *CBQ* 35 (1973) 2-3, n. 6; KNAPP, *Deuteronomium 4*, 17; MAYES, *Deuteronomy*, 36-37; *Story of Israel*, 29-30; McCONVILLE, *Law and Theology*, 65. One explanation for the variation in number in later texts is that the authors/editors were imitating the style of the texts before them, which already had a mixture of both singular and plural forms of address. Cf. R. NELSON, *The Double Redaction of the Deuteronomistic History* (JSOTSS 18; Sheffield 1981) 92. However BEGG, "Literary Criticism of Deut 4,1-40," 19, n. 50, finds little or no evidence for such a proposal.

[65] BUIS, *Le Deutéronome*, 30; MITCHELL, "The Use of the Second Person in Deuteronomy," 63-66; MORAN, "Deuteronomy," 257. MITCHELL lists other examples in Exodus and Leviticus (e.g., Exod 10,2; 12,24; 15,26; 19,4-6; 33,2-8; 34,13).

[66] Certain sections of Matthew and Luke, where Jesus addresses the crowds, alternate between singular and plural forms. Some New Testament scholars also use the phenomenon as a literary critical criterion (passages in the second person plural reveal Q), although it could also be a deliberate rhetorical device. Cf. G. KENNEDY, *New Testament Interpretation through Rhetorical Criticism* (Chapel Hill 1984), 41-42.

[67] The Greek literary critic LONGINUS (third century C.E.) already recognized and analyzed the shift in number in *Oedipus* (23.2-3), Xenophon (25.1), and the *Iliad* (27.1-2): "The use of this figure is appropriate when the urgency of the moment gives the writer no chance to delay, but forces on him an immediate change from one person to another." Quoted in B. VICKERS, *In Defence of Rhetoric* (Oxford 1988) 310.

[68] McCARTHY, *Treaty and Covenant*, 158, n. 2; D. HILLERS, *Treaty-Curses and the Old Testament Prophets*, (BibOr 16; Rome 1964) 32.

[69] BREIT, *Die Predigt*, 25-26; NTAGWARARA, "Alliance d'Israël," 197. The LXX normally follows MT in translating singular and plural forms of address, but in at least 147 places they disagree. This discrepancy can also be found in the first and third persons. L. LABERGE, "La Septante de Dt 1-11: Pour une étude du 'texte,'" *Das Deuteronomium: Entstehung, Gestalt und Botschaft* (ed. N. LOHFINK) 131, calls for caution when comparing MT with the versions.

[70] MAYES, *Story of Israel*, 30; BEGG, "Literary Criticism of Deut 4,1-40," 28-29.

historical memory (that is, historical genre tends to prefer it) and the singular hints at the personal involvement found in parenesis.[71] In fact, narrative or historical sections of Dt (where the listeners are described as having participated in the events mentioned) generally seem to be in the plural, while parenetic sections tend to be mixed, even if predominantly singular.[72] History is supposedly more "objective" and therefore in the plural, while parenesis is aimed at the listener and therefore in the singular.[73]

Long ago König suggested that singular and plural address alternated to avoid certain problems in language and style.[74] In other words, the main reasons for this variety were stylistic. This notion of variation because of style and emphasis has been resurrected in the past thirty years. The sudden change in number emphasizes or underlines a word, phrase, or paragraph.[75] Every change of number is a new form of address, and every new address forces the listener to pay attention. Thus the purpose of the variation is effect and emphasis. So it is a question of style, not of sources or redaction.[76] Another important reason for such a variation in number is the creation of a particular relationship with one's audience. The change emphasizes both the corporate identity of the community and its collectivity.[77]

1.4 Aural Nature of Deuteronomy

In Dt 31,9-13 we learn that Moses wrote down this *torah* and entrusted it to the levitical priests and to all the elders of Israel. Then he

---

[71] LOHFINK, *Das Hauptgebot*, 239-258. See also MAYES, "Deuteronomy 4," 28-29; McCARTHY, *Treaty and Covenant*, 158, n. 2; MINETTE DE TILLESSE, "Tu et vous," 43-44.

[72] LOHFINK, *Das Hauptgebot*, 246, 250; MORAN, "Deuteronomy," 257.

[73] Note that this interpretation contradicts the usual understanding of the singular as directed toward the community as a whole and the plural as directed toward individuals. Cf. n. 57.

[74] E. KÖNIG, "The Unity of Deuteronomy," *ExpTim* 10 (1898-99) 124-126; *Stilistik, Rhetorik, Poetik in Bezug auf die biblische Litteratur* (Leipzig 1900) 232-236.

[75] LOHFINK, *Das Hauptgebot*, 247-248. He sees the change from singular to plural as more important or more striking. Cf. LABUSCHAGNE, "Divine Speech." 115.

[76] W. BEYERLIN, "Die Paränese im Bundesbuch und ihre Herkunft," *Gottes Wort und Gottes Land* (FS. Hans-Wilhelm Hertzberg; ed. H. G. REVENTLOW) (Göttingen 1965) 20; BRAULIK, "Das Deuteronomium und die Geburt des Monotheismus," *Gott, der einzige: Zur Entstehung des Monotheismus in Israel* (ed. E. HAAG; Quaestiones Disputatae 104) (Freiburg 1985) 139; BREIT, *Die Predigt*, 25, n. 2; LABUSCHAGNE, "Divine Speech," 114; LOHFINK, *Das Hauptgebot*, 242. Such a style of rapid change in number exists even today in some oral societies of Africa. See BUIS, *Le Deutéronome*, 31; BUIS and LECLERCQ, *Le Deutéronome*, 9.

[77] Y. GITAY, "Deutero-Isaiah: Oral or Written?" *JBL* 99 (1980) 195; KÖNIG, *Stilistik, Rhetorik, Poetik*, 232-236; S. D. McBRIDE, JR., "Polity of the Covenant People: The Book of Deuteronomy," *Int* 61 (1987) 237.

commissioned them to read it aloud before all Israel. How seriously are we to take this commission? Whether or not Dt had any previous oral traditions, it is eminently a written document, a piece of literature, as it likes to remind us (a "book" or "scroll" of instruction — ספר — 28,58.61; 29,20; 30,10; cf. Josh 1,8; 8,34; 24,26). Indeed, the speeches in Dt indicate that they were already written down before being delivered (28,58; 29,19-20.26).[78]

But there are also clear indications that Dt was meant to be read aloud, that is, it was composed for oral recitation. Its very form as speeches to an assembly and its direct address demonstrate that. For Dt itself, Moses doesn't really write (except when it's all over: 31,9) — he *speaks*. The *torah* of Dt is meant to be proclaimed aloud, it is meant to be heard (31,11: תקרא ... באזניהם). Although Dt may have introduced the notion of a written law, it is one which is entirely at the service of an oral law, for tradition teaches that Moses spoke to the people with his own voice.[79]

We must bear in mind that the ancients were much more oriented toward the spoken word than we are. Most likely the ancient Hebrews and their Canaanite neighbors were literate, at least during the seventh and late eighth centuries B.C.E.[80] (But widespread distribution of written materials was impossible, since few could afford to buy books or writing materials).[81] Nevertheless all ancient writing was meant to be read aloud.

---

[78] A. CHOLEWINSKI, *Deuteronomio* (lecture notes; Rome 1982) II, 11; D. CHRISTENSEN, "Form and Structure in Deuteronomy 1-11," *Das Deuteronomium: Entstehung, Gestalt und Botschaft* (ed. N. LOHFINK) 135; MAYES, *Deuteronomy*, 359; PREUSS, *Deuteronomium*, 127; WEINFELD, *Deuteronomy and the Deuteronomic School*, 51-53.

[79] S. AMSLER, "Loi orale et loi écrite dans le Deutéronome," *Das Deuteronomium: Entstehung, Gestalt und Botschaft* (ed. N. LOHFINK), 51, 54. The word *torah* may even be associated with oral proclamation: LIEDKE and PETERSEN, תּוֹרָה *THAT* II, 1034, 1036.

[80] Y. AHARONI, *The Archaeology of the Land of Israel: From the Prehistoric Beginnings to the End of the First Temple Period* (ed. M. AHARONI; Trans. A. F. Rainey; Philadelphia 1982) 277; A. DEMSKY, Response to "An Assessment of the Evidence for Writing in Ancient Israel," by A. MILLARD, in *Biblical Archaeology Today: Proceedings of the International Congress on Biblical Archaelogy: Jerusalem, April 1984* (ed. A. BIRAN et al.; Jerusalem 1985) 349-353; C. GORDON, *The Common Background of Hebrew and Greek Civilizations* (New York 1965) 282-283; A. LEMAIRE, "Sagesse et écoles," *VT* 34 (1984) 280; A. MILLARD, "The Question of Israelite Literacy," *Bible Review* 3 (1987) 22-31; "An Assessment of the Evidence for Writing in Ancient Israel," *Biblical Archaeology Today* (ed. A. BIRAN et al.; Jerusalem 1985) 301-312; J. NAVEH, Response to "An Assessment of the Evidence for Writing in Ancient Israel," by A. MILLARD, in *Biblical Archaeology Today* (ed. A. BIRAN et al.; Jerusalem 1985) 354; G. WIDENGREN, *Literary and Psychological Aspects of the Hebrew Prophets* (Uppsala 1948) 62.

[81] FERGUSON, *Biblical Hermeneutics,* 70; GITAY, "Deutero-Isaiah," 191; E. NIDA and W. REYBURN, *Meaning across Cultures* (American Society of Missiology Series 4; Maryknoll, N. Y. 1981) 23. AHARONI, *The Archaeology of the Land of Israel,* 276, suggests that inexpensive writing material may have been available in the last phase of the Judean monarchy.

Generally speaking, whether or not a biblical text was originally written down, it was meant for public oral recitation. It was composed to be heard, not just to be seen. Moreover, reading quietly to oneself was a later development. In the ancient world reading was done aloud. This is evident in the Hebrew word קרא, "read," for it also means "call" or "shout." Even today Jews use a related term for the Bible: מקרא, ("reading aloud"). Thus understanding came through the ear, not the eye.[82]

It should be fairly obvious that prophetic oracles and many poems were meant to be heard. Even when these were written down, they were afterwards proclaimed. Baruch read the scroll of Jeremiah before the people assembled at the Temple in Jerusalem (Jer 36,8-9). But the same scroll was also read aloud by someone to the king, who could easily have read it privately but did not choose to do so (Jer 36,21.23). It's also likely that all the lawcodes were associated with cultic celebrations where their contents were read before the people.[83]

Dt too was meant to be heard, not simply read in silence.[84] The style and structure of biblical literature may be explained by its aural nature, and this is no less true of Dt. The very repetitiveness of much of Dt may result from the fact that it was written for oral presentation. Direct address, the appeal to the individual, the almost dramatic urgency of this appeal, and the constant variety within this repetitiveness point to the aural nature of the book.[85] Dt even emphasizes the aural over the visual

---

[82] L. ALONSO SCHÖKEL, *A Manual of Hebrew Poetics* (Subsidia Biblica 11; Rome 1988) 20; R. ALTER, *The Art of Biblical Narrative* (New York 1981) 90; J. GABEL and C. WHEELER, *The Bible as Literature: An Introduction* (New York/Oxford 1986) 33; GITAY, "Deutero-Isaiah," 191-194; C. J. LABUSCHAGNE, "קרא." *THAT* II, 672; R. LIWAK, *Der Prophet und die Geschichte: Eine literar-historische Untersuchung zum Jeremiabuch* (BWANT 121; Stuttgart 1987) 2; H. PARUNAK, "Some Axioms for Literary Architecture," *Semitics* 8 (1982) 2-3; A. STOCK, "Chiastic Awareness and Education in Antiquity," *BTB* 14 (1984) 26; WIDENGREN, *The Literary and Psychological Aspects,* 59. Cf. also G. KENNEDY, *The Art of Persuasion in Greece* (Princeton 1963) 3-4; *New Testament Interpretation,* 5-6.
[83] GEMSER, "The Importance of the Motive Clause," 62; B. ANDERSON, "Martin Noth's Traditio-Historical Approach in the Context of Twentieth-Century Biblical Research," introduction to *A History of Pentateuchal Traditions* by M. NOTH (Chico, California 1981) xvi.
[84] This was first suggested, at least for chaps. 5-11, by A. KLOSTERMANN, *Der Pentateuch: Beiträge zu seinem Verständnis und seiner Entstehungsgeschichte,* Neue Folge, II (Leipzig 1907) 348. See BREIT, *Die Predigt,* 24; CHRISTENSEN, "Form and Structure in Dt 1-11," 136; F. GARCÍA LÓPEZ, "Le Roi d'Israël: Dt 17,14-20," *Das Deuteronomium: Entstehung, Gestalt und Botschaft* (ed. N. LOHFINK) 290; GREENWOOD, "Origins," 194-195; N. LOHFINK, *Höre, Israel! Auslegung von Texten aus dem Buch Deuteronomium* (Die Welt der Bibel 18; Düsseldorf 1965) 24; D. SKWERES, *Die Rückverweise im Buch Deuteronomium* (AnBib 79; Rome 1979) 1.
[85] ALTER, *The Art of Biblical Narrative,* 90; L. EINHORN, "Oral and Written Style: An

theologically. For during the theophany at Horeb Israel could only see fire — not God, who reveals himself through his voice. It is God's voice which causes the people to fear, and they beg Moses to become their mediator by listening to it alone and reporting to them later (Dt 4,12.15.33.36; 5,22-27).[86]

1.5 The Roots of Deuteronomy's Rhetoric

We have seen that Dt is a book which presents itself as Moses' farewell address or valedictory oration to the people of Israel on the plains of Moab. It has been described as rhetorical, didactic, homiletic, and with a style peculiarly its own. It was meant to be read aloud, to be heard. What are the roots of this highly rhetorical work?

1.5.1 Cult

The highly stylized character of Dt as an oration easily suggests that it is largely liturgical material shaped by frequent repetition. The call to read "this *torah*" before an assembly of the entire people every seven years (Dt 31,10-13) contributes to this impression. The very fact that Dt can be called a sermon or a series of sermons leads us to think of Israel's worship. Most scholars would agree that the roots of Dt lie in the cult.[87] One of the most cited indications of cult influence upon Dt has been the use of the word "today," which occurs 27 times in the book. This word has been described as a liturgical device which wipes away time and permits Israel to identify itself with the ancestors who entered into the covenant at Horeb (and again in Moab).[88] The suggestion has been made

---

Examination of Differences," *The Southern Speech Communication Journal* 43 (1978) 306-307; H. Parunak, "Transitional Techniques in the Bible," *JBL* 102 (1983) 546. Aristotle, *Rhetoric* (ed. F. Solmsen; New York 1954), 1413b, commented on the differences in style between written prose and spoken oratory. He associated variety, repetition, and dramatic delivery with what is spoken.

[86] Weinfeld, *Deuteronomy and the Deuteronomic School*, 207-208.

[87] Braulik, *Deuteronomium 1-16,17*, 15-16; Claburn, "Deuteronomy and Collective Behavior," 60-61; Lohfink, *Höre, Israel!*, 11, 24; Nicholson, *Deuteronomy and Tradition*, 38-39, 46; Von Rad, *Deuteronomium-Studien*, 19; "Das formgeschichtliche Problem des Hexateuch," 32, 35, 41; *Das fünfte Buch Mose*, 8; Watts, "The Deuteronomic Theology," 323; Weinfeld, *Deuteronomy and the Deuteronomic School*, 32-45.

[88] R. Murphy, "Deuteronomy — A Document of Revival," *Concilium* 9 (1973) 28. J. Van Goudoever, "The Liturgical Significance of the Date in Dt 1,3," *Das Deuteronomium: Entstehung, Gestalt und Botschaft* (ed. N. Lohfink) 148, calls Dt "the most liturgical book of the Bible." At least for Dt 1,3 the word "today" can have three meanings: 1) today = the time of Moses; 2) today = the cultic festival day on which these words were read, i.e., the time of Josiah; and 3) the future. In the cult all three meanings can be found at the same time. See Lohfink, *Höre, Israel!*, 50; Nicholson, *Deuteronomy and Tradition*, 45; Von Rad, "Das formgeschichtliche Problem des Hexateuch," 36.

that Dt is associated with a particular cultic festival, that of the annual covenant renewal, which is often linked with the autumn Feast of Tabernacles (*Sukkoth*).[89] However, in its present form Dt is a literary product and no text for a specific cult ceremony.[90]

1.5.2 Law

There is another side of Dt which may or may not be associated with the cult. For this book contains numerous commandments, laws, statutes, and decrees which cover much of Israel's social, political, religious, and even economic life. "Deuteronomy presents itself as the written authoritative Law which provides the basis of Israel's life."[91] In Dt the written laws and instructions, the *torah,* begin to assume a character and an importance which is independent of the lawgiver, Moses. It is entrusted to the levites and the elders (31,9), it is read publicly every seven years (31,10-11), and it functions as a witness against Israel (31,26). Except for the decalogue, which is announced by Yahweh himself, these laws, statutes, decrees, and instructions of Dt are promulgated by Moses. They too, however, were revealed by Yahweh to Moses on Mt. Horeb.

Dt uses a variety of words to name these laws: דרך, דברים/דבר, ברית, תורה, עדות, משפטים, משמרת, מצות/מצוה, חקות/חקים. These words can be combined into expressions of varied order and number, a technique which Dt freely makes use of. The only principle to which the authors of Dt seem to conform in their use of these various expressions is that of

---

However, not everyone recognizes the expressions "today" and "this day" as holdovers from the cult. After all, the expressions have a powerful influence on an audience, for they bring a sense of presence to it. R. Polzin, "Deuteronomy," *The Literary Guide to the Bible* (ed. R. Alter and F. Kermode; London 1987) 92-93, sees the expression as a device to help put the recitation of the law into context. Weinfeld, *Deuteronomy and the Deuteronomic School,* 174-175, also sees the expressions as rhetorical devices used in deuteronomic orations to stress the present reality of the author.

[89] Von Rad, "Das formgeschichtliche Problem des Hexateuch," 41-48, suggested and promoted this association of Dt and a covenant renewal festival. See also his *Das fünfte Buch Mose,* 16; *Theologie des Alten Testaments,* I, 233. Cf. Nicholson, *Deuteronomy and Tradition,* 40-47. On pp. 44-45 Nicholson proposes the pattern that this covenant renewal festival could have followed: 1) parenesis and a historical retrospect of Yahweh's saving deeds on Israel's behalf; 2) the setting forth of the divine stipulations; 3) the making of a covenant; and 4) the setting forth of blessings and curses. He sees Dt following this pattern closely. Cf. also Bee, "Statistical Propeties," 4, 14; Blair, "An Appeal to Remembrance," 44; Buis and Leclercq, *Le Deutéronome,* 14. E. Kutsch, *Verheißung und Gesetz: Untersuchungen zum sogenannten "Bund" im alten Testament* (BZAW 131; Berlin 1973) 172, denies that there ever was such a covenant renewal festival.

[90] Brekelmans, "Wisdom Influence in Deuteronomy," 31; Von Rad, *Das fünfte Buch Mose,* 16; Weinfeld, *Deuteronomy and the Deuteronomic School,* 51, 53, 57.

[91] L. Hoppe, "The Meaning of Deuteronomy," *BTB* 10 (1980) 115.

variety.[92] The expression which became the most important, of course, is תורה, *torah*, for this is the term which Dt calls itself and which became so important for Judaism.

The laws of Dt are removed from any orginal setting in the cult or jurisprudence. If Dt was originally a lawcode in form, it no longer appears that way. For the laws are not directed towards the judiciary but to all Israel. In fact, they are not presented so much as *laws* but as *teaching* (*torah*). They are embedded in parenesis, influenced by the cult, and given a style which is didactic and peculiar. This is no corpus of civil or ceremonial statutes. It is more a "manual," as Driver calls it, for it is addressed to the people and meant for popular use.[93]

1.5.3 Vassal Treaties

For more than one thousand years the peoples and rulers of the ancient Near East made use of a special form of agreement to establish legal and political relationships with each other. Such treaties conformed to specific language and conventions, and despite differences in time (approximately 2500–700 B.C.E.) and locality (Mesopotamia, Asia Minor, Syria), such language and conventions remained relatively uniform and stable. The *parity* treaty (one between equals, such as the treaty between Rameses II of Egypt and Hattusilis III of Hatti in the early 13th century B.C.E.) has rarely come down to us. But numerous examples of the *vassal* or *suzerainty* treaty have been discovered. Such vassal treaties generally conform to the following pattern[94]:

---

[92] G. BRAULIK, "Die Ausdrücke für 'Gesetz' im Buch Deuteronomium," *Bib* 51 (1970) 39-66; and LOHFINK, *Das Hauptgebot*, 54-58, especially p. 54, tried to show that all these individual words for law are more or less interchangeable and that each word or combination of words tends to refer to the entire corpus of laws. However, LOHFINK has since backed away from this position in "Die *ḥuqqîm ûmišpaṭîm* im Buch Deuteronomium und ihre Neubegrenzung durch Dtn 12,1," *Bib* 70 (1989) 1-29. LINDARS, "Torah in Deuteronomy," 126-127, also sees some nuanced differences between some of the words, such as that between חק and חקה. But he feels that otherwise it is impossible to distinguish between these expressions. He concludes that מצוה, the predominating term (it occurs 14 times in the singular and 30 times in the plural in Dt: PENNA, *Deuteronomio*, 34), has assimilated to itself the meaning of the others. He associates מצוה with the absolute demands of the king. Such demands became identified with all the commandments, statutes, and decrees of Yahweh (129).

[93] DRIVER, *Deuteronomy*, xxvi; MAYES, *Deuteronomy*, 71.

[94] VON RAD, *Das fünfte Buch Mose*, 15: 1. Präambel; 2. Vorgeschichte; 3. Grundsatzerklärung; 4. Einzelbestimmungen; 5. Anrufung der Götter als Zeugen; 6. Fluch und Segen. He uses the analysis of K. BALTZER, *Das Bundesformular* (WMANT 4; Neukirchen 1960) 20-25. The classic analysis of Hittite vassal treaties by KOROŠEC is slightly different: 1) the titulary (here the king presents his titles); 2) the history (relations between the two parties are reviewed); 3) the stipulations (the specific obligations to which the vassal must submit); 4) the document clause (regulations about the preservation and

1. Preamble
2. Previous history (or historical prologue)
3. Declaration of basic principle
4. Regulations/stipulations in detail
5. Invocation of the gods as witnesses
6. Curse and blessing.

The vassal traties can be roughly divided into two groups, the second-millennium Hittite (and Syrian) treaties and the first-millennium Mesopotamian (usually Assyrian) treaties. The two types differ in that the later Mesopotamian treaties usually lack a previous history while often containing long and colorful curses without any corresponding blessings.[95]

The present form of Dt reflects to some extent these vassal treaties of the ancient Near East. Many scholars have observed all or at least some of these elements within the book.[96] They don't always agree on the details or the meaning of such patterns, but many are willing to admit at least some influence on Dt.

There are other features of the ancient vassal treaty which may be even more important for Dt than the structure. For example, the treaties demand exclusive allegiance to an overlord. This central demand is reflected in Dt's command to love God with all one's heart, soul, and energy — an expression reminiscent of the juridical and political language of the second millennium B.C.E.

---

reading of the treaty); 5) the god list (the divine witnesses); and 6) the blessings and curses (invoked upon those who keep or violate the treaty). Cf. McCARTHY, *Treaty and Covenant*, 51-52. G. MENDENHALL, *Law and Covenant in Israel and the Ancient Near East* (Pittsburgh 1955) 32-34, follows KOROŠEC's analysis.

[95] G. GARCÍA LÓPEZ, *Le Deutéronome: Une loi prêchée* (Cahiers Evangile 63; Paris 1988) 15; MAYES, *Deuteronomy*, 32; PREUSS, *Deuteronomium*, 64-65.

[96] For example, BRAULIK, *Deuteronomium 1-16,17*, 7. CRAIGIE, *Deuteronomy*, 24, lists the following: 1) preamble (1,1-5); 2) historical prologue (1,6-4,49); 3) general stipulations (chaps. 5-11); 4) specific stipulations (chaps. 12-26); 5) blessings and curses (chaps. 27-28); 6) witnesses (30,19; 31,19; 32,1-43). THOMPSON, *Deuteronomy*, 19, sees the analysis of the treaty form in Dt slightly differently: 1) historical prologue (1,6-3,29); 2) basic stipulations (4,1-40; 5,1-11,32); 3) detailed stipulations (12,1-26,19); 4) document clause (27,1-26); 5) blessings (28,1-14); 6) curses (28,15-68); 7) "recapitulation" (29,1-30,20). WEINFELD, *Deuteronomy and the Deuteronomic School*, 66, sees the following format in Dt: 1) preamble (1,1-6a; 5,6a); 2) historical prologue (1,6b-3,29; 5; 9,7-10,11); 3) basic stipulation of allegiance (4,1-23; 6,4-7,26; 10,12-22); 4) covenant clauses (chaps. 12-26); 5) invocation of witnesses (31,28); 6) blessings and curses (chap. 28); 7) oath-imprecation (29,9-28); 8) the deposit (10,1-5; 31,24-26); 9) periodic reading (31,9-13); 10) duplicates and copies (17,18-19; 31,25-26). McCARTHY, *Treaty and Covenant*, 186, sees the treaty pattern in Moses' Second Address: 1) *mise en scène* (normal opening for treaties-turned-speeches: 4,44-49); 2) historical-parenetic prologue (chaps. 5-11); 3) stipulations (12,1-26,15[16]); 4)

Expressions such as "to go after ... others" אחרים (אלהים) ללכת אחרי; "to turn to ... others" אחרים (אלהים) פנה אל; "to serve ... others" ... עבד אחרים; "to love, to cleave" אהב, דבק; "to fear" ירא; "to swear" נשבע; "to listen to (or obey) the voice of" שמע בקול; "to be perfect (תמים) with (blameless before) him"; "to act in truth" באמת; "the good/welfare" טובה; "personal property/favored vassal" סגלה; recognize ידע;"uphold or stand by one's covenant" הקים ברית; "remember" זכר; "peace" שלום are also common to both Dt and the diplomatic letters and state treaties of the first and second millennia B.C.E., especially in the vassal treaties of Esarhaddon of Assyria (680–669 B.C.E.).[97]

Moreover, Dt 28,1-2.15 connects the laws with the curses and blessings of that chapter: happiness or disaster depend on obedience to the laws. Similar language is to be found in the treaties. The curses of Dt 28,20-57 are parallel to those of Assyrian treaty texts, and many see this as evidence that Dt is the product of the eighth or seventh century B.C.E.[98] It is quite tempting to see Dt as the written treaty with Yahweh which was a substitution for a former treaty between Judah and the king of Assyria.[99]

---

invocation-adjuration (26,[16]17-19); 5) blessings and curses (28,1-46[69]). MAYES, *Deuteronomy*, 32-34, admits that there is some connection between Dt and this extrabiblical treaty tradition. However, he denies that Dt is a treaty document or that it follows the treaty pattern. PREUSS, *Deuteronomium*, 65-73, likewise denies that Dt follows the treaty pattern.

[97] WEINFELD, *Deuteronomy and the Deuteronomic School*, 83-84. See also R. FRANKENA, "The Vassal-Treaties of Esarhaddon and the Dating of Deuteronomy," *OTS* 14 (1965) 140; LOHFINK, *Das Hauptgebot*, 278; MAYES, *Deuteronomy*, 33; McCARTHY, *Treaty and Covenant*, 288-289. Even the reference to stipulations written in a "book" may be normal treaty terminology: see HILLERS, *Treaty-Curses*, 32.

[98] P.E. DION, "Quelques aspects de l'interaction entre religion et politique dans le Deutéronome," *ScEs* 30 (1978) 44-51; FRANKENA, "The Vassal-Treaties of Esarhaddon," 144-149; McCARTHY, *Treaty and Covenant*, 171-175; W. MORAN, "The Near Eastern Background of the Love of God in Deuteronomy," *CBQ* 25 (1963) 83-84; WEINFELD, *Deuteronomy and the Deuteronomic School*, 60-61, 66-67, 121-122.

[99] FRANKENA, "The Vassal-Treaties of Esarhaddon," 153; LOHFINK, "Culture Shock," 16. LOHFINK believes that the treaty form was made use of by the authors of Dt because it was understandable and acceptable at the time: "... The new Assyrian empire was held together through a multiplication of oath-takings and treaties of every kind. To conclude a treaty was the great fashion. The mania for pacts went so far that ... Assahadan (sic!), the overlord of Manasses of Judah, through the Istah (sic!) priest, even concluded a treaty between the god Ashur, himself the king, and the people of Assyria!" (20). However, some scholars feel that the comparison between the treaty texts and Dt has led others to draw hasty conclusions, especially about the date of Dt: PREUSS, *Deuteronomium*, 66; McCONVILLE, *Law and Theology*, 37, 159. Some scholars see the relationship between Dt and the vassal treaties in terms of the Hittite treaties of the second millennium B.C.E. This would give a much earlier date to Dt: G. WENHAM, "The Date of Deuteronomy: Linch-Pin of Old Testament Criticism," *Them* 10 (1985) 19; CRAIGIE, *Deuteronomy*, 25-28.

The language of the treaties has been recognized as having its own peculiar rhetorical qualities and emphases. Treaties were, after all, proclaimed publicly (therefore orally) on certain specified occasions. The language was conventional and the style corresponded to the practice of ancient ministries of foreign affairs. This style tended to be wordy, repetitious, grandiloquent, and "baroque".[100] One of the purposes of the treaty was to instill an obedient attitude in the vassal, an attitude which Dt also seeks to inspire. The treaties accomplished this by means of parenesis or exhortation, especially in the historical prologue. Here they recalled past favors and promised future benefits to motivate such obedience. All available means were used to persuade the vassals and their subjects to follow the stipulations and to "love" the overlord, who was politically not only their master but also their father.[101] The treaties were also concerned with passing on the knowledge of their contents to future generations.[102] Thus we can see that much of the language, didacticism, style and rhetoric of Dt may owe its existence to the ancient Near Eastern vassal treaties.

Despite so many contacts with and similarities to the ancient vassal treaty, however, Dt cannot be seriously considered a treaty document itself. Whoever wrote Dt probably made use of the language, ideas, and even form of the treaties to render Israel's covenant and legal traditions faithful to both past and present. Unlike the treaty, however, Dt is not a legal document but an oration with the style of a sermon.[103] It deviates at times from the treaty form.

The most apparent and most important deviation from this form is the large section of Dt devoted to civil, cultic, and criminal law. This section is rather different from the normal stipulations of the treaty. One must keep in mind that ancient lawcodes also often contained historical prologues, laws, blessings, and curses. The treaties had no monopoly over

---

[100] BRAULIK, *Deuteronomium 1-16,17*, 8; N. LOHFINK, "Deuteronomy," *IDBSup* 229; *Das Hauptgebot*, 111; *Höre, Israel!*, 22-23; "Gott im Buch Deuteronomium," *La Notion biblique de Dieu: Le Dieu de la Bible et le Dieu des philosophes* (ed. J. COPPENS; BETL 41) (Leuven 1976) 111-112.

[101] W. BEYERLIN, "Die Paränese im Bundesbuch," 27; F.C. FENSHAM, "Father and son as Terminology for Treaty and Covenant," *Near Eastern Studies in Honor of William Foxwell Albright* (ed. H. GOEDICKE; Baltimore/London 1971) 121-135, especially 129, 131; McCARTHY, *Treaty and Covenant*, 53-54, 77-79, 169-170; MORAN, "Near Eastern Background," 78-80.

[102] LOHFINK, *Das Hauptgebot*, 115-116; McCARTHY, *Treaty and Covenant*, 200; D.J. WISEMAN, *The Vassal Treaties of Esarhaddon, Iraq* 20 (1958) 49-52.

[103] E. GERSTENBERGER, "Covenant and Commandment," *JBL* 84 (1965) 48-49; MAYES, *Deuteronomy*, 33; F. NÖTSCHER, "Bundesformular und 'Amtsschimmel': Ein kritischer Überblick," *BZ*, N.F. 9 (1965) 199; WEINFELD, *Deuteronomy and the Deuteronomic School*, 157.

such things, so the lawcode and the treaty might overlap somewhat. Dt is neither lawcode nor treaty document; but deep in its roots there are elements of both.[104]

1.5.4. Wisdom

Another less obvious but no less important influence on the book of Dt is that of wisdom traditions. The didactic tone of Dt resembles wisdom literature, the central concern of which is education. Indeed, wisdom traditions and writings played an important role in the educational systems of all ancient Near Eastern cultures, and we possess a great amount of sapiential literature largely because it was reproduced for study and teaching purposes. Israel, like many other peoples, proceeded from the assumption that truth could be grasped in the world and that knowledge, even of God's will, could be obtained. That such truth could be written down as *torah* and taught to future generations would make sense in wisdom circles. For in biblical wisdom literature תורה is used in a general way to express the instruction of the sage. In Prov 1,8; 3,1; 4,2; 6,20.23; 7,2; 13,14 it is used of the teaching given to the young.[105]

In Dt the laws of the *torah* are identified with wisdom (4,6), and like wisdom, it is accessible and can be understood (30,11-14). The relationship between Yahweh and Israel in Dt is similar to that between father and son or teacher and student — precisely those relationships found in wisdom literature. Certain words, expressions, and concerns are shared by Dt and wisdom literature: the removal of landmarks, the falsification of weights and measures, "an abomination to Yahweh," "perfect" (תמים), partiality in justice, fear of God, etc.[106] Connections with biblical wisdom literature have been found in Dt 1,13.15-17.31a; 4,1.6.9-14; 14,29; 16,20; 17,1; 23,16.23-24; 30,11-14.15-20; 31,11-13; 32; 34,9.[107]

---

[104] CHRISTENSEN, "Form and Structure in Dt 1-11," 135; MAYES, "Deuteronomy: Law of Moses or Law of God?" *PIBA* 5 (1981) 37-38; WEINFELD, *Deuteronomy and the Deuteronomic School,* 148-151.

[105] M. FISHBANE, *Biblical Interpretation in Ancient Israel* (Oxford 1988) 35; LIEDKE and PETERSEN,"תּוֹרָה," *THAT* II, 1034; LINDARS, "Torah in Deuteronomy," 122; G. VON RAD, *Weisheit in Israel* (Neukirchen/Vluyn 1970) 376, 379; WEINFELD, *Deuteronomy and Deuteronomic School,* 256, 280, 298. GERSTENBERGER, "Covenant and Commandment," 49-50 sees a connection between collections of proverbs, discourses, parables and other materials which are normally associated with wisdom literature and the collections of commandments and laws in the legal sections of the Old Testament.

[106] LOHFINK,"Deuteronomy," 229; WEINFELD, *Deuteronomy and the Deuteronomic School,* 265-274.

[107] J. BOSTON, "The Wisdom Influence upon the Song of Moses," *JBL* 87 (1968) 198-202; FISHBANE, *Biblical Interpretation,* 540, n. 24; J.W. McKAY, "Man's Love for God in Deuteronomy and the Father/Teacher–Son/Pupil Relationship," *VT* 22 (1972) 426-435; PREUSS, *Deuteronomium,* 88.

Wisdom traditions would account not only for the didacticism and pedagogical aims of Dt but even for its parenetic style and rhetoric. Egyptian texts indicate that scribes there considered the ability to speak effectively as one of the chief purposes of their training and education. To reach a position of influence at the royal court required not only a mastery of intellectual but also theorical skills. To become an eloquent and intelligent speaker was an ideal to which every Egyptian (and probably also Israelite) scribe aspired. In the book of Genesis Joseph is presented as a wise man who possesses both eloquence and good counsel. He represents an ideal found even in Israel. David, like Joseph, is praised for being skilled in speech (נבון דבר: 1 Sam 16,18). A large number of maxims in the book of Proverbs deals with right speaking, right silence, and the art of the "pleasant word" (אמרי נעם: Prov 16,24). The cultivation of rhetoric, then, pervaded the Ancient Near East, and Israel was no exception to this practice.[108]

However, it should be noted that Dt is not, strictly speaking, wisdom literature — just as it is not simply a cultic document, a lawcode, or a treaty text. Didactic tendencies and parenesis can be found not only in wisdom circles but also in treaties and in worship. Wisdom was not the exclusive property of royal counselors but could be taught to all learned classes. Treaty language, educational motifs, and religious ideas could be shared by all who had an education. The ancient world did not tend to separate the religious from the secular in the manner that modern Westerners do. We ought not to think of priests, prophets, and scribes (the three groups most closely associated with education in the ancient world) in terms of watertight compartments where communication and contact was forbidden or impossible.[109]

1.5.5 Purpose of Deuteronomy: Reform and Renewal

Can we discern a purpose or task for the book of Dt? Many scholars believe so. Obviously Dt was not written merely to reproduce a civil lawcode or to preserve various liturgical and wisdom traditions. The tone of Dt is urgent, the style didactic, and it strongly appeals to the

---

[108] Dion, "Quelques aspects," 54; A. Rose, "The 'Principles' of Divine Election: Wisdom in 1 Samuel 16," *Rhetorical Criticism* (FS. James Muilenburg; ed. M. Kessler and J.J. Jackson) (Pittsburgh 1974) 64; G. Von Rad, "Josephsgeschichte und ältere Chokma," *Gesammelte Studien zum Alten Testament* I, 274-275; *Theologie des Alten Testaments* I, 443-444.

[109] Brekelmans, "Wisdom Influence in Deuteronomy," 36; J. Levenson, "The Theologies of Commandment in Biblical Israel," *HTR* 73 (1980) 27; McCarthy, *Treaty and Covenant*, 164, n. 16; Review of *Deuteronomy and the Deuteronomic School*, by M. Weinfeld, in *Bib* 54 (1973) 452; Von Rad, *Theologie des Alten Testaments* I, 441; Weinfeld, *Deuteronomy and the Deuteronomic School*, 298.

individual. At the same time it reminds the community of its important religious traditions and speaks in the name of Moses, Israel's lawgiver. The authors seem to have felt that they had an important task to perform: to present and reinterpret Israel's traditions in the light of new and pressing problems. In other words, Dt is a document of reform, of revival.[110]

A reform program by its nature necessitates both an appeal to the past and a new beginning. It was no accident that Dt reviewed Israel's historical and legal traditions. Its relationship with Yahweh depended upon these. But the authors of Dt could not settle for a mere recall of the past. They had to make the old cultic and legal material relevant for their time, a time which had outgrown the past. Dt seems to have been written to respond to some major crisis in Israel's history — a crisis not of politics but of faith. That crisis can be faced and overcome only with a new understanding of what Israel's relationship with Yahweh means. If the religious life of the nation was to be reformed, the exclusive claims of Yahweh upon Israel's loyalty had to be reasserted and redefined.

After a shameful history Israel had to rediscover what that relationship might be and whether it still even existed. Dt insisted that God's covenant and faithfulness were still in force and that the promised blessing was still a possibility. To demonstrate this the authors placed Israel once again in the wilderness with Moses speaking to it. Israel was called upon to listen and respond *today*. Only this time the appeal is to every Israelite, to the individual; and that appeal is made not only to the individual's intelligence but also to his or her conscience, feelings, and soul. If not a detailed program of reform, Dt was at least its manifesto, for it aimed at the education of public opinion and sought to provoke the adherence of every group and every individual in Israel to that reform.[111]

---

[110] BUIS and LECLERCQ, *Le Deutéronome*, 18; DION, "Quelques aspects," 46; LACONI, *Deuteronomio*, 29; MORAN, "Deuteronomy," 259; R.E. MURPHY, "Deuteronomy — A Document of Revival," *Concilium* 9 (1973) 26-36; VON RAD, *Deuteronomium-Studien*, 43; *Das fünfte Buch Mose*, 14. Many of Dt's laws, for example, may be viewed as updated or reinterpreted versions of previous legal material. See FISHBANE, *Biblical Interpretation*, 164-166, 175-179, 201-208, 217-221, 229-230, 307-317, 321-322, etc.

[111] BUIS and LECLERCQ, *Le Deutéronome*, 18; R.E. CLEMENTS, *Old Testament Theology: A Fresh Approach* (Marshalls Theological Library; Basingstoke 1978) 89, 102; DRIVER, *Deuteronomy*, xxiv, lii-liii; HOPPE, "The Meaning of Deuteronomy," 117; MORAN, Review of *Israel und die Völker*, 375; MYERS, "The Requisites for Response," 15-16, 29; ORMANN, "Die Stilmittel," 52; A. PHILLIPS, *Deuteronomy* (The Cambridge Bible Commentary on the New English Bible; Cambridge 1973) 8-10; VON RAD, *Deuteronomium-Studien*, 51; *Das fünfte Buch Mose*, 14; *Theologie des Alten Testaments* I, 244; WEINFELD, *Deuteronomy and the Deuteronomic School*, 95-96, 190.

1.5.6 Author and Date

Three groups in ancient Israel were associated with teaching and preaching: the priests, the prophets, and the wise (Jer 18,18). And all three groups have been named by scholars as possible authors of Dt.[112] This study will make no attempt to further resolve the problems of Dt's authorship. However, there will be an attempt to discover the audience of this work.[113] For Dt is neither lawcode, treaty form, liturgical document, nor wisdom literature. It seems to have been written for the layperson, the non-expert, the "man in the street."[114] Whoever wrote the book — whether levite, prophet, elder, or scribe — wrote it for a general audience. Although Dt's author was obviously familiar with treaty terminology, laws, wisdom traditions, and cultic practices, he or she also made it a point to communicate to a general audience, and not only to experts.

The majority of biblical critics accept the theory that Dt was written during the eighth or seventh centuries B.C.E., although the exact time is still disputed. Possibly begun in the northern kingdom of Israel before its destruction, Dt as we know it is an effort to reform the southern kingdom of Judah. It has connections with the reforms of both Hezekiah and Josiah, although those connections are much stronger with Josiah.[115]

---

[112] PHILLIPS, *Deuteronomy*, 7-8. VON RAD has proposed and defended the thesis that country levites were responsible for Dt. He bases this claim on the practice of the levites in Neh 8, 7-9: *Deuteronomium-Studien*, 8-11, 41-49; *Das fünfte Buch Mose*, 16-19; *Theologie des Alten Testaments* I, 234. Cf. BLAIR, "An Appeal to Remembrance," 43; BUIS, *Le Deutéronome*, 456; BUIS and LECLERCQ, *Le Deutéronome*, 7; D.N. FREEDMAN, "The Deuteronomic History," *IDBSup* 227; B. HALPERN, "The Centralization Formula in Deuteronomy," *VT* 31 (1981) 37-38; WRIGHT, *Deuteronomy*, 315-316. Others have defended a prophetic origin of Dt: NICHOLSON, *Deuteronomy and Tradition*, 69; GREENWOOD, "Origins," 195-196. WEINFELD strongly defends the scribes (חכמים סופרים) as the authors, since they were capable of developing a literary technique and would have been familiar with treaty and wisdom traditions: *Deuteronomy and the Deuteronomic School*, 9, 158-178; "The Present State of Inquiry," 262; "Traces of Assyrian Treaty Formulae in Deuteronomy," *Bib* 46 (1965) 427. Cf. also CAZELLES, "Passages in the Singular," 207; MALFROY, "Sagesse et loi," 55. A fourth group which has been defended as responsible for the authorship of Dt is that of the elders. See L. HOPPE, "Elders and Deuteronomy: A Proposal," *EgT* 14 (1983) 259-272; "The Levitical Origins of Deuteronomy Reconsidered," *BR* 28 (1983) 27-36. Cf. J. BUCHHOLZ, *Die Ältesten Israels im Deuteronomium* (GTA 36; Göttingen 1988).

[113] See 3.1.

[114] McCONVILLE, *Law and Theology*, 54, 105; WEINFELD, "The Present State of Inquiry," 259; *Deuteronomy and the Deuteronomic School*, 188, 233-243; WRIGHT, *Deuteronomy*, 315.

[115] BRAULIK, *Deuteronomium 1-16,17*, 10-11; *Deuteronomio: Il testamento di Mosè*, 12-13; BUIS and LECLERCQ, *Le Deutéronome*, 16; CLEMENTS, *Deuteronomy*, 71-74; DRIVER, *Deuteronomy*, xlvi; GREENWOOD, "Origins," 191; LOHFINK, "Die Bundesurkunde des Königs Josias," 261-288, 461-498; "Culture Shock," 13-14; MAYES, *Deuteronomy*, 81-103;

There is much in Dt which associates the work with the period of Assyrian power in the eighth and seventh centuries. More than one hundred years of Assyrian dominance had strongly affected Judah's religion, society, and world view. The collapse and destruction of the northern kingdom in 721 B.C.E. and the failure of King Hezekiah to win independence from Assyria no doubt provided an atmosphere which permitted syncretism and the acceptance of foreign customs. Judah's own existence was threatened, for it could easily have been overwhelmed by the religious and social ideas of its overlord and oppressor. The reforms of Dt would then be linked to a political reaction against Assyria's dominance and a religious reaction against foreign and syncretistic ideas.[116]

The style and rhetoric of Dt may imitate Near Eastern oratory of the eighth and seventh centuries B.C.E. In Assyrian culture the "baroque" style (pompous, verbose, flowery) became popular. A notable example of such a style is the inflated curse-section of Assyrian vassal treaties. Dt's interest in past traditions may even reflect similar interests in Egypt and Assyria, for the seventh century saw many movements to recapture the glorious past. Ashurbanipal (668-633 B.C.E.) was known for the collection of ancient Babylonian myths and epics in his library at Nineveh, while in Egypt his contemporary Psamtik I (Psammeticus I: 663-610 B.C.E.) was also encouraging the copying of ancient texts and the revival of ancient cultic practices. It would seem that the entire Near East of this period was turning with nostalgia to the past in an effort to recapture its spirit and vivacity. The later Nabonidus of Babylonia

---

NICHOLSON, *Deuteronomy and Tradition,* 1-2, 94, 101-102; J.A. SOGGIN, *Storia d'Israele: Dalle origini a Bar Kochbà* (Biblioteca di Cultura Religiosa 44; Brescia 1984) 366-367; H. SPIECKERMANN, *Juda unter Assur in der Sargonidenzeit* (FRLANT 129; Göttingen 1982). Of course, these and other scholars do not often agree on the relationship between Josiah's (and Hezekiah's) reforms and Dt. GINSBERG, *Israelian Heritage,* 37, sees the reform of Hezekiah as based on an already-existing Dt. BEE, "Statistical Properties," 16, dates Dt after Josiah but before the exile. There are some scholars who disagree that the origins of Dt are connected with either Hezekiah or Josiah. Some tend to see a much earlier date for the book. These include: CH. RABIN, "Discourse Analysis and the Dating of Deuteronomy," *Interpreting the Hebrew Bible: Essays in Honour of E.I.J. Rosenthal* (ed. J.A. EMERTON and S. REIF; Cambridge 1982) 177 (early monarchy); THOMPSON, *Deuteronomy,* 48-68 (he refuses to commit himself but is critical of the "late" date of common opinion); CRAIGIE, *Deuteronomy,* 25-29 (Mosaic period). Others see an exilic date for all or at least much of the book: O. KAISER, *Einleitung in das Alte Testament: Eine Einführung in ihre Ergebnisse und Probleme,* 5th ed. (Gütersloh 1984) 134; HOPPE, "The Meaning of Deuteronomy," 116; LACONI, *Deuteronomio,* 29.

[116] LOHFINK, "Culture Shock," 18; NICHOLSON, *Deuteronomy and Tradition,* 98-99, 105; WATTS, "The Deuteronomic Theology," 324; WEINFELD, *Deuteronomy and the Deuteronomic School,* 51. For background information, cf. M. COGAN, *Imperialism and Religion: Assyria, Judah and Israel in the Eighth and Seventh Centuries B.C.E.* (SBLMS 19; Missoula 1974) and SPIECKERMANN, *Juda unter Assur in der Sargonidenzeit.*

(556-539 B.C.E.) was so zealous for antiquity that he ordered excavations of many well-known temple sites.[117]

To claim that Dt is the product of the seventh century B.C.E. does not mean that the entire book was written at the same time by the same author. There are indications that parts of the work may have been composed only during the exile. Those sections of Dt most strongly defended as exilic include 4,1-40; 29,21-27; 30,1-10; and perhaps parts of chapter 28.[118] Thus it is unlikely that Dt is the work of a single author who wrote during a relatively short span of time. The book is probably the product of a long evolutionary development. Scholars, however, do not agree on the precise stages of this development.[119]

---

[117] W. ALBRIGHT, *From Stone Age to Christianity: Monotheism and the Historical Process,* 2nd ed. (Garden City, N.Y. 1957) 315-319; H. DONNER, *Geschichte des Volkes Israel und seiner Nachbarn in Grundzügen* (Grundrisse zum Alten Testament: Das Alte Testament Deutsch — Ergänzungsreihe 4/1 and 4/2). Teil II: *Von der Königszeit bis zu Alexander dem Großen: Mit einem Augenblick auf die Geschichte des Judentums bis Bar Kochba* (Göttingen 1986) 368-369; J. FINEGAN, *Light from the Ancient Past: The Archeological Background of the Hebrew-Christian Religion* (Princeton 1959) I, 128, 216-217; S. HERRMANN, "Die konstruktive Restauration: Das Deuteronomium als Mitte biblischer Theologie," *Probleme biblischer Theologie* (FS. Gerhard von Rad; ed. H.W. WOLFF) (München 1971) 169-170; LIWAK, "Literary Individuality and the Problem of Hermeneutics," 92; LOHFINK, "Culture Shock," 20; "Gott im Buch Deuteronomium," 114-115; MAYES, *Deuteronomy,* 83; J.A. SOGGIN, *Storia d'Israele,* 351. However, NELSON, *Double Redaction,* 26-27, argues that such an interest in the past (and the imitation of language that went with it) could also have been prevalent during the exilic and postexilic periods.

[118] N. LOHFINK, "Deuteronomy," *IDBSup* 230. In "Verkündigung des Hauptgebots," 251-252, 255, LOHFINK sees 4,1-10 as a unity and is impressed by the exilic implications of vv. 26-28 and especially vv. 29-31. LACONI, *Deuteronomio,* 26, lists 4,29-40; 28,47-69; and 30,1-10 as exilic. J. LEVENSON, "Who Inserted the Book of the Torah?" *HTR* 68 (1975) 221, sees an exilic frame to Dt in 4,1-40; 29,21-28; 30; 31,16-22.24-29; 31,30-32,44. G. VANONI, "Der Geist und der Buchstabe: Überlegungen zum Verhältnis der Testamente und Beobachtungen zu Dtn 30,1-10," *BN* 14 (1981) 85, sees 4,1-40; 28; and 30,1-10 as exilic. VERMEYLEN, "Les sections narratives," 179, n.16, assigns 28,15-68; 29,21-27; 31,16-18 to a Dtr1 who wrote at the beginning of the exile. Some authors see an exilic hand throughout all of Dt. For example, MAYES, *Deuteronomy,* 46, assigns to an exilic second deuteronomistic editor such passages as 6,10-18; 7,4-5.7-16.25-26; 8,1-6.11b.15-16.18b-20; 10,12-11,32; 12,1-7.32; 14,1.4-21; 15,4-6; 17,2-3; 25,17-19; 26,1-15; 26,16-27,26; 31,9-13.24-29; 32,45-47. Even this doesn't seem to exhaust his list of possible exilic additions.

[119] The *Urdeuteronomium,* or original copy of Dt, has been the subject of much debate. Most scholars admit that the book found in the temple during the reign of Josiah is not Dt as we know it today: PHILLIPS, *Deuteronomy,* 3; WEINFELD, *Deuteronomy and the Deuteronomic School,* 158-159. WELLHAUSEN saw the *Urdeuteronomium* in chaps. 12-26, while DRIVER, *Deuteronomy,* lxv, saw it in chaps. 5-26, 28; M. NOTH, *Überlieferungsge-schichtliche Studien* I (Schriften der Königsberger Gelehrten Gesellschaft 18; Halle 1943) 16, holds that it is to be found in 4,44-30,20. MAYES, *Deuteronomy,* 48, includes the following in an original edition of Dt: 4,45; 6,4-9.20-24; 7,1-3.6.17-24; 8,7-11a. 12-14.17-18a; 9,1-7a.13-14.26-29; 10,10-11; 12,13-15.17-19.(20-28.)29-31; 13,1-18*; 14,2-

It is not the aim of this study to enter into the heated discussion regarding the evolutionary development of the book of Dt. The focus of this work will be on Dt's rhetoric or argumentation. This assumes a synchronic approach to the text. Thus it will tend to avoid or bracket out historical and diachronic considerations. The cultic, legal, diplomatic, and wisdom roots have been examined because they appear to have influenced Dt's rhetoric. It is good to be aware of that historical context, even if diachronic features are not essential to a rhetorical-critical analysis.

3.21*; and nearly all of 14,22-25,16, with a few isolated exceptions. Cf. also KAISER, *Einleitung in das Alte Testament*, 134-135. B. CHILDS, *Introduction to the Old Testament as Scripture*, 2nd ed. (London 1979) 206, points out that there is little agreement on the nature or the scope of the earliest Dt or even on the criteria by which it can be discovered. FREEDMAN, "The Deuteronomistic History," 226, doubts if Josiah's Dt can be rediscovered by critical techniques.

The evolution of Dt is complicated by its relationship to the Deuteronomistic History. It was NOTH who first proposed that Dt and the Former Prophets constituted a continuous historical and theological work encompassing the period of Israel's history from just prior to the conquest of the land to the end of the monarchy. NOTH's theory has been modified by many and challenged by a few. Just some of the works discussing this Deuteronomistic History are: A. CHOLEWINSKI, "Zur theologischen Deutung des Moabbundes," *Bib* 66 (1985) 102; F.M. CROSS, *Canaanite Myth and Hebrew Epic* (Cambridge, Mass. 1973) 274-289; W. DIETRICH, *Prophetie und Geschichte* (FRLANT 108; Göttingen 1972); D.N. FREEDMAN, "The Deuteronomic History," *IDBSup* 226-228; R.E. FRIEDMAN, *The Exile and Biblical Narrative: The Formation of the Deuteronomistic and Priestly Works* (HSM 22; Chico, Calif. 1981); P. KEARNEY, "The Role of the Gibeonites in the Deuteronomic History," *CBQ* 35 (1973) 1-19; J. LEVENSON, "Who Inserted the Book of the Torah?" *HTR* 68 (1975) 203-233; N. LOHFINK, "Kerygmata des deuteronomistischen Geschichtswerks," *Die Botschaft und die Boten* (FS. H.W. Wolff; ed. J. JEREMIAS and L. PERLITT) (Neukirchen/Vluyn 1981) 87-100; D.J. McCARTHY, "II Samuel 7 and the Structure of the Deuteronomic History," *JBL* 84 (1965) 131-138; "The Wrath of Yahweh and the Structural Unity of the Deuteronomistic History," *Essays in Old Testament Ethics: J.P. Hyatt Memorial* (ed. J.L. CRENSHAW and J.T. WILLIS; New York 1974) 99-110; A.D.H. MAYES, "Deuteronomy: Law of Moses or Law of God?" *PIBA* 5 (1981) 41, 49-51; *Story of Israel*; J. MEJIA, "The Aim of the Deuteronomic Historian: A Reappraisal," *Proceedings of the Sixth World Congress of Jewish Studies*, I (ed. A. SHINAN; Jerusalem 1977) 291-298; MINETTE DE TILLESSE, "Martin Noth et la Redaktionsgeschichte des livres historiques," 51-76; "Tu et vous"; NELSON, *Double Redaction*; NOTH, *Überlieferungsgeschichtliche Studien* I; M. O'BRIEN, *The Deuteronomistic History Hypothesis: A Reassessment* (OBO 92; Fribourg/Göttingen 1989); B. PECKHAM, *The Composition of the Deuteronomistic History* (HSM 35; Atlanta 1985); POLZIN, *Moses and the Deuteronomist*; A. RADJAWANE, "Das deuteronomistische Geschichtswerk: Ein Forschungsbericht," *TRu* 38 (1974) 177-216; R. SMEND, "Deuteronomistisches Geschichtswerk, *EKL*, 3rd ed. (1986) I, 821-823; *Die Entstehung des Alten Testaments*, especially 62-81, 110-139; "Das Gesetz und die Völker: Ein Beitrag zur deuteronomistischen Redaktionsgeschichte," *Probleme biblischer Theologie* (FS. G. von Rod; ed. H.W. WOLFF) (München 1971) 494-509; H.W. WOLFF, "Das Kerygma des deuteronomistischen Geschichtswerks," *ZAW* 73 (1961) 171-186.

This chapter has attempted to investigate the rhetorical nature of the book of Dt. We have noted that this book presents itself as the valedictory address of Moses, or rather as a series of farewell discourses given by him to the assembled people of Israel. Its style is peculiar, didactic, and homiletic. Its parenesis expresses a certain urgency, and it speaks to Israel in direct address. The roots of Dt's rhetoric lie in Israel's legal, cultic, political, and wisdom traditions. Possibly written by levites, elders, court scribes, or prophets, its purpose seems to lie in a reform of the religion and society of Israel. Meant to be read aloud, it presents a program of religious instruction and an urgent call to renewal. We will now turn to a specific section of Dt, the Third Address of Moses. This, the shortest of the three orations, reflects all the concerns thus far examined.

1.6 The Third Address of Moses

In Dt 28,69 – 30,20[120] is found the third and last prose speech of Moses on the plains of Moab, and it has often been described as a "supplement," "peroration," or even "conclusion" to chapters 1-28. Whoever composed this discourse was familiar with the original Dt (at least chapters 5 – 28), to which it refers as "this book" הספר הזה: 29,19.26) or "this book of the *torah*" (ספר התורה הזה: 29,20; 30,10).[121] The concerns of "this book" are reflected in the Third Address of Moses.

In general chapters 29 – 30 are considered to be later additions to an original Dt. Yet this Third Address shares much with what precedes it. In fact, the common features are numerous enough to lead some authors to conclude that there is at least a general kind of unity with chapters 1 – 28.[122] Dt 29 – 30 have been described as a series of speeches or

---

[120] In this study the Third Address of Moses is considered to include not only Dt 29-30 but also the last verse of chap. 28 (v.69). The reasons for this delimitation can be found in 5.1. The determination of the rhetorical unit has been delayed in order to follow more closely the *parts* of ancient rhetoric. Since the beginning and the end of a text are associated with its organization, they will be discussed under *dispositio*.

[121] Buis and Leclercq, *Le Deutéronome*, 181; Cholewinski, *Deuteronomio* II, 41; Knapp, *Deuteronomium 4*, 139; Laconi, *Deuteronomio*, 197; Nicholson, *Deuteronomy and Tradition*, 21; Reiter, "Der Bundesschluß," 60, 302; Von Rad, *Das fünfte Buch Mose*, 129; *Theologie des Alten Testaments* I, 234-235; Wright, *Deuteronomy*, 312-313, 502. ספר התורה הזה is also found in 31,26, while ספר התורה הזאת is found in 28,61. ספר התורה is also found in Josh 8,34; 2 Kgs 22,8.11; הספר הזה is also found in Dt 28,58; 2 Kgs 22,13; 23,3. See Cholewinski, "Deutung des Moabbundes," 101; Lohfink, "Die Bundesurkunde des Königs Josias," 285-288.

[122] Breit, *Die Predigt*, 29; F. Montet, *Le Deutéronome et la question de l'Hexateuque: étude critique et exégétique* (Paris 1891) 97; Thompson, *Deuteronomy*, 20-21. Also Von Rad admits to an essential unity of some unspecified kind within the entire book: *Das fünfte Buch Mose*, 8.

sermons whose main theme is obedience to the covenant law which has just been proclaimed. Here again the sermon or address is largely parenetic as it attempts to persuade Israel to obey Yahweh. This section also exhibits the use of rhetorical skills to appeal to the individual.[123] Many of the characteristic words and expressions found in the rest of Dt appear in these two chapters.[124] Even the problem of variation in singular and plural forms of address is to be found here. Dt 29 is largely in the second person plural, although singular forms occur now and then. Dt 30 is mostly singular with an occasional plural form. Both chapters also have some first person plural forms (Dt 30 only in vv. 12-14).

Like the rest of Dt, the Third Address has its roots in Israel's cult. There is a marked liturgical interest here: the recitation of a salvation history (29,1-7); the solemn charge to accept the covenant (29,8-14); warnings of the disastrous consequences of idolatry (29,15-18); the promise of restoration and mercy in the case of repentance (30,1-10), and a solemn appeal to freely choose this relationship with Yahweh (30,11-20). All this may even be based on a specific liturgy. Some scholars believe that Dt 29-30 could have been used in a covenant renewal festival, even if it is not a proper liturgical text as it stands,[125] Lohfink sees the outline of such a liturgy especially in 29,1-20 and 30,11-20. This outline includes: 1) the recitation of a salvation history; 2) the proclamation of the making of a covenant; 3) sermons; 4) blessings, curse, calling upon witnesses, closing parenesis.[126] One sign of such a liturgy is the persistent use of the word "today," which occurs seven times in chapter 29 and six times in chapter 30.[127]

---

[123] LOERSCH, *Das Deuteronomium und seine Deutungen*, 33; McCARTHY, *Treaty and Covenant*, 188, 204-205; MAYES, *Story of Israel*, 36; "Deuteronomy 4," 44-45; VANONI, "Der Geist und der Buchstabe," 81.

[124] Of the 249 words, expressions, and combinations of expressions which WEINFELD lists as characteristic of or at least common in both Dt and the Deuteronomistic History, 46 are found in Dt 29-30. Twelve of these expressions are shared exclusively with Dt 1-4, the Deuteronomistic History, or Jeremiah C, those prose sections in the book of Jeremiah which may have been added by the Deuteronomistic School. This still leaves 34 expressions in Dt 29-30 which are shared with chaps. 5-28. Cf. WEINFELD, *Deuteronomy and the Deuteronomic School*, 320-359. DRIVER, *Deuteronomy*, 320, lists words and expressions found in Dt 29-30 which are not otherwise found in Dt: השכיל (29,8); אלה (29,11.13.18.19.20; 30,7); גללים and שקוצים (29,16); פן יש (29,17); שררות (29,18); עשן אף (29,19); סלח (29,19); לרעה (29,20); תחלואים (29,21); עזבו את ברית (29,24); נתש (29,27); הדיח (30,1.4). Cf. also VANONI, "Der Geist und der Buchstabe," 80.

[125] BEE, "Statistical Properties," 14; CHOLEWINSKI, *Deuteronomio II*, 27; DRIVER, *Deuteronomy*, ii; LACONI, *Deuteronomio*, 198; NICHOLSON, *Deuteronomy and Tradition*, 21-22; THOMPSON, *Deuteronomy*, 279; WRIGHT, *Deuteronomy*, 317, 502.

[126] LOHFINK, "Der Bundesschluß im Land Moab," 44.

[127] Dt 29,3.9.11.12.14[2X].17; 30,2.8.11.16.18.19. Cf. also כיום הזה in 29,27. See NICHOLSON, *Deuteronomy and Tradition*, 45; VON RAD, "Das formgeschichtliche Problem des Hexateuch," 35-36; *Das fünfte Buch Mose*, 129.

The ancient Near Eastern vassal treaties also have left traces upon this Third Address of Moses. Many scholars see an internal structure to these two chapters which reflects the treaty form.[128] The appeal for absolute fidelity to Yahweh (30,2.6.10.20) and some of the vocabulary also call to mind the vassal treaties. For we hear of cities being overthrown (הפך), burned (שׂרף), and strewn with sulphur and salt (29,22) — all conventional methods of retaliation for breach of treaty in the ancient Near East.[129]

---

[128] For example, LOHFINK, "Der Bundesschluß im Land Moab," 43, sees six treaty elements in the structure of the Third Address:
1. Vorgeschichte (29,1-8);
2. Protokoll des Bundesschlusses (29,9-14);
3. (warnende) Predigt (29,15-20);
4. anknüpfender Fluchabschluß und Segen in exilischer Weiterentwicklung (29,21-30,10);
5. (empfehlende) Predigt (30,11-14);
6. Segen, Fluch, Zeugenanrufung und Schlußparänese (30,15-20).

Actually LOHFINK himself feels that this structure shows only traces of the treaty form, so he does not follow the formula suggested by K. BALTZER, *Das Bundesformular* (WMANT 4; Neukirchen 1960) 44, who finds the following structure in the Third Address: Vorgeschichte (29,1-7); Grundsatzerklärung (29,8.12.17); Fluch und Segen (29,21-30,10); Segen- und Fluchformel (30,16-18); Erwähnung der Anrufung von Himmel und Erde zu zeugen (30,19). McCARTHY, *Treaty and Covenant,* 202, prefers to see ten elements in the structure:
1. *Mise en scène* (28,69);
2. Historical prologue (29,1b-8);
3. List of parties (29,9-14);
4. Stipulations (29,15-18);
5. Curse (29,19-27);
6. Blessing (30,1-10);
7. Exhortation (30,11-14);
8. Curse-blessing (30,15-19);
9. Witnesses (30,19);
10. Exhortation (30,19b-20).

CHOLEWINSKI, *Deuteronomio* II, 6, corrects three of McCARTHY's ten elements:
4. Esigenza fondamentale   29,15-20
5. Maledizioni   29,21-28
8. Appello a fare la scelta 30,15-20

Cf. also NTAGWARARA, "Alliance d'Israël," 89, 227; PHILLIPS, *Deuteronomy,* 198-199; VON RAD, *Das fünfte Buch Mose,* 128. A. ROFÉ. "The Covenant in the Land of Moab (Dt 28,69-30,20): Historico-literary, Comparative, and Formcritical Considerations," *Das Deuteronomium: Entstehung, Gestalt und Botschaft* (ed. N. LOHFINK) 317, sees the structure more closely approximating that of the Hittite treaties rather than that of the Assyrian treaties: a) inscription (28,69); b) the historical prologue (29,1-9); c) the statement of bond (29,10-14); d) stipulation (29,15-19a.28); e) and f) witness and "concised" curse and blessing (30,15-20). He considers 29,21-27 and 30,1-10 to be secondary additions. VON RAD, *Das fünfte Buch Mose,* 129, 132, points out that even 29,16-21 and 30,15-20 can be seen as microcosms or fragmentary forms of the covenant pattern.

[129] WEINFELD, *Deuteronomy and the Deuteronomic School,* 142.

Yet it is also clear that no matter how much treaty language, ideas, and forms may have influenced these chapters, there is no treaty ceremony or document standing directly behind them. One essential element of the form (the stipulations) is missing. The elements of the treaty which do appear here are not really formal parts of a treaty document. Rather, they are embedded in the speech or sermon which Dt 29–30 purports to be. These chapters give the impression of being an artistically formed literary creation. Rather than a "living text," it's an artificial composition.[130]

Wisdom traditions also link these two chapters with the rest of Dt. In 29,3 we read about a "heart to know" (לב לדעת), while 29,28 speaks of a hidden wisdom known only to God (cf. Job 28). This wisdom is not only accessible to every human being but is even in the mouth and the heart (30,11-14) — for God makes it possible for Israel to know wisdom (Job 28,12-23; Bar 3,29-31; Sir 24,4; Ps 37,31). The second half of chapter 30 is no less influenced by themes common to sapiential literature, for it imitates Wisdom's imploring call to choose from two ways what is life, what is wise, what is good. This choice is a personal one, another concept found in wisdom traditions (cf. Prov 1,1-7; 2,4; 3,13.16; 4,6-7.13; 8,35-36).[131]

Dt 29–30 have especially strong links to Dt 4,1-40. Klostermann in 1871 already noted the relationship between the two sections, which serve as a kind of frame to Moses' Second Address.[132] In chapters 29-30, just as in 4,1-40, a treaty scheme of history, law, and sanction serves as a background. Both sections treat curse and blessing not as alternatives but rather as historical fact: blessing follows curse (30,1-10; 4,25-30). The correspondence of content in the two sections has long been noted: announcements of exile (29,21-27; 4,25-28); restoration (30,1-10; 4,29-30); the nearness of God (30,11-14; 4,7-8). Both share much of the same vocabulary: idols of wood and stone (29,16; 4,28); trials, signs, and wonders (29,2; 4,34), etc. Both sections treat of wisdom themes, especially that of the ease and sweetness of the law. Both issue a call to conversion, and both are believed to be exilic, possibly even by the same hand. McCarthy suggests that the reasons why these chapters frame the kernel

---

[130] Buis and Leclercq, Le Deutéronome, 181; Cholewinski, Deuteronomio II, 11; Mayes, Deuteronomy, 359; "Deuteronomy 4," 45; Nötscher, "Bundesformular und 'Amtsschimmel,'" 199; Penna, Deuteronomio, 37; Preuss, Deuteronomium, 159-160.

[131] Kearney, "The Role of the Gibeonites," 6; Loersch, Das Deuteronomium und seine Deutungen, 93; McCarthy, Treaty and Covenant, 203; Preuss, Deuteronomium, 88; Von Rad, Theologie des Alten Testaments I, 457; Weisheit in Israel, 192; Weinfeld, Deuteronomy and the Deuteronomic School, 308.

[132] A. Klostermann, "Das Lied Mose (Deut 32) und das Deuteronomium: Ein Beitrag zur Entstehungsgeschichte des Pentateuchs," TSK 44 (1871) 259-260. Cf. Begg, "Literary Criticism of Deut 4,1-40," 13.

of Dt is to surround the obligations and curses of the deuteronomic code with a message of hope.[133]

There are, of course, differences between the second and third discourses of Moses, differences which lead most scholars to accept that all or at least part of 28,69 – 30,20 is exilic. The Third Address of Moses seems to presume that the covenant relationship has been ended because of Israel's infidelity and that the curses have fallen upon the people. The land is desolate and its citizens are scattered. It has already been noted that the existence of Dt 5-28 is taken for granted in this section and that curses and blessings are not viewed as alternative possibilities but as succeeding phases of Israel's history. The Third Address may contain some old material, especially in 30,11-20, but otherwise most scholars are convinced that this section is late.[134]

Are the two chapters a unity? Few scholars who approach the Third Address of Moses diachronically seem to think so. Driver already saw "imperfect" connections in chapter 29 between vv. 20 and 21 and in chapter 30 between vv. 10 and 11. Others have separated the two chapters from one another, pointing out that Dt 30 is a logical continuation of chapter 28, not of chapter 29.[135] Often 30,1-10 is considered a secondary insertion within the unit 29,1-20; 30,11-20.[136] Some scholars prefer to slice up the two chapters into a number of independent pieces.[137]

---

[133] McCarthy, *Treaty and Covenant*, 204. See Begg, "Literary Criticism of Deut 4,1-40," 49; Driver, *Deuteronomy*, lxxvi; Knapp, *Deuteronomium 4*, 129-138, 158-163; Levenson, "Who Inserted... the Torah?" 212-214; Lohfink, *Höre, Israel!*, 119-120; Mayes, *Story of Israel*, 36-37; "Deuteronomy 4," 44-46; Wolff, "Kerygma," 184.

[134] Cholewinski, *Deuteronomio II*, 6, 19-20, 27; "Deutung des Moabbundes," 107; Mayes, *Deuteronomy*, 44-45; McCarthy, *Treaty and Covenant*, 137, 147; Phillips, *Deuteronomy*, 198. It is especially 29,21-27 and 30,1-10 which are considered late: Friedman, *The Exile and Biblical Narrative*, 18-19; Ginsberg, *Israelian Heritage*, 80; Wolff, "Kerygma," 181. Buis, *Le Deutéronome*, 394, points to common themes of conversion and return in Dt 30,1-10 and Deutero-Isaiah (Isa 43,18-21; 48,20-21; 50,2-3; 51,10-11). This is probably not the result of dependence of one work upon the other but of common ideas during the exilic period. Mayes, *Deuteronomy*, 367-368, also sees affinities with Jeremiah as clear indications for an exilic date for Dt 29-30. Those who accept some older material in these chapters (especially in 30,11-20) include: Buis and Leclercq, *Le Deutéronome*, 16; Driver, *Deuteronomy*, lxxv; Ntagwarara, "Alliance d'Israël," 220, 228; Wright, *Deuteronomy*, 317-318.

[135] Driver, *Deuteronomy*, lxxiii; Kearney, "The Role of the Gibeonites," 14, n. 46; Mitchell, "Use of the Second Person," 106; Nicholson, *Deuteronomy and Tradition*, 35; Rofé, "The Covenant in the Land of Moab," 311-312; Wolff, "Kerygma," 181.

[136] Begg, "Literary Criticism of Deut 4,1-40," 50; Mendecki, "Dtn 30,3-4," 267.

[137] Knapp, *Deuteronomium 4*, 128-163, divides Dt 29-30 into three blocks which supposedly correspond with similar layers in Dt 4: 29,1-14*; 29,15-27*; and 30,1-10*. The remainder of this section, 30,11-14.15-20, is not supposed to correspond with chapter four. This analysis and the process used to reach such results have been criticized sharply by G. Braulik, review of *Deuteronomium 4: Literarische Analyse und theologische Interpretation*, by D. Knapp, in *RB* 96 (1989) 266-286. Another scholar who divides Dt

1.7 Conclusion

This first chapter has been an attempt to explore the rhetorical nature of the book of Dt in general and of the Third Address of Moses (Dt 28,69 – 30,20) in particular. We have noted that the book has the form of a valedictory address to the people of Israel on the plains of Moab just prior to their entrance into the promised land. Chapters 29 and 30 form the last of three prose speeches in the work. They form a kind of peroration for Dt.

The speeches of Dt have a didactic and homiletic thrust. The work has its roots in the liturgy, jurisprudence, diplomacy, and wisdom traditions of ancient Israel. Dt is *torah,* a persuasive and didactic reform program designed to teach Israel its traditions and to remind it of its obligations to Yahweh. Dt seeks to convince its audience to renew its special relationship with Yahweh, and it does this through its peculiar style and its parenesis — an insistent, personal appeal to the mind and emotions of every individual in the audience. Whether composed by levites, scribes, elders, or prophets, the book has an urgent tone and demands from the people an exclusive loyalty to its God.

The nature of Dt, then, is highly rhetorical. The book is didactic and argumentative, for it seeks to persuade and to convince. It is meant to be read aloud, to be heard. The distinctive style and argumentation of Dt are apparent even in chapters 29 – 30. The liturgical, political, legal, and pedagogical elements found throughout Dt are also to be found here. Dt 29-30 is cast in the form of an oration, an oration which seeks to convince its listeners of the necessity of reform. If Dt in general is rhetorical, we can say the same of its third address.

Biblical experts have used a variety of methods to investigate Dt. Is there possibly any method which has been overlooked so far which might help to cast light on the text? The next chapter will suggest that there is. If Dt is cast in the form of a speech which is meant to be read aloud, if it is by nature rhetorical, why can't we attempt to apply the insights of the art of rhetoric to the book?

29-30 into even smaller pieces is PREUSS, *Deuteronomium,* 60, 159 (despite the comment that chaps. 29 and 30 are closely related!). In his "layer four" is to be found 29,1.2?3.6-7.8-10aα.13-14.15-20; 30,1-10.11-14.15-20; "layer five" contains 29,2?4-5. 10aβ-12?28?; 30,18.19a?. However, CHOLEWINSKI, *Deuteronomio* II, 38, sees both chapters as more or less a unity.

CHAPTER 2

RHETORIC AND RHETORICAL CRITICISM

2.1 Rhetorical Criticism

In the first chapter we explored the rhetorical nature of Dt. Past research has demonstrated that this book is homiletic, didactic, and recognizable by its peculiar style and parenesis. Its rhetoric is rooted in the liturgy, laws, diplomacy, and wisdom traditions of ancient Israel. Whether written by levites, prophets, elders, or scribes, Dt is a reform program addressed to every member of God's chosen people.

This description is largely the product of historical-critical investigations. Historical criticism, which has dominated biblical exegesis for the past two centuries, actually consists of a number of different methodologies, all of which try

> to reconstruct in a critical way the historical context in which the biblical texts had their origin. The critic sets out to discover the historical meaning of the text — the meaning that the text had for the community for which it was destined.[1]

Traditional historical-critical methods then are diachronic, that is, they are concerned with the history or evolution of a text.[2]

In recent years, however, there has been a growing dissatisfaction with historical criticism and its diachronic reading of a text. Despite its contribution to our understanding of the Bible, the historical-critical "method" is losing its status as the only acceptable approach to Scripture. Its presuppositions have been challenged, its results sometimes

---

[1] A. STOCK, "The Limits of Historical-Critical Exegesis," *BTB* 13 (1983) 28.

[2] D. PATTE, *What Is Structural Exegesis?* (GBS, New Testament Series; Philadelphia 1976) 13. The terminology *diachronic/synchronic* comes from linguistics, specifically from F. DE SAUSSURE, *Cours de linguistique générale* (reprint of Édition critique préparée par TULLIO DE MAURO, Paris 1916; reprint: Paris 1972) 117. Synchrony refers to a language-state, while diachrony refers to the evolution of language, its historical aspects. N. FRYE, *The Great Code: The Bible and Literature* (San Diego 1982) 15, notes that in contemporary thought the emphasis is on language and linguistic models. The term "historical criticism" could include such methodologies as source criticism (sometimes also called literary criticism), form criticism, tradition history, and redaction criticism.

have been rejected, and its criteria have been questioned.³ Many scholars
have been searching for new methods and models for approaching
ancient biblical texts.⁴ Such new methodologies or approaches often

---

³ See, for example: ALTER, *The Art of Biblical Narrative,* 47-48; B.W. ANDERSON, "The
New Frontier of Rhetorical Criticism: A Tribute to James Muilenburg," introduction to
Rhetorical Criticism (FS. James Muilenburg; ed. M. KESSLER and J.J. JACKSON) (Pittsburgh
1974) xvii; J. BARTON, *Reading the Old Testament: Method in Biblical Study* (London 1984)
77-78, 105-106; S. BROWN, "Biblical Philology, Linguistics and the Problem of Method,"
HeyJ 20 (1979) 296; B. CHILDS, *Introduction to the Old Testament as Scripture,* 2nd ed.
(London 1979) 13, 71, 79, 83; "Response to Reviewers of *Introduction to the OT as
Scripture,*" *JSOT* 16 (1980) 57-58; G. COATS, "Humility and Honor: A Moses Legend in
Numbers 12," *Art and Meaning: Rhetoric in Biblical Literature* (JSOTSS 19; ed. D. CLINES,
D. GUNN, and A. HAUSER) (Sheffield 1982) 97; J.D. CROSSAN, "Perspectives and Methods in
Contemporary Biblical Criticism," *BR* 22 (1977) 39; ESLINGER, *Into the Hands of the Living
God,* 9; FERGUSON, *Biblical Hermeneutics,* 67; N. FRYE, *Anatomy of Criticism:* Four Essays
(Princeton, N.J. 1957) 315; *The Great Code,* xvii; N. GOTTWALD, *The Hebrew Bible: A
Socio-Literary Introduction* (Philadelphia 1985) 20-21; R. GRANT and D. TRACY, *A Short
History of the Interpretation of the Bible,* 2nd ed. (London 1984) 130-131; M. KESSLER, "A
Methodological Setting for Rhetorical Criticism," *Semitics* 4 (1974) 32-33; "An
Introduction to Rhetorical Criticism of the Bible: Prolegomena," *Semitics* 7 (1980) 10, 20;
R. KNIERIM, "Old Testament Form Criticism Reconsidered," *Int* 27 (1973) 449; E. KRENTZ,
The Historical-Critical Method (GBS, Philadelphia 1975) 85; W. LASOR, "The *Sensus Plenior*
and Biblical Interpretation," *A Guide to Contemporary Hermeneutics: Major Trends in
Biblical Interpretation* (ed. D. McKIM; Grand Rapids 1986) 53; LOHFINK, "Kerygmata des
deuteronomistischen Geschichtswerks," 89; McCARTHY, *Treaty and Covenant,* 175; P.
MACKY, "The Coming Revolution: The New Literary Approach to New Testament
Interpretation," *A Guide to Contemporary Hermeneutics* (ed. D. McKIM, 1986) 263-279,
especially 265-267; T. MERRIAM, "Dissociation and the Literal Interpretation of the Bible,"
DRev 96 (1978) 84; R. MORGAN and J. BARTON, *Biblical Interpretation* (Oxford Bible Series;
Oxford 1988) 287; A. NATIONS, "Historical Criticism and the Current Methodological
Crisis," *SJT* 36 (1983) 63-64; PATTE, *What Is Structural Exegesis?,* 9-10, 14; POLZIN, *Moses
and the Deuteronomist,* 13; M. POWELL, *What Is Narrative Criticism?* (GBS, New Testament
Series; Minneapolis 1990) 2; D. ROBERTSON, *The Old Testament and the Literary Critic*
(GBS, Old Testament Series; Philadelphia 1977) 7; G. SOARES-PRABHU, "The Historical
Critical Method: Reflections on its Relevance for the Study of the Gospels in India Today,"
Theologizing in India (ed. M. AMALADOSS, T.K. JOHN, and G. GISPERT-SAUCH; Bangalore
1981) 317-319, 340-341; D. STEINMETZ, "The Superiority of Pre-critical Exegesis," *TToday*
37 (1980) 27-38; STOCK, "Limits," 28; W. WINK, *The Bible in Human Transformation:
Toward a New Paradigm for Biblical Study* (Philadelphia 1973) 1-15.
    ⁴ ALONSO SCHÖKEL, "Of Methods and Models," 3-13; GOTTWALD, *The Hebrew Bible,*
7-8, 20-22; T. LONG, "Committing Hermeneutical Heresy," *TToday* 44 (1987) 165. I
cannot begin to do justice with the recent materials on some of these methods, and in any
case it would go beyond the scope of this book to do so. One can note, for example, the
storm of controversy raised over the form of canonical criticism proposed by CHILDS in
his *Introduction to the Old Testament as Scripture.* See, for example, J. BARR, "Childs'
Introduction to the Old Testament as Scripture," *JSOT* 16 (1980) 12-23; BARTON, *Reading
the Old Testament,* 77-103; J. BLENKINSOPP, "A New Kind of Introduction: Professor
Childs' *Introduction to the Old Testament as Scripture,*" *JSOT* 16 (1980) 24-27; H.
CAZELLES, "The Canonical Approach to Torah and Prophets," *JSOT* 16 (1980) 28-31; B.
CHILDS, "Response to Reviewers," 52-60; T. KEEGAN, *Interpreting the Bible: A Popular
Introduction to Biblical Hermeneutics* (New York/Mahwah, N.J. 1985) 131-144; B. KITTEL,

emphasize synchronic aspects over diachronic ones.[5] Dissatisfaction with historical criticism, of course, cannot deny its achievements and its continuing value.[6] But the way has been opened to new avenues of exploring the Bible. Today's research often seeks a variety of methods and a plurality of meanings in a text.[7]

One of these new methodologies is called *rhetorical criticism*. The name "rhetorical criticism" was proposed by Muilenburg in his presidential address to the Society of Biblical Literature on December 18, 1968.[8] Muilenburg's rhetorical criticism concentrates its energies on the unique features of a text. Its concerns are *structural* (defining the limits of a literary unit, discerning the configuration of its parts) and *stylistic* (such as the use of rhetorical figures, particles, and repetition). Such a

---

"Brevard Childs' Development of the Canonical Approach," *JSOT* 16 (1980) 2-11; G. LANDES, "The Canonical Approach to Introducing the Old Testament: Prodigy and Problems," *JSOT* 16 (1980) 32-39; R.E. MURPHY, "The Old Testament as Scripture," *JSOT* 16 (1980) 40-44; D. PATRICK and A. SCULT, *Rhetoric and Biblical Interpretation* (JSOTSS 82; BLS 26; Sheffield 1990) 130-133; and R. SMEND, "Questions about the Importance of the Canon in an Old Testament Introduction," *JSOT* 16 (1980) 45-51. Controversy has also centered around so-called "structural exegesis": BARTON, *Reading the Old Testament*, 104-139; R. CULLEY, "Some Comments on Structural Analysis and Biblical Studies," *VTS* 22 (1971) 129-142; KEEGAN, *Interpreting the Bible*, 40-72; R. JACOBSON, "The Structuralists and the Bible," *Int* 28 (1974) 146-164; PATTE, *What Is Structural Exegesis?*; R. POLZIN, *Biblical Structuralism: Method and Subjectivity in the Study of Ancient Texts* (SBLSS 5; Philadelphia/Missoula 1977); R. SPIVEY, "Structuralism and Biblical Studies: The Uninvited Guest," *Int* 28 (1974) 133-145.

[5] KESSLER, "Methodological Setting," 34; S. BOORER, "The Importance of a Diachronic Approach: The Case of Genesis-Kings," *CBQ* 51 (1989) 206. It should be noted that English literary criticism had its own period of rejection of diachronic approaches in favor of synchronic ones. This period is associated with the so-called "New Criticism." See BARTON, *Reading the Old Testament*, 140-157; KESSLER, "Introduction to Rhetorical Criticism," 8-12.

[6] SOARES-PRABHU, "The Historical Critical Method," 345. It's unlikely that historical critical methodologies will disappear (it would also be a great loss). It still has staunch defenders: BARTON, *Reading the Old Testament*, 43; KRENTZ, *The Historical-Critical Method*, 61, 63; MORGAN and BARTON, *Biblical Interpretation*, 172; NATIONS, "Historical Criticism," 65-67. Some scholars question whether modern literary criticism will open new avenues in Bible interpretation, since it may be too subjective: BUIS, *Le Deutéronome*, 475; J. KUGEL, "On the Bible and Literary Criticism," *Prooftexts* 1 (1981) 228-232; PERLITT, "Deuteronomium 1-3," 153, 158-159; D. PATRICK and A. SCULT, *Rhetoric and Biblical Interpretation* (JSOTSS 82; BLS 26; Sheffield 1990) 18; L. POLAND, "The Bible and the Rhetorical Sublime," *The Bible as Rhetoric* (ed. M. WARNER; London/New York 1990) 31.

[7] BARTON, *Reading the Old Testament*, 5-6; CROSSAN, "Perspectives and Methods," 40-42; KESSLER, "Introduction to Rhetorical Criticism," 7.

[8] See J. MUILENBURG, "Form Criticism and Beyond," *JBL* 88 (1969) 1-18. He calls the compositional and structural patterns of a text "rhetoric" and the methodology used to describe them "rhetorical criticism" (p. 8).

rhetorical criticism focuses on "the particular linguistic features of a given text"[9] and thus emphasizes its synchronic aspects.

Studies since Muilenburg have been struggling to work out an acceptable definition and methodology for this new approach to biblical texts. Melugin criticizes Muilenburg for neglecting the study of genre but agrees that exegesis must study both the typical and the unique.[10] Greenwood follows Muilenburg in criticizing form criticism and associating rhetorical criticism with the literary features of a text. He feels that Hebrew literature has to be related to other literature in the ancient Near East. For Greenwood rhetorical criticism is an art.[11]

Kessler observes that English literary critics themselves do not agree on what the term "rhetoric" means or ought to mean.[12] He notes that such critics often distinguish between a narrower and a broader notion of rhetorical criticism. The narrower conception follows the traditional concerns of rhetoric, especially the investigation of stylistic devices; the wider conception often includes developments in linguistics, critical theory, and semantics.[13] Kessler suggests that the term "rhetorical criticism" be used for a broad-based type of literary criticism which deals with an exclusively structural and synchronic investigation of a text.[14]

Anderson sees rhetorical criticism as a methodology which gives its attention to the text itself, to the final literary work as we have it.[15] Kikawada sees it as a synchronic study of a text which aims to recover the meaning of the units of a literary work. This is done by tracing the process of composition through the examination of content, grammar, rhetorical features, structural devices and poetic parallelism.[16] Kikawada does stress that rhetorical criticism should reveal not only what the text says but how it conveys that message. Gottwald relates rhetorical

---

[9] R. MELUGIN, "Muilenburg, Form Criticism, and Theological Exegesis," *Encounter with the Text: Form and History in the Hebrew Bible* (SBLSS 8; ed. M.J. BUSS) (Philadelphia/Missoula 1979) 91.

[10] Ibid., 94.

[11] D. GREENWOOD, "Rhetorical Criticism and Formgeschichte: Some Methodological Considerations," *JBL* 89 (1970) 418-426, especially 422-423.

[12] KESSLER, "Methodological Setting," 22.

[13] Ibid., 24.

[14] Ibid., 35-36. In a later article, "Introduction to Rhetorical Criticism," 1-27, KESSLER virtually identifies biblical criticism with literary study. He examines modern literary criticism and encourages biblical scholars to do the same.

[15] ANDERSON, "The New Frontier," xvii.

[16] I. KIKAWADA, "Some Proposals for the Definition of Rhetorical Criticism," *Semitics* 5 (1977) 67, 70, 74. KIKAWADA's methodology is basically one of dividing a text into units which are then analyzed stylistically. See M. SAVAGE, "Literary Criticism and Biblical Studies: A Rhetorical Analysis of the Joseph Narrative," *Scripture in Context: Essays on the Comparative Method* (ed. C. EVANS, W. HALLO, and J. WHITE; PTMS 34) (Pittsburgh 1980) 86-87.

criticism to the "Bible as literature" movement, since it seeks to establish the literary individuality of a text by analyzing its structure and the dynamic interrelationship of its parts.[17]

Such notions of rhetorical criticism are thus closely related to, or form a division of, literary-critical analysis of texts. The attention of the rhetorical critic seems to be focused on three elements: the author's intention, the specific devices or tools the author uses (especially structural and rhetorical devices), and its effect on an audience.

Kennedy proposes the following definition:

> Rhetorical criticism takes the text as we have it, whether the work of a single author or the product of editing, and looks at it from the point of view of the author's or editor's intent, the unified results, and how it would be perceived by an audience of near contemporaries.[18]

This definition is broad enough to include most, if not all, of the understandings of rhetorical criticism as practiced by biblical scholars today. Nevertheless, at least in Old Testament studies, rhetorical criticism has most often emphasized the literary criticism of a text.[19]

However, such a literary notion of rhetoric has been sharply criticized. Fox faults Kikawada and others for missing the main point of rhetoric: suasion.[20] Rhetorical criticism of the Old Testament has too

---

[17] GOTTWALD, *The Hebrew Bible*, 23.

[18] KENNEDY, *New Testament Interpretation*, 4. Note that such rhetorical criticism would study a text from all three points of view in communication: that of sender, that of message/text, and that of receiver. W. BOOTH, a literary critic who stirred up great interest in the rhetorical analysis of literature, defined "rhetorical study" as "study of *use*, of purposes pursued, targets hit or missed, practices illuminated for the sake not of pure knowledge but of further (and improved) practice." See *The Rhetoric of Fiction*, 2nd ed. (Chicago 1983) 441. B. VICKERS, *In Defence of Rhetoric* (Oxford 1988) 306, defines rhetorical criticism very simply as "the analysis of texts in terms of specific rhetorical devices."

[19] See, for example, BRAULIK, *Die Mittel*; I. BALL, Jr., *A Rhetorical Study of Zephaniah* (Berkeley 1988); D. CLINES, D. GUNN, and A. HAUSER, ed., *Art and Meaning: Rhetoric in Biblical Literature* (JSOTSS 19; Sheffield 1982); J.J. JACKSON and M. KESSLER, ed., *Rhetorical Criticism: Essays in Honor of James Muilenburg* (PTMS 1; Pittsburgh 1974). New Testament rhetorical-critical studies have seen more emphasis on rhetoric as argumentation. See KENNEDY, *New Testament Interpretation*; B. MACK, *Rhetoric and the New Testament* (GBS, New Testament Series; Minneapolis 1990). Nevertheless, there have been proponents of a more literary and structural approach. See, for example, R. MEYNET, *Initiation à la rhétorique biblique: "Qui donc est le plus grand?"*, 2 vols. (Paris 1982); "Analyse rhétorique du prologue de Jean," *RB* 96 (1989) 481-510. MEYNET's notion of rhetorical criticism is very structural. He explains his method in *L'analyse rhétorique: Une nouvelle méthode pour comprendre la Bible: Textes fondateurs et exposé systématique* (Paris 1989).

[20] M. FOX, "The Rhetoric of Ezekiel's Vision of the Valley of the Bones," *HUCA* 51 (1980) 1, n. 1. C.C. BLACK, "Rhetorical Criticism and Biblical Interpretation," *ExpTim*

often restricted itself to investigating the formal literary aspects of a text
and thus has neglected the argumentative or persuasive aspects. Literary
features certainly contribute to the meaning of a text, and rhetoric has
traditionally concerned itself with style; but the real rhetorical force is to
be found in those features which seek to gain the adherence of an
audience.[21]

Wuellner has campaigned to bring rhetorical criticism back to its
proper focus: argumentation and persuasion. He rejects the association of
the method with literary criticism. He claims that this association can
only lead to a distorted and paralyzing criticism, since it concentrates on
stylistics. Such an approach led to the decline of rhetoric after two
millennia of esteem in Western academic circles.[22] Rhetorical criticism,
according to Wuellner, must choose between an identification with
literary criticism or an identification with what he calls "practical
criticism," a criticism directed towards the persuasive aspects of the text
or discourse.[23]

To appreciate rhetorical criticism, it is necessary to understand the
interests, applications, and tasks of rhetoric.

2.2. Rhetoric

What is rhetoric? What fields or areas does it cover? Such questions
are actually not easy to answer, since there has been some disagreement

---

100 (1988-89) 254, also criticizes the "Muilenburg method" as being too narrow and
tending toward distortion.

[21] Fox, "The Rhetoric of Ezekiel's Vision," 1-4. Cf. KENNEDY, *New Testament
Interpretation,* 159; PATRICK and SCULT, *Rhetoric and Biblical Interpretation,* 8, 11-19;
CH. PERELMAN, *L'empire rhétorique: Rhétorique et argumentation* (Paris 1977), 35, 53; M.
WARNER, "Introduction," *The Bible as Rhetoric: Studies in Biblical Persuasion and
Credibility* (ed. M. WARNER; Warwick Studies in Philosophy and Literature)
(London/New York 1990) 2, 4. Among Old Testament exegetes who emphasize the
argumentative nature of a text can be included R. DUKE, *The Persuasive Appeal of the
Chronicler: A Rhetorical Analysis* (JSOTSS 88; BLS 25) (Sheffield 1990); Y. GITAY,
"Deutero-Isaiah"; "The Effectiveness of Isaiah's Speech," *JQR* 75 (1984) 162-172;
"Isaiah and His Audience," *Prooftexts* 3 (1983) 223-230; "Reflections on the Study of
the Prophetic Discourse: The Question of Isaiah I 2-20," *VT* 33 (1983) 207-221; "A
Study of Amos's Art of Speech: A Rhetorical Analysis of Amos 3:1-15," *CBQ* 42 (1980)
293-309.

[22] W. WUELLNER, "Where Is Rhetorical Criticism Taking Us?" *CBQ* 49 (1987) 451;
see also "Paul as Pastor: The Function of Rhetorical Questions in First Corinthians,"
L'Apôtre Paul: Personnalité, style et conception du ministère (BETL 73; ed. A. VANHOYE)
(Leuven 1986) 49-77.

[23] WUELLNER, "Where Is Rhetorical Criticism Taking Us?" 453. KESSLER,
"Introduction to Rhetorical Criticism," 4-5, also speaks of "pragmatic theories," which
stress that literature has a purpose and that its authors want to achieve certain effects,
such as to please or teach. Its focus is effect on an audience.

over the centuries as to what rhetoric is and just what it includes. This lack of agreement is reflected in the confusion over the meaning, task, and methodology of rhetorical criticism. There seems to be three general areas with which rhetoric has been traditionally associated: persuasion, poetics or literature, and philosophy.[24]

2.2.1 Persuasion/Argumentation

Rhetoric has often been defined broadly as "the art of persuasion."[25] Aristotle more precisely defined it as "the faculty of observing in any given case the available means of persuasion."[26] Corbett summarizes classical ideas in the following way:

> Rhetoric is the art or the discipline that deals with the use of discourse, either spoken or written, to inform or persuade or move an audience, whether that audience is made up of a single person or a group of persons.[27]

In this definition there is a distinction between "inform," "persuade," and "move." (This distinction resembles the traditional *offices* or *duties* of an orator.[28]) The emphasis is upon the speaker's or writer's intention to make an impact on an audience, to work an effect. Rhetoric is communication with a purpose, the purpose of persuasion, that is, moving the will by speech or by the written word. Thus it is no mere communication of knowledge. It aims at agreement and consensus.[29]

---

[24] C.C. BLACK, "Rhetorical Criticism and Biblical Interpretation," 253.

[25] R. LANHAM, *A Handlist of Rhetorical Terms: A Guide for Students of English Literature* (Berkeley, 1968) 86.

[26] ARISTOTLE, *Rhetoric*, I.2.1355b: Ἔστω δὴ ῥητορικὴ δύναμις περὶ ἕκαστον τοῦ θεωρῆσαι τὸ ἐνδεχόμενον πιθανόν.

[27] E. CORBETT, *Classical Rhetoric for the Modern Student*, 2nd ed. (New York 1971) 3; O. REBOUL, *Introduction à la rhétorique: Théorie et pratique* (Collection Premier Cycle; Paris 1991) 4, gives a similar but shorter definition: "la rhétorique est l'art de persuader par le discours."

[28] The traditional *offices* of rhetoric are three: *probare* or *docere* ("teach"), *flectere* or *movere* ("move" or "persuade"), and *delectare* ("delight" or "please"). CICERO, *Orator*, xxi.69, says: "Erit igitur eloquens... is qui in foro causisque civilibus ita dicet, ut probet, ut delectet, ut flectat. Probare necessitatis est, delectare suavitatis, flectere victoriae..." Cf. his *Brutus*, xlix.185: "Tria sunt enim, ut quidem ego sentio, quae sint efficienda dicendo: ut doceatur is apud quem dicetur, ut delectetur, ut moveatur vehementius." Cf. also lxxx.276. AUGUSTINE cites CICERO's statement from *Orator* in *De doctrina christiana*, IV.12.27. Cf. also QUINTILIAN, *Institutio oratoria*, VIII. prooemium.7.

[29] H. LAUSBERG, *Handbuch der literarischen Rhetorik: Eine Grundlegung der Literaturwissenschaft*, 2 vols. (München 1960), I, 41; *Elemente der literarischen Rhetorik: Eine Einführung für Studierende der klassischen, romanischen, englischen und deutschen Philologie* (München 1963) 13; G. UEDING and B. STEINBRINK, *Grundriß der Rhetorik: Geschichte – Technik – Methode* (Stuttgart 1986) 4; VICKERS, *In Defence of Rhetoric*, 92.

The first theorizing about rhetoric took place in ancient Greece. There ἡ τέχνη ῥητορική, the art of discourse, referred basically to oral discourse — persuasive public *speaking*.[30] However, the theory of rhetoric has always tended to outgrow its original concern with public oratory. From the earliest times it was also applied to written discourse and to all problems of communication and language. Such problems were faced not only by the orator but also by the poet, the philosopher, the scientist — by anyone who tries to communicate his or her message effectively.[31] Thus the definition and meaning of rhetoric expanded from the notions of speaking and persuasion toward literature and philosophy.

2.2.2 Rhetoric and Literature/Poetics

Like many arts, rhetoric has been considered pragmatic, that is, it functions to produce action or change, it performs a task. Through discourse one can somehow affect or change reality.[32] This pragmatic function, as we have already noted, was quickly applied to the written word. Booth remarks that the term "rhetoric" can refer to any and all possible ways to change people's minds, from seemingly pointless classifications to the attractive language of literature to the intellectual language of philosophy.[33]

Rhetoric has also been defined very generally as a "way of arranging words"[34] and as "that quality in discourse by which a speaker or writer

---

[30] "Rhetoric," *The Great Ideas: A Synopticon of Great Books of the Western World* (ed. M. ADLER), vol. 3: *The Great Ideas*, II (Chicago 1952) 647; W. ONG, *Oralità e scrittura: Le tecnologie della parola* (Intersezioni 26), trans. Alessandra Calanchi (Bologna 1986) 28. On p. 155, however, ONG notes that although rhetoric was directed toward speaking, theorizing about this art took place — and could only take place — after the invention of and through the mediation of writing.

[31] E. BLACK, *Rhetorical Criticism: A Study in Method* (Madison, Wis. 1979) 11; ONG, *Oralità e scrittura*, 162; LANHAM, *Handlist*, 87; "Rhetoric," *Synopticon*, II, 651. VICKERS, *In Defence of Rhetoric*, 1, notes that rhetoric "has long been recognized as the systematization of natural eloquence."

[32] C. ARNOLD, "Oral Rhetoric, Rhetoric, and Literature," *Rhetoric in Transition: Studies in the Nature and Uses of Rhetoric* (ed. E. WHITE; University Park, Pa./London 1980) 158. This would be an intentional change on the part of the speaker or writer. R. SCOTT, "Intentionality in the Rhetorical Process," *Rhetoric in Transition*, 49, defines rhetoric as "communicative behavior that is highly intentional and that occurs in public circumstances." LAUSBERG, *Elemente*, 13, gives a definition of "rhetoric in its wider sense" which emphasizes its effects: "Die Rhetorik ist ein mehr oder minder ausgebautes System gedanklicher und sprachlicher Formen, die dem Zweck der vom Redenden in der Situation beabsichtigten Wirkung dienen können."

[33] W. BOOTH, *Now Don't Try to Reason with Me: Essays and Ironies for a Credulous Age* (Chicago/London 1970) 35-36; Cf. J. HEXTER, *Doing History* (Bloomington, Ind./London 1971) 40.

[34] FRYE, *The Great Code*, 81. Cf. G. GENETTE, *Figures I* (Points 74; Paris 1966) 208: "la rhétorique est un *système* des figures."

seeks to accomplish his purposes."[35] Any literary work intended for the public may be described as rhetorical, since it involves a person who intends to communicate something to an audience. Since most of our speaking and writing involves some kind of audience, rhetoric then concerns itself with communicating through language. An author deliberately writes so as to attract and involve his or her reader. The reader has to work to put together a story, a thought, a message, and the author uses certain techniques to involve, even "control" the reader.[36] Such attraction is associated with ornamental speech, with the beautiful. And from the beginning rhetoric was associated not only with persuasive speech but also with ornamental discourse. Ornamental rhetoric is inseparable from literature, and Frye even defines literature as "the rhetorical organization of grammar and logic."[37] Thus there has been a close relationship between literature (or poetics) and rhetoric since the days of ancient Greece.[38]

But sometimes the definition of rhetoric seems to expand until it covers all communication and communicative acts. Valesio, for example, claims that "rhetoric is *all* of language, in its realization of discourse."[39] The problem with such a wide definition is that it tends to include too much and thus works itself out of a job. To talk about everything is to talk about nothing. This tendency of rhetoric to expand its subject of inquiry risks a loss of identity, for rhetoric could become confused with literary criticism or with philosophy.[40]

This tendency of rhetoric to associate itself with literature eventually led to its decline. Rhetoric became more and more associated with stylistics, esthetics, and the manipulation of language for doubtful ends. It was identified with verbalism and empty forms. This distortion of rhetoric could only lead to its demise. Eventually rhetoric, after more

---

[35] KENNEDY, *New Testament Interpretation*, 3.

[36] KEEGAN, *Interpreting the Bible*, 84; cf. W. BOOTH, *A Rhetoric of Irony* (Chicago/London 1974) 41; *The Rhetoric of Fiction*, xiii, 105.

[37] FRYE, *Anatomy of Criticism*, 245; cf. D. BRYANT, "Uses of Rhetoric in Criticism," *Papers in Rhetoric and Poetic* (ed. D. BRYANT; Iowa City 1965) 1.

[38] B. GARAVELLI, *Manuale di retorica* (Studi Bompiani; Milano 1988) 288; LAUSBERG, *Handbuch*, I, 41-44; "Rhetoric," *Synopticon*, II, 651; VICKERS, *In Defence of Rhetoric*, 334-335. REBOUL, *Introduction à la rhétorique*, 72, claims that "l'elocution est donc le point où la rhétorique rencontre la littérature." Today there has also been a revival of the ·identification of rhetoric with poetics or literature. See, for example, Groupe μ, *Rhétorique générale* (Points 146; Paris 1982); P. RICŒUR, "Rhétorique – Poétique – Herméneutique," *De la métaphysique à la rhétorique: Essais à la mémoire de Chaïm Perelman* (ed. M. MEYER; Bruxelles 1986) 147.

[39] P. VALESIO, *Novantiqua; Rhetorics as a Contemporary Theory* (Bloomington, Ind. 1980) 7. Cf. RICŒUR, "Rhétorique – Poétique – Herméneutique," 144.

[40] GARAVELLI, *Manuale di retorica*, 11.

than two thousand years as a major factor in the education of Westerners, was finally rejected as irrelevant, inappropriate, or useless.[41]

2.2.3 Rhetoric and Philosophy

Almost from its inception rhetoric has been involved with and related to philosophy. It could hardly have been otherwise once its definition expanded to include nearly all language. In the ancient Greco-Roman world rhetoric was the rival of philosophy, and training in this subject was considered the final stage and highest level of education and of the formation of culture and intellect.[42] For the Romans rhetoric was *ars bene dicendi*[43] (the art of speaking well) and the orator was *vir bonus dicendi peritus*[44] (a good man skilled in speaking). For Cicero and Quintilian, philosophy was the servant of rhetoric, for it was knowledge of philosophy that helped the orator to speak well on every subject.

The boundary between philosophy and rhetoric has always been rather fluid and thus difficult to define. Like grammar, literature, and poetics, rhetoric concerns itself with language and discourse; but like logic and philosophy, it also has to do with thought, reason, and argument.[45] So rhetoric has even been defined very broadly as "a way of knowing."[46] Such a definition presupposes that we cannot easily separate our knowing from language and communication.

---

[41] W. BRANDT, *The Rhetoric of Argumentation* (Indianapolis 1970) 93; P. DIXON, *Rhetoric* (The Critical Idiom 19; London/New York 1971) 5; KENNEDY, *New Testament Interpretation,* 3; CH. PERELMAN, "The New Rhetoric: A Theory of Practical Reasoning," *The Great Ideas Today* (Chicago 1970) 277; A. PLEBE and P. EMANUELE, *Manuale di retorica* (Universale Laterza 720; Roma/Bari 1989) 29; P. RICŒUR, *La métaphore vive* (L'ordre philosophique; Paris 1975) 13-14, 41; VICKERS, *In Defence of Rhetoric,* 215. This decline is blamed especially on the separation of rhetoric from *inventio* and *dispositio* (and therefore its concentration on *elocutio* or style) by Petrus RAMUS in the sixteenth century. See R. BARILLI, "Rhétorique et culture," *RIP* 33 (1979) 74; GARAVELLI, *Manuale di retorica,* 47; O. REBOUL, *La rhétorique* (Que sais-je? 2133; Paris 1984) 110.

[42] VICKERS, *In Defence of Rhetoric,* 460.

[43] QUINTILIAN, *Institutio oratoria,* II.17.37. In II.14.5 he defines rhetoric as *bene dicendi scientia.* Although these definitions do not limit rhetoric to persuasive discourse, it seems that QUINTILIAN actually had only persuasive discourse in mind (E. BLACK, *Rhetorical Criticism,* 12).

[44] QUINTILIAN, *Institutio oratoria,* XII.1.1 It was CATO who first described the orator in this fashion.

[45] "Rhetoric," *Synopticon,* II, 645; R. BROWN, *Society as Text: Essays on Rhetoric, Reason, and Reality* (Chicago/London 1987) 63-79.

[46] C. ARNOLD and K. FRANDSEN, "Conceptions of Rhetoric and Communication," *Handbook of Rhetorical and Communication Theory* (ed. C. ARNOLD and J. BOWERS; Boston 1984) 29; R. OLIVER, *Culture and Communication: The Problem of Penetrating National and Cultural Boundaries* (American Lecture Series 506; Springfield, Ill. 1962) 77-78. Cf. RICŒUR, "Rhétorique – Poétique – Herméneutique," 146.

However, philosophy and rhetoric have been rivals and even archenemies since the days of Plato, who attacked rhetoric and accused it of not seeking the truth but rather of pleasing an audience.[47] A dichotomy was set up between truth and rational knowledge on the one hand, and opinion, probability, and emotions on the other. Plato associated philosophy with the first and rhetoric with the second. His problem with rhetoric was that in saying something well one could ignore the truth. And so there seemed to be a choice between truth and pleasure, truth and opinion, truth and the emotions.[48]

Such dichotomies, however, may be false or at least overvalued.[49] Modern philosophers have challenged the assumptions of such dualities. The boundary between the demonstrable (that is, the scientific or philosophical) and the probable (that is, the rhetorical) has become blurred. Mathematical rationalism, which rejected every opinion, itself can lead to immobility and conformism. All knowledge is not built on unshakable self-evidence but must also be examined through reasonable and probable argumentation.[50] By stressing only what is rational one ignores a good part of human life, making it unavailable for reflection.[51] Thus rhetoric is indispensable, and its dispute with philosophy is unreal. For rational thought needs to be expressed, and language cannot exist without ideas.[52] Grassi would thus define rhetoric as "the speech which is the basis of rational thought."[53]

Aristotle tried to reconcile rhetoric and philosophy by admitting that rhetoric was the counterpart of dialectic[54] and that it dealt not with the

---

[47] VICKERS, *In Defence of Rhetoric*, 107. PLATO, *Gorgias*, 120, identifies rhetoric with the desire for power and selfishness. In his *Phaedrus*, 134, PLATO acknowledges that rhetoric may teach the plausible, but he claims that only his philosophy has access to the truth. See PLEBE and EMANUELE, *Manuale di retorica*, 5.

[48] "Rhetoric," *Synopticon*, II, 648; E. GRASSI, *Rhetoric as Philosophy: The Humanist Tradition* (University Park/London 1980) 18; D. JASPER, " 'In the Sermon Which I Have Just Completed, Wherever I Said Aristotle, I Meant St. Paul,' " *The Bible as Rhetoric* (ed. M. WARNER 1990) 135.

[49] K. BURKE, *A Rhetoric of Motives* (Berkeley 1969), 54; T. SLOAN and CH. PERELMAN, "Rhetoric," *Encyclopedia Britannica*, 15th ed. (1977) XV, 799.

[50] PERELMAN, *L'empire rhétorique*, 173, 175-176; W. KLUBACK and M. BECKER, "The Significance of Chaim Perelman's Philosophy of Rhetoric," *RIP* 33 (1979) 34; R. OLIVER, *Culture and Communication*, 108-109.

[51] GRASSI, *Rhetoric as Philosophy*, 40; KLUBACK and BECKER, "The Significance of Chaim Perelman's Philosophy of Rhetoric," 40-41.

[52] VICKERS, *In Defence of Rhetoric*, 212; GRASSI, *Rhetoric as Philosophy*, 34. Already CICERO had bemoaned the separation between philosophy and rhetoric, which he tried to unite in the orator (*De oratore* III.61; III.72-73). R. BROWN, *Society as Text*, 85, claims that not only "rhetoric is epistemic, but also that epistemology and ontology are themselves rhetorical."

[53] GRASSI, *Rhetoric as Philosophy*, 65.

[54] ARISTOTLE, *Rhetoric*, I.1.1354a.

demonstrable but with the probable (τὸ εἰκός).[55] Aristotle's link between
rhetorical persuasion and the logical concept of the probable made a
relationship between philosophy and rhetoric possible.[56] In human affairs
we must live with uncertainties and make our decisions on the basis of
probabilities. The tradition of argumentation presumes listeners and
readers who are willing to give (conditional) assent to probable
statements if they seem reasonable enough.[57]

2.3 The New Rhetoric

Rhetoric declined as a serious intellectual field of endeavor as a
result of its identification with stylistics and the technicalities of
producing a work of art. In the seventeenth and eighteenth centuries it
was relegated to the sidelines, and by the nineteenth century it seemed to
have died a natural death.[58] But notices of rhetoric's demise were
premature: in this century, especially since World War II, rhetoric has
made a comeback. Since it has changed some of its approaches, it is often
called the "New Rhetoric":

> The new rhetoric is defined as a theory of argumentation that has as its
> object the study of discursive techniques and that aims to provoke or to
> increase the adherence of men's minds to the theses that are presented for
> their assent. It also examines the conditions that allow argumentation to
> begin and be developed, as well as the effects produced by this
> development.[59]

This New Rhetoric is a reaction to logical empiricism and other
forms of purely rationalistic philosophy. It opposes classical and modern
rationalism and attempts to enlarge the domain of reason to include
reasonableness (probability) and pluralism in values. For there exists not

---

[55] Ibid., I.2.1357a.

[56] Ricœur, *La métaphore vive*, 16-18; Perelman, *L'empire rhétorique*, 171; E. Black,
Rhetorical Criticism, 116-118, however, criticizes Aristotle for not allowing emotional
appeals ever to be considered a primary force in argumentation.

[57] Brandt, *The Rhetoric of Argumentation*, 42-43; Corbett, *Classical Rhetoric*, 73;
Plebe and Emanuele, *Manuale di retorica*, 18.

[58] R. Barthes, *L'ancienne rhétorique: Aide-Mémoire*, in *L'aventure sémiologique*
(Paris 1985) 89, 118-120; Groupe μ, *Rhétorique générale*, 8; Reboul, *Introduction à la
rhétorique*, 86. Cf. n. 41.

[59] Sloan and Perelman, "Rhetoric," 803. Cf. Ch. Perelman and L. Olbrechts-
Tyteca, *Traité de l'argumentation: La nouvelle rhétorique*, 5th ed. (Bruxelles 1988) 5: "En
effet, l'objet de cette théorie est l'étude des techniques discursives permettant de *provoquer
ou d'accroître l'adhésion des esprits aux thèses qu'on présente à leur assentiment*." Burke, *A
Rhetoric of Motives*, 43, prefers to define rhetoric as "the use of language as a symbolic
means of inducing cooperation in beings that by nature respond to symbols."

only a reason which demonstrates through formal logic but also a reason which argues.[60] The New Rhetoric avoids the pitfalls of the old rhetoric by concentrating on argumentation and not on stylistics or literature. Its proponents, Perelman and Olbrechts-Tyteca, in *Traité de l'argumentation: La nouvelle rhétorique*,[61] re-established rhetoric as an intellectual field of endeavor.

The New Rhetoric does not limit itself to formally correct logical statements nor to purely stylistic considerations. In fact, Perelman and Olbrechts-Tyteca rejected the notion of rhetoric as merely the art of good speaking and writing. For them such a conception was the source of the degeneration, sterility, and verbalism of classical rhetoric.[62] Instead the New Rhetoric emphasizes argumentative and persuasive aspects. It is a theory of argumentaion.[63] The nature of all argumentation is the engagement of others for the purpose of eliciting or increasing adherence or allegiance to ideas.[64] Thus the New Rhetoric is a theory of practical

---

[60] R. DEARIN, "The Philosophical Basis of Chaim Perelman's Theory of Rhetoric," *The Quarterly Journal of Speech* 55 (1969) 214, 218, 222; SLOAN and PERELMAN, "Rhetoric," 803; UEDING and STEINBRINK, *Grundriß*, 171; H. ZYSKIND, "The New Rhetoric and Formalism," *RIP* 33 (1979) 19.

[61] In English: *The New Rhetoric: A Treatise on Argumentation* (Notre Dame 1969). GARAVELLI, *Manuale di retorica*, 11, acknowledges that this work, more than any other, contributed to the present renewal of rhetorical studies. VICKERS, *In Defence of Rhetoric*, 215, also sees a renaissance of rhetoric in recent years. ARNOLD and FRANDSEN, "Conceptions," 3-4, note the rise of interest not only in rhetoric but in communication in general in the twentieth century. See also M. BEAUJOUR, "Rhétorique et littérature," *De la métaphysique à la rhétorique* (ed. M. MEYER, 1986) 157; C.C. BLACK, "Rhetorical Criticism and Biblical Interpretation," 253; Groupe μ, *Rhétorique générale*, 12; MACK, *Rhetoric and the New Testament*, 14-15; REBOUL, *La rhétorique*, 7, 31-32; H. SUHAMY, *Les figures du style* (Que sais-je? 1809) 18-19.

[62] PERELMAN and OLBRECHTS-TYTECA, *Traité de l'argumentation, 192*.

[63] Ibid.; PERELMAN, *L'empire rhétorique*, 19; "The New Rhetoric," 284. J. CONDON and F. YOUSEF, *An Introduction to Intercultural Communication* (The Bobbs-Merrill Series in Speech Communication; Indianapolis 1975), 213, define argumentation as "... the process of determining and providing "proofs" — going from evidence to conclusions, making inferences and deductions, and in one way or another going from what is known or assumed to an appropriate conclusion." BRANDT, *The Rhetoric of Argumentation*, 22, points out that "the essence of argumentation is the establishment of a convincing connection between two terms." Since the connections must be made in the minds of the members of an audience, PERELMAN and OLBRECHTS-TYTECA, *Traité de l'argumentation*, 18, argue that the aim of argumentation is the gaining of the adherence of minds.

[64] C. ARNOLD, Introduction to *The Realm of Rhetoric* by CH. PERELMAN (Notre Dame/London 1982) xii; PERELMAN and OLBRECHTS-TYTECA, *Traité de l'argumentation*, 18; PERELMAN, "The New Rhetoric," 282, 290; *L'empire rhétorique*, 23-25. Cf. P. OLÉRON, *L'argumentation*, 2nd ed. (Que sais-je? 2087; Paris 1987), 4-5. Note that "argumentation" is defined somewhat differently in rhetoric than it is in logic. Logicians tend to define argumentation as "a kind of perfect composite expression in which one thing having been given, something else follows." See D. KANE, *Logic: The Art of Inference and Predication* (New York 1969) 126.

reasoning and decision-making, and it espouses the view that the human mind is essentially argumentative.[65]

Perelman makes the following claims about argumentation:

1. Argumentation proceeds informally and not according to the rules of logic.
2. Arguments are always addressed to audiences to induce or increase their adherence to certain theses.
3. Arguments must proceed from premises acceptable to the audience addressed.
4. Argumentation can be advanced when ideas and values are given *presence* in the minds of those addressed.
5. Since language is equivocal, ambiguity is always present in argumentation.
6. Certain verbal techniques create or dissolve relationships or concepts and attitudes which make argumentation possible. These include:
   a. Quasi-logical arguments which resemble formal reasoning;
   b. Arguments which resemble the structure of reality;
   c. Arguments based on examples, illustrations, and models;
   d. Analogy and metaphor;
   e. Dissociation;
   f. Amplification or abridgment of ideas or values;
   g. Systematizing or ordering ideas and arguments.[66]

Perelman's own experience with law and justice led him to adapt a juridical model for philosophy. The reasoning process in the law court is justificatory and argumentative, and his understanding of rhetoric comes from such a model.[67] Instead of basing philosophy on unquestionable truths, Perelman and Olbrechts-Tyteca start from the presumption that all people adhere to opinions of various kinds with variable intensity.[68] It is the process of argumentation that increases or lessens adherence to these opinions or promotes new ones. Rhetoric is thus that theory of argumentation which aims to provoke or increase such adherence.

Not everyone totally agrees with the thesis of Perelman and Olbrechts-Tyteca. Plebe and Emanuele claim that rhetoric is the art of *invention,* not that of argumentation.[69] However, such criticism seems to

---

[65] H. ZYSKIND, Introduction to *The New Rhetoric and the Humanities: Essays on Rhetoric and its Applications* (Synthese Library 140) by CH. PERELMAN (Dordrecht 1979) xi, xx.

[66] ARNOLD, Introduction to *The Realm of Rhetoric,* x-xi; ZYSKIND, "The New Rhetoric and Formalism," 28.

[67] ZYSKIND, Introduction to *The New Rhetoric and the Humanities,* xvii; DEARIN, "The Philosophical Basis," 219-220.

[68] PERELMAN and OLBRECHTS-TYTECA, *Traité de l'argumentation,* 677-678.

[69] PLEBE and EMANUELE, *Manuale di retorica,* vii; 98-99.

be the result of a difference in perspective and emphasis. Aristotle's definition of rhetoric, as noted above, is "the faculty of observing in any given case the available means of persuasion." Plebe and Emanuele emphasize "the faculty of observing" or finding, and thus they see in rhetoric the foundation of new thinking, of *invention*. Perelman and Olbrechts-Tyteca, on the other hand, coming out of their own juridical perspective, emphasize "the available means of persuasion," the argumentation side of rhetoric. This emphasis on persuasion and argumentation is a valid and genuine continuation of Aristotelian and classical rhetorical tradition.[70]

Another criticism of the New Rhetoric concerns this continuation of the Aristotelian tradition. Perelman, like Aristotle, tends to limit himself to the intellectual aspects of rhetoric, neglecting the affective aspects. The danger is that the New Rhetoric may itself become too rigidly rational a process.[71] Perelman and Olbrechts-Tyteca also reject all notions of style and esthetics in their view of argumentation. This is because they blame rhetoric's decline on its identification with stylistics. But is this not a neglect of an area traditionally important for rhetoric?[72]

Despite these criticisms, the New Rhetoric has revealed itself as a practical methodology in that it evaluates the various types of arguments and figures in terms of argumentation. Even Plebe and Emanuele admit that the argumentative techniques offered and evaluated by Perelman and Olbrechts-Tyteca are invaluable.[73] For that reason this work will often draw from the New Rhetoric as it seeks to evaluate the argumentation within the Third Address of Moses.

2.4 Rhetorical Genres

Traditionally rhetoricians have distinguished three types of persuasive discourse. Aristotle was the first to divide oratory into three genres: deliberative, forensic, and epideictic.[74]

---

[70] OLÉRON, *L'argumentation*, 7; REBOUL, *Introduction à la rhétorique*, 97; UEDING and STEINBRINK, *Grundriß*, 172.

[71] A. LEMPEREUR, "Les restrictions de deux néo-rhétoriques," *Figures et conflits rhétoriques* (ed. M. MEYER and A. LEMPEREUR; Bruxelles 1990) 148-153 (LEMPEREUR also questions whether the model of judge is suitable for rhetoric); OLÉRON, *L'argumentation*, 8; REBOUL, *Introduction à la rhétorique*, 122; *La rhétorique*, 113-114.

[72] Groupe μ, *Rhétorique générale*, 12; M. MEYER and A. LEMPEREUR, ed., *Figures et conflits rhétoriques* (Bruxelles 1990); REBOUL, *La rhétorique*, 32-33.

[73] PLEBE and EMANUELE, *Manuale di retorica*, 102.

[74] ARISTOTLE, *Rhetoric*, I.3.1358b. Cf. SLOAN and PERELMAN, "Rhetoric," 800; WUELLNER, "Paul's Rhetoric of Argumentation," 165.

Deliberative or *political* oratory (*genus deliberativum*; συμβουλευτι-κὸν γένος) in ancient Greece concerned itself with politics and originated in popular assemblies. It was the rhetoric employed to convince political groups to take or avoid a course of action. According to Aristotle, deliberative oratory was always concerned with the future (since it deals with something we shall or shall not do), and its focus is on self-interest and the expedient. In broad terms, we can say that deliberative rhetoric is that in which a speaker attempts to persuade another to do something or to accept a point of view.[75]

An important topic in deliberative discourse is happiness, since we seek what is worthy or advantageous for the sake of our own happiness. Other topics include the possible and the impossible, advantage or disadvantage, more and less.[76] Cicero notes that in political oratory one makes use of exhortation and appeals to emotions such as hope, fear, desire, ambition, and anger.[77] In deliberative rhetoric there are often inductive arguments based on past examples, and frequently the audience is directly involved in the matter under discussion.[78] Deliberative discourse has often been associated with sermons, theology, and even letter writing (during the Middle Ages).[79]

The second genre of oratory is called *judicial* or *forensic* (*genus iudiciale*; δικανὸν γένος). In ancient Greece and Rome this was the oratory of the law court, and it became the most important genre in imperial Rome. With this genre a speaker attacks or defends someone, and he or she is concerned with past action as well as with justice and injustice. The special topics of judicial rhetoric concern the *status* of a case, that is, what precisely is the issue that is to be discussed.[80]

The third rhetorical genre is known as *epideictic* or *ceremonial* oratory (*genus demonstrativum*; ἐπιδεικτικὸν γένος). Aristotle said that ceremonial oratory praises or censures someone and is concerned with the present. Its special topics are praise and blame, and it generally deals with

---

[75] CORBETT, *Classical Rhetoric*, 26, 39; KENNEDY, *New Testament Interpretation*, 46. ARISTOTLE discusses deliberative rhetoric in Book I, chaps. 4-8 of *Rhetoric*.

[76] CORBETT, *Classical Rhetoric*, 146-149.

[77] CICERO, *De oratore*, II, 337.

[78] KENNEDY, *New Testament Interpretation, 36-37*.

[79] DIXON, *Rhetoric*, 22; J. MESSER LEON, *The Book of the Honeycomb's Flow: Sēpher Nōpheth Ṣūphīm*, ed. and trans. I. RABINOWITZ (Ithaca, N.Y. 1983) I.2.13, says that in theology much of the speaking is deliberative; in II.18.8 he considers much of what is found in the Bible, especially "commandments, admonitions, and reproofs" as deliberative. KENNEDY, *New Testament Interpretation*, 45, calls the Sermon on the Mount an example of deliberative rhetoric.

[80] ARISTOTLE, *Rhetoric*, I.3.1358b. ARISTOTLE dedicates all of Book I, chap. 10, to a discussion of forensic oratory. This discussion actually extends to the end of chap. 15. Cf. CORBETT, *Classical Rhetoric*, 149-152; DIXON, *Rhetoric*, 22.

a person's moral character and with virtues or vices.[81] In ancient Greece it arose from public ceremonies and rituals, where it was used to praise gods and outstanding citizens. This type of rhetoric included funeral addresses and congratulatory speeches as well as oratorical exhibitions. Christian sermons have also been classified under this genre.[82]

Epideictic rhetoric is the most "literary" and ornate of the three kinds of discourse.[83] It is fond of amplification and repetition, ornament and description, digression and imagination.[84] The judicial and deliberative genres tend to be practical, since they aim to change a situation, whether that be legal or political. The epideictic genre, on the other hand, is more difficult to define, although it tends to deal with already established values and usually does not aim for immediate changes. Its chief goal is the strengthening of audience adherence to some value.[85] Because of its literary characteristics, during the Middle Ages and the Renaissance practically all literature was influenced by epideictic oratory.[86]

Epideictic oratory also has a tendency to blend with both deliberative and judicial discourse. In praising a person one suggests to an audience that its members ought to act similarly — which is deliberative rhetoric. Or like a lawyer in the courtroom the speaker or writer moves into forensic rhetoric when he or she seems to be

---

[81] ARISTOTLE, *Rhetoric,* I.3.1358b. He develops the notion of epideictic oratory in Book I, chap. 9. See CORBETT, *Classical Rhetoric,* 152. MESSER LEON, *Honeycomb's Flow,* I.3.3, differs from the ancient rhetoricians by associating epideictic with past time, since praise and blame contemplates the past.

[82] CICERO, *Orator,* xi.37-xii.38; CORBETT, *Classical Rhetoric,* 40; DIXON, *Rhetoric,* 23.

[83] ARISTOTLE, *Rhetoric,* III.12.1414a; BURKE, *A Rhetoric of Motives,* 72; CORBETT, *Classical Rhetoric,* 40; PERELMAN and OLBRECHTS-TYTECA, *Traité de l'argumentation,* 64.

[84] KENNEDY, *New Testament Interpretation,* 75.

[85] LAUSBERG, *Elemente,* 18-19; KENNEDY, *New Testament Interpretation,* 74. CICERO, *Orator,* xi.37; xii.38; xiii.42; lx.208, seems to limit epideictic to what will give pleasure ("quia quasi ad inspiciendum delectationis causa comparatum est": xi.37). However, he also credits epideictic with the inculcation of virtue (*De oratore* II.342-348). L. ROSENFIELD, "The Practical Celebration of Epideictic," *Rhetoric in Transition: Studies in the Nature and Uses of Rhetoric* (ed. E. WHITE; University Park/London 1980) 133-146, contends that it is a misunderstanding of epideictic to consider its tactics to be only praise and blame. Rather it concerns itself with a view of reality which recognizes certain values. The virtues of a person cry out for recognition and make a claim on us. Epideictic is not "showing *off*" but "showing *forth.*" Thus epideictic evokes an immediacy or urgency which might be lacking and thus functions to provoke thought.

[86] VICKERS, *In Defence of Rhetoric,* 54; KENNEDY, *New Testament Interpretation,* 74. Rhetoric in its prime was associated with democratic political institutions. Thus in periods of democratic decline deliberative (and even forensic) rhetoric would be curtailed and epideictic would assume a greater importance. This could explain why epideictic had such predominance during the Middle Ages and Renaissance. See BURKE, *A Rhetoric of Motives,* 71-72.

exonerating or discrediting someone. Then again, both deliberative and judicial discourse regularly use epideictic passages in their approaches.[87] So it is understandable why Perelman calls the division of rhetoric into these three genres "artificial."[88]

Nevertheless, since the division is traditional and useful, Perelman and Olbrechts-Tyteca develop the notion of epideictic: "Les discours épidictiques ont pour but d'accroître l'intensité d'adhésion aux valeurs communes de l'auditoire et de l'orateur...."[89] The role of this type of rhetoric, then, is to appeal to common values (which are normally undisputed but also unformulated) and to strengthen adherence to them. Associated thus with education, epideictic oratory creates a disposition toward action by increasing adherence to certain values.[90] Perelman and Olbrechts-Tyteca can conceive of all argument — including epideictic discourse — "in terms of the action for which it paves the way or which it actually brings about."[91] The association of epideictic with education is a major contribution to rhetoric by these two philosophers.[92]

2.5 Parts of Rhetoric

Traditional rhetoric was divided into five parts:[93]

1. Invention (*inventio*; εὕρεσις);
2. Arrangement (*dispositio*; τάξις);
3. Style (*elocutio*; λέξις or φράσις or ἑρμενεία);
4. Memory (*memoria*; μνήμη);
5. Delivery (*actio* or *pronuntiatio;* ὑπόκρισις).

The last two parts, *memory* (concerned with the memorizing of speeches) and *delivery* (the rules for control of the voice and the use of gestures), despite their importance, were often neglected in rhetorical

---

[87] BRANDT, *The Rhetoric of Argumentation,* 13; CORBETT, *Classical Rhetoric,* 152; KENNEDY, *New Testament Interpretation,* 74-75. Cf. QUINTILIAN, *Institutio oratoria,* III.4.16.

[88] PERELMAN, "The New Rhetoric," 279; *L'empire rhétorique,* 33.

[89] PERELMAN and OLBRECHTS-TYTECA, *Traité de l'argumentation,* 71.

[90] Ibid., 53; PERELMAN, "The New Rhetoric," 279. In *L'empire rhétorique,* 33, PERELMAN says that epideictic rhetoric seeks to create a feeling or disposition to act at the appropriate moment rather than immediately. He also feels that all practical philosophy arises from epideictic.

[91] PERELMAN and OLBRECHTS-TYTECA, *The New Rhetoric,* 54. The original text is found in *Traité de l'argumentation,* 71: "toute argumentation ne se conçoit, dans cette perspective, qu'en fonction de l'action qu'elle prépare ou qu'elle détermine."

[92] WUELLNER, "Where Is Rhetorical Criticism Taking Us?" 460.

[93] CICERO, *De oratore,* I.31.142-143; KENNEDY, *New Testament Interpretation,* 13-14; LANHAM, *Handlist,* 106.

treatises. With the concentration of rhetoric on written discourse, these two parts were often omitted or ignored. The invention of printing reinforced this neglect. Since it would be impossible (as well as irrelevant) to deal with these two areas in Hebrew rhetoric and the book of Dt, they will not be considered in this essay.

2.5.1 Invention (*Inventio*)

Invention refers to the planning of a discourse and its arguments. It is that part of the rhetorical process which concerns itself with research, for it seeks to discover the possibilities of argumentation. One could call this the theoretical side of rhetoric. With invention the speaker or writer 1) seeks to understand and evaluate the nature of the issue and 2) attempts to "find" or "create" appropriate proof and arguments.[94]

Some modern philosophers of rhetoric see in invention the foundation of philosophy, since philosophic first principles cannot be proved but only "found" or "invented." Thus all thinking and philosophy originates with rhetorical invention.[95] Since invention concerns itself with the understanding of the issue and the finding of proofs and arguments, it is that part of rhetoric which can be identified most strongly with argumentation.

Aristotle noted that persuasive speech is used to lead to decisions or judgments.[96] A more contemporary interpretation would say that argumentation "always tends to modify a preexisting state of affairs."[97] The purpose of a discourse is to bring an audience to the conclusions offered by the speaker or writer. Argumentation is no formal, logical procedure in which conclusions are deduced from premises. Rather it is a process which aims to elicit or increase the adherence of an audience to the conclusions offered by the speaker or writer.[98] In this process the audience must not only be persuaded to accept certain ideas or theses, but it must also be *dissuaded* from other convictions as well.[99]

---

[94] UEDING and STEINBRINK, *Grundriß*, 195; BRANDT, *The Rhetoric of Argumentation*, 14.

[95] ARNOLD and FRANDSEN, "Conceptions," 21; GRASSI, *Rhetoric as Philosophy*, 19, 41-42, 44; PLEBE and EMANUELE, *Manuale di retorica*, 30-46, 99.

[96] ARISTOTLE, *Rhetoric*, II.18.1391b.

[97] PERELMAN and OLBRECHTS-TYTECA, *The New Rhetoric*, 54. (*Traité de l'argumentation*, 72: "L'argumentation est une action qui tend toujours à modifier un état de choses préexistant.")

[98] Cf. n. 64.

[99] E. BLACK, *Rhetorical Criticism*, 161. On p. 15 he notes that persuasion refers to intent, not necessarily to accomplishment. Whether or not a particular discourse is successful in influencing an audience has no bearing on whether it is rhetorical.

Rhetorical proof is never completely necessary proof, as in logic. For all argumentation is indicative of doubt.[100] Since the conclusions we present are not self-evidently true, they must be made to seem reasonable. The audience must make a judgment whether or not they are. As Aristotle observed, the listener or reader must make a decision or a judgment when he or she gives some degree of acceptance to a claim.[101]

2.5.1.1 Modes of Argumentation

Traditional rhetoric saw three "modes" of argumentation: *ethos, pathos,* and *logos.*[102] Logos is associated with logical or rational argumentation, while both pathos and ethos are associated with emotions.[103]

Ethos (ἦθος) is the credibility which a speaker or an author has, and so it is normally associated with his or her character, especially moral character. This credibility is established in the work itself, although a well-known person brings a certain ethos to a work even before it has begun.[104] Aristotle said that confidence is inspired in a speaker's character when he or she displays good sense, good moral character, and good will.[105]

---

[100] PERELMAN and OLBRECHTS-TYTECA, *Traité de l'argumentation,* 82-83, 635-636; O. REBOUL, "La figure et l'argument," *De la métaphysique à la rhétorique* (ed. M. MEYER, 1986) 185-186.

[101] ARNOLD, Introduction to *The Realm of Rhetoric,* xi. One can never hope that adherence to a thesis will be total and irrevocable. It is in the nature of argumentation that there is room for doubt and for a change of view. One can only seek a *degree* of acceptance (xii).

[102] ARISTOTLE, *Rhetoric,* I.2.1356a. These were considered modes of "artificial" or "artistic" proof, since the orator had to produce them through his or her own creativity and "invention." Inartificial proof is what we would today call *evidence*: sworn testimony, documents, scientific analysis, laws. See DIXON, *Rhetoric,* 24; LANHAM, *Handlist,* 106-107.

[103] LAUSBERG, *Elemente,* 35. The ethos or character of a speaker, however important it may be, is not established on some rational basis. It tends to be a subjective element, dependent upon each member of an audience, who must "catch" the tone or mood for himself or herself. Every speaker or writer projects a particular and unique mood or tone — an ethos. See D. CLINES, "The Arguments of Job's Three Friends," *Art and Meaning* (JSOTSS 19; ed. D. CLINES, D. GUNN, and A. HAUSER) (Sheffield 1982) 199.

[104] ARNOLD and FRANDSEN, "Conceptions," 14; CORBETT, *Classical Rhetoric,* 93-94; DIXON, *Rhetoric,* 24; KENNEDY, *New Testament Interpretation,* 15.

[105] ARISTOTLE, *Rhetoric,* II.1.1378a; cf. CORBETT, *Classical Rhetoric,* 19. In I.2.1356a ARISTOTLE claims that ethos could be the most effective means of persuasion. This is because even the soundest arguments will be rejected if an audience doesn't trust a speaker. See CICERO, *De oratore,* II.184; QUINTILIAN, *Institutio oratoria,* III.8.13; CORBETT, *Classical Rhetoric,* 35, 93; ROSENFIELD, "The Practical Celebration of Epideictic," 145. UEDING and STEINBRINK, *Grundriß,* 261, note that the character of a speaker is revealed not only by what he or she says but also by his or her entire appearance, actions, attire, and impression.

Modern rhetoricians seem to understand the concept of ethos as a complex of relationships. For every speaker or writer from the start must establish a relationship with the audience, an attitude towards the subject matter, and some sense of the kind of person he or she is or chooses to be thought.[106] Any opposition from the audience is harmful for a speaker's purposes, and thus the orator will use every means possible to promote communion with it.[107] At the same time ethos also establishes a relationship between speaker and speech or writer and text, for an audience tends to regard the communicator as intimately connected with his or her message.[108]

Pathos (πάθος), or emotional appeal, is the second mode of persuasion. Aristotle recognized that speech stirs emotions, and emotions affect our judgments.[109] He dedicated the first eleven chapters of Book II of his *Rhetoric* to a description of various emotions and how to arouse them. Although some philosophers have attacked rhetoric's appeal to the emotions, rhetoricians have recognized that it is perfectly normal to be moved to action through our feelings. For it is our will that moves us to action, and emotions have a powerful influence on our will.[110] To minimize or eliminate emotions in a discourse is to risk losing an audience, for it denies listeners a meaningful understanding of that discourse.[111] Human beings tend to link the truth of certain propositions to their own past experiences, and these include emotional experiences: "If I feel this strong emotion, then a certain set of propositions must be true."[112]

The various ways of producing emotions in an audience can be reduced to two. First of all, a speaker or writer can lower the level of abstraction, that is, can become very concrete. The ancients often described this technique as ἐνάργεια or *demonstratio* (vividness): "when an event is so described in words that the business seems to be enacted

---

[106] BRANDT, *The Rhetoric of Argumentation,* 32, 55. ARNOLD and FRANDSEN, "Conceptions," note that communication among human beings automatically entails certain personal obligations by those involved. That obligation on the part of the speaker or writer could be called ethos.

[107] PERELMAN and OLBRECHTS-TYTECA, *Traité de l'argumentation,* 430-431.

[108] Ibid., 426-427.

[109] ARISTOTLE, *Rhetoric,* I.2.1356a.

[110] CORBETT, *Classical Rhetoric,* 99-100; UEDING and STEINBRINK, *Grundriß,* 95, 256-257. REBOUL, *Introduction à la rhétorique,* 7, claims that "en rhétorique raison et sentiments sont inséparables." Cf. BOOTH, *Now Don't Try to Reason with Me,* 13; VALESIO, *Novantiqua,* 104. Cf. also CICERO, *Brutus,* lxxx.279: "Quis enim non fateatur, cum ex omnibus oratoris laudibus longe ista sit maxima, inflammare animos audientium et quocumque res postulet modo flectere, qui hac virtute caruerit, id ei quod maximum fuerit defuisse?"

[111] ROSENFIELD, "The Practical Celebration of Epideictic," 144.

[112] E. BLACK, *Rhetorical Criticism,* 146.

and the subject to pass vividly before our eyes."[113] Secondly, the speaker
or writer can simulate within himself or herself the emotions he or she
wishes the audience to feel, for emotions stimulate others' emotions.[114]
Parenesis or exhortation in a speech or a literary work, for example, is
associated with pathos, for it arouses emotion which produces belief.[115]

The third mode of persuasion is *logos* (λόγος), or rational appeal.
With this mode the speaker appeals to the audience's reasoning or
understanding, and normally the word "argumentation" is associated
with this mode.[116] Logical argumentation was normally divided into
inductive and *deductive* reasoning. Inductive reasoning uses a series of
particular examples to draw a general conclusion, while deductive
reasoning begins with general premises acceptable to an audience and
from them draws a conclusion.[117]

In logic deductive reasoning normally takes place formally through
the *syllogism*.[118] In rhetoric the equivalent of the syllogism is the
enthymeme. The enthymeme has been defined as "a syllogism with one
premise (usually the major) omitted"[119] or as "a statement with a
supporting reason."[120] It is certainly the most common logical figure used
in argumentation, and one reason for its popularity is its brevity. The
function of an enthymeme is to move from what is already accepted by an
audience to that which is problematic, the conclusion. The enthymeme
differs from the syllogism in that a premise is missing and is taken for
granted by the audience. It also has probable rather than necessary
conclusions. An audience can be satisfied with the probable conclusions of
an enthymeme because it recognizes the contingent nature of rhetoric and
is willing to accept a certain amount of common opinions which may be
self-evident within a particular cultural, religious, or political system.[121]

---

[113] *Rhetorica ad Herennium*, IV.55.68: "cum ita verbis res exprimitur ut geri
negotium et res ante oculos esse videatur." Cf. QUINTILIAN, *Institutio oratoria*, VIII.3.61;
IX.2.40; E. BLACK, *Rhetorical Criticism*, 144; BRANDT, *The Rhetoric of Argumentation*, 224.

[114] BRANDT, *The Rhetoric of Argumentation*, 224; UEDING and STEINBRINK, *Grundriß*,
258, 262; QUINTILIAN, *Institutio oratoria*, VI.2.26 ("Summa enim, quantum ego quidem
sentio, circa movendos adfectus in hoc posita est, ut moveamur ipsi").

[115] E. BLACK, *Rhetorical Criticism*, 138.

[116] CORBETT, *Classical Rhetoric*, 34.

[117] Ibid.; KENNEDY, *New Testament Interpretation*, 16.

[118] CORBETT, *Classical Rhetoric*, 34, 56-72.

[119] BRANDT, *The Rhetoric of Argumentation*, 32. Cf. ARISTOTLE, *Rhetoric*, I.2.1357a.

[120] KENNEDY, *New Testament Interpretation*, 7.

[121] E. BLACK, *Rhetorical Criticism*, 125-126; BRANDT, *The Rhetoric of Argumentation*,
33; CORBETT, *Classical Rhetoric*, 73; DIXON, *Rhetoric*, 14; UEDING and STEINBRINK,
Grundriß, 247. Cf. D. KANE, *Logic: The Art of Inference and Predication* (New York 1969)
157: "We know that in contemporary society to say more than is polite or expedient, to
make explicit what could normally be presupposed, and to assert or support opinions in a
highly formal way are unacceptable modes of social behavior."

Thus rhetorical arguments are based on what is generally true or probable, and its conclusions are particular, not general. In comparison with syllogisms, enthymemes may seem not only abbreviated but also distorted. However, these differences are essential in both oral and written discourse, since an audience's attention will wane if an argument does not have a certain momentum. Barthes suggests that the enthymeme provides enticement or pleasure for readers or listeners, since it allows the audience to finish the construction of an argument for itself. Thus the argument becomes stronger by permitting an audience a certain freedom and creativity.[122] Thus the "logic" of rhetoric is persuasive.[123]

2.5.1.2 Topics

The method devised by ancient rhetoricians to discover material for these three modes involved *topics* (τόποι; *loci*). A *topos* or *locus* was a "place" where one could find or "invent" something to say about a subject. Topics were associated both with the material with which arguments are made and the form of those arguments. They were tested and approved ways of investigating a subject and conducting an argument.[124]

Aristotle distinguished two kinds of topics, special and common. The special topics were arguments that could be applied to particular kinds of discourse; the common topics (*loci communes* or "commonplaces") were those which could be used for any occasion or type of speech. Aristotle named four common topics: 1) more or less (the topic of degree); 2) the possible and the impossible; 3) past fact and future fact; 4) greatness and smallness (the topic of size).[125] Later the term "commonplace" was applied to practically any observation or truth (often appearing in the form of a maxim or saying).

---

[122] BARTHES, *L'ancienne rhétorique,* 133. Cf. W. ISER, *The Implied Reader: Patterns of Communication in Prose Fiction from Bunyon to Beckett* (Baltimore/London 1974) 278-279.

[123] BRANDT, *The Rhetoric of Argumentation,* 39; A.-E. CHAIGNET, *La rhétorique et son histoire* (Paris 1888) 214; CORBETT, *Classical Rhetoric,* 77.

[124] CORBETT, *Classical Rhetoric,* 35; DIXON, *Rhetoric,* 26; LANHAM, *Handlist,* 99-100; UEDING and STEINBRINK, *Grundriß,* 218; S. VAN NOORDEN, "Rhetorical Arguments in Aristotle and Perelman," *RIP* 33 (1979) 184. CICERO, *Orator,* xiv.46, defined topics as "quasi argumentorum notas tradidit unde omnis in utramque partem traheretur oratio." REBOUL, *Introduction à la rhétorique,* 62-64, points out that "topics" actually had three different meanings: 1) an argument "type"; 2) a "type" of argument corresponding to commonplaces; and 3) a question "type" which permitted the discovery of both arguments and counter-arguments.

[125] ARISTOTLE, *Rhetoric,* II.19.1392a-1393a; KENNEDY, *New Testament Interpretation,* 21; CORBETT, *Classical Rhetoric,* 35. On p. 110 CORBETT lists a number of common topics with their subtopics: definition, comparison, relationship, circumstance, and testimony.

So the term "commonplaces" has two meanings: 1) titles or headings under which arguments could be classified; and 2) collections of formulas or themes, observations or wisdom sayings which served as subject matter for arguments.[126] The fact that such "commonplaces" are stylized approaches to reality does not mean that they are mere cliches or stereotypes, for they are able to provoke contrasts.[127] Perelman and Olbrechts-Tyteca remind us that the *loci* have argumentative value and thus form an indispensable arsenal on which one can draw for arguments. They list *loci* of quantity, quality, order, the existing, essence, and the person.[128]

2.5.1.3 The New Rhetoric

As noted above, Perelman and Olbrechts-Tyteca see the aim of argumentation in the eliciting or increasing of adherence to theses presented to an audience. Such adherence presupposes a meeting of minds between speaker and audience. Argumentation is that process which attempts to modify the audience's convictions. The speaker therefore must begin with premises already accepted by the audience. The transfer of adherence to the speaker's theses is possible only if a bond has been established between the premises of the audience and the theses whose acceptance the speaker wants to achieve.[129]

Argumentation occurs through *association* or *dissociation* of ideas. Processes of association (or *liaison*) bring separate elements together and establish some kind of unity among them. Processes of dissociation are techniques of separation.[130] Perelman and Olbrechts-Tyteca list and describe many types of arguments which fall under these two categories,

---

[126] DIXON, *Rhetoric*, 27; LANHAM, *Handlist*, 100; ONG, *Oralità e scrittura*, 156; PERELMAN and OLBRECHTS-TYTECA, *Traité de l'argumentation*, 112.

[127] VALESIO, *Novantiqua*, 33.

[128] PERELMAN and OLBRECHTS-TYTECA, *Traité de l'argumentation*, 114-128; see also PERELMAN, *L'empire rhétorique*, 43-44. Their understandings of these *loci*: *Loci of quantity* affirm one thing is better than another for quantitative reasons. For example, a greater number of good things is more desirable than a smaller number; a good thing useful for a comparatively large number of ends is more desirable than one useful to a lesser degree; that which is more lasting or durable is more desirable than that which is less so. *Loci of quality* give a high rating to the unique. *Loci of order* affirm the superiority of that which is earlier over that which is later; sometimes they affirm the superiority of the cause, the principle, the end, or the goal. *Loci of the existing* affirm the superiority of that which exists, the actual, the real, over the possible, the contingent, or the impossible. *Loci of essence* accord higher value to individuals to the extent that they embody the essence of something. *Loci of the person* affirm the dignity, the worth, and the authority of the individual person. REBOUL, *Introduction à la rhétorique*, 168-169, has reduced these *loci* to three: *loci* of quantity, quality, and unity.

[129] PERELMAN, *L'empire rhétorique*, 35.

[130] Ibid., 64; PERELMAN and OLBRECHTS-TYTECA, *Traité de l'argumentation*, 255.

but they give special attention to three general kinds of arguments which establish liaisons: quasi-logical arguments, arguments that are based on the structure of reality, and arguments which establish the structure of reality.

Quasi-logical arguments are similar to the formal reasoning of logic or mathematics; nevertheless, they are nonformal in character. Such quasi-logical arguments include those which involve incompatibility, identity, definition, tautology, reciprocity, division, dilemma, weights and measures, probabilities, and comparisons.[131]

Arguments based on the structure of reality make use of reality to establish a relationship between accepted judgments and those one wishes to promote. Most arguments of this type appeal either to relations of *succession* (such as cause and effect) or of *coexistence* (which unite a person to his or her actions, a group to its individual members, or an essence to its manifestations). Liaisons of succession would include cause and effect, pragmatic arguments, and arguments of direction and development. Liaisons of coexistence unite two realities which are not on the same level. Thus they include arguments involving an essence and its manifestations or acts, arguments of authority, and qualitative or quantitative hierarchies.[132]

Arguments which establish the structure of reality normally establish relations through particular cases (example, illustration, model) or through reasoning by analogy or metaphor.[133]

2.5.2 Arrangement (*Dispositio*)

"The second part of rhetoric, arrangement, seeks to determine the rhetorically effective composition of the speech and mold its elements into a unified structure."[134] Once material and arguments have been found in order to present an idea, it is necessary to give these a certain order or structure. Without some order even the strongest arguments will become weak or ineffective. And not just any order will do. The arrangement of arguments is no matter of indifference, for arrangement can strengthen or vitiate adherence to the theses the arguments are defending or attacking.

---

[131] PERELMAN, *L'empire rhétorique*, 69-94; PERELMAN and OLBRECHTS-TYTECA, *Traité de l'argumentation*, 259-350.

[132] PERELMAN, *L'empire rhétorique*, 95-117; PERELMAN and OLBRECHTS-TYTECA, *Traité de l'argumentation*, 351-470.

[133] PERELMAN, *L'empire rhétorique*, 119-138; PERELMAN and OLBRECHTS-TYTECA, *Traité de l'argumentation*, 471-549.

[134] KENNEDY, *New Testament Interpretation*, 23.

Aristotle felt that the only necessary parts of a speech are the statement and the argument.[135] He was willing to concede, however, that in practice many orators also added an introduction and a conclusion.[136] Eventually classical Latin rhetoricians saw a seven-part arrangement of a speech, especially for forensic discourse:[137]

1. Entrance or Prooemium (*exordium*), which catches the audience's attention.
2. Narration (*praecognitio* or *narratio*), which sets forth the facts.
3. Exposition or Definition (*explicatio* or *definitio*), which defines terms and opens issues to be proven.

---

[135] ARISTOTLE, *Rhetoric,* III.13.1414b. PLATO, *Phaedrus,* 264C, says that a discourse must be arranged like a body with head, feet, middle, and members.

[136] CORBETT, *Classical Rhetoric,* 36; BRANDT, *The Rhetoric of Argumentation,* 51, reduces these four parts to three: introduction, argument, and conclusion.

[137] LANHAM, *Handlist,* 112. To some extent this list is a simplification, since all authors do not agree on seven parts. However, the disagreements are not major ones, since they are often but subtle refinements of this list. *Rhetorica ad Herennium,* I.iii.4, lists six elements: introduction (*exordium*); statement of facts (*narratio*); division (*divisio*); proof (*confirmatio*); refutation (*confutatio*); and conclusion (*conclusio*). It is to be noted that the discussion about such structure in *Rhetorica ad Herennium,* as well as in most ancient rhetorical works, takes place under *inventio*. CICERO, *De oratore,*. II.80, knows these parts even without giving their names. He describes the order of a discourse in the following manner: "iubent enim exordiri ita, ut eum, qui audiat, benevolum nobis faciamus et docilem et attentum; deinde rem narrare, et ita ut veri similis narratio sit, ut aperta, ut brevis; post autem dividere causam aut proponere; nostra confirmare argumentis ac rationibus; deinde contraria refutare; tum autem alii conclusionem orationis et quasi perorationem conlocant, alii iubent, ante quam peroretur, ornandi aut augendi causa digredi, deinde concludere ac perorare," QUINTILIAN, *Institutio oratoria,* describes seven parts in discourse: *exordium* (IV.1), *narratio* (IV.2), *digressio* or *egressio* (IV.3), *propositio* (IV.4), *partitio* (IV.5), *refutatio* (V.13), and *peroratio* (VI.1). He doesn't list *confirmatio*, yet he does speak about proofs and arguments in V.1-12. BARTHES, *L'ancienne rhétorique,* 90, points out that CORAX, one of the first Greek rhetoricians (fifth century B.C.E. in Sicily) already described five parts of an oration: exordium, narration or action, argumentation or proof, digression, and epilogue. GARAVELLI, *Manuale di retorica,* 63, sums up the parts of discourse mentioned in ancient times with the following table:

1.	*prooimion*	1.	*exordium/prooemium/principium*
2.	*(diégesis)*	2.	*narratio*
2a.	*parékbasis*	2a.	*digressio/egressus*
2b.	*próthesis*	2b.	*propositio/expositio*
		2c.	*partitio/enumeratio*
3.	*pístis*	3.	*argumentatio*
3a.	*kataskeué*	3a.	*confirmatio/probatio*
3b.	*anaskeué*	3b.	*refutatio/confutatio/reprehensio*
4.	*epílogos*	4.	*epilogus/peroratio/conclusio*

4. Proposition (*partitio*), which clarifies the points at issue and states exactly what is to be proved.
5. Confirmation (*amplificatio*), which sets forth the arguments for and against; this is the proof.
6. Confutation or Refutation (*refutatio* or *reprehensio*), which refutes the opponent's arguments.
7. Conclusion or Epilogue (*peroratio* or *epilogus*), which sums up arguments and stirs the audience.

Such a scheme could be followed by an orator to help him or her arrange the material to present a strong case. However, adherence to this type of order in a discourse is hardly mandatory. It was imitated widely not only in ancient Greece and Rome but also in Christian Europe during the Middle Ages and the Renaissance. But it is possible, even likely, that other cultures would not follow such a scheme in arranging their own discourses.

The author of *Rhetorica ad Herennium,* who favors this kind of arrangement, admits that a speaker may depart from it when he or she judges the circumstances favorable for such a change.[138] The speaker or writer must arrange the material in accordance with the kind of discourse used, the nature of the subject, his or her own personality, and the nature of the audience.[139] Perelman and Olbrechts-Tyteca see three elements which affect the order of a discourse: the argumentative situation (that is, the influence of earlier discussion or other outside factors on the argumentative possibilities open to the speaker), the conditioning of the audience by the speech itself, and the reactions of the audience during the speech.[140]

Arrangement is significant because the whole must work together to cause an effect, that is, to promote or strengthen the adherence of an audience to the ideas of the orator. The audience is therefore of utmost importance for arranging one's arguments. It should be noted that order has no special role in a purely formal demonstration, but in argumentation the arrangement can drastically affect the conditions for the acceptance of one's theses.[141] For as the discourse develops, it changes the situation of the audience — it does not leave its hearers the same as at

---

[138] *Rhetorica ad Herennium,* III.ix.17: "Est autem alia dispositio, quae, cum ab ordine artificioso recedendum est, oratoris iudicio ad tempus adcomodatur."

[139] CORBETT, *Classical Rhetoric,* 300. CICERO, *Brutus,* lvii.209, comments that all discourse has a beginning and an ending, but the significance of the other parts depends on their relationship to one another.

[140] PERELMAN and OLBRECHTS-TYTECA, *Traité de l'argumentation,* 651. Cf. C.C. BLACK, "The Rhetorical Form of the Hellenistic Jewish and Early Christian Sermon: A Response to Lawrence Wills," *HTR* 81 (1988) 7; CHAIGNET, *La rhétorique et son histoire,* 400-401.

[141] PERELMAN, *L'empire rhétorique,* 161.

the beginning. "The order adopted is crucial precisely because the changes in the audience are both effective and contingent."[142]

In argumentation one always begins with premises acceptable to an audience. The speaker or writer will need to arrange the material in such a way as to bring forward new premises, to confer presence on certain elements, and to extract certain agreements from the listeners or readers.[143] Thus normally the statement of facts is placed near the beginning of a discourse, since facts are quick to command a large measure of agreement.[144] In the past orators have favored order based on the strength of arguments: the order of increasing strength, the order of decreasing strength, and the Nestorian order (where one begins and ends with the strongest arguments, leaving the weaker ones in between).[145]

But such rigid arrangements of arguments fail to take into account the audience and the rhetorical situation. It is difficult to give rigid rules on the order of arguments, since so much depends on the audience and the way in which the arguments are received. Argumentation is marked by a constant interaction among numerous factors, and thus arguments cannot be evaluated in isolation. Their strength depends on their arrangement, their development, and their reception by the audience. *Context* is all-important for the effectiveness of arguments.[146]

---

[142] PERELMAN and OLBRECHTS-TYTECA, *The New Rhetoric*, 491. The original text can be found in *Traité de l'argumentation*, 650: "C'est précisément parce que les modifications de l'auditoire sont à la fois effectives et contingentes que l'ordre adopté importe tant."

[143] PERELMAN and OLBRECHTS-TYTECA, *Traité de l'argumentation*, 651.

[144] Ibid., 654.

[145] GARAVELLI, *Manuale di retorica*, 106-107; *Rhetorica ad Herennium*, III.ix.18, recommends the Nestorian order. The term comes from Homer's *Iliad*, where Nestor arranged his command in such a way that the weakest soldiers were placed between two ranks of his strongest troops. See also CICERO, *Orator*, xv.50.

[146] PERELMAN and OLBRECHTS-TYTECA, *Traité de l'argumentation*, 650; PERELMAN, *L'empire rhétorique*, 163. REBOUL, *Introduction à la rhétorique*, 104-105, comments that the order in argumentation is not linear or chain-like (as in a demonstration) but more like that of a spindle or a bundle: "...l'argumentation serait plutôt semblable à un *fuseau* d'arguments, indépendants les uns des autres et convergeant vers la même conclusion..." He illustrates his point in the following fashion:

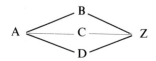

Such an order is not so much *logical* as *psychological*.

2.5.3 Style (*Elocutio*)

Despite its importance, style is a rather difficult concept to define. It seems that none of the ancient works on rhetoric attempted to give a definition, although they had much to say on the subject.[147] Style is normally associated with the individuality or personality of the author or speaker.[148]

> In all literary structures we are aware of a quality that we may call the quality of a verbal personality or a speaking voice — something different from direct address, though related to it. When this quality is felt to be the voice of the author himself, we call it style: *le style c'est l'homme* is a generally accepted axiom. The conception of style is based on the fact that every writer has his own rhythm, as distinctive as his handwriting, and his own imagery, ranging from a preference for certain vowels and consonants to a preoccupation with two or three archetypes.[149]

Elocutio for the ancients was the expression of the ideas "found" in *inventio*. It was the act of giving linguistic form to ideas. But there is a danger of establishing a dichotomy between form and content, style and meaning, or — as the Romans put it — *verba* and *res*. The problem with such a dichotomy is that style could be considered only an embellishment or decoration. This notion paved the way for rhetoric's later exclusive association with stylistics, which led to its decline.[150] Genuine rhetorical

---

[147] CORBETT, *Classical Rhetoric*, 37.

[148] E. BLACK, *Rhetorical Criticism*, xiii. A. MARCHESE, *Dizionario di retorica e stilistica: Arte e artificio nell'uso delle parole: Retorica, stilistica, metrica, teoria della letteratura*, 5th ed. (Milano 1989), 305, defines style as "l'espressione personale, e dunque fortemente autonoma e creativa, di uno scrittore." But one can speak not only of the style of an author but also of a work (p. 307). The *Dictionnaire encyclopédique des sciences du langage* (ed. O. DUCROT and T. TODOROV; Points 110; Paris 1972) 382, defines style as "le choix que tout texte doit opérer parmi un certain nombre de disponibilités contenues dans la langue."

[149] FRYE, *Anatomy of Criticism*, 268.

[150] GARAVELLI, *Manuale di retorica*, 111-112; KENNEDY, *New Testament Interpretation*, 25. CICERO, *De oratore*, I.142, in listing the five parts of rhetoric, describes *elocutio* in the following words: "tum ea denique vestire atque ornare oratione." Such a description in terms of a garment or an ornament was unfortunate, for it reinforced the dichotomy between *res* and *verba* (see UEDING and STEINBRINK, *Grundriß*, 199). However, the word used to describe style, *ornatus,* does not mean merely "ornament" or "decoration." For the Roman *ornatus* was associated with "equipment" or a soldier's "gear," and it suggested excellence, preparedness, and usefulness. (See VICKERS, *In Defence of Rhetoric,* 314; GARAVELLI, *Manuale di retorica 139.* D.P. SIMPSON, *Cassell's New Latin Dictionary* [New York 1959] 417, gives the definition for *ornatus* as "dress, attire, equipment." The secondary meanings are "embellishment, ornament." The verb *ornare* has as its first meaning "to equip, furnish, provide with necessaries, fit out." Only afterwards comes "to adorn, decorate, embellish.") GRASSI, *Rhetoric as Philosophy,* 48, claims that QUINTILIAN proposed that any content of speech has its own rhetorical form and that originally the dichotomy between *res* and *verba* did not exist. See QUINTILIAN, *Institutio oratoria,* I.intro.5.

teaching, both ancient and modern, recognizes that speech and thought, form and content, style and meaning are inseparable, and thus style cannot be seen as mere clothing or ornamentation for ideas. There is an integral relationship between the two. In literature as well as in a speech the form is meaningful, and meaning exists in and through the form. Style is thus another means of persuasion, another way of promoting or increasing adherence to proposed theses.[151]

Aristotle[152] observes that each rhetorical genre has its own appropriate style, and he also distinguishes between written and oral styles. Cicero[153] describes three levels of style: 1) the low, plain, or subdued style (*genus humile* or *extenuatum*), which explains everything and makes every point clear rather than impressive; 2) the high, majestic, or grandiloquent style (*genus grande* or *grave*), which is forceful, versatile, copious, and emotional; and 3) the middle or temperate style (*genus medium* or *modicum* or *mediocre* or *temperatum*), which was somewhere between the other two. The plain style was considered the best for teaching, the middle style for pleasing, and the majestic or grand style for moving or persuading.[154] Such a three-part division is rather ambiguous, however, since it is difficult to distinguish where one style ends and another begins. The distinctions were normally based on considerations of subject, diction, effect on the audience, and syntax or composition.[155]

---

[151] L. ALONSO SCHÖKEL, "Hermeneutical Problems of a Literary Study of the Bible," *VTS* 28 (1975) 1-15; CORBETT, *Classical Rhetoric*, 415; FISHBANE, *Text and Texture*, 8; UEDING and STEINBRINK, *Grundriß*, 200.

[152] ARISTOTLE, *Rhetoric*, III.12.1413b.

[153] CICERO, *Orator*, v.20-vi.21; *De oratore*, III.199; see CORBETT, *Classical Rhetoric*, 37; LANHAM, *Handlist*, 113; MESSER LEON, *Honeycomb's Flow*, I.14.1-8.

[154] CICERO, *Orator*, xxi.69: "Sed quot officia oratoris tot sunt genera dicendi: subtile in probando, modicum in delectando, vehemens in flectendo." CICERO goes on to describe the plain style in xxiii.76; xxiv.81-xxvi.90; the middle style in xxvi.91-xxvii.96; and the grand style in xxviii.97-99. However, CICERO also writes about style in terms of the two contemporary categories of *Attic* (a plainer style) and *Asiatic* (a grander style). See *Orator*, xxiii.75-76; *Brutus*, lxxxii.284-lxxxiv.289; xcv.325. Cf. BURKE, *A Rhetoric of Motives*, 73; UEDING and STEINBRINK, *Grundriß*, 260-262; *Rhetorica ad Herennium*, IV.viii.11-x.14. AUGUSTINE, *De doctrina christiana*, IV, chaps. 17-26, speaks about these three styles. In IV.17.34 he quotes CICERO, *Orator*, xxix.101, on their use. Then he rephrases this quotation in his own words: "Is erit igitur eloquens, qui ut doceat, poterit parva submisse, ut delectet, modica temperate, ut flectat, magna granditer dicere." This division of style into three types seems to have originated with THEOPHRASTUS and was adopted by CICERO and others (see DIXON, *Rhetoric*, 33).

[155] LANHAM, *Handlist*, 113-114. In terms of the subject, it was felt that the more important the subject, the grander should be the style. AUGUSTINE, *De doctrina christiana*, IV.18.35-37, felt that the majestic style could be used often, since the Christian preacher or teacher was speaking about the most essential of subjects, salvation and damnation. Regarding *diction* or language use, the higher the style the greater the use of figures and other rhetorical devices. As for *effect on the audience*, the grandiloquent style was

The ancients also insisted on certain qualities of style. The *Rhetorica ad Herennium* recommended taste (*elegantia*), artistic composition (*conpositio*), and distinction (*dignitas*).[156] Cicero, following Theophrastus, recommended the virtues of purity or correctness of language (*puritas* or *latinitas*; καθαρότης or ἑλληνίσμος), clarity (*perspicuitas;* σαφήνεια), appropriateness or suitability (*aptum*; τὸ πρέπον), and ornamentation (*ornatus*; κατασκευή). Purity refers to correctness or the good use of language. Each language, of course, will have its own proper usage of sounds, words, rhythm, and grammar. Clarity refers to the intelligibility of language, to the avoidance of ambiguity or unnecessary complexity. Language must first be understood before it can persuade, and to be understood it must be clear. Appropriateness concerns itself with the context of a discourse. Style must be suitable to the subject matter, the purpose, the occasion, and the audience. Ornamentation refers to the decorative aspects of style, to what is pleasing to our senses.[157]

Among the decorative aspects of style are *figures* and *tropes,* which were among the most studied features of ancient rhetorical theory. A figure is "any device or pattern of language in which meaning is changed or enhanced."[158] Rhetoricians disagree with one another in the classification of these rhetorical devices, but they generally speak about schemes, tropes, figures of speech, and figures of thought.[159]

---

considered to be more effective for moving and thus persuading an audience. In terms of *syntax* or *composition,* the majestic style made use of balanced elements in complex arrangements, while the plain style used shorter periods.

[156] *Rhetorica ad Herennium,* IV.xii.17-xiii.18. *Elegantia* concerns itself with purity of language (*latinitas*) and clarity (*explanatio*); *conpositio* concerns itself with the arrangement of words and sounds; and *dignitas* concerns itself with embellishment, especially with figures of speech and figures of thought.

[157] CICERO, *De oratore,* III.37-55. QUINTILIAN, *Institutio oratoria,* VIII.2-3, writes about *perspicuitas* and *ornatus.* Cf. DIXON, *Rhetoric,* 34; GARAVELLI, *Manuale di retorica,* 115-140; LAUSBERG, *Elemente,* 44-62, 153; UEDING and STEINBRINK, *Grundriß,* 201-211; CICERO is especially concerned with propriety or appropriateness (see *Orator,* xxi.70-xxii.74). ARISTOTLE, *Rhetoric,* III.2.1404b, mentions both clarity and appropriateness, but he emphasizes clarity. Cf. KENNEDY, *New Testament Interpretation,* 25. PERELMAN and OLBRECHTS-TYTECA, *Traité de l'argumentation,* 168, doubt if language can eliminate ambiguity sufficiently to make absolute clarity possible.

[158] LANHAM, *Handlist,* 116. QUINTILIAN, *Institutio oratoria,* IX.1.14, after a discussion on figures and schemes, finally defines a figure: "Ergo figura sit arte aliqua novata forma dicendi." This notion of a figure as a change of meaning or form has led to its description as an "écart" or "gap, space." See, for example, R. BARTHES, "Style and Its Image," *Literary Style: A Symposium* (ed. S. CHATMAN; London/New York 1971) 6-7; DUCROT and TODOROV, ed., *Dictionnaire encyclopédique des sciences du langage,* 349-350; G. GENETTE, *Figures I,* 207; *Figures II* (Points 106; Paris 1969) 127; Groupe μ, *Rhétorique générale,* 173-174; MARCHESE, *Dizionario di retorica e di stilistica,* 305; REBOUL, *Introduction à la rhétorique,* 75-77.

[159] CORBETT, *Classical Rhetoric,* 460-461, divides all "figures of speech" into the two categories of *schemes* and *tropes.* A *scheme* (from the Greek word σχῆμα: "form,"

A *scheme* is associated with a deviation from the ordinary arrangement of words; it is contrasted with a *trope,* which is a deviation from the ordinary meaning of a word. Both involve a transference, whether of order/form (scheme) or of meaning (trope). Metaphor, synecdoche, metonymy, and hyperbole would be examples of tropes. All tropes work through some type of substitution (based on resemblance and/or difference), in which the reader or listener is expected to relate two terms to one another mentally. Thus a trope reveals some tension between the particular use of a word and some perceived normative use.[160]

Figures have also been traditionally divided into figures of speech (λέξεως σχήματα or *figurae verborum*: literally, figures of *words*) and figures of thought (διανοίας σχήματα or *figurae sententiae*).[161] Figures of

---

"shape") involves a deviation from the ordinary pattern or arrangement of words. A *trope* (from the Greek word τρόπος, a "turn," "direction," or "way"; it comes from the verb τρέπειν, which means "to lead," "to guide," or "to turn") is a deviation from the ordinary meaning of a word. LANHAM, *Handlist,* 116, prefers to divide all figures into figures of words and figures of thought. The figures of words would then be subdivided into tropes and schemes. GARAVELLI, *Manuale di retorica,* 140, divides all devices of *ornatus* into those of single words and those of groups of words or connections between words. Tropes are included among the devices of single words, while figures of speech and figures of thought are among the devices of groups of words and the connections between words. VICKERS, *In Defence of Rhetoric,* 315-316, mentions that a trope involves a change or transference of meaning and therefore works on a conceptual level, while a figure involves the placing of words in a structure which goes beyond the normal or minimal needs of communication. DIXON, *Rhetoric,* 37, acknowledges some confusion with these terms, since "trope" covers certain figures, while "scheme" and "figure" somehow cover the rest. UEDING and STEINBRINK, *Grundriß,* 266, maintain that it is often difficult to differentiate between figures and tropes. MARCHESE, *Dizionario di retorica e di stilistica,* 116, admits that there is no commonly agreed classification of figures. He lists the following as an ancient classification: 1) figure di pensiero; 2) figure di significazione o tropi; 3) figure di dizione; 4) figure di elocuzione; 5) figure di costruzione; and 6) figure di ritmo. However, he finds such classifications unsatisfactory and arbitrary. GENETTE, *Figures I,* 216-217, gives a slightly different list: tropes, figures de diction, figures de construction, figures d'élocution, figures de style, and figures de pensée. Groupe μ, *Rhétorique générale,* divides all figures and tropes into métaplasmes, métataxes, métasémèmes, and métalogismes.

[160] VICKERS, *In Defence of Rhetoric,* 444; BRANDT, *The Rhetoric of Argumentation,* 101, 135. BRANDT comments that tropes obtain our attention and help us to get to an experience itself rather than being a mere statement about experience. *Rhetorica ad Herennium,* IV.xxxi.42-xxxiv.46, discusses ten tropes, although the author does not call them by that name (he uses the term *exornationes verborum*). CICERO was probably the first rhetorician to theorize about tropes. See *Brutus,* xvii.69, where he tells us that the name comes from the Greeks. Cf. PLEBE and EMANUELE, *Manuale di retorica,* 160. QUINTILIAN, *Institutio oratoria,* VIII. 6.1, defines trope in the following terms: "Tropus est verbi vel sermonis a propria significatione in aliam cum virtute mutatio." He speaks about tropes throughout chap. 6 of Book VIII.

[161] *Rhetorica ad Herennium,* IV.xiii.18, already expressed this division: "Haec in verborum et in sententiarum exornationes dividitur. Verborum exornatio est quae ipsius

speech include such devices as repetitions (for example, *anaphora, epiphora*), synonyms, climax, enumeration, and puns. Figures of thought include rhetorical questions, oxymoron, allegory, allusion, self-correction, and apostrophe.[162] However, the distinction between the two has often been vague and confusing, and so has the distinction between figure and trope.[163] Perelman and Olbrechts-Tyteca, in fact, believe that the division into figures of thought and figures of speech has only obscured their real role in argumentation.[164] They prefer to divide the rhetorical devices into figures of choice, figures of presence, and figures of communion.[165]

Admittedly figures are decorative devices in language, but it would be a mistake to regard them merely as ornamentation. For they give clarity, liveliness, and energy to discourse. Figures are functional devices important for a speaker or writer in argumentation, for they portray character, support arguments, and induce emotions.[166] Their effectiveness is especially notable in the inducing of emotional responses in audiences.[167]

Figures, however, do not merely act on the feelings of an audience. They have other persuasive or argumentative functions as well. A figure

---

sermonis insignita continetur perpolitione. Sententiarum exornatio est quae non in verbis, sed in ipsius rebus quandam habet dignitatem." The *Rhetorica ad Herennium,* however, did not distinguish between tropes and schemes/figures, and even the distinction between figures of speech and figures of thought could be vague. CICERO, *De oratore,* III.200, sees the difference between the two types of figures in this way: when one changes the wording of a figure of speech, it disintegrates as a figure; but when one changes the wording of a figure of thought, the figure remains. QUINTILIAN, *Institutio oratoria,* IX.1.17, formulates the classic understanding of figures of speech and figures of thought: "...duas eius esse partes, διανοίας, id est mentis vel sensus vel sententiarum, nam his omnibus modis dictum est, et λέξεως, id est verborum vel dictionis vel elocutionis vel sermonis vel orationis...." He dedicates chap. 2 of Book IX to figures of thought and chap. 3 to figures of speech. In IX.3.1-102 QUINTILIAN divides figures of speech into four types: 1) variations of syntax; 2) modes of iteration; 3) word-plays; and 4) balance and antithesis. See VICKERS, *In Defence of Rhetoric,* 316. MESSER LEON, *Honeycomb's Flow,* I.14.14, describes a figure of speech as one where the wording contains no small amount of embellishment and adornment, while a figure of thought contains its beauty within the thought itself.

[162] GARAVELLI, *Manuale di retorica,* 188, 239.

[163] Ibid., 235-236; A. SNYMAN, "On Studying the Figures (*schēmata*) in the New Testament," *Bib* 69 (1988) 94.

[164] PERELMAN and OLBRECHTS-TYTECA, *Traité de l'argumentation,* 232.

[165] Ibid., 232-241. A *figure of choice* imposes or suggests that a choice or a judgment must be made; a *figure of presence* makes an object present in the mind; a *figure of communion* increases communion with the audience.

[166] BRANDT, *The Rhetoric of Argumentation,* 101; CORBETT, *Classical Rhetoric,* 459; DIXON, *Rhetoric,* 40-41; KENNEDY, *New Testament Interpretation,* 29; REBOUL, *La rhétorique,* 36, 40.

[167] VICKERS, *In Defence of Rhetoric,* 304-305, 309-310. Cf. QUINTILIAN, *Institutio oratoria,* IX.1.21: "Iam vero adfectus nihil magis ducit." See also MESSER LEON, *Honeycomb's Flow,* IV.82.3.

is argumentative if its use leads to a change of perspective.[168] Thus it is impossible to determine in advance if a given structure is a figure, and whether or not that figure is argumentative or merely stylistic. This is because all depends on the context, and the context includes the audience and the rhetorical situation. Categorizing figures outside their contexts has led to the impression that such devices are merely decorative. One cannot understand a figure outside its argumentative context.[169]

2.6 Rhetorical Criticism and the Hebrew Bible

The theory of rhetoric, whether ancient or modern, is basically a European or Western phenomenon. Thus the question arises whether it can be applied to the Bible, an ancient text written in a Semitic tongue unrelated to Greek, Latin, or any modern European language. In fact, our knowledge of ancient Hebrew rhetoric is minimal, and even our knowledge of the language itself is far from complete.[170]

This does not mean that the ancient Hebrews made no use of rhetoric. Rhetoric is a universal aspect of language, even if a particular culture does not recognize this nor theorize about it. "Rhetoric is coextensive with human discourse, and it is no more possible to speak without being rhetorical than it is to live without breathing."[171] According to Messer Leon, God himself created rhetoric and put it within the human spirit.[172] Rhetoric is the manipulation of language to create particular effects; such effects include persuading, convincing, and inducing emotions. As a result, it is an art that human beings have used whenever they have communicated. Persuasion is thus implicit within language.[173] For "the very acts of thinking, talking, and writing

---

[168] PERELMAN and OLBRECHTS-TYTECA, *Traité de l'argumentation*, 229; PERELMAN, *L'empire rhétorique*, 52-53. Cf. BURKE, *A Rhetoric of Motives*, 57.

[169] PERELMAN and OLBRECHTS-TYTECA, *Traité de l'argumentation*, 229-231; SNYMAN, "On Studying the Figures," 100-102. Cf. R. WELLEK and A. WARREN, *Theory of Literature*, 3rd ed. (Harmondsworth 1985) 178.

[170] NIDA and REYBURN, *Meaning across Cultures*, 12.

[171] VALESIO, *Novantiqua*, 60. See BEAUJOUR, "Rhétorique et littérature," 158; FRYE, *Anatomy of Criticism*, 331; JASPER, "Wherever I Said Aristotle," 134; OLÉRON, *L'argumentation*, 3; PATRICK and SCULT, *Rhetoric and Biblical Interpretation*, 13.

[172] MESSER LEON, *Honeycomb's Flow*, I.4.11; cf. I. RABINOWITZ, Introduction to *The Book of the Honeycomb's Flow: Sēpher Nōpheth Ṣūphīm*, by Judah MESSER LEON, liii.

[173] BRANDT, *The Rhetoric of Argumentation*, 3; BURKE, *A Rhetoric of Motives*, 274; GRASSI, *Rhetoric as Philosophy*, 26; REBOUL, *La rhétorique*, 6; "Rhetoric," *Synopticon*, II, 652; SLOAN and PERELMAN, "Rhetoric," 803. For an example of argumentation or persuasive speech in an isolated culture of Papua New Guinea see J. LARSON, "The Dynamics of Enga Persuasive Speech," *Exploring Enga Culture: Studies in Missionary Anthropology* (ed. P. BRENNAN; Second Anthropological Conference of New Guinea Lutheran Mission — 1970) (Wapenamanda, Papua New Guinea 1970) 1-16.

presuppose the existence of other people, the act of communication, and therefore the desire to persuade." [174]

Burke sees the origin of rhetoric in the strife implicit in human society. Language is a natural if symbolic means of defending one's own interests, gaining advantage, or inducing cooperation in beings that by nature respond to symbols.[175] Grassi likewise sees rhetoric rising from language's function of overcoming isolation.[176] Persuasion or argumentation is the result of the human need to defend one's interests as well as to overcome potential conflicts. From such needs originates every possible form of persuasion, whether that be sales promotion, propaganda, courtship, etiquette, education, theology, or politics.[177]

Nevertheless rhetoric is affected by the particular culture in which it takes shape. Western rhetoric, for example, has developed an "agonistic" orientation, that is, it tends to accentuate opposition and differences. As such it would be quite different from an Indian or a Chinese rhetoric, which minimizes conflict and opposition and denies duality.[178] Particular cultures develop their own forms of discourse, and these will be affected by the attitudes, experiences, traditions, and language of the culture involved.[179] We cannot expect uniform principles of rhetoric which can be applied indiscriminately to every culture and every age. One must keep in mind the cultural context of argumentation. Arguments are assertions

---

[174] VICKERS, *In Defence of Rhetoric*, 212; see also 23, 301. CORBETT, *Classical Rhetoric*, 41, points out that there are four conventional forms of spoken or written discourse — description, exposition, argumentation, and narration. Of these, argumentation is the most frequent. NIDA and REYBURN, *Meaning across Cultures*, 42, also see four different types of "discourse structure": narrative, description, argument, and dialogue.

[175] BURKE, *A Rhetoric of Motives*, 22-23, 43. He sees all human effort aiming at *advantage* of one sort or another. This promotes strife. Rhetoric's goal of identification is one way of overcoming this strife. See pp. 20, 60-61. VALESIO, *Novantiqua*, 65-66, would probably agree with BURKE, since he recognizes that rhetoric is dialectical and that all cultural contrasts are conflicts that need to be resolved. Rhetoric is one important way of dealing with such conflicts. ARISTOTLE, *Rhetoric*, I.1.1354a, was the first to observe that all people attempt to defend themselves and attack others when discussing. Cf. also P. OLÉRON, *L'argumentation*, 11, 57.

[176] GRASSI, *Rhetoric as Philosophy*, 110. L. BITZER, "Functional Communication: A Situational Perspective," *Rhetoric in Transition* (ed. E. WHITE; University Park/London 1980) 21-22, sees rhetoric as rising from the human being's need to interact functionally with the environment.

[177] BURKE, *A Rhetoric of Motives*, xiv.

[178] G. MANETTI, *Le teorie del segno nell'antichità classica* (Strumenti Bompiani; Milano 1987) 52; ONG, *Oralità e scrittura*, 157. OLIVER, *Culture and Communication*, 79, points out that the presumptions and values of Western rhetoric are not universal.

[179] J. LYONS, *Language and Linguistics: An Introduction* (Cambridge 1981) 144; PERELMAN and OLBRECHTS-TYTECA, *Traité de l'argumentation*, 27; RABIN, "Discourse Analysis," 173-174; SLOAN and PERELMAN, "Rhetoric," 802; D. TANNEN, "Repetition in Conversation as Spontaneous Formulaicity," *Text* 7 (1987) 225; ZYSKIND, Introduction to *The New Rhetoric and the Humanities*, xii.

about reality, and they revolve around cultural topics as well as common topics. This means that arguments will cluster around questions of importance to a particular group.[180]

Thus one cannot apply Greek, Latin, or even modern Western rhetorical theory to ancient Hebrew (and its foremost literary product, the Bible) without modification.[181] We may not presume that the canons and principles of Greek and Latin rhetorical art were operable in the ancient Israelite culture, such as Messer Leon did when he wrote *Sēpher Nōpheth Ṣūphīm*.[182] If rhetorical criticism is to be valid, it must be practiced with some awareness of both the fundamental and universal features of rhetoric and the particular traditions of Hebrew speech and culture. Rhetoric is a universal phenomenon "built into" the workings of every human society.[183] At the same time it is definitely affected by the traditions and conventions of particular cultures.

---

[180] J. ANDREWS, "'Charting Cultural Paths': Toward a Method for Investigating Rhetorical-Cultural Interaction," *Rhetoric in Transition: Studies in the Nature and Uses of Rhetoric* (ed. E. WHITE; University Park/London 1980), 102-103. Cf. J. CONDON and F. YOUSEF, *An Introduction to Intercultural Communication,* 185. On pp. 185-187, 232-236, they list examples of "cultural rhetoric" from the United States: Americans often speak in game terminology, in series of three, with superlatives, and with dichotomous patterns. OLIVER, *Culture and Communication,* 85, 155, says there is no such thing as a universal rhetoric. Rather, since each culture has its own rhetoric, there are many rhetorics.

[181] A weakness of Aristotelian rhetoric is ARISTOTLE's limited knowledge of different cultures. He tended to assume that all human beings were basically like the Greeks of Athens. Modern anthropology has taught us that our perceiving and thinking is profoundly affected by our language, customs, history, and accepted system of values. See OLIVER, *Culture and Communication,* 110-111. Cf. also C.C. BLACK, "Rhetorical Criticism and Biblical Interpretation," 257; E. BLACK, *Rhetorical Criticism,* 124; ESLINGER, *Into the Hands of the Living God,* 4; G. KENNEDY, "'Truth' and 'Rhetoric' in the Pauline Epistles," *The Bible as Rhetoric* (ed. M. WARNER, 1990) 195.

[182] RABINOWITZ, Introduction to *The Book of the Honeycomb's Flow,* lxv. He adds: "The identical suspicion, we hasten to add, for the same reason — though with far less excuse than in the case of our fifteenth-century scholar — attaches to practically the whole of our modern rhetorical and literary criticism of the Hebrew Bible. A valid rhetorical understanding of the Hebrew Bible is still, as it was in JML's day, a prime desideratum of biblical scholarship." Judah MESSER LEON's work is actually a work on rhetoric written in Hebrew, and it is a continuation of ancient Greek and Roman theory. He illustrated the principles of rhetoric with examples from the Hebrew Bible. AUGUSTINE in *De doctrina christiana* also gave examples from the Old Testament and the New Testament, but his efforts were aimed at writing a rhetoric for the Christian orator. He points out that pagan science and philosophy may be adapted for Christian use, and he recommends Scripture as a model for eloquence. Thus for him the Bible also serves as a source of models and examples of good oratory. E. BULLINGER, *Figures of Speech Used in the Bible Explained and Illustrated* (London 1898; reprint: Grand Rapids 1968), despite the title, merely lists various figures found in the Bible. He does not provide an explanation about their argumentative significance. E. KÖNIG, *Stilistik, Rhetorik, Poetik in Bezug auf die biblische Litteratur* (Leipzig 1900), makes an attempt to evaluate figures in terms of style or poetics, but he generally does not comment on their argumentative value.

[183] KENNEDY, *New Testament Interpretation,* 10, 12. NIDA and REYBURN, *Meaning*

This means that rhetorical criticism must be more than a mere study of style and rhetorical devices, more than a study of structure or arrangement, even if such studies have their place. It is especially within the area of *inventio* that the universal features of rhetoric will be found, while *dispositio* and *elocutio* tend to display more readily the influences of a particular culture.[184] What is useful about ancient Greek and Latin rhetoric is the degree to which their rhetoricians conceptualized the art. They organized rhetorical techniques into a system that can be applied (with modifications) to the rhetoric of other cultures and other times.[185] All modern rhetoricians, including Perelman and Olbrechts-Tyteca, acknowledge their debt to these ancient Greek and Roman masters. Both ancient and modern rhetoricians can aid us in this area of *inventio*, the discovery of arguments. For even the Israelites had to discover arguments when they were writing the Bible.

In contrast to Greek and Latin discourse, Hebrew rhetoric tends to avoid logical argumentation and aims to impress by its force and its concreteness. For the ancient Israelites believed that truth would make itself felt by its own power.[186] The Hebrews also made use of linguistic patterns, particular word formations, and literary genres which we may not always recognize today — certainly chiasm, inclusion, and keywords are among the conventions which they used.[187] A Hebrew audience knew what to expect, and thus perhaps its members could grasp a totality even when discourse presented itself in a form which to us seems rather fragmentary.[188] We must also bear in mind that the ancient Hebrew culture, despite its literacy, was still fundamentally oral in many of its

---

across Cultures, 41, point out that figurative language is closely related to culture and differs from one language to another. However, the use of figurative language is universal. LYONS, *Language and Linguistics,* 323, observes that despite the impossibility of translating all the sentences of one language into another, human beings have always been successful at getting members of other language groups to understand them.

[184] KENNEDY, *New Testament Interpretation,* 8. Cf. R. BARILLI, "Rhétorique et culture," *RIP* 33 (1979) 74.

[185] KENNEDY, *New Testament Interpretation,* 10-11. REBOUL, *La rhétorique,* tells us: "La Grèce n'a pas inventé la rhétorique, mais son enseignement; ce qu'on pratiquait jusque-là sans le savoir, on s'est préoccupé de savoir le pratiquer."

[186] SOGGIN, *Introduzione all'Antico Testamento,* 113. J. PEDERSEN, *Israel: Its Life and Culture* (London 1926) I-II, 115, 123, claims that Hebrew thought sought totality and movement.

[187] M. KESSLER, "Inclusio in the Hebrew Bible," *Semitics* 6 (1978) 45; MUILENBURG, "Form Criticism and Beyond," 18; PATRICK and SCULT, *Rhetoric and Biblical Interpretation,* 31.

[188] J. LUNDBOM, *Jeremiah: A Study in Ancient Hebrew Rhetoric* (SBLDS 18; Missoula, Mont. 1975) 114. ALTER, *The Art of Biblical Narrative,* 20, comments that our expectations of what is logical or contradictory may be different from those of ancient Israel.

habits and attitudes.[189] This residual orality certainly affected rhetorical practices.

Rhetorical criticism of the Bible must also recognize that there is a distinctive rhetoric of religion. This rhetoric tends to be authoritative, oracular, and demanding. It often contains paradoxes, obscurity, repetitions, and the rejection of worldly reasoning. Religious rhetoric tends to emphasize authoritative proclamation and not rational persuasion.[190] All religious systems are rhetorical in that they attempt to communicate religious truth in a particular way: they aim to convince their hearers or readers that this message is vital and important. Rhetoric has even been described as "religion's closest ally," for rhetoric makes possible reflection upon and communication of ultimate reality and ultimate values.[191]

There is another problem associated with any rhetorical-critical approach to a biblical text which emphasizes argumentation or persuasion. This problem was exposed by E. Black, who made a blistering attack on rhetorical criticism as practiced by certain literary critics in the United States in the twentieth century. He condemned this "neo-Aristotelianism" (as he called it). He did not actually condemn the attempt to investigate argumentation or persuasion; rather he disagreed with the narrow way in which it was done, especially through its historicism. This literary movement tended to judge a discourse *only* by its effects on an audience; thus it neglected the intent of the author. Neo-Aristotelianism understands the historical context of a discourse in a limited way, and it fails to appreciate discourse as an art.[192]

A rhetorical-critical evaluation of a biblical text would do well to keep his criticisms in mind. Black, however, never directed his attention to either the Bible or to rhetorical-critical studies of biblical texts. The Bible has special problems of its own, since the author is generally unknown, the reactions of the audience are normally impossible to ascertain, and the historical context is often disputed.

The book of Dt is an argumentative work with its own rhetorical purposes, as we noted above in the first chapter.

---

[189] ONG, *Oralità e scrittura*, 101.

[190] FRYE, *The Great Code*, 29; JASPER, "Wherever I Said Aristotle," 136; KENNEDY, *New Testament Interpretation*, 6, 158. GRASSI, *Rhetoric as Philosophy*, 103-104, sees five traits of sacred language: 1) a directive, revealing, or evangelical character; 2) its formulations are without mediation; 3) it tends to be metaphorical; 4) it is urgent; and 5) its announcements stand outside of time.

[191] WUELLNER, "Where Is Rhetorical Criticism Taking Us?" 449; KENNEDY, *New Testament Interpretation*, 158. Cf. FRYE, *The Great Code*, 28.

[192] E. BLACK, *Rhetorical Criticism*, especially 75, 131.

... In Dt this more objective point of view has been covered over by the desire to persuade. Thus the blessings and curses doubtless remain effective in themselves, but the full rhetorical expansion, the vivid picture of the promised good or evil, turns them into a means of convincing, or producing in the hearer or reader the will to obey because he is moved and persuaded.... In the Dtic use of the covenant the desire to produce an internal consent, a conviction which will move one to obedience has been given an exceptionally important place.[193]

Dt is an eminently suitable subject for rhetorical analysis. This work is an attempt to apply rhetorical criticism to a particular section of Dt, the Third Address of Moses. No doubt such an attempt is full of pitfalls. After all, it will certainly be limited by our lack of knowledge of ancient Hebrew rhetoric. Nevertheless, it is worth a try, since the argumentative aspects of the Book of Dt have been neglected thus far. A rhetorical-critical investigation offers good possibilities for increasing our understanding of Dt 28,69 – 30,20.

This investigation will follow the traditional parts of rhetoric but will also adapt itself to the New Rhetoric.[194] Thus chapter three of this essay will examine the audience and the rhetorical situation of Dt 28,69 – 30,20. Chapter four will concern itself with *inventio,* chapter five with *dispositio,* and chapter six with *elocutio.* Finally chapter seven will summarize and conclude this rhetorical-critical investigation of the Third Address of Moses.

2.7 Methodological Considerations

This essay is an attempt to discover and apply a rhetorical-critical approach to a particular biblical text. How does this approach differ from that of other critics?

First of all, it is a *synchronic* approach. Diachronic questions, problems, and solutions for the most part will be bracketed out. This investigation will limit itself to the final form of the text. Thus there will

---

[193] McCARTHY, *Treaty and Covenant,* 187. LOHFINK, *Höre, Israel!,* 11, agrees that Dt is basically an argumentative work: "Im Deuteronomium will jedes Wort und jede Zeile erklären und überzeugen."

[194] KENNEDY, *New Testament Interpretation,* 33-38, proposes a rhetorical-critical methodology. His process has five steps:.

1. The definition of the rhetorical unit.
2. The identification of the rhetorical situation.
3. The identification of rhetorical disposition or arrangement.
4. The identification of rhetorical techniques or style.
5. The identification of rhetorical criticism as a synchronic whole.

KENNEDY does not specifically include *inventio* (which is the heart of rhetoric) in his scheme, and he tends to break up the classical order of the parts of rhetoric. This work will follow the traditional order more closely.

be no attempt to distinguish an original text from other layers, glosses, additions, or editorial comments. It is possible that the Third Discourse of Moses is the product of more than one real author or editor. But no effort will be made to distinguish them or even to discover their existence.

In fact, in comparison with many other exegetical works, the real authors and their intentions will be neglected here. This makes it possible to concentrate more attention on the audience. This work points out the importance which the audience has in a communication act, for argumentation must not only acknowledge the existence of its receivers but also pay close attention to them. So no suggestions will be made whether the authors of Dt were priests, levites, prophets, elders, or scribes.

The emphasis in this rhetorical-critical approach is on argumentation. Thus it often refers to both ancient Greek and Roman as well as to modern Western rhetoric in order to understand the process of argumentation within Dt 28,69–30,20. Unfortunately we have no ancient Hebrew theory of rhetoric to shed light on this process. Thus it is possible — perhaps even likely — that something will be overlooked in the attempt to analyze this text.

This emphasis on argumentation leads to a search for logical, emotional, and ethical arguments within the text. An attempt will be made to isolate rational arguments according to traditional enthymemes as well as according to arguments of association and dissociation as described by Perelman and Olbrechts-Tyteca. To my knowledge no previous investigator of Dt has ever attempted such a detailed analysis of both rational and affective arguments.[195]

Historical-critical exegesis of Dt has often concentrated its efforts on distinguishing the various historical layers of a text. Sometimes this appears to be the only goal of some exegetes who practice *Literarkritik*. A few critics, however, have adapted a literary-structural approach to the text. Let us briefly review some of the recent commentators on Dt's Third Discourse (and the related text in Dt 4).

Mayes[196] concludes that Dt 29-30 is (more or less) a unity which forms part of the Dtr² edition of Dt. He believes that the notion of Dt as a covenant text following ancient treaty practice is a late one. Dt 29 – 30,

---

[195] To the best of my knowledge there exists only one other thorough study of logical argumentation within a biblical text of any size. This appears in DUKE, *The Persuasive Appeal of the Chronicler*, 81-104. DUKE investigates the enthymemes, examples, and topics within Chronicles. Elsewhere he also examines pathos and ethos. However, he bases his study solely on ARISTOTLE and ancient rhetoric and makes no references to PERELMAN.

[196] MAYES, *Deuteronomy*, 55, 358-371. MAYES calls Dt 30,7 a later addition.

as part of Dtr², makes a contribution by presenting the Horeb and Moab covenants as equals. Mayes does not evaluate the argumentation process within the text.

Preuß[197] prefers to divide Dt 29-30 into a number of subsections which belong to two general layers, layer four (deuteronomistic) and layer five (later additions). He points out references to other parts of Dt, to the Deuteronomistic History, and to Deutero-Isaiah. He also mentions connections with wisdom traditions and downplays the influences of treaty traditions. Other than summarizing them as punishment for Israel's sin and conversion founded upon God's mercy, Preuß has little to say about the content of these two chapters. He says nothing at all about argumentation here.

Reiter[198] investigates Dt 29,1-20. He approaches the text with the tools of text criticism, *Literarkritik,* form analysis (grammar, division into *Sprechzeilen,* repetitions, stylistic considerations), and tradition history. He devotes much of his attention to an attempt to discover layers in the text. He concludes that there is a basic, original layer (29,1-6a [without 5a].9-12 [without 10aβγb]); a reworked editorial layer (vv. [5a].8. [10aβγb].13-19); and other additions (vv. 6b-7.20).

The basic layer, which Reiter considers early exilic, demonstrates that only the acknowledgment of Yahweh can establish a relationship between God and Israel. The covenant is thus based on a historical situation where Yahweh on his own initiative has approached Israel and established a relationship with it. The editorial layer adds a notion of obligation on the part of Israel, whose loyalty is demanded exclusively for Yahweh. Finally, the later additions consider the East Jordan land as part of the benefits of salvation and establish connections between covenant and oath. Literary features and rhetorical devices are analyzed only as evidence of various textual layers. Reiter says little or nothing about argumentation.

Ntagwarara[199] also explores the Third Discourse of Moses from a traditional historical-critical point of view. He suggests that Dt 28,69–30,20 is a covenantal text between God and his people. He first makes a textual-critical analysis, then he examines the structure, the

---

[197] PREUSS, *Deuteronomium,* 60, 157-162. In layer four, which is deuteronomistic, he sees different sublayers: 29,1.(2?).3.6-7; 8-10aα; 13-14; 15-20; 21-27.(28?); 30,1-10; 11-14; 15-20. In layer five he sees the following sublayers: 29,(2?).4-5; 10aβ-12(?); (28?); 30,18.19a(?).

[198] J. REITER, "Der Bundesschluß im Land Moab: Eine exegetische Studie zum Deuteronomium 29,1-20," (Diss. Univ. Wien, 1984).

[199] J. NTAGWARARA, "Alliance d'Israël au pays de Moab (Dt 28,69-30,20): Analyse exégétique, histoire rédactionelle et théologie," (Diss. Univ. de Sciences Humaines de Strasbourg, 1983).

literary form, literary connections, and the tradition history of each section of the text (which he divides into 28,69-29,8; 29,9-14; 29,15-20; 29,21-28; 30,1-10; 30,11-14; and 30,15-20).

Ntagwarara devotes much attention to the problem of singular and plural direct address and to similarities to the Near Eastern treaty form. His chief interest lies with the growth or expansion of this text and with literary connections to other texts. He offers suggestions concerning the sources of the Third Discourse of Moses. However, he makes no attempt to analyze the argumentation within Dt 28,69 – 30,20. For Ntagwarara stylistic and rhetorical devices are useful only as evidence of connections with other texts. In his theological comments on the Third Discourse he ignores his own emphasis on the literary growth of the text and treats it as one uniform block.

Knapp[200] investigates Dt 4, but he does include a study of Dt 29 – 30, which he considers related to chapter 4. He tries to answer questions concerning the unity of Dt 4 and its literary-historical position in Dt. He concludes that Dt 4,1-40 is not the original continuation of Dt 1 – 3, and that it is no unit but the product of several hands. He sees three major blocks of material in 4,1-40: vv. 1-4.9-14; vv. 15-27*; and vv. 29-35. Knapp then devotes his attention to demonstrating that there are similarities between 1) 29,1-14* and 4,1-4.9-14; 2) 29,15ff.* and 4,15-27*; and 3) 30,1-10 and 4,29-35. Making use of various word studies, he claims that Dt 29 – 30 is relatively late. He also notes that each of the three sets of related blocks have different theological interests: block one is interested in the law and obedience; block two is concerned with the first and second commandments; and block three deals with Israel's conversion and a new understanding of obedience to the law.

Knapp bases his analysis on breaks in the thought and syntax, on repetitions and vocabulary patterns. However, it seems a risky venture to ignore such common rhetorical devices such as anacoluthon or amplification when proposing such blocks of material. It would be even more dangerous to presume that every author or editor is capable of only one single fixed thought. Undoubtedly it would be unfair to accuse Knapp of such a presumption, but one cannot help wondering if it is somehow lurking in the background.

Historical-critical studies have traditionally viewed repetition and amplification as signs of various layers within a text. Rhetorical criticism, however, sees these devices as attempts to provide presence, stir emotions, give emphasis, and "fill out" an argument. This is certainly a notable

---

[200] D. KNAPP, *Deuteronomium 4: Literarische Analyse und theologische Interpretation* (Göttingen 1987).

departure from the investigations of scholars such as Mayes, Preuß, Reiter, Ntagwarara, and Knapp.[201]

Braulik[202] investigates Dt 4 (he includes no study of chapters 29–30). In contrast with the previously-mentioned scholars, he abandons the methods of *Literarkritik* and tradition history to concentrate on what he seems to feel is a rhetorical approach. For him, however, rhetoric is understood exclusively in terms of literary, stylistic, and structural analysis. He sees Dt 4,1-40 as a unit, since he finds no sure signs of different layers within the text. He makes no specific references to argumentation, logic, pathos, or ethos. Braulik devotes much of his attention to rhetorical devices (especially those involving sound patterns, syntax, rhyme schemes, and figures of speech), but for him their function is stylistic and structural rather than persuasive. Thus he concludes that the author of Dt 4,1-40 uses these devices for emphasis, contrast, and development of meaning.

In contrast with all these authors, I will concentrate my efforts on the argumentation within the Third Discourse of Moses. Rhetorical devices will be seen in functional terms, since they promote the theses of the communicator and seek the adherence of the audience. Figures and tropes may please, excite emotions, establish presence, or promote communion with the audience. They also contribute to the logical argumentation within a communication act.

Rhetorical arrangement also differs from a structure dependent upon diachronic layers or literary considerations. A structure based on a diachronic study reflects (supposed) breaks, interruptions, and inconsistencies within a text; a structure based on literary factors may reflect motifs, chiasms, and key words; whereas a rhetorical structure reflects the argumentation of a text (its premises, topics, ethos, pathos, logic, etc.).

Whether or not Dt 28,69–30,20 is a diachronic unity, it can be viewed rhetorically as a single unified discourse. It addresses a widely-inclusive audience in a direct and personal fashion. Basing itself on certain premises (historical facts, an established social organization, common presumptions about God, common values) and making use of recognized topics (definition, comparison, relationship, the possible and the impossible, authority, etc.), this text appeals to the emotions and involves the mind in a rational process. The authority of Moses, and

---

[201] This presumption that repetition and amplification reveals various hands has been frequently questioned. See BRAULIK, *Die Mittel,* 128-129; LEVENSON, "Who Inserted ... the Torah?" 205; LOHFINK, *Das Hauptgebot,* 28; *Höre Israel!,* 75; J. MUILENBURG, "The Form and Structure of the Covenantal Formulations," *VT* 9 (1959) 357.

[202] G. BRAULIK, *Die Mittel deuteronomischer Rhetorik* (AnBib 68; Rome 1978).

behind him that of God, strongly reaffirms the message: the worship of both Yahweh and other gods is incompatible; the worship of other gods results in punishment; the observance of the covenant results in blessing and prosperity. Everything leads toward the resolution of the incompatibility by choosing Yahweh and his covenant, life, good, and blessing over other gods, death, evil, and curse. Of course, this simple message is reiterated and amplified by numerous arguments and devices which claim and promote the possibility — and *necessity* — of a choice for Yahweh and his covenant.

CHAPTER 3

AUDIENCE AND RHETORICAL SITUATION

This chapter will examine two important preliminary considerations in rhetorical criticism: the audience and the rhetorical situation of a particular text.

3.1 Audience

3.1.1 Introduction

Every written or oral discourse presumes an audience, for no sender would bother to begin a communication act where there is no receptor.[1] The necessity for an audience becomes even more obvious in argumentation, since argumentation is always persuasive in intention.[2] A speaker or writer, then, will have a particular audience in mind (if only subconsciously) when he or she begins the communication act.

The role of listener or reader is not merely passive, for "it is as legitimate to take the listener as the maker of a message as the speaker."[3] Every discourse is actually an *interaction* between communicator and audience, thus something that both do together.[4] Without this interaction, without audience involvement, the communication act fails. Thus "no analysis of communication can be complete without a thorough study of the role of the receptors of a message."[5]

For effective argumentation the speaker or writer must adapt to his or her audience. "In fact, every persuasive discourse is an adaptation to the audience."[6] In practice this means that the communicator can begin

---

[1] BOOTH, *Now Don't Try to Reason with Me*, 27; *The Rhetoric of Fiction*, 397; R. CULLEY, "An Approach to the Problem of Oral Tradition," *VT* 13 (1963) 121-122; DIXON, *Rhetoric*, 1; ONG, *Oralità e scrittura*, 243; PERELMAN and OLBRECHTS-TYTECA, *Traité de l'argumentation*, 8-9, 22.

[2] BRANDT, *The Rhetoric of Argumentation*, 205; BURKE, *A Rhetoric of Motives*, 38; SLOAN and PERELMAN, "Rhetoric," 798.

[3] SCOTT, "Intentionality in the Rhetorical Process," 54.

[4] ARNOLD, "Oral Rhetoric, Rhetoric, and Literature," 159; BOOTH, *Now Don't Try to Reason with Me*, 162.

[5] NIDA and REYBURN, *Meaning across Cultures*, 9. ARISTOTLE, *Rhetoric*, I.9.1367b; and CICERO, *De oratore*, II. 17 and 186, would agree.

[6] PERELMAN, *The New Rhetoric and the Humanities*, 57. See also PERELMAN, *L'empire rhétorique*, 35; PERELMAN and OLBRECHTS-TYTECA, *Traité de l'argumentation*, 31-34; CICERO, *Orator*, viii.24.

only with theses or premises already accepted by those he or she addresses.[7] The aim of argumentation is to transfer to the conclusions the adherence the audience already accords to the premises.[8] Thus the speaker or writer can only start from and build upon what is already acceptable to a particular audience. The process of argumentation is not one of deduction but rather one of transference, for the communicator seeks to induce an audience to transfer its acceptance of certain premises to an as-yet unaccepted conclusion.

Seldom if ever can a single argument lead immediately to such adherence. Rather argumentation is a kind of system which reinforces premises, makes new ideas present and acceptable, and involves an audience not only intellectually but also emotionally. To do this the orator or author tries to secure from the audience its attention, its goodwill, and its identification or solidarity with the communicator.[9]

The audience, by the way, may not be limited to those whom the speaker or writer expressly addresses, and the effect of a discourse also may not be limited to its intended hearers.[10] Modern readers, for example, can be moved by Lincoln's Gettysburg Address or Jesus' Sermon on the Mount as easily as (and even more than) their original counterparts. In a book like Dt, the audience can be a complex notion, for it includes Israel before the conquest, Judah in the days of Josiah, an exilic religious community, and even modern Jews and Christians. For the purposes of rhetoric, Perelman and Olbrechts-Tyteca defined an audience as "l'ensemble de ceux sur lesquels l'orateur veut influer par son argumentation."[11] But even this definition may be extended to all those who may eventually hear a discourse or read a text.

3.1.2 The Audience of Deuteronomy

Modern biblical scholarship has tended to emphasize the role of the author of a text (and his or her intention) rather than its audience. Yet

---

[7] PERELMAN, *L'empire rhétorique*, 35, 37; "The New Rhetoric," 286; PERELMAN and OLBRECHTS-TYTECA, *Traité de l'argumentation*, 611-612; RICŒUR, "Rhétorique – Poétique – Herméneutique," 145.

[8] PERELMAN, *L'empire rhétorique*, 35, 153; SLOAN and PERELMAN, "Rhetoric," 803-804.

[9] ARISTOTLE, *Rhetoric*, III.14.1415a-1415b; CICERO, *De oratore*, II.178; ARNOLD and FRANDSEN, "Conceptions," 39; BOOTH, *The Rhetoric of Fiction*, 124; KENNEDY, *New Testament Interpretation*, 45; PERELMAN and OLBRECHTS-TYTECA, *Traité de l'argumentation*, 23.

[10] PERELMAN and OLBRECHTS-TYTECA, *Traité de l'argumentation*, 24-25; FOX, "The Rhetoric of Ezekiel's Vision," 4.

[11] PERELMAN and OLBRECHTS-TYTECA, *Traité de l'argumentation*, 25; see also PERELMAN, *L'empire rhétorique*, 27. They develop the notion of an ideal or "universal" audience, which would be made up of all mankind or at least of all competent and reasonable persons. See *Traité de l'argumentation*, 40-46; *L'empire rhétorique*, 28. Cf. also BRANDT, *The Rhetoric of Argumentation*, 200.

some scholars have also given some attention to the receptors of a particular biblical text (especially in New Testament studies). It is generally acknowledged that Dt has been written for a lay audience rather than for priests. For it is not a specialized work for officials and administrators, whether those be priests, judges, or kings.[12] In this it differs from the books of Leviticus and Numbers, whose laws are often meant for the instruction of the priests themselves.[13]

Dt's audience of lay people is an ideal community of "brothers."[14] This group of brothers seems to live in a time of agricultural prosperity or at least has enough to provide also for the poor.[15] Lohfink sees the readers of Dt as a group which still attends cultic functions which have lost much of their relevance. But at least the narrative and cultic traditions are known to this audience.[16]

An outstanding feature of Dt is that it names its audience as "all Israel" (כל ישראל: Dt 1,1; 5,1; 27,9; 29,1; 31,1.11[2X]; 32,45; 31,30 uses the expression כל-קהל-ישראל).[17] The use of this term is considered to be

---

[12] CLEMENTS, *Deuteronomy*, 63; VON RAD, *Das fünfte Buch Mose*, 13; WRIGHT, *Deuteronomy*, 312, 315.

[13] MORAN, "Deuteronomy," 270. He notes that Dt 14,4-20 is in sharp contrast with the rest of Dt, since it deals with some fine distinctions meant for priests. He considers this a later addition to Dt.

[14] C. LEVIN, *Die Verheißung des neuen Bundes in ihrem theologiegeschichtlichen Zusammenhang* (FRLANT 137; Göttingen 1985) 93, n. 82; BRAULIK, *Deuteronomio: Il testamento di Mosè*, 20; *Deuteronomium 1-16,17*, 16; "Das Deuteronomium und die Menschenrechte," *TQ* 166 (1986) 22; GARCÍA LÓPEZ, *Le Deutéronome*, 8, 35; L. HOPPE, "Deuteronomy and the Poor," *TBT* 24 (1986) 371-375; "Deuteronomy on Political Power," *TBT* 26 (1988) 261-266; N. LOHFINK, "Botschaft vom Bund: Das Deuteronomium," *Wort und Botschaft des Alten Testaments*, 2nd ed. (ed. J. SCHREINER; Würzburg 1969) 191; NICHOLSON, "Deuteronomy's Vision of Israel," 191-192, 202; PERLITT, "'Ein einzig Volk von Brüdern,'" 27-52. The word "brother" (אח) is used 48 times in Dt, of which three occurrences (Dt 10,9; 18,2.7) refer to fellow levites and 32 to fellow Israelites (Dt 1,16[2X].28; 3,18.20; 15,2.3.7[2X].9.11.12; 17,15[2X].20; 18,15.18; 19,18.19; 20,8; 22,1[2X].2[2X].3.4; 23,20.21; 24,7.14; 25,3.11. It is to be noted that Dt is not the only work in the Hebrew Bible which considers Israelites as brothers. The same concept can be found in the Holiness Code (see, for example, Lev 25,25.35.39).

[15] On the basis of texts such as Dt 12,12.19; 14,22-29; 16,11.14; and 17,8-11, CAZELLES feels that the Deuteronomic Code is addressed to the rich landed proprietor. Cf. "Droit public dans le Deutéronome," *Das Deuteronomium: Entstehung, Gestalt und Botschaft* (BETL 68; ed. N. LOHFINK) (Leuven 1985) 101. See also BRAULIK, *Deuteronomium 1-16,17*, 50; GARCÍA LÓPEZ, *Le Deutéronome*, 9, also feels that the earliest layers of Dt demonstrate a flourishing economic period in a rich land. He concludes that this could only indicate the northern kingdom of Israel.

[16] LOHFINK, *Das Hauptgebot*, 266-267.

[17] Other instances of the use of כל ישראל in Dt are 11,6; 13,12; 18,6; 21,21; 31,7; 34,12 (14 occurrences in all). The name ישראל appears alone in Dt 1,38; 4,1; 5,1; 6,3.4; 9,1; 10,12; 17,4.12.20; 18,1; 19,13; 20,3; 21,8; 22,19.21.22; 25,6.7.10; 26,15; 27,1.9.14; 29,9.21; 31,9; 33,5.10.21.28.29; 34,10; while בני ישראל appears in 1,3; 3,18; 4,44-46; 10,6; 23,18; 24,7; 28,69; 31,19.22.23; 32,8.49-52; 33,1; 34,8-9. See PREUSS, *Deuteronomium*, 182. G.

deuteronomic or deuteronomistic.[18] "All Israel," according to Flanagan, has three meanings in the Deuteronomistic History: 1) the non-Judahite unit within the united monarchy; 2) both kingdoms in the united monarchy; and 3) the territory of the northern kingdom after the break with Jerusalem.[19] But many have seen in כל ישראל an idealistic concept of a united people, a collective identity which perhaps never existed in reality.[20] In fact, in Dt Israel is considered a collective personality which can be addressed in the vocative as a single individual (Dt 4,1; 5,1; 6,3.4; 9,1; 10,12; 27,9).[21]

At the same time Dt strongly appeals to the individual members of the community, as we have seen above.[22] Even the term כל ישראל may be seen more in a distributive sense and not only in a collective sense, for groups of individuals are identified within "all Israel": *your* heads of your tribes, elders, officers, all the men of Israel, plus children, women, and resident aliens (Dt 29,9-10).[23]

GERLEMAN, "ישראל," *THAT* I, 783, lists 72 occurrences of the name Israel in Dt, of which 21 occur as בני ישראל. According to A. BESTERS, "'Israël' et 'fils d'Israël' dans les livres historiques (Genèse — II Rois)," *RB* 74 (1967), 5-23, especially p. 21, the term בני ישראל is a collective term which is (usually) later than the use of a simple ישראל. However, it cannot be used to distinguish layers in a work like Dt. A.R. HULST, "Der Name 'Israel' im Deuteronomium," *OTS* 9 (1951) 82, 104, agrees that בהי ישראל may reflect Israel's plurality, while ישראל alone emphasizes the religious unity of God's people. However, he does not observe any great difference between these two terms. H. HAAG, "בֶּן," *TWAT* I, 673, says that בני ישראל "bezeichnet die gegliederte Gemeinschaft Israels als Einheit und ist nicht als Betonung eines einzigen leiblichen Stammvaters des Volkes aufzufassen." H.-J. ZOBEL, "ישראל," *TWAT* III, 994, calls בני ישראל "das individualisierende Wort," at least in comparison with ישראל alone, which he calls a "Kollektivwort."

[18] BUIS, *Le Deutéronome*, 43; J. FLANAGAN, "The Deuteronomic Meaning of the Phrase '*kol yiśrā'ēl*,'" *SR* 6 (1976/77) 162. On p. 163 FLANAGAN points out that there are predeuteronomic occurrences of כל ישראל, but he claims that the term had not been used for a while until its reintroduction by Dt. See also J. L'HOUR, "Une législation criminelle dans le Deutéronome," *Bib* 44 (1963) 10, n. 3; J.N. SCHOFIELD, "'All Israel' in the Deuteronomic Writers," *Essays and Studies Presented to Stanley Arthur Cook* (ed. D.W. THOMAS; London 1950) 27; G. SEITZ, *Redaktionsgeschichtliche Studien zum Deuteronomium* (BWANT 93; Stuttgart 1971) 32. WEINFELD, *Deuteronomy and the Deuteronomic School*, 173, notes that the emphasis on vast audiences and the detailed enumeration of participants is also peculiar to Dt and the Deuteronomistic History.

[19] FLANAGAN, "*kol yiśrā'ēl*," 164-165. Cf. SCHOFIELD, "All Israel," 34.

[20] Ibid., 166; S. HERRMANN, "Die konstruktive Restauration: Das Deuteronomium als Mitte biblischer Theologie," *Probleme biblischer Theologie* (FS. Gerhard von Rad; ed. H.W. WOLFF) (München 1971) 160-162; MAYES, *Deuteronomy*, 55-56; NICHOLSON, "Deuteronomy's Vision of Israel," 191. כל ישראל is thus an ideal text-world audience, but the expression is used as well to indicate a widely-inclusive real audience which extends through time.

[21] BUIS, *Le Deutéronome*, 211. LOHFINK, *Das Hauptgebot*, 66, sees the vocative "Israel" as a structural signal in Dt 5-11.

[22] Cf. 1.2.3.

[23] BUIS, *Le Deutéronome*, 212; VERMEYLEN, "Les sections narratives de Deut 5-11," 192.

Polzin points out that Dt in fact has more than one audience. The first audience is the fictive audience which Moses addresses on the plains of Moab (this is the text-world audience); a second audience is that of the narrator/author of Dt (we can probably identify this as the real [original or later] audience).[24] Polzin suggests that the author of Dt (for him the Deuteronomist) gradually obliterates the distinction between Moses and the narrator in order to enhance the authority of his narrator.[25] This implies that the two audiences must also somehow lose their distinctiveness. More and more the listeners of Dt must identify themselves with the original Israelites who escaped from Egypt and were about to embark on the conquest of the land.

Let us now take a closer look at the audience in Dt 28,69 – 30,20.

3.1.3 The Audience of the Third Discourse

The Third Discourse of Moses gives a fair number of indications of its audience. In Dt 28,69 and 29,1 the narrator twice tells us that Moses speaks directly to Israel. These two verses are the only ones in the Third Discourse which are reporting speech (given by the narrator). The next 47 verses are reported speech (given by Moses, although he himself quotes others).

Dt 28,69 has the narrator announcing that these are the words of the covenant which the Lord commanded Moses to make את־בני ישראל in the land of Moab. The emphasis in this verse, however, is on neither the speaker (Moses) nor the audience (the people of Israel) but on the message. The covenant (ברית) is mentioned twice. Such an introduction has led some scholars to suggest that the following discourse is a kind of covenant document, a covenant sermon, or a text used in a covenant renewal ceremony.[26]

---

[24] POLZIN, *Moses and the Deuteronomist*, 72, 92. The audience may be even more complicated than POLZIN suggests. Although the narrative within Dt is minimal, one could follow some of the insights of narrative criticism and accept the notion of implied author and implied audience. In that case there would be four levels of sender and receiver within the text of Dt: 1) Moses and his actual audience on the plains of Moab; 2) the narrator and his narrative audience (an ideal audience of brothers?); 3) the implied author and the implied audience; and 4) the actual author(s) and the actual readers or listeners. In such a scheme the level of rhetoric would probably be that of the implied author and implied audience. See, for example, BOOTH, *The Rhetoric of Fiction*, 137-138, 151-152, 421-431; G. BROWN, *Society as Text*, 146; ESLINGER, *Into the Hands of the Living God*, 4-15; ISER, *The Implied Reader*, 274-294; KEEGAN, *Interpreting the Bible*, 92-108. G. GENETTE, *Nouveau discours du récit* (Paris 1983) 93-107, denies the existence of the implied author and implied audience. This work limits itself to the text-world audience and the real (especially the original) audience.

[25] POLZIN, *Moses and the Deuteronomist*, 57. See 1.3.1, especially n. 51.

[26] For example, WRIGHT, *Deuteronomy*, 317; BUIS and LECLERCQ, *Le Deutéronome*,

The term בני־ישראל occurs 21 times in Dt, of which only four appear in Dt 5–30. The use in 28,69 is its only occurrence in the Third Discourse. Here it is a collective and very general term, referring to Israel as an organized whole.[27] It could refer to any particular audience of Israelites, from a few to the whole nation.

3.1.3.1 "All Israel"

Much more can be said about the reference to כל ישראל in 29,1. כל ישראל appears 14 times in Dt,[28] but not all of these occurrences are alike. Dt 29,1, for example, repeats the words of 5,1: ויקרא משה אל־כל־ישראל ויאמר אלהם. *All* Israel is summoned and spoken to. Similarly Moses addresses all Israel in 1,1; 31,1; and 32,45. In 27,9 the הכהנים הלוים join Moses in speaking to all Israel. Here the audience remains the same but the speakers increase in number. In 31,30 Moses addresses כל־קהל ישראל. קהל is a "convocation," "assembly," or "congregation" which often has cultic overtones (see, for example, Josh 8,35; Joel 2,16; Ps 22,23; Neh 8,2).

These six occurrences of כל ישראל (plus the כל־קהל ישראל of Dt 31,30) share in common a *narrator's* report of a communication act, for in each case both sender and receiver are mentioned in the third person. By contrast both occurrences in Dt 31,11 are included in a command of *Moses* that all Israel should present itself to the Lord every seven years at the feast of Booths. On this occasion the message he has just delivered should be communicated to the same audience: all Israel.

The other occurrences of כל ישראל in Dt do not assume an assembly or a communication act, even if communication is possible. In 31,7 and 34,12 all Israel bears witness, for something takes place before its eyes. In 31,7 Moses commissions Joshua before all Israel. Joshua is the immediate receiver of the message, and yet all Israel is also there to see, hear, and understand. Dt 34,12 is a general report of all that Moses did in the sight of the people. This does not imply a communication act.

181; THOMPSON, *Deuteronomy,* 279. There has been considerable discussion about the meaning of the term ברית. Although it has been traditionally translated as "covenant," some prefer to translate it as "obligation." Cf. BRAULIK, "Ausdrücke für Gesetz," 43-45; review of KNAPP, *Deuteronomium 4,* 272; CROSS, *Canaanite Myth and Hebrew Epic,* 265-273; P. KALLUVEETTIL, *Declaration and Covenant: A Comprehensive Review of Covenant Formulae from the Old Testament and the Ancient Near East* (AnBib 88; Rome 1982) 7-9; E. KUTSCH, *Verheißung und Gesetz;* "תּוֹרָה," *THAT* I, 339-352; McCARTHY, *Treaty and Covenant, 14-22;* PREUSS, *Deuteronomium,* 197; SOGGIN, *Introduzione all'Antico Testamento,* 169-174; M. WEINFELD,"*Berît* — Covenant vs. Obligation," *Bib* 56 (1975) 120-128; "בְּרִית," *TWAT* I, 781-808.

[27] Cf. n. 17.

[28] Dt 1,1; 5,1; 11,6; 13,12; 18,6; 21,21; 27,9; 29,1; 31,1.7.11[2X]; 32,45; 34,12.

In Dt 13,12 and 21,21 there is a lesson for Israel which suggests a prior communication act. All the people are to hear of a punishment (the execution of a family member for apostasy or for rebelliousness). In these cases the lesson is the result of a general report with the hope that a specific lesson (fear of God) is learned. No sender is mentioned.

The final two occurrences of כל ישראל (Dt 11,6 and 18,6) have nothing to do with communication acts.

Outside of Dt the expression כל ישראל appears 117 times in the Hebrew Bible. All occur in deuteronomistic passages or in the two books of Chronicles.[29] Of these, only 13 occur in situations where a communication act takes place (or may take place) and where כל ישראל refers to the receiver or audience. Seven of these are very general, only hinting that Israel heard or may have heard some kind of communication (1 Sam 4,1; 7,5; 13,4; 17,11; 2 Sam 16,21; 1 Kgs 3,28; 12,20). Thus they are not specific enough to be of use for this study.

Six occurrences of כל ישראל, however, do parallel the seven appearances in Dt in which all Israel is the audience of a discourse. In Josh 23,2 Joshua is the speaker; in 1 Sam 12,1 it is Samuel; in 1 Sam 14,40 it is Saul; in 2 Chr 1,2[30] it is Solomon; in 2 Chr 11,3 it is God speaking to Shemaiah the man of God, who is to address the following words to the king and to all Israel;[31] and in 2 Chr 13,4 it is Abijah, king of Judah.[32] Thus, of the numerous occurrences of the expression כל ישראל in the Hebrew Bible, only 13 (seven of which are found in Dt) occur in communication acts in which all Israel is the audience.

Considering the frequency of discourses in Sacred Scripture, it is notable that *all Israel* is so seldom explicitly mentioned as an audience.

---

[29] The expression occurs only twice in the Pentateuch outside Dt: Exod 18,25 and Num 16,34. FLANAGAN, "*kol yiśrā'ēl*," 162, says these are "deuteronomic additions."

[30] The expression לכל־ישראל occurs twice in 2 Chr 1,2, but the second occurrence is not a specific reference to Israel as an audience. After having addressed all Israel, Solomon directs his discourse to various leaders, including לכל נשׂיא לכל־ישראל (RSV: "and to all the leaders in all Israel"). It is important to note here that after the description of the audience and the mentioning of a discourse, no actual address is reported.

[31] 2 Chr 11,3 is different from all the other occurrences of כל ישראל as an audience in a communication act in that 1) it is God who speaks; 2) the sender is telling the receiver to give the following message, so the receiver becomes a new sender; and 3) an imperative is used. Here כל ישראל is only the second, and probably minor, component of the audience, since the message is meant especially for the king. Similar patterns occur in the prophetic books, where God commands the prophet to deliver a particular message to the king, the priests, the people, etc. (for example, Isa 37,6.21; 38,5; 39,5; Jer 21,3; 22,2; 28,13; 37,7; Am 7,17).

[32] In 2 Chr 13,4 the pattern deviates from the norm, since usually the speaker mentions כל ישראל as the audience in the third person. Here Abijah addresses Rehoboam and all Israel directly, therefore it is in the vocative.

Let us examine parallel situations to Dt in the other books of the Pentateuch where all or a large part of Israel is an audience.[33]

The first impression one receives when comparing the discourses in Dt with those in Exodus through Numbers is the simplicity of Dt. Its few discourses are long and contain little reporting material (i.e., references to speakers and audience). For the most part it is Moses who speaks, and God is heard only in citation. The picture is vastly different in Exodus, Leviticus, and Numbers. Here God does most of the communicating, what Moses says is often but a citation of God's words, and the introductions and references to sender and receiver (reporting material) occur frequently. Discourses also tend to be short.

In most of Dt Moses is speaking to an assembly of all Israel. What can we say about the discourses in Exodus, Leviticus, and Numbers? To begin with, both speakers and audiences in these books are quite diverse, but the principal sender is God and his usual audience is Moses.[34] At times it seems that God may be speaking to both Moses *and* Israel, but his words are addressed only to Moses. On a few occasions God may include others in his messages to Moses: Aaron, Aaron and Miriam, and Eleazar.[35] The only individuals who are addressed without Moses are Aaron (Num 18,1.8.20) and Aaron and Miriam together (Num 12,5-6). God addresses the people directly on only one occasion, and even that event is ambiguous.[36] Otherwise God never addresses the people without the mediation of Moses or Aaron or both.

---

[33] The following comments cover Exod 16 to Num 36. It begins somewhat arbitrarily with Exod 16, since only after the Exodus does Israel begin to take shape as an audience with its own identity.

[34] God addresses Moses alone in Exod 16,4.11.32; 17,5.14; 19,10; 30,11.17.22.34; 31,1; 32,7.9.33; 33,1.17; 34,1.27; 40,1; Lev 5,14.20; 6,1.12; 8,1; 14,1; 16,1; 22,26; 23,26; 24,13; Num 1,1.48; 3,1.5.11.14.40; 4,21; 5,4; 7,4; 8,5.23; 9,1; 10,1; 11,16.23; 12,14; 13,1; 14,11.20; 15,35; 17,1.9.25; 18,25; 20,7; 21,8.34; 25,4.10.16; 26,52; 27,6.12.18; 31,1.25; 34,16. On some of these occasions Israel may also be part of God's audience, but the words are addressed to Moses.

[35] God addresses both Moses and Aaron in Lev 11,1; 13,1; 14,33; 15,1; Num 2,1; 4,1.17; 14,26; 16,20; 19,1; 20,23. He addresses Moses, Aaron, and Miriam in Num 12,4. Finally God addresses Moses and Eleazar in Num 26,1.

[36] The only place where God directly addresses Israel is in Exod 20,1: וידבר אלהים את כל־הדברים האלה לאמר. The Ten Commandments follow this introduction. Interestingly enough, no specific audience is actually mentioned. The previous verse (19,25) tells us that Moses went down to the people to speak to them (ויאמר אלהם). Exod 20,18-19 recounts that the people heard thunder and trumpets and asked Moses to arrange that God not speak directly to them lest they die. One gets the impression that the audience neither understood the message nor wanted to hear it! Their request that Moses become their mediator and God's spokesman (similar to that of Dt 5,24-27) was granted, for they never again hear God's words directly.

A very common communication act which occurs between Exod 16 and Num 36 is a kind of *double discourse* or *mediated discourse*. This is where God commands Moses (or Moses and Aaron) to give the following address or instructions to a particular audience.[37] Thus there are really two communication acts, since God's command to Moses (and Aaron) is to initiate a discourse. Normally it is Moses who receives this command to speak to the people, although occasionally God may give such instructions to both Moses and Aaron.[38] Such commands to Moses are directed toward various audiences: Aaron alone, the priests, or a group composed of Aaron, his sons, and all the people of Israel.[39] This "mediated discourse" has even been adapted by Moses for his own communication acts, since on one occasion (Lev 9,3) he himself commands Aaron to say something to the people.

There are other *speakers* as well in the section which covers Exod 16 to Num 36. Here we will ignore private conversations (which are numerous enough) and concentrate only on those who address Israel as a group. These are few: Moses and Aaron together (Exod 16,6; Num 20,10 — in this example actually only a single person speaks, and that is probably Moses); Moses and Eleazar (Num 26,3); Aaron (Exod 16,10; 32,2.5); Caleb and Joshua (Num 14,6-7); the scouts (Num 13,26-27.31); and an imprecise "they" (probably referring to Israel itself) in Exod 32,4. At some time or other all of these address the assembly.

Just who are the *receivers,* the audiences of the discourses of Moses in Exod 16 – Num 36? Unlike Dt, individuals and small groups are often the receivers of communication acts in this part of the Pentateuch. Moses directs his words to the heads of the tribes (Num 30,2); the officers in the army (Num 31,15); the leaders or elders (Exod 16,23; 19,7); the scouts (Num 13,17); the judges (Num 25,5); the priests and elders (Lev 9,1); Aaron and/or his sons (Exod 16,33; Lev 8,31; 9,2.7; 10,3.4.6.8.12.16) and Hobab (Num 10,29).[40] In Num 32,28 Moses gives

---

[37] Often the imperative is used: דַּבֵּר, אֱמֹר or צַו.

[38] God commands Moses alone to speak to the people in Exod 20,22; 25,1-2; 31,12-13; 33,5; Lev 1,1-2; 4,1-2; 7,22-23; 12,1-2; 18,1-2; 19,1-2; 20,1-2; 23,1-2.9-10.23-24.33-34; 24,1-2.15; 25,1-2; 27,1-2; Num 5,1-2.5-6.11-12; 6,1-2; 9,9-10; 15,1-2.17-18.37-38; 16,23-24; 17,16-17; 28,1-3; 33,50-51; 34,1-2; 35,1-2.9-10. God commands both Moses and Aaron to speak to the people in Lev 11,1-2; 15,1-2; Num 14,28.

[39] God commands Moses to speak to Aaron in Lev 16,2; 21,16-17; Num 8,1-2; to the priests, whether to Aaron's sons only or to Aaron and his sons, in Lev 6,17-18; 21,1; 22,1-3; Num 6,22-23; and to Aaron, his sons, and all the people in Lev 17,1-2.8; 22,17-18.

[40] This list could be expanded considerably if we include all the narrative sections within Exod 16-Num 36. Sometimes the "discourse" involved however, is a conversation or part of a narrative, with which we are not concerned in this work. It can be difficult to decide where an address ends and where a conversation or a narrative begins.

instructions to a wide group of specifically mentioned individuals: Eleazar the priest, Joshua, and the heads of the fathers' houses.

In Dt such appeals to individuals in an audience occur rarely. The only analogous situations in Dt appear at the end of the book (Dt 31; 32,44-52; 34) in what is mostly reporting speech. One might also include certain narrative sections where Moses cites others, such as Dt 1–3; 9,6–10,11. Here discourses with sender and receiver are mentioned within Moses' discourse. In a history or a narrative the naming of individuals in an audience gives them special presence and may add vivacity to the discourse. But citing individuals of an audience also makes the discourse more exclusive. When a discourse is meant for individuals or a small group, others may listen in, but the message may not seem to be for them.

But let us return to the people of Israel. Are they ignored in Exod 16 to Num 36? Despite the constant naming of Moses and other individuals or groups as receivers, Israel is always nearby, listening in or at least ready to receive God's messages through Moses. With only a few exceptions,[41] the "mediated discourse" or "double discourse" is normally addressed to the people of Israel. A few times Moses addresses only a part of the people, such as when he converses with the tribes of Reuben and Gad (Num 32,6.20). At times no audience is mentioned, but the people are implied (Exod 36,6; Lev 9,6; Num 16,28); or else the people are referred to only with a pronoun and with no specific reference other than to "them" (Exod 16,15.19; 17,2; 19,25; 34,31; 35,1).

How is Israel addressed as an audience from Exod 16 to Num 36? There seem to be several choices. A few times the people are referred to simply as עם (Exod 19,25; 24,3.7; 32,20; Num 13,30; 31,3). On other occasions Israel is called an עדה ("congregation," "gathering," or "company"): Exod 16,9.10; 35,1.4; Lev 8,5; 19,2; Num 13,26; 14,7; 16,24.(26). On one occasion the people are referred to as a קהל ("convocation" or "assembly"): Num 20,10. But the name used overwhelmingly for the audience which is the people of Israel is בני ישראל.[42] This seems to be the preferred general term for the people when are gathered together to listen to Moses and to others.

The term כל ישראל as the reference to an audience does not occur in Exod 16 to Num 36. But there are equivalents. On seven occasions the

---

[41] See n. 39.

[42] בני ישראל as an audience occurs in the following passages: Exod 16,6.9.10; 20,22; 25,2; 31,13; 33,5; (34,32); 35,1.4.30; Lev 1,2; 4,2; 7,23; 11,2; 12,2; 15,2; 17,2; 18,2; 19,2; 20,2; 21,24; 22,18; 23,2.10.24.34.44; 24,2.15.23; 25,2; 27,2; Num 5,2.6.12; 6,2.23; 9,4.10; 13,26; 14,7.39; 15,2.18.38; 17,17; 28,2; 30,1; 33,51; 34,2.13; 35,2.10; 36,5.13. Of the occurrences of עדה as an audience, only Lev 8,5 and Num 16,24 do not also include בני ישראל.

audience is called "all the assembly of the people of Israel" (כל־עדת
בני ישראל): Exod 16,9.10; 35,1.4; Lev 19,2; Num 13,26; 14,7. There are also
six occurrences of כל־בני ישראל: Exod 16,6; (34,32 — not actually
addressed here but later referred to as "he commanded *them*"); Lev 17,2;
21,24; 22,18; Num 14,39.

Thus in Exod 16–Num 36 there are the same number of occurrences
of כל־(עדת)־בני ישראל as there are of כל ישראל in Dt to 2 Kgs and 1–2
Chr. If כל ישראל is considered a collective term for Israel before the
Lord (especially in the cult), כל־(עדת־)בני ישראל must be more or less
equivalent. Perhaps בני ישראל is more individualizing or distributive than
כל ישראל, [43] yet so far one can hardly see much difference in the two
expressions for the comprehensive audience which is Israel.

3.1.3.2 Participant Lists

The occurrences of כל ישראל and בני ישראל are not the only audience
indicators in Dt 28,69-30,20. Within his own discourse Moses also refers
to those who are listening to him.

The first audience indicator in Moses' address occurs in 29,9; it is the
simple word כלכם. "All of you (plur.)" is certainly a way of including
everyone, of trying to draw every individual in the audience into the
group so that he or she will pay attention and also identify with all the
other members of the audience. The use of כלכם excludes the speaker
from the audience but joins the listeners together. Moses (and through
him the author) is attempting to establish a relationship between the
group and its members, for the members can be as much the
manifestation of a group as the act can be the expression of a person. The
relationship between individual and group can be important in
argumentation, for individuals influence our impression of a group and
vice versa.[44] Identification with a group can influence our willingness to
accept certain arguments, for example. The need for identification results
because division is a natural state.[45] Here Moses (and the author) seeks to
establish an identification with the group of the various individuals and
smaller groups within his audience.

---

[43] Cf. n. 17. The investigation here was limited to Dt and to parallel passages in
Exod 16-Num 36. The term כל ישראל also appears in an audience situation in Josh 8,33;
23,2; 2 Chr 1,2; Ezra 10,5; while כל־בני ישראל appears in Judg 20,1. Parallel or equivalent
terms used outside the Pentateuch for the audience which is all Israel include: כל־קהל
ישראל (Josh 8,35); כל־שבטי ישראל (Josh 24,1; Judg 20,2; 1 Sam 10,20); כל־העם (Josh 24,2;
2 Kgs 23,2; Jer 29,1; Neh 8,1.3; 2 Chr 34,30); כל־עדת ישראל (2 Kgs 8,5; 2 Chr 5,6); כל־יהודה
(2 Chr 20,13.15); and כל־הגולה (Jer 29,4).
[44] PERELMAN and OLBRECHTS-TYTECA, *Traité de l'argumentation*, 432-434.
[45] BURKE, *A Rhetoric of Motives*, 20-22.

To continue this identification and to reinforce it, Moses gives some vague details on time (היום) and place (ראשיכם שבטיכם). If Dt is read every seven years in a liturgical-communal assembly, as Dt 31,10-13 suggests, these time and location markers will serve to remind the audience where it is and why it has gathered there.

More importantly, Moses then proceeds to draw up a "participant list," an enumeration of those present in his audience. He mentions no names (that would tend to exclude others), but rather he lists some wide and rather inclusive groupings: ראשיכם שבטיכם זקניכם ושטריכם כל איש (Dt ישראל : טפכם נשיכם וגרך אשר בקרב מחניך מחטב עציך עד שאב מימיך 29,9-10).

Before investigating these groups, it is necessary to pause one moment at the first two words of this listing, for ראשיכם שבטיכם represent a textual critical problem. By themselves they make good sense: "your heads, your tribes." But in the context of a participant list the שבטיכם sounds strange indeed. Would tribes be mentioned in a list of heads, officers, men, women, children, and resident aliens?

Several solutions have been proposed: 1) It is possible that the כם of ראשיכם was tacked on by mistake (dittography), and thus the reading should be ראשי שבטיכם, "the heads/chief of your tribes."[46] 2) ראשיכם שבטיכם can be understood as a rare variant of the construct relationship, and thus the meaning would still be "the heads/chiefs of your tribes."[47] 3) It's best not to tamper with the text and simply accept "your heads, your tribes."[48] 4) שבטיכם here actually has a rare meaning of "leaders."[49] 5) שבטיכם should be emended to שפטיכם, "judges."[50]

---

[46] A solution favored by NTAGWARARA, "Alliance d'Israël," 56-57; PHILLIPS, *Deuteronomy*, 194; and VON RAD, *Das fünfte Buch Mose*, 127. This is the reading of Syriac and T^J.

[47] Favored by REITER, "Der Bundesschluß," 17-19; and also probably by RASHI. Cf. M. ROSENBAUM and A.M. SILBERMANN (ed.) et al., *Pentateuch with Targum Onkelos, Haphtaroth and Rashi's Commentary* (Jerusalem 1934) 144.

[48] Favored by C. BEGG, "The Reading *šbṭy(km)* in Deut 29,9 and 2 Sam 7,7," *ETL* 58 (1982) 87-105; "The Reading in 2 Sam 7,7: Some Remarks," *RB* 95 (1988) 551-558. See also BUIS, *Le Deutéronome*, 383; BUIS and LECLERCQ, *Le Deutéronome*, 180 (in a footnote they suggest that it may be necessary to read "judges" instead of "tribes"); CRAIGIE, *Deuteronomy*, 354; PENNA, *Deuteronomio*, 237.

[49] D. BARTHÉLEMY, *Critique textuelle de l'Ancien Testament* (OBO 50/1; Fribourg, Suisse 1982) 245-246, suggests this possibility in a reference to 2 Sam 7,7. BEGG, "The Reading *šbṭy(km)*," 89, also discusses this possibility.

[50] Favored by DRIVER, *Deuteronomy*, 322; LACONI, *Deuteronomio*, 198 (although he seems to follow LXX, which contains both οἱ ἀρχίφυλοι ὑμῶν and οἱ κριταὶ ὑμῶν; LXX itself is ambiguous, according to BEGG, "The Reading *šbṭy(km)*," 89-91); MAYES, *Deuteronomy*, 362-363; and WEINFELD, *Deuteronomy and the Deuteronomic School*, 101, n. 5. S. GEVIRTZ, "On Hebrew *šebeṭ* = 'Judge,'" *The Bible World: Essays in Honor of Cyrus H. Gordon* (ed. G. RENDSBURG et al.; New York 1980), 61-66, suggests that the text does not need to be emended, since שבט already means "judge."

I doubt if rhetorical criticism can resolve this thorny problem. As far the audience is concerned, only the reading "your tribes" (such as is found in MT) would affect our understanding, since that would be a strange all-inclusive item in a list of relatively small groups of individuals. Therefore I would favor solutions 1 or 2. This would give a balanced list of three groups of leaders (tribal heads, elders, and officers) followed by a summary statement (all the men of Israel), followed then by three groups of marginalized or less important individuals (children, women, and resident aliens).[51] If שבטיכם is emended to שפטיכם (or if it already means "judges" or "leaders"), this would add a fourth group of leaders to the beginning of the list. Regardless of which solution is accepted, there's no doubt about the intention of the participant list: all individuals in Israel, whether in leadership positions or serving as servants with few rights, are to be included in Moses' audience.

It has already been noted that this list of seven (or eight) component groups appears in a kind of symmetry. First various officials are mentioned, then all the men, and finally those without responsible positions within the worshipping community of Israel. The three classes of leaders (or four, if one includes judges or assumes that שבטיכם are leaders of some kind) are all lay authorities. Although the difference between secular and religious authority in ancient Israel may have been blurred, it is still apparent that none of the officials mentioned has a priestly office.

In fact, neither כהנים nor לוים are mentioned in this participant list. Priests and levites may be part of the assembly listening to Moses, but they are deliberately excluded by name from the audience. One might get the impression that the priests and levites (better: the levitical priests) were excluded from כל ישראל! In Dt 27,9 the levitical priests share with Moses the role of sender (as do the elders in 27,1, but they remain part of the audience in 29,9). They also are charged with obligations to speak by Moses in Dt 27,14; 31,9-13 (again, so are the elders in 31,9). There is also no mention of prophets. Prophets, however, were probably a rather small if vociferous group.

One could assume that Dt, or at least the Third Discourse, was written by a priestly group. This could explain why they are not included in Moses' audience. Nevertheless, one could as easily defend the position

---

[51] NTAGWARARA, "Alliance d'Israël," 57. REITER, "Der Bundesschluß," 229-230, sees the first three groups as those which have a role to play in a covenant ceremony. Both NTAGWARARA and REITER translate שטרים as "scribes." HULST, "Der Name 'Israel' im Deuteronomium," 104-105, notes that the קהל originally was a cult community that included only adult males (and not even all of them). Only gradually it began to loosen its ties to the cult and to include anyone who observed the *torah*.

that Dt was written by lay scribes (the חכמים סופרים).[52] However, it seems that Dt is saying much more about its *audience* than about its authors here. The audience is an assembly of lay people, whether they be officials, the average adult male with religious obligations, or those who normally have no privileges or obligations in the congregation: children, women, and immigrants or resident aliens. In no part of Dt 28,69 – 30,20 are levitical priests considered part of the audience toward which this discourse is directed.

One gets the impression that the functions and roles of the various officials are left vague here. Of course, the ancient Hebrews undoubtedly had a better idea than we have of who could be included within ראשיכם שבטיכם זקניכם ושטריכם.[53] Terms such as ראשיכם שבטיכם and זקניכם seem to be rather broad, for they probably describe a wide-ranging group of leaders. Such an impression is reinforced by the mention of women, children and כל איש ישראל.

Outside of Dt 29,9 the expression כל איש ישראל appears 17 times in the Hebrew Bible. It expresses the notion of an entire body of men acting in concert, so it is usually translated by "all the men of Israel" rather than "every man of Israel." Ten of the 17 occurrences of the phrase concern military activities (Josh 10,24; Judg 7,8; 20,11.33; 1 Sam 14,22; 17,19.24; 2 Sam 17,24; 20,2; 1 Chr 10,7), four occurrences are very general (2 Sam 16,18; 17,14; 19,42; 1 Chr 16,3), while only three refer specifically to an audience of a discourse (Dt 27,14; 1 Kgs 8,2; 2 Chr 5,3; Josh 10,24 may also be considered here, since Joshua summoned all the men of Israel, although he spoke directly only to their chiefs). In each of these discourses, as well as in Dt 29,9, the narrator wishes to include the entire group of men of Israel, even every single individual, within his audience.[54]

---

[52] WEINFELD, *Deuteronomy and the Deuteronomic School*, 158-178.

[53] שטרים, for example, can be translated as "record keepers," "officers," "officials," or "scribes." Their function seems to have been more secretarial or scribal than anything else, even when they were associated with military forces. See CAZELLES, "Droit public dans le Deutéronome," 103-105; M. WEINFELD, "Judge and Officer in Ancient Israel and in the Ancient Near East," *IsrOrSt* 7 (1977) 65-88. Cf. also BUCHHOLZ, *Die Ältesten im Deuteronomium*, 85-100.

[54] See REITER, "Der Bundesschluß," 152, n. 156, who mistakenly adds one more reference in 2 Sam 23,9 (only כל ישראל is involved here). On p. 230 he comments that "der Ausdruck kennzeichnet deutlicher als andere das demokratische Element in der Gesellschaft Israels." The word כל generally means "the whole," "the whole of," although in English it is often translated "all" or "every." Hebrew has a tendency to use כל with an entire class, whereas English tends to describe the individuals of a class ("each," "every," "any"). Thus it seems that כל איש ישראל describes that group which includes every man of Israel. See F. BROWN, S.R. DRIVER, and C.A. BRIGGS, *A Hebrew and English Lexicon of the Old Testament* (Oxford 1972; first issued 1907) 481-482; H. RINGGREN, "כל," *THAT* I, 828-830. Note that the Hebrew Bible also uses כל איש יהודה as an expression parallel to כל איש ישראל in 2 Sam 19,15.43; 2 Kgs 23,2; Jer 44,26.27; 2 Chr 20,27; 34,30.

Moses, and through him the author(s), is attempting to include as wide an audience as possible in this address. Even the immigrant or resident alien is included. Everyone in Israel should hear this message. The original real audience, like the text-world audience, is a widely inclusive one.

Dt 29,9-10 is not the only place in the Hebrew Bible where a "participant list" occurs, that is, where the constituent parts of a large assembly (which is an audience) are enumerated. But no other similar list takes the exact form as this one.

In Dt there are three places where possible parallels occur.[55] In 5,23 כל־ראשי שבטיכם וזקניכם are listed among those who hear God's voice on Mt. Horeb. They speak for the people, requesting Moses to listen to God's voice and communicate his message to them (5,24-27). Here these leaders are entrusted with a task which they perform for the people, that is, they speak in the name of all the people. The participant list in 5,23 is rather restricted.

Dt 31,9-12 actually includes more than one participant list. Moses wrote down the *torah* and handed it over אל־הכהנים בני לוי ואל־כל־זקני ישראל. They are thus not included within the wider audience of Israel but rather are an exclusive audience which is addressed in vv. 10-13. This exclusive group received the obligation to communicate this *torah* to a much wider audience, all Israel, כל ישראל (mentioned twice in v. 11). The audience is then redefined as העם האנשים והנשים והטף וגרך אשר בשעריך (v. 12). This list approximates the list in Dt 29,9-10, although it doesn't use the exact same words. Men, women, children, and resident aliens are included in the audience which is all Israel. The difference comes with the addition of the priests, the subtraction of a list of officials (here only the זקנים are associated with the priests), and the separation of the priests and the elders from the people. The priests and elders are thus among the speakers or senders, whereas everyone else mentioned is part of the audience or receivers. Moses' command is that the *torah* be read to this audience every seven years. But no reading or discourse actually follows. Dt. 29,9-10, however, seems to assume that this is just what is happening when Moses addresses his audience.

---

[55] In two other places in Dt there are related parallels, but these are not really audience situations. The first occurs in Dt 1,13-16. In v. 13 Moses addresses the people and commands them to choose from among themselves wise, understanding, and experienced men to become ראשיכם. In v. 15 Moses reports that he took these ראשי שבטיכם and made them ראשים עליכם שרי אלפים ושרי מאות ושרי חמשים ושרי עשרת ושטרים לשבטיכם. He also gave instructions to שפטיכם. The second parallel apears in Dt 33,5.21, which are a part of Moses' blessing. V. 5 mentions the gathering of the heads of the people (ראשי עם) and the tribes of Israel (שבטי ישראל), while v. 21 mentions the heads of the people (ראשי עם). However, these are not enumerations of particular audiences for particular discourses.

The third parallel in Dt occurs in 31,28.30. Moses has finished writing the *torah* and commands the levites to put it by the ark. Then he commands them to assemble את־כל־זקני שבטיכם ושטריכם (v. 28), that he may recite a song to them. When he actually speaks the words of the song, כל־קהל ישראל are included in the audience (v. 30). Men, women, children, and resident aliens are not specifically mentioned.

Outside of Dt there are a number of audience participant lists in the Hebrew Bible.[56] In Lev 9,1-2 Moses addresses Aaron, his sons, and the elders of Israel (although according to v. 2 he speaks *only* to Aaron). Here the wider audience of the people is not included. In Lev 17,1-2 and 22,17-18 we have two discourses with the same audience situation and the same participant list. In a "double discourse" or "mediated discourse" God addresses Moses, who doesn't actually speak but is supposed to address Aaron, his sons, and כל־בני ישראל. Thus only Aaron and his sons, that is, the priests, are specifically mentioned apart from the wide assembly of all the people. Such a mention of certain individuals makes them stand out from the crowd. Similarly in Lev 21,24 Moses mentions that his audience is Aaron, Aaron's sons, and all the people of Israel. This verse is a concluding statement, since it indicates that Moses faithfully carried out his instructions to speak to Aaron (and to a wider audience).

In Num 32,28 Moses addresses Eleazar the priest, Joshua, and ראשי אבות המטות לבני ישראל and gives them instructions regarding the Reubenites

---

[56] In Exod 19,7 only the זקני העם are listed as Moses' audience for a discourse which is not recorded. In the following verse all the people (כל־העם) answer, so they must also have been included in the audience, even though they are not mentioned. But this hardly comprises a list.

Num 11,16-17.24 is similar to Dt 1,13-16. Here God commands Moses to gather seventy men מזקני ישראל who are זקני העם and שטרים. These men will receive some of the spirit which is on Moses. Moses explains these instructions to the people in v. 24. Although an audience is present, these men are actually separated from the people and thus this is no participant list.

In Josh 22,30 the Reubenites, Gadites, and Manassites address Phinehas the priest ונשאי העדה וראשי אלפי ישראל. Only officials are addressed, since they are a delegation from the rest of Israel. All the people hear a report from these officials afterwards (vv. 32-33).

In 1 Sam 10,17.19-20 Samuel speaks to the people (העם, v. 17), who want a king. He instructs them to present themselves to the Lord לשבטיכם ולאלפיכם (v. 19). He brings כל־שבטי ישראל near in order to cast lots to choose a king. The divisions here are quite large, since they concern tribes and groups of one thousand. If it is a participant list, it is extremely vague.

In 1 Chr 23,2 David assembles כל־שרי ישראל והכהנים והלוים in order to appoint officers and judges and to divide temple obligations among the priests and levites. This audience is relatively small, since it does not include all the people, and the subject matter is highly specialized. It's obvious that David addresses this audience (the first person verb עשיתי is used), but there are no formal indications of speaking (such as "he said").

and the Gadites. This is a rather exclusive and narrow audience, however, since the people in general do not seem to be included.

The book of Joshua contains four participant lists. Two occur in Josh 8,33.35. Joshua addresses כל־ישראל וזקניו ושטרים ושפטיו ... נגד הכהנים הלוים כגר כאזרח ... (v. 33). Joshua is fulfilling Moses' command that a special ceremony of curse and blessing take place in front of Mounts Gerizim and Ebal. This ceremony takes place around the ark of the covenant and is obviously connected with the cult. Thus far we have a list of officials similar to what we find in Dt 29,9, except that there is no mention of the heads of tribes but rather of judges. Although the priests are not listed with the other officials, there is no doubt that they are present, since they are carrying the ark. So they seem to be part of the audience and yet are separated from everyone else. All Israel is included, but there is no specific mention of women and children.

A second list occurs in v. 35. Here Joshua reads the commands of Moses before כל־קהל ישראל והנשים והטף והגר ההלך בקרבם. Women and children are finally listed, but they and the resident alien are specifically named in addition to and apart from the congregation (קהל). These two lists together are a rather close parallel to Dt 29,9-10. No discourse, however, is actually reported, and the priests are mentioned if kept apart. Otherwise these lists are also rather inclusive.

Joshua's two farewell addresses to the people of Israel also contain participant lists. In Josh 23,2 he speaks לכל־ישראל לזקניו ולראשיו ולשפטיו ולשטריו.Here the whole assembly and four groups of officials are enumerated. In Josh 24,1 the audience is listed as כל־שבטי ישראל ... לזקני ישראל ולראשיו ולשפטיו ולשטריו V. 2 adds simply "all the people" (כל־העם). For this discourse the larger group is listed twice ("all the tribes of Israel" and "all the people"), while four groups of leaders are also enumerated. In both of these lists priests are not reported.

The only audience participant list reported in the book of Judges is found in 20,1-2. All Israel, except for the tribe of Benjamin, gathers to learn of an atrocity in the land. A levite, the husband of the murdered woman, addresses the assembly. This group is composed of כל־בני ישראל, which makes up the עדה (v. 1). This group includes כל העם פנות כל־העם. שבטי ישראל בקהל עמהאלהים ארבע מאות אלף איש רגלי שלף חרב Although called an עדה and a קהל, the purpose of this assembly is war, which is emphasized by the indication of 400,000 foot soldiers who know how to handle the sword. No women, children, or resident aliens are included here.

In 1 Kgs 8,1-3 (and its parallel 2 Chr 5,2-4) Solomon assembles the people in order to bring the ark to the temple and to dedicate this new sanctuary. Solomon's address begins only in v. 12 (2 Chr 6,1), so the list of audience participants occurs long before the discourse itself. Only the first verse has the form of a list, but other groups appear sporadically in the next verses as their role in the ceremony is mentioned. We first learn that Solomon assembled את־זקני ישראל את־כל ראשי המטות נשיאי האבות לבני ישראל in Jerusalem (1 Kgs 8,1; 2 Chr 5,2). All the men of Israelכל־איש (ישראל) gather (1 Kgs 8,2; 2 Chr 5,3), as well as כל־זקני ישראל and the priests (הכהנים)who carry the ark (1 Kgs 8,3; 2 Chr 5,4 — where הלוים replaces הכהנים). The priests and levites are mentioned again (1 Kgs 8,4; 2 Chr 5,5) as is the whole congregation of Israel (כל־עדת ישראל — 1 Kgs 8,5; 2 Chr 5,6). So the elders, the heads of the tribes and clans, and the men of Israel are participants at this important cultic event, as well as the priests and the levites. Women, children, and resident aliens seem not to be part of the קהל or עדה, since they are not mentioned.

The situations in 2 Kgs 23,1-2 and 2 Chr 34,29-30 are also parallel. Josiah gathers the people and reads the book of the covenant to them,. Included in this audience are כל־זקני יהודה וירושלם (2 Kgs 23,1; 2 Chr 34,29), plus וכל־איש יהודה וכל־ישבי ירושלם ...והכהנים והנביאים וכל־העם למקטן ועד־גדול (2 Kgs 23,2; 2 Chr 34,30 changes the section after the priests to והלוים וכל־העם מגדול ועד־קטן). This participant list does not include many officials, since only the elders are mentioned. But it specifies that the priests (and for the Chronicler, the levites) and the prophets (not in 2 Chr) were present, while all the inhabitants of Jerusalem and all the people both great and small were included. This list is similar to Dt 29,9-10 in that it is quite inclusive. It differs by adding priests, levites (only in 2 Chr), prophets (only in 2 Kgs), and the inhabitants of Jerusalem to the audience. It also makes no mention of women, children, and resident aliens (these might be considered as belonging to the "small") nor most officials (who could be considered as belonging to the "great").

In Jer 29,1 we find the introduction to a written rather than an oral discourse, for Jeremiah writes a letter to the exiled community in Babylon. He writes אל־יתר זקני הגולה ואל־הכהנים ואל־הנביאים ואל־כל־העם. He includes no references to men, women, children, or resident aliens; the only officials mentioned are the elders. But he does include priests and prophets in his audience.

The prophet Joel twice gives brief lists for those who should participate in an assembly. Whether he considers these groups his audience, however, is difficult to ascertain. In Joel 1,14 a solemn assembly (עצרה) is called in which participate the זקנים and כל ישבי הארץ. A more extensive participant list is found in Joel 2,15-16 for this solemn assembly: עם, קהל, זקנים, עוללים, יונקי שדים, חתן, and כלה. This audience includes no specific mention of priests (they appear later in v. 17), and the only officials mentioned are the elders. However, to emphasize the emergency nature of this assembly, the prophet calls upon those who are normally exempt from such obligations: newlyweds, children, small babies.

Again in Ezra 10,1 there is a very great assembly of men, women, and children: מישראל קהל רב מאד אנשים ונשים וילדים (see also העם). However, it is difficult to ascertain whether this is really an audience. Ezra prays, weeps, and makes confession, but he becomes the audience when Shecaniah addresses *him*. The fact that Ezra made את־שׂרי הכהנים הלוים וכל ישׂראל take an oath in v. 5 indicates that he must have addressed this group at some time. Thus here we have an assembly of priests and people, but no elders or officials are listed in this group.

Neh 8,1-3 speaks of another assembly (כל־העם: v. 1). Ezra brings the ספר תורת משה before הקהל מאישׁ ועד־אשׁה וכל מבין לשׁמע (v. 2). He then reads this *torah* to האנשׁים והנשׁים והמבינים ... כל העם (v. 3). Here it is again an assembly of lay people who hear the words of the *torah*. Officials and resident aliens seem to have disappeared, for they are not mentioned. The audience is composed of men, women, and those who can understand (presumably children after a certain age).

The final two examples of audience participant lists come from 2 Chronicles. In 2 Chr 1,2 Solomon speaks לכל־ישׂראל לשׂרי האלפים והמאות ולשׁפטים ולכל נשׂיא לכל־ישׂראל ראשׁי האבות. No recorded discourse follows. The words are addressed to all Israel, but only military officers, judges, leaders/princes, and heads of clans are specifically enumerated as members of this audience.

In 2 Chr 20,13.15 Jahaziel prophesies in the midst of an assembly of כל יהודה ... גם טפם נשׁיהם ובניהם (v. 13). When he begins speaking he specifically addresses כל־יהודה וישׁבי ירושׁלם והמלך יהושׁפט. In this discourse the king is part of an audience which includes women and children. No priests or officials are specifically mentioned.

In summary, scattered throughout the Hebrew Bible are situations in which an audience is described in a kind of "participant list." The audiences we have examined have been assemblies which included all or a large part of Israel. Priests and levites, various public officials, individuals, men, women, children, and resident aliens are among those included in such lists. Some participant lists are quite short and/or their audiences rather restricted (e.g., Lev 9,1-2; 17,1-2; 21,24; 22,17-18; Num 32,28; Dt 31,28.30).

Generally speaking, those lists enumerating officials don't mention men, women, and children (e.g., Josh 23,2; 24,1-2; 1 Kgs 8,1-2; 2 Chr 5,2-3); while those enumerating men, women, and children mention few if any officials (e.g., Ezra 10,1; Neh 8,1-3; 2 Chr 20,13.15). The closest parallels to Dt 29,9-10 appear in Dt 31,9-12 and Josh 8,33.35. But even Dt 31,9-12 lists only priests and elders among the officials, while Josh 8,33.35 includes judges (and priests) in its list but neglects the ראשׁי שׁבטיכם. In other words, there is no participant list in the Hebrew Bible identical to that in Dt 29,9-10.[57]

---

[57] REITER, "Der Bundesschluß," 153, agrees: "Dtn 29,9-10 bringt eine Aufzählung von Personen wie es in ihrer Art keine mehr im AT gibt."

The participant list of Dt 29,9-10 is one in which all are included —
those with privileges and obligations (the officials) and those without
(children, women, resident aliens). Also included are כל איש ישראל, male
members of the assembly who have religious obligations and yet play no
official role. This is an exclusively lay audience which encompasses all of
Israel. No one is left out *except* those with religious offices (priests,
levites, prophets).

3.1.3.3 Other Audience Indicators

The participant list of Dt 29,9-10 is expanded to unknown limits in
vv. 13-14, for Moses declares that he is making this covenant ולא אתכם
לבדכם but also את־אשר ישנו פה עמנו עמד היום לפני יהוה אלהינו ואת אשר איננו
פה עמנו היום. Moses' audience does not include merely those who have
gathered on this one occasion to hear his final words. They include both
those present and those absent.

This expansion of Moses' audience is repetitious and a bit more
complicated than one might expect. V. 13 begins with a separation
between speaker and audience, for אתכם לבדכם is second person plural,
while אנכי is first person singular. But in v. 14 the speaker associates
himself with his audience, since the double use of עמנו is in the first person
plural. I (the speaker says) am not making this covenant with you (plural)
alone, but with him who is *here* with us and with him who is *not here* with
us. Somehow all those others (for ישנו [singular] and איננו [which may be
either singular or plural] hardly refer to one single individual) here with
us standing before the Lord and all those others who are not here *today*
are involved in this common action of ours (a covenant and an oath, that
is, a sworn covenant).

Once again we see how the author is appealing to a widely inclusive
audience. Who belongs to those who are not with us today? Obviously
Moses is not seeking a universal audience.[58] He has no intention of
including those outside the community (the גר seems to have had a
specific if subordinate position within ישראל [59]). His comments on
Egyptians (Dt 29,1-2.15-16), Sihon and Og (29,6-7), and foreigners in

---

[58] PERELMAN and OLBRECHTS-TYTECA, *Traité de l'argumentation,* 39, define the
universal audience as "l'humanité tout entière, ou du moins par tous les hommes adultes
et normaux." See their discussion on pp. 40-46. Cf. PERELMAN, *L'empire rhétorique,* 28.

[59] BRAULIK, "Das Deuteronomium und die Menschenrechte," 14-15; "Die Freude des
Festes: Das Kultverständnis des Deuteronomium — die älteste biblische Festtheorie,"
Theologische Jahrbuch 1983 (ed. W. ERNST et al.; Leipzig 1983) 45; BREIT, *Die Predigt,*
186-188; D. KELLERMANN, "גור," *TWAT* I, 983-984, 986; R. MARTIN-ACHARD, "גור," *THAT*
I, 410-411. See also M. COHEN, "Le 'ger' biblique et son statut socio-religieux," *RHR* 207
(1990) 131-158; F. CRÜSEMANN, "Fremdenliebe und Identitätssicherung: Zum Verständnis
der 'Fremden'-Gesetze im Alten Testament," *Wort und Dienst* N.F. 19 (1987) 11-24.

general (29,21.23; 30,1.2.7) leave no doubt that these are excluded from his audience. In argumentation exclusion from an audience may be just as important as inclusion. For the identity of an audience can also result from disagreement with and dissociation from those who have nothing to do with the group.[60]

Who then is included among those who are not with us today? There are two possibilities. It could refer to those who, for some reason or other, stayed at home and were not present for this particular occasion. Or else "those not present" refers to future generations. This seems the more likely possibility. Moses' audience expands to include all future Israelites or Jews.[61] This discourse is not restricted to those who actually heard the words of Moses on a particular occasion (the text-world audience). It is also applicable to future listeners (the original real audience or later real audiences). This interpretation makes sense in a book which often refers to future generations.[62] Within the Third Discourse itself there are also other indicators that the audience includes future generations: טפכם (29,10); חרעך (30,6.19); ובניך (30,2).[63]

The statement ולא אתכם לבדכם ...כי את־אשר ישנו פה עמנו ... ואת אשר איננו פה עמנו is unique in the Hebrew Bible. There is no other audience indicator quite like it. לבד occurs 156 times in the Hebrew Bible, but only twice in the form לבדכם. Besides our occurrence in Dt 29,13, it appears in Isa 5,8. In this passage God addresses the rich, but the לבדכם is no audience indicator here. There are 17 occurrences of the term in the second person singular, of which eleven are addressed to God, who is a unique audience.[64] These examples don't help very much in the search for the audience of Moses' Third Discourse.

---

[60] PERELMAN and OLBRECHTS-TYTECA, Traité de l'argumentation, 436-437; KENNEDY, New Testament Interpretation, 45.

[61] This is the interpretation favored in commentaries. See BUIS, Le Deutéronome, 389; BUIS and LECLERCQ, Le Deutéronome, 183; CRAIGIE, Deuteronomy, 357; DRIVER, Deuteronomy, 323; MAYES, Deuteronomy, 363-364; PENNA, Deuteronomio, 238; PHILLIPS, Deuteronomy, 200; RASHI (in ROSENBAUM and SILBERMANN, Pentateuch with Targum Onkelos, Haphtaroth and Rashi's Commentary, 145); THOMPSON, Deuteronomy, 281-282; and VON RAD, Das fünfte Buch Mose, 129.

[62] Cf. Chap. 1, n. 47. In Dt 31,13 there is a reference to future generations who have not known the message (ובניהם אשר לא־ידעו) but will some day become an audience to hear it and learn it (ישמעו ולמדו). POLZIN, Moses and the Deuteronomist, 69-70, notes that the third address of Moses, as opposed to the first two, concentrates on the future.

[63] Dt 29,21 specifically mentions הדור האחרון בניכם, but Moses quotes their future words. Thus they are senders/speakers rather than receivers/audience here.

[64] God (alone) is addressed in 1 Kgs 8,39; 2 Kgs 19,15.19; Isa 37,16.20; Ps 51,6; 71,16; 83,19; 86,10; Neh 9,6; 2 Chr 6,30. Other occurrences of לבדך are in Exod 18,14.18; Num 11,17; 1 Sam 21,2; Prov 5,17; 9,12.

Of the 138 occurrences of יֵשׁ, only in Dt 29,14 does it concern an audience.[65] The word אֵין occurs 789 times in the Hebrew Bible, 30 of which are in Dt. Generally speaking, the word is used merely as a negation. In five places in Dt, however, the word is used in an "exclusive" sense,[66] for it intends to deny participation by others (Dt 4,35.39; 32,12.39; 33,26?). All of these concern the uniqueness of God. However, not a single one of them involves an audience situation, since in none of these passages is God addressed. The passage in Dt 29,14 is unique in that it uses the exclusion of some as a way to *include* them in an audience: those who are *today* excluded from this audience (i.e., those not present) will be part of the audience in the future.

Dt 29,13-14 contrasts with 5,2-3, which states: יהוה אלהנו כרת עמנו ברית בחרב: לא את־אבתינו כרת יהוה את־הברית הזאת כי אתנו אנחנו אלה פה היום כלנו חיים. This passage is intent on emphasizing the role of the audience actually present, and thus it excludes the participants' ancestors from the covenant being made. In Dt 29,13-14 Moses becomes much more inclusive, for he mentions future generations. He ignores the past; he doesn't deliberately exclude the ancestors here, but neither are they mentioned. Dt 29,13-14 doesn't really contradict 5,2-3, however, for the latter has a different emphasis. In chapter five the aspect of presence[67] is accentuated; chapter 29 actually does the same thing but in a roundabout way. Any audience later than that of Moses should conclude that it too was being addressed. So 29,13-14 recalls and expands the notion of audience that appeared in Dt 5,2-3.

There is yet another passage in Dt which may seem to contradict 29,13-14. That is Dt 11,2: וידעתם היום כי לא את־בניכם אשר לא־ידעו ואשר לא־ראו את־מוסר יהוה אלהיכם. This flatly denies that the audience's children experienced the Lord's discipline. Moses' direct appeal to adults gives a strong sense of *presence* to the following recitation of history by reminding those listening that they themselves were witnesses to these mighty acts. It is an exclusion of children from the audience which 29,13-14 corrects, since this passage is much more inclusive. However, Dt 11,2 does not actually exclude future generations from its potential

---

[65] The form found in Dt 29,14 (ישנו) occurs elsewhere only in 1 Sam 14,39; 23,23; and Est 3,8.

[66] Occurrences involving some kind of exclusion from a group seem to occur only with את, עם, or (אחר): Gen 44,26.30.34 (all with את); 2 Sam 3,22 (עם); and 1 Sam 11,7 (which uses both אחרי and אחר). Only this last one concerns an audience, for Saul sends a message throughout the territory of Israel with a threat for all those who did not follow him and Samuel.

[67] "Presence" involves making something immediately present, i.e., it brings a person, thing, or idea to an audience's attention so that listeners or readers will focus on it. See PERELMAN, "The New Rhetoric," 289. Cf. 4.4.1.

audience; rather, it simply brackets them out for the moment in order to emphasize the experience of the present adult audience.

A final audience indicator occurs in Dt 29,17-18. It is possible that יֵשׁ בָּכֶם אִישׁ אוֹ אִשָּׁה אוֹ מִשְׁפָּחָה אוֹ שֵׁבֶט can turn away from the Lord within (לְבָבוֹ). This could happen if such an individual or social unit could somehow make mental reservations about one's relationship with the Lord (וְהִתְבָּרֵךְ בִּלְבָבוֹ לֵאמֹר). It is no surprise in a work which often appeals to an individual's conscience and feelings that one is capable of a private or personal sin and is answerable for it on a personal basis (cf. Dt 17,2-7). Individuals and social units are both capable of self-reflection. Here אִישׁ and אִשָּׁה are not collective terms but refer to individual members of the community, just as מִשְׁפָּחָה and שֵׁבֶט refer to individual families/clans and tribes within כֹּל יִשְׂרָאֵל.

There is a recognition that the audience here is not only an integral whole. It is also composed of individuals. There seems to be a healthy tension between group and individual, collectivity and distribution in the Third Discourse of Moses. It may be true that the ancient Israelites had a strong sense of solidarity within the group,[68] but this doesn't exclude the possibility of individual awareness. That individual awareness, if not explicit at least latent in כֹּל אִישׁ יִשְׂרָאֵל (Dt 29,9), seems to come to expression here in 29,17-18.

3.1.3.4 Speaker and Audience

The relationship between the speaker and his audience in Dt 29–30 is a complicated one. This relationship is revealed somewhat through the use of the first and second persons, both singular and plural. In chapter one of this essay it was noted that Dt frequently varies its direct form of address between the singular and the plural. This is no less true for Moses' Third Discourse.

Generally speaking, Dt 29 uses the plural forms while Dt 30 uses the singular. But there are exceptions. Already in 29,2 a singular form (עֵינֶיךָ) is found,[69] while in v. 4 two singular forms appear among all the plurals (רַגְלֶךָ and וְנַעֲלְךָ).[70] Again in v. 10, after two plural words, the sentence continues in the singular until the end of v. 12, when it reverts to the

---

[68] This strong sense of solidarity is the basis for what has been called the "corporate personality." See, for example, L'HOUR, "Une législation criminelle dans le Deutéronome," 13, n. 1; J.R. PORTER, "The Legal Aspects of the Concept of 'Corporate Personality' in the Old Testament," *VT* 15 (1965) 361-380.

[69] The Lucianic recension of LXX, the Syriac, and T^J have the second person plural here.

[70] In both cases there is good evidence for plural forms, since the plural is found in Sam, LXX, Syriac, T^J, and Vg. It should be noted that 8,2-4, upon which 29,4 may be based, is in the singular.

plural. Dt 30 is much more uniformly singular, but in vv. 18-19 the plural appears.

Such sudden shifts from singular to plural or vice versa were probably noticeable to listeners of the discourse. Members of the audience were addressed both as individuals and as a whole, reinforcing both these identities. The audience is not merely a mass of individuals, nor is it merely a cohesive whole. It is somehow both, and the speaker appeals to both. His appeal to the solidarity of the group reinforces his appeal to each individual.

The relationship between speaker and audience is complicated by the use of the *first person* in the discourse. There are not many occurrences, yet these are sufficient to add certain nuances. The first person singular appears three times in Dt 29 (vv. 4.5.13) and nine times in Dt 30 (vv. 1.2.8.11.15-16.18-19). The first person plural appears as well in 29,6-7.14-15.17.28; 30,12-13.

The use of the first person singular establishes a separation between the sender and the receiver(s), for distinguishing between "I" and "you" (whether singular or plural) tends to exclude. In 11 of the 12 occurrences of the first person singular it is apparent that Moses is the speaker. But in one place (Dt 29,5) it is obviously God who is speaking. Perhaps Moses cites God's words, but such a citation is not apparent. In 29,1-2 Yahweh is mentioned in the third person, but suddenly in v. 5 he interjects an "I am Yahweh your (plur.) God." This is also the only place in the two chapters where אני is used as a first person pronoun. Usually אנכי is used.[71]

The fact that God intervenes in the middle of Moses' speech (the only time in the Third Discourse that this happens) must come as something of a shock to the audience.[72] There is no indication on the part of Moses or the narrator that such an intervention will occur. Other than תדעו כי, there is no sign that this could be a quotation. The activities that Moses cites in the first person singular outside of v. 5 in Dt 29 are activities that God could perhaps also claim: leading the Israelites in the desert for forty years (v. 4) and making a covenant with them (v. 13). It leads to the impression that the roles of Moses and God could at times be interchanged. Perhaps Polzin is correct in claiming that the voices of God and of Moses in Dt tend at times to blend, adding extra authority (ethos) to the words of Moses.[73]

---

[71] אנכי appears in Dt 29,13; 30,2.8.11.16. All the occurrences in chap. 30 are part of a stereotyped phrase, אשר אנכי מצוך היום. According to FISHBANE, *Biblical Interpretation*, 164, this stereotyped phrase is used whenever Dt refers to its own teachings.

[72] It was enough of a shock that LXX (B) changed the expression to ὅτι οὗτος κύριος ὁ θεὸς ὑμῶν. However, J. RENNES, *Le Deutéronome* (Genève 1967) 136, comments that such interruptions are common in the Bible, especially in the Psalms. Cf. also MAYES, *Deuteronomy*, 361. See also chap. 5, n. 32.

[73] POLZIN, *Moses and the Deuteronomist*, 55, 57. Cf. 1.3.1, especially n. 50 and n. 51.

The majority of Moses' first person singular comments concerns the covenant or instructions which are related to that covenant. In Dt 29,13 Moses says אנכי כרת את־הברית הזאת ואת־האלה הזאת. In 30,1 Moses speaks of כל־הדברים האלה הברכה והקללה אשר נתתי לפניך. Four times the first person singular reference is to something אשר אנכי מצוך היום. Six of the first person singular comments are not in the form of personal pronouns but are verbs: ואולך (29,4); נתתי (30,1.15.19); הגדתי (30,18); and העידתי (30,19). Moses' (and God's) separation from his audience, then, concerns chiefly the covenant relationship. Moses is God's spokesman, the mediator between God and the people. As such he separates himself from the people with I-you statements. As God's mouthpiece he proclaims (הגדתי), testifies (העידתי), and offers a choice (נתתי לפניך) to the people. For this part of his message Moses distances himself from his audience.

But there are other occasions when Moses deliberately identifies himself with his audience. This seems to occur especially when Moses recites Israel's history, a history which he himself shares with his audience. Moses uses the first person plural when he speaks of the battles with Sihon and Og and the division of their lands (29,6-7) and when he reminds the Israelites of their time in Egypt and in the desert (29,15.17). Such uses of the first person plural, however, are brief and sometimes mixed with second person plural passages. In Dt 29,14 there is also the reference to those who are here "with us" and those who are not here "with us." So when it comes to the present moment and the present locality, Moses has no difficulty identifying with his audience. Such identity probably enhances the notion of *presence*.

The other uses of the first person plural are not necessarily identifications of Moses with his audience. Both probably involve citations of some kind. In Dt 30,12-13 there are imaginary citations from the audience itself, as its members wonder who will find God's commands for them. However, the use of such quotations in the first person plural is ambiguous enough that the audience could assume that Moses is identifying himself with them in these cases as well.

3.1.3.5 Summary

Moses for the most part remains separated from his audience, which is a collective whole and yet full of individuals. This is especially the case when he speaks for God as the mediator of the covenant. On one occasion he even seems to disappear as God speaks, or at least the voices of Moses and God tend to blend or to become confused. Every now and then Moses does identify with this audience before him, an all-inclusive audience of lay people who are brothers and sisters. This audience includes men, women, and children, leaders in responsible positions and the "emarginalized." It is an audience so vast that it takes in even future generations. Yet it also excludes foreign elements.

For the most part we have been describing the audience of Moses, for he is the one who is defining his audience through participant lists, inclusive terms, and the use of the first and second persons. The narrator adds the notions of בני ישראל and כל ישראל, the only audience indicators of the reporting speech in Dt 28,69 – 30,20. However, the audiences of Moses and the narrator are but creations of the author. Thus these audience indicators say more about the audience of the author of the Third Address than about the audience of Moses. For we don't even know exactly who was included in the Israel of Moses' time.[74]

That Moses would include in his audience future generations may itself be an indication that a later author had in mind an audience that was different from Moses' own. It is an audience that ideally includes all men, plus women and children and resident aliens (could such a class exist in Moses' day, when he and the Israelites *themselves* were the aliens?). It is an audience of a literary work, a book (ספר: Dt 29,19.20.26; 30,10). And it is a widely-inclusive lay audience, an ideal audience which will take these words to heart in a personal way, an audience which consists of individuals and yet is strongly identified with this nation Israel. The author does not specifically mention that his or her audience comes from sixth- or seventh- or eighth-century B.C.E. Israel. But we have a good idea of what kind of audience was expected to listen to the words which Moses (and his narrator) proclaims.

3.2 Rhetorical Situation

3.2.1 Introduction

Every discourse has a context, that is, certain circumstances contribute to the origin and the understanding of a communication act.[75] That context may include historical, sociological, psychological, or cultural factors. Biblical studies in the past century have investigated historical and sociological contexts of texts through the examination of their *Sitz im Leben* or "life setting." This term, coined by Gunkel,

---

[74] I will not attempt to go into the very thorny problem of the historicity of Moses and what Israel may have meant for him. See, for example, GERLEMANN, "ישראל," *THAT* I, 782-785; M. NOTH, *Geschichte Israels,* 7th ed. (Göttingen 1969) 11, 127-130; *Überlieferungsgeschichte des Pentateuch* (Stuttgart 1948) 172-191; SOGGIN, *Storia d'Israele,* 46-57, 213-218; ZOBEL, "ישראל," *TWAT* III, 986-1012 (with extended bibliography). In this study references have been to Moses' text-world audience rather than to some real audience from his day.

[75] In a communication act the "universal factors" include the sender, the receiver, the message, and "the occasion or context in which the work is composed or delivered." KENNEDY, *New Testament Interpretation,* 15; see also SNYMAN, "On Studying the Figures," 106.

concerns "the social usage in which a genre originates, to be distinguished from the contexts in which individual instances or applications of the genre may occur."[76] The search for the *Sitz im Leben* and for genre classification of a particular text have characterized that part of biblical studies known as "form criticism."[77]

The context of a discourse, however, can also be seen from a different viewpoint — the viewpoint of rhetoric. In rhetoric the context of a communication act is called the *rhetorical situation*. In general terms one can define such a rhetorical situation as "the context in which rhetoric occurs, that the rhetorical act is 'grounded in,' is dependent upon..."[78] Bitzer defines it as

> a complex of persons, events, objects, and relations which presents an exigence that can be completely or partially removed if discourse — introduced into the situation — can influence audience thought or action so as to bring about positive modification of the exigence.[79]

Such a concept of rhetorical situation goes beyond the notion of *Sitz im Leben* or the historical context of a discourse.[80] It is concerned with the relationship between persons and their environment and with the origin and goal of the communication act. There are three constituents of a rhetorical situation:

---

[76] M. Buss, "The Idea of Sitz im Leben — History and Critique," *ZAW* 90 (1978) 157. See also Alonso Schökel, *A Manual of Hebrew Poetics*, 10; Barton, *Reading the Old Testament*, 32-34; G. Tucker, *Form Criticism of the Old Testament* (GBS, Old Testament Series; Philadelphia 1971) 15.

[77] In recent years such attempts at discovering the historical and/or sociological setting of a particular text have been criticized, especially since reliable information from independent sources is lacking. Thus some reconstructions of the *Sitz im Leben* have been rather tenuous. See, for example, Alonso Schökel, "Of Methods and Models," 12; Buss, "The Idea of Sitz im Leben," 157-170; Knierim, "Old Testament Form Criticism Reconsidered," 435-468; B. Long, "Recent Field Studies in Oral Literature and the Question of *Sitz im Leben*," *Semeia* 5 (1976) 35-49; Melugin, "Muilenburg, Form Criticism, and Theological Exegesis," 95-96.

[78] A. Brinton, "Situation in the Theory of Rhetoric," *Philosophy and Rhetoric* 14 (1981) 234.

[79] L. Bitzer, "Functional Communication: A Situational Perspective," *Rhetoric in Transition: Studies in the Nature and Uses of Rhetoric* (ed. E. White; University Park/London 1980) 24. E. Black, *Rhetorical Criticism*, 133, writes: "*Situation* here refers to the prevailing state of the audience's convictions, the reputation of the rhetor, the popularity and urgency of his subject; in sum, to all the extralinguistic factors that influence an audience's reactions to a rhetorical discourse." Burke, *A Rhetoric of Motives*, 130, sees the "basic" rhetorical situation as economic.

[80] E. Black, *Rhetorical Criticism*, 38-39, criticizes neo-Aristotelian critics of rhetorical discourse for their restricted view of situation as historical context and their tendency to understand rhetorical discourse as merely a design to achieve certain results with a particular audience on a particular occasion.

First, there must be an exigence — a problem or defect, something other than it should be. Second, there must be an audience capable of being constrained in thought or action in order to effect positive modification of the exigence. Third, there must be a set of constraints capable of influencing the rhetor and an audience.[81]

Communication arises out of a felt need. Somehow a problem exists which *must* be resolved. Human beings respond to situations where there is need, perplexity, or a lack of some kind. The environment (and other persons within that environment) invites change, a change which communication can effect. "An exigence is an imperfection marked by some degree of urgency; it is a defect, an obstacle, something to be corrected. It is necessarily related to interests and valuations."[82] Every communication act is thus provoked, for as human beings we respond to needs which require modification. Or perhaps we could say that a situation "invites" utterance. Purposeful communication responds to urgent needs and seeks to make changes.[83]

Not every need in our environment, however, produces a communication act. An audience is also required. The exigence must be connected with other persons who are capable of interests and evaluations. There are also *constraints,* codes or structures which influence decisions and actions necessary to modify an exigence. Such constraints may include other persons, events, objects, relations, rules, facts, laws, interests, emotions, and conventions — these regard historical and social factors, cultural codes, personal or psychological factors, and what structuralists like to call "deep structures".[84]

Unlike form criticism, which seeks the typical or conventional in biblical literature, rhetorical criticism recognizes that all rhetorical

---

[81] Bitzer, "Functional Communication," 23.

[82] Ibid., 26. Interest in a subject often depends on its *presence* to an audience. Bitzer, pp. 32-33, lists six factors which influence such an interest: 1) Interest is generated in proportion to the probability of a subject's facticity. 2) Possessing knowledge is different from truly *knowing* a situation. 3) An exigence near in time and place generates more interest than one distant in both. 4) Interest will depend on the numbers and importance of the participants. 5) "An exigence that involves speaker or audience personally will generate more interest than one in which they are not directly involved" (p. 32). 6) The quality of an interest is also involved, since some emotions are more powerful than others. See Perelman and Olbrechts-Tyteca, *Traité de l'argumentation,* 123-124.

[83] E. White, "Rhetoric as Historical Configuration," *Rhetoric in Transition: Studies in the Nature and Uses of Rhetoric* (ed. E. White; University Park/London 1980) 14; Kennedy, *New Testament Interpretation,* 34-35; Lausberg, *Elemente,* 15; Patrick and Scult, *Rhetoric and Biblical Interpretation,* 54.

[84] Bitzer, "Functional Communication," 23-24; Keegan, *Interpreting the Bible,* 47-49.

[85] Booth, *A Rhetoric of Irony,* 227-228; Muilenburg, "Form Criticism and Beyond," 4-5.

situations are unique.[85] The rhetorical situation depends not only on historical, social, or cultural factors, but also on the audience, the speaker, and the particular circumstances of a rhetorical act. A central concept for rhetoric, then is its appropriateness or fitness: how well the communication act applies to the rhetorical situation.[86] This is actually no new concept, since it was also known to the ancient rhetoricians.[87] However, they usually saw appropriateness in terms of style, whereas actually effects every part of argumentation. It will influence the available arguments about the subject, the interests and peculiarities of the audience, and the personality (ethos) of the speaker or writer.[88]

If every rhetorical situation is unique, then it is a much more fluid concept than that of *Sitz im Leben*. Every new audience will be different, and every set of circumstances facing a speaker or writer will have its own characteristics and its own problems. The premises given may differ in each situation, since we can argue effectively only if we begin with premises a particular audience accepts. And every argumentative situation changes as the discourse progresses, for no communication act leaves the receiver the same as he or she was at the beginning.[89]

Traditional rhetoric defined a text's rhetorical situation in three ways: 1) through the notion of a text's *status* or basic issue; 2) through *topoi*; and 3) through rhetorical genres.[90] The first area, that of the *status causae,* was especially well developed in the judicial or forensic genre, where it was important to determine the basic issue at hand before beginning one's argumentation.[91] *Topoi* or *loci* are often chosen because of the argumentative situation which a speaker or writer must face. For the rhetorical situation also includes the goals the communicator has and the arguments he or she may encounter. Thus the choice of *topoi* and arguments depends on the attitudes and arguments of one's opponents as well, whether they be vocal or silent, present or absent, or even just imaginary.[92]

---

[86] BITZER, "Functional Communication," 36-37; BRINTON, "Situation in the Theory of Rhetoric," 238.

[87] ARISTOTLE addresses himself to appropriateness in his *Rhetoric,* Book III, especially chaps. 2-7. However, he normally is speaking about the suitability of style here. Appropriateness in style is also mentioned in CICERO, *Orator,* xxxv. 123 - xxxvi. 125; and in *Rhetorica ad Herennium,* III.ix.17 and IV.xii.17.

[88] BOOTH, *Now Don't Try to Reason with Me,* 27, calls this the "rhetorical stance."

[89] PERELMAN and OLBRECHTS-TYTECA, *Traité de l'argumentation,* 650.

[90] WUELLNER, "Where Is Rhetorical Criticism Taking Us?" 456. Cf. W. WUELLNER, "Paul as Pastor: The Function of Rhetorical Questions in First Corinthians," *L'Apôtre Paul: Personnalité, style et conception du ministère* (ed. A. VANHOYE; BETL 73) Leuven 1986) 60; "Paul's Rhetoric of Argumentation in Romans: An Alternative to the Donfried—Karris Debate over Romans," *The Romans Debate* (ed. K. DONFRIED: Minneapolis 1977) (First published in *CBQ* 38 [1976] 330-351) 156.

[91] LAUSBERG, *Handbuch,* 64-85 (§§ 79-138).

[92] PERELMAN and OLBRECHTS-TYTECA, *Traité de l'argumentation,* 128-129.

3.2.2 The Rhetorical Situation of Dt 29–30

Discovering the rhetorical situation of an ancient written document can be problematic. The differences in time, culture, and language between us and the authors and audience of Dt obscure many of the indications the text might give. Yet there are some hints which help us to understand a bit the particular rhetorical situation of the Third Discourse of Moses.

A communication act arises from an exigence, a need. What kind of exigence inspired the authors of Dt? In the first chapter of this book it was noted that Dt is characterized by didacticism, an appeal to the individual, and a parenesis which has an urgent tone. These characteristics are also found in Dt 29–30. Despite the witness of the great things God has done for Israel, Moses tells his audience ולא־נתן יהוה לכם לב לדעת ועינים לראות ואזנים לשמע עד היום הזה (29,3). They are still lacking in insight and understanding, and Moses wants to change that situation.

There is a real danger which Moses sees: the danger of apostasy (Dt 29,17-18.24-25; 30,17) and thus also the danger of punishment from God, a punishment which includes the loss of the land (29,19-22.26-27; 30,18). Because of this danger Moses exhorts the Israelites ושמרתם את־דברי הברית הזאת ועשיתם אתם למען תשכילו את כל־אשר תעשון (29,8; see 30,2.8.10.16.20). The people are encouraged to be faithful, to obey, and to love God with all their heart and soul (בכל־לבבך ובכל־נפשך: 30,3.6.10). The urgency of this message is emphasized by the word היום, "today" (29,3.9.11.12.14[2X].17; 30,2.8.11.16.18.19: 13 times; כיום הזה also appears in 29,27) and the fourfold use of אשר אנכי מצוך היום (30,2.8.11.16). Moses *commands* obedience and love, using not only the word צוה but also שמע בקול (30,2.8.10.20), עשה (29,8.28; 30,8.12.13.14), and שמר (29,8; 30,10.16).

The narrator in Dt 28,69 and Moses in 29,11-13 reveal their intentions in the Third Discourse. In 28,69 the narrator announces that אלה דברי הברית אשר־צוה יהוה את־משה לכרת את־בני ישראל בארץ מואב. Moses has been commanded to make a covenant with this people. Moses himself reaffirms this task in 29,11-13. Actually the sentence begins in v. 9 with אתם נצבים היום כלכם, followed by the participant list. "All of you" are standing here today to enter[93] into the Lord's covenant and oath. The discourse then has as its aim the preparation or inducement of the people to enter into a covenant with God. The covenant relationship between the

---

[93] The use of עבר בברית in Dt 29,11 is a hapax in the Hebrew Bible. It is not the normal way to express the making of a covenant. In fact, עבר ברית usually means the breaking or transgressing of a covenant (such as in Dt 17,2). The normal expression for making a covenant is כרת ברית, which is found in Dt 28,69[2X]; 29,(11).13.24. In 29,11 עבר בברית may literally mean "to pass over into the covenant." See DRIVER, *Deuteronomy*, 323, n. 11; PENNA, *Deuteronomio*, 238; REITER, "Der Bundesschluß," 154-155.

two parties is expressed in v. 12: למען הקים־אתך היום לו לעם והוא יהיה־לך
לאלהים. Moses (and through him the author) is encouraging the people to
renew their covenant relationship with Yahweh and to be faithful to that
relationship.

The notion of entering into a covenant relationship with Yahweh is
not unique to Moses' Third Discourse, although the occurrences of כרת
ברית are relatively frequent in comparison with the rest of Dt.[94] The
unique element in 28,69 – 30,20 is that Moses offers his audience a choice:
החיים והמות נתתי לפניך הברכה והקללה (30,19). And he insists that the people
make a proper choice, that of life (ובחרת בחיים). This is the high point of
Moses' Third Discourse, and perhaps the high point of all Dt.[95]

In Dt 11, 26 Moses also presents the alternatives to Israel, a choice
between a blessing and a curse: ראה אנכי נתן לפניכם היום ברכה וקללה. These
alternatives are offered at the end of the long parenesis of chapters 5 – 11
and before the presentation of the statutes and laws. However, no choice
is insisted upon at this point. The people must hear their obligations first
before deciding. The issue of Moses' Third Discourse lies in the necessity
of making a decision, of making or renewing the covenant with God. No
indication is given of the audience's response,[96] but there's no doubt that
each individual is expected to make a personal decision about this
all-important matter.

In the first part of this chapter we explored the audience of Dt
28,69-30,20, which is the second important element for the rhetorical
situation. The widely inclusive audience of Moses should also affect the
rhetorical situation, especially if Dt 31,10-13 is to be taken seriously.
There Moses commands that every seven years on the feast of Sukkoth
כל־ישראל should come לראות את־פני יהוה אלהיך במקום אשר יבחר, and there
the priests and elders should read את־התורה הזאת נגד כל־ישראל באזניהם
(v. 11).

This command seems to assume some kind of cultic situation, for the
reading of the *torah* is to take place during a religious feast (v. 10: בחג
הסכות) and at a sanctuary (v. 11: במקום אשר יבחר). There are other indi-

---

[94] The expression כרת ברית can be found in Dt 4,23; 5,2.3; 7,2; 9,9; 28,69[2X];
29,11.13; 31,16. The expression הקים ברית is used in 8,18. The only occurrence of the word
ברית in all Dt 12-26 is in 17,2, where לעבר בריתו refers to the *transgressing* of the covenant.

[95] CHOLEWINSKI, *Deuteronomio* II, 40.

[96] In Exod 19,3-8 the people of Israel also make a choice, but the circumstances differ
markedly from those of Dt 30,19. First Moses ascends Mt. Sinai and has a conversation with
God, who offers to make the people his own kingdom of priests and a holy nation (ואתם
תהיו־לי ממלכת כהנים וגוי קדוש v. 6). Moses presents this offer to the people, who immediately
accept it. So their response is recorded. In Josh 24,14-24 we have a conversation between
Joshua and the people. In 24,15 Joshua orders the people to choose (בחרו לכם) whom they will
serve. Again the people respond immediately and favorably (vv. 16-18), to which Joshua
expresses his doubts (vv. 19-20). In vv. 21 and 24 the people again respond and insist that they
can follow their choice.

cations within the Third Discourse that confirm this cultic setting. For standing לפני יהוה (Dt 29,9.14) is a technical term for the worship of God.[97] There is also the frequent use of היום, which is often considered a cultic indicator.[98] Such evidence has led many scholars to propose a cultic *Sitz im Leben* for the Third Discourse of Moses.[99] The presence of women, children, and resident aliens, however, points to an expansion or development of the cult congregation, since the קהל was originally composed only of adult males.[100]

3.2.3 References to Dt 1–28

The rhetorical situation of a communication act is affected by what has been communicated previous to it. Dt 28,69 – 30,20 follows two other discourses, one of which is fairly long. The Third Discourse makes a new start in order to bring the people to a decision for the Lord. To do this it actually repeats in summary fashion much of what has already been said, using even the same formulas. It is worth noting how extensively 28,69 – 30,20 repeats expressions and ideas already given in Dt 1 – 28 (especially chapters 4 – 28).[101]

Dt 28,69 begins with אלה דברי הברית, which sounds something like the opening of Dt in 1,1 (אלה הדברים). The same words are used in reverse order in 30,1 (הדברים האלה).

---

[97] S. AMSLER, "עמד," *THAT* II, 331. "Standing before the Lord" in the sense of a worshipping stance occurs normally with עמד. עמד לפני יהוה is found for example in Lev 9,5; Dt 4,10; 10,8; 18,7; 19,17; 2 Chr 20,13. נצב לפני יהוה is found only in Dt 29,9; but standing before God (אלהים) is found in Josh 24,1, while התיצב לפני יהוה is found in 1 Sam 10,19.

[98] See chap. 1, n. 88.

[99] BUIS and LECLERCQ, *Le Deutéronome*, 182; LACONI, *Deuteronomio*, 198; LOHFINK, "Der Bundesschluß im Land Moab," 43; PENNA, *Deuteronomio*, 237; VON RAD, *Das fünfte Buch Mose*, 129; WRIGHT, *Deuteronomy*, 317, 502.

[100] HULST, "Der Name 'Israel' im Deuteronomium," 104-105. N. LOHFINK, "Glauben lernen in Israel," *Katechetische Blätter* 108 (1983) 84-99; and "Der Glaube und die nächste Generation: Das Gottesvolk der Bibel as Lerngemeinschaft," *Das Jüdische am Christentum: Die verlorene Dimension* (Freiburg 1987) 144-166, suggests that the public recitation of the *torah* every seven years was actually a *communal* recitation, since all would learn it by heart. It's an interesting suggestion, although it would be hard to prove. But even if that was the result of the development of Israel's understanding of how one should learn and teach the *torah*, it doesn't seem to be that of Dt's authors, who require that the *torah* should be *proclaimed* to all Israel — literally "read ... into their ears" (תקרא ... באזניהם). GORDON, *The Common Background*, 293, suggests that the Pentateuch was actually chanted or sung at public ceremonies.

[101] Many of the following connections have been suggested by WEINFELD, *Deuteronomy and the Deuteronomic School*, 320-359 (his appendix on deuteronomic phraseology) and by REITER, "Der Bundesschluß," 138-177.

The repetition of words, phrases, and ideas which have appeared in previous sections of Dt is seen here as part of the rhetorical situation of the Third Discourse. Such

Dt 29,1 begins with the exact same words as 5,1: ‏ויקרא משה אל־כל־‏
‏ישראל ויאמר אלהם‏. This same verse mentions the eyes which have seen certain things in Egypt, which recalls what was said in 1,30; 6,22; 7,18; 11,3.7. Certain words and expressions found in 29,2 also refer to historical events already recalled in earlier sections of Dt: ‏אתות‏ and ‏מופתים‏ can be found in 4,34; 6,22; 7,19; and 26,8; ‏המסות‏ can be found in 4,34 and 7,19; and expressions similar to ‏אשר ראו עיניך‏ can be found in 4,9; 7,19; and 10,21.

In 29,3 ‏לב לדעת‏ is similar to various expressions combining ‏ידע‏ and ‏לבב‏ in 4,39 and 8,5. In this verse also appears the first of 13 occurrences of "today" (‏היום‏) or "this day" (‏כיום הזה‏ — 29,27) in Dt 29–30. These expressions are found quite extensively in the rest of Dt.[102] The descriptions in 29,4 of clothing and shoes not wearing out is also similar to that of 8,4.

In 29,5 we read ‏כי אני יהוה אלהיכם‏, which has parallel expressions (using ‏אנכי‏ instead of ‏אני‏) in 5,6.9. The expresson ‏ותבאו אל־המקום הזה‏, found in Dt 29,6, has parallels in 1,31; 9,7; 11,5 (cf. 26,9). References to Sihon, Og, and the distribution of their land after their defeat appear in 2,24-37 and 3,1-17. The leaders mentioned in the participant lists appear also in 1,15 and 5,23, but in a different context and without mentioning all of them together at the same time.

---

repetition thus establishes links with the rest of Dt and can contribute to ethos and pathos. One can also view some of these repetitions in terms of "inner-biblical exegesis," that is, they may actually reflect exegetical revisions of earlier biblical material. For example, Dt 29,4-5 repeats the ideas and many of the words of Dt 8,3-4. Both of these passages not only summarize but also expand the traditions of the people's wandering in the wilderness (cf. Exod 16-17; Num 11). Dt 29,12 refers to the promises made to the ancestors, yet it focuses only on a promise that the audience would be Yahweh's people and he would be their God. 30,20 presents those promises in different terms, this time emphasizing the land. 30,9 states that God rejoiced over the ancestors, yet nowhere else in the Pentateuch is such a declaration (using the word ‏שוש‏) to be found. Similarly there is no explicit mention in earlier traditions that the Israelites saw the idols of Egypt and other nations with their own eyes, such as 29,15-16 claims. The Third Discourse also refers to curses (29,19.20.26) and laws (30,10) already written down in a book. These (and perhaps other) verses could be explored from a diachronic point of view to reveal inner-biblical exegesis. However, that would be beyond the scope of the present work. See L. DOZEMAN, "Inner-Biblical Interpretation of Yahweh's Gracious and Compassionate Character," *JBL* 108 (1989) 207-223; L. ESLINGER, "Hosea 12:5a and Genesis 32:29: A Study in Inner Biblical Exegesis," *JSOT* 18 (1980) 91-99; "Inner-Biblical Exegesis and Inner-Biblical Allusion: The Question of Category," *VT* 42 (1992) 47-58; M. FISHBANE, *Biblical Interpretation*; "Inner Biblical Exegesis: Types and Strategies of Interpretation in Ancient Israel," *Midrash and Literature* (ed. G. HARTMAN and S. BUDICK; New Haven/London 1986) 19-37; S. SANDMEL, "The Haggadah within Scripture," *JBL* 80 (1961) 105-122.

[102] Outside of chaps. 29-30, ‏היום‏ occurs in Dt 1,10.39; 2,18.22.25; 3,14; 4,4.8.26.39.40; 5,1.3; 6,6; 7,11; 8,1.11.19; 9,1.3; 10,8.13; 11.2.4.8.13.26.27.28.32; 12,8; 13,19; 15,5.15; 19,9; 20,3; 26,3.17.18; 27,1.4.10; 28,1.13.14.15; 31,2.21.27; 32,46.48; 34,6. Similar expressions are ‏כהיום הזה‏, which occurs in 6,24; and ‏כיום הזה‏, which occurs not only in 29,27 but also in 2,30; 4,20.38; 8,18; and 10,15.

In Dt 29,12 appears the formula לו לעם והוא יהיה־לך לאלהים.
Although these exact words do not occur again in Dt, similar phrases
occur in 4,20; 7,6; 14,2; 26,18; 27,9; 28,9. God's oath to the fathers,
whether specifically by name (לאברהם ליצחק וליעקב) or more generally, also
occurs in 1,8.35; 4,31; 6,10.18.23; 7,8.12.13; 8,1.18; 9,5; 10,11; 11,9.21;
13,18; 19,8; 26,3.15; 28,11.[103] Normally God's oath to the fathers
concerns the land.

In Dt 29,17 the reference to איש או אשה או משפחה או שבט could easily
recall the laws against those individuals or groups who apostatize and
worship other gods or encourage their fellow Israelites to do the same:
the prophet (13,1-5), a near relative (13,6-11), or a city (13,12-18).
Perhaps Dt 17,2-7 could also be called to mind by such a reference.

In Dt 29,19 we have the expression כל־האלה הכתובה בספר הזה,
followed by references to God's anger and the consequences of
disobedience. Coming so soon after chapter 28, this expression would
easily recall to the audience the curses so recently pronounced before them.
A similar phrase, את־כל־הקללה הכתובה בספר הזה appears in 29,26.[104]

The crime of serving other gods, ויעבדו אלהים אחרים, is mentioned in
Dt 29,25 (with similar words in 30,17). This expression is also found in
7,4; 11,16; 13,7.14; 17,3; 28,36.64. Equivalent expressions occur in 4,19
and 8,19. These other gods are אלהים אשר לא ידעום, an expression which
also occurs in 11,28; 13,3.7.14; and 28,64. In Dt 29,27 the punishment is
that וישם יהוה מעל אדמתם. Similar expressions occur in 4,26; 6,15; 11,17;
28,21.63.

In Dt 29,28 occurs the phrase לעשות את־כל־דברי התורה הזאת, which
also appears in 17,19 and 28,58.

The formula בכל־לבבך ובכל־נפשך, which occurs in 30,2.6.10, is also
found in 4,29; 6,5; 10,12; 11,13; 13,4; 26,16. Another popular phrase in
Dt is אשר אנכי מצוך היום, which in Moses' Third Discourse can be found
four times: 30,2.8.11.16. It is also found in this or similar forms in
4,2[2X].40; 6,6; 7,11; 8,1.11; 10,13; 11,8.13.22.27.28; 12,11.14.28; 13,1.19;
15,5; 19,9; 27,1.4.10; 28,1.13.14.15.

In 30,3 Moses mentions exile (מכל־העמים אשר הפיצך). Similar
expressions occur only twice in earlier sections of Dt (4,27 and 28,64), but
the second appeared recently among the curses of chapter 28. The verb ירש
occurs in one or another of its forms four times in Dt 30 (vv. 5[2X].16.18)
and 61 times in previous sections of Dt.[105] A much more "deuteronomic"

_____

[103] Such an oath is mentioned as well in 31,7.20.21.23; 34,4.
[104] Outside of the Third Discourse the word ספר occurs in Dt 17,18; 24,1.3; 28,58.61;
31,26.
[105] Dt 1,8.21.39; 2,12.21.22.24.31[2X]; 3,12.18.20; 4,1.5.14.22.26.38.47; 5,28.30(33);
6,1.18; 7,1.17; 8,1; 9,1.3.4[2X].5[2X].6.23; 10,11; 11,1.8[2X].10.11.23[2X].29.31;
12,2.29[2X]; 15,4; 16,20; 17,14; 18,12.14; 19,1.2.14; 21,1; 23,21.63; 25,19; 26,1; 28,42.

expression which contains this verb is found in 30,16: בארץ אשר־אתה בא־שמה לרשתה. This and similar phrases occur in 4,1.5; 6,18; 7,1; 8,1; 9,5; 11,8.10.29; 12,29; 28,21. An expression with a similar idea is found in Dt 30,18: האדמה אשר אתה עבר את־הירדן לבא שמה לרשתה. This same expression or its equivalent occurs in 4,14.22.26; 6,1; 9,1; 11,8.11.31.

Dt 30,6 mentions the circumcision of the heart, which also appears in 10,16. Also in 30,6 appears a favorite deuteronomic expression, לאהבה את־יהוה. It not only reappears twice in 30,16.20 but also occurs in 6,5; 10,12; 11,1.13.22; 13,4; 19,9. In Dt 30,7 we have the promise that God will transfer these curses to Israel's enemies, an idea found also in 28,7.

In Dt 30,8 we find ושמעת בקול יהוה. Obeying (listening to the voice of) the Lord or obeying *him* (where it refers to God) appears elsewhere in the Third Discourse in 30,2.8.10.20. Before this it also occurs in 4,30; 8,20; 9,23; 13,5.19; 15,5; 26,14.17; 27,10; 28,1.2.15.45.62.

In Dt 30,9 appears the blessing of מעשה ידך. Similar expressions occur in 2,7; 14,29; 15,10.18; 16,15; 23,21; 24,19; 28,8.12. Also within 30,9 is found בפרי בטנך ובפרי בהמתך ובפרי אדמתך. The same expression is used in 7,13; 28,4.11. A third phrase in this verse, לשוש עליך לטוב, is found elsewhere only once, but that happens to be in the curses which have been recently proclaimed (28,63).

Dt 30,10 places together מצותיו וחקתיו, a combination found later in the Third Discourse (30,16) as well as in 6,2; 10,13; 28,15.45. These and other words for laws, legal stipulations, and the covenant are combined with the verb שמר quite often in Dt. In the Third Discourse such expressions can be found in 29,8; 30,10.16. Before this they can be found in Dt 4,2.40; 5,10.26; 6,2.17.25; 7,9.11; 8,1.2.6.11; 10,13; 11,1.8.22.32; 12,28; 13,5.19; 15,5; 16,12; 17,19; 19,9; 23,24; 26,17.18; 27,1; 28,1.9.15.45.58.

In Dt 30,11 we find המצוה הזאת, which also occurs in 6,25; 11,22; 15,5; 19,9. As mentioned above, the choice between life and death, good and evil, blessing and curse, found in Dt 30,15.19, reflects the choice already offered in 11,26 between blessing and curse.

The phrase ללכת בדרכיו appears in Dt 30,16 and also in 8,6; 19,9; 26,17; and 28,9. This same verse also combines מצותיו וחקתיו ומשפטיו, something which also occurs in 8,11; 11,1; and 26,17. The expression וברכך יהוה אלהיך, also found in Dt 30,16, has parallels in 12,7; 14,24; 15,6.14; 16,10; 26,15.

Dt 30,18 contains the expression תאריכן ימים. It is also to be found in 4,26.40; 5,33; 11,9; 17,20; 22,7. In Dt 30,19 Moses says העידתי בכם היום את־השמים ואת־הארץ. The exact same words are to be found in 4,26. There these words are followed by כי־אבד תאבדון, which in the Third Discourse is found in 30,18, a clause which is parallel to v. 19. Also in 30,19 we find the phrase למען תחיה. The conjunction למען followed by a form of the verb חיה is also found in 4,1; 5,30; 8,1; 16,20.

Finally, in Dt 30,20 occurs the expression ולדבקה־בו. It is also found in 4,4; 10,20; 11,22; and 13,5.

This long list of connections between Dt 28,69–30,20 and what precedes it suggests that the author was familiar with Dt 1–28 (especially Dt 4–28) or with the traditions behind these chapters and that he or she wanted to continue their style, phraseology, and even some of their ideas. In any case the Third Discourse of Moses becomes a reminder and summary of what has already been read. The author does not want the audience to forget what has just been proclaimed, even if now there is something more to be said.

3.2.4 Summary

The rhetorical situation of a communication act is the context in which a discourse takes place and by which it is influenced. It includes the notion of exigence, which is a problem or defect, something which provokes the communication act. In Dt 28,69–30,20 the Israelites are charged with not yet understanding the great works which God has performed for them. The danger of apostasy and of God's punishment requires a change of heart (a "circumcision") and a choice for life and blessing. The Third Discourse of Moses finally insists that every member of its widely inclusive audience personally make that decision.

The short address that we find in Dt 29–30 comes after two other discourses by Moses, and its rhetorical situation is affected by what has been mentioned in these two addresses. There are numerous references in the Third Discourse to laws, historical events, and even the phraseology mentioned in chapters 1–28. Obviously the authors do not want the audience to forget what has been said before this. At the same time they don't waste much time on this speech, for in a mere 47 verses they attempt to bring the people to a choice, a decision.

The specific devices and rhetorical strategies used by the author to convince the audience to choose properly will be explored in the following three chapters.

INVENTIO

Chapter three investigated the audience and the rhetorical situation of Dt 28,69 – 30,20. In this chapter we want to look at the Third Discourse of Moses from the point of view of *inventio* or invention, that is, the finding of arguments for a particular thesis. Invention flows naturally out of the rhetorical situation. An exigence exists: the lack of understanding on the part of the people and the danger of apostasy with its consequent punishment from God. Moses is attempting to persuade Israel to choose the way of obedience and love. What means does the human author use to get this point across? This chapter will first investigate the premises and topics upon which argumentation in the Third Discourse of Moses is based. Then it will explore the various means by which ethos, pathos, and logos are pursued in Dt 28,69 – 30,20.

4.1 Premises

The aim of argumentation is the eliciting or increasing of the adherence of an audience to the theses of the speaker or writer. Thus the communicator must begin with premises already accepted by the audience. According to Perelman and Olbrechts-Tyteca, such premises can be divided into two classes: 1) the *real* (facts, truths, and presumptions); and 2) the *preferable* (values, hierarchies, and *loci* of the preferable).[1] What premises appear in Moses' Third Discourse?

In terms of the *real,* Dt 28,69 – 30,20 accepts as *facts* certain events which are part of the history of Israel: a sojourn in Egypt, an escape from slavery, wanderings in the wilderness for forty years, and battles with some of the peoples of Transjordan (29,1-7.15.24). Other events accepted as historical facts are the destruction of Sodom, Gomorrah, Admah, and Zeboiim (29,22); and the making of covenants with God on Mt.Horeb and in the land of Moab (28,69; 29,8.11.13.20.24). Accepted social facts

---

[1] PERELMAN and OLBRECHTS-TYTECA, *Traité de l'argumentation,* 88. They discuss the subdivisions on pp. 89-132. The premises upon which argumentation is based are, at least in comparison with those of scientific demonstration, often rather ill-defined. Cf. PERELMAN, *L'empire rhétorique,* 64.

include an organization of the people into tribes and families (29,7.9.17) who have common ancestors (29,12.24; 30,20). This nation is considered a single whole (28,69; 29,1.9) with an established hierarchy (29,9-10). In other words, the authors assume that the audience accepts the notions of a common history and a common identity.

There are also *truths* accepted without question by the audience. The author does not need to defend the idea that blessings and curses are powerful and effective (29,19-20.26; 30,1.7.19). The written word also has a certain power or effectiveness or authority, for what is written will surely happen (29,19.20.26; 30,10). Evil thoughts will be punished (29,18-20), while conversion brings blessing and reward (30,1-2).

The audience accepts certain notions about God as well: He acts in history (e.g., he makes covenants and performs wonders [28,69; 29,1-2.11-12]); he speaks to human beings (28,69; 29,12); he experiences emotions such as joy, pity, and anger (29,19.22-23.26-27; 30,3.9); he can forgive or he can punish (29,19-27; 30,1-10.18). Thus God is powerful, establishes relations with individuals and nations, and should be listened to when he or his representative speaks.

It's a bit more difficult to ascertain the *presumptions* inherent in the text. Presumptions are associated with the normal and the reasonable. Of course "normality" is subject to interpretation and depends largely on one's culture. But the immediate effect of a presumption is that it imposes the burden of proof on anyone who wants to oppose it.[2]

In the Third Discourse of Moses one presumption may be that you can trust what your eyes see, that is, personal witness or experience is valuable (29,1.2.3.16). The text also presumes that the heart is the seat of thought and decision-making (29,3.17-18; 30,6.14.17). War, blessing and curse, reward and punishment by God are considered to be normal events

---

[2] PERELMAN, *L'empire rhétorique,* 39; PERELMAN and OLBRECHTS-TYTECA, *Traité de l'argumentation,* 94, list "quelques présomptions d'usage courant: la présomption que la qualité d'un acte manifeste celle de la personne qui l'a posé; la présomption de crédulité naturelle qui fait que notre premier mouvement est d'accueillir comme vrai ce que l'on nous dit, et qui est admise aussi longtemps et dans la mesure où nous n'avons pas de raison de nous méfier; la présomption d'intérêt d'après laquelle nous concluons que tout énoncé porté à notre conaissance est censé nous intéresser; la présomption concernant le caractère sensé de toute action humaine." Presumptions may also be associated with *conventions* in literature and oral discourse. In our well-ordered world, every culture has unspoken but fixed rules for greetings, for beginning a conversation, for telling a story, for writing poetry, or for having a debate. Such fixed notions, which involve communication acts, have been called *conventions.* Cf. BOOTH, *The Rhetoric of Fiction,* 433; PERELMAN and OLBRECHTS-TYTECA, *Traité de l'argumentation,* 20; ROBERTSON, *The Old Testament and the Literary Critic,* 8-9. KUGEL, "On the Bible and Literary Criticism," 222, tells us that "convention determines perception."

in the life of a person. The necessity of worshipping the divine is also accepted as normal.

What are some of the premises of our text in the realm of the *preferable*? Certain *values* do appear in Dt 28,69 – 30,20. Children are considered an important asset (29,10.18.21; 30,2.6.19) — they were even part of the audience! One's name was also valuable, for the threat to blot it out seems to be a powerful motivating factor (29,19). The land (and its productivity) was a particularly valuable gift, so exile or the loss of the land's productivity was a terrible punishment (29,7.20-23.26-27; 30,1-5.9.16.18). Other important values for the audience are fertility or productivity (30,9), blessing (30,1.19), and life (especially a long life: 30,6.15.16.18-20). Obviously family relationships, including those with the ancestors, were also important (29,12.24; 30,20).

The values which appear as premises in the Third Discourse (children, family, land, productivity, blessing, and [long] life) are what Perelman and Olbrechts-Tyteca would call *concrete* values as opposed to *abstract* values.[3] Abstract values also appear in Dt, but these for the most part seem to be part of the thesis that the author is trying to promote — such as love for God (30,6.16.20) and obedience to the *torah* (29,8.28; 30,2.8.10.12-14.16.20).[4]

Values are crucial in argumentation, even if they are rejected in formal demonstration. Not only is it impossible to eliminate values in argumentation, but it would also seem to be unwise. "One appeals to values in order to induce the hearer to make certain choices rather than others and, most of all, to justify those choices so that they may be accepted and approved by others."[5] When inserted into a system of beliefs, values can even be accepted as facts or truths by an audience.[6] Thus values presented in a religious text like Dt help to persuade, since the audience tends to accept them as solid evidence in favor of a thesis.

---

[3] PERELMAN and OLBRECHTS-TYTECA, *Traité de l'argumentation*, 103-107; PERELMAN, *L'empire rhétorique*, 41-42.

[4] Thus one gets the impression that in the Third Discourse of Moses, if not in all of Dt, there is a movement from concrete (conservative) values to abstract values, which are essentially connected with criticism and change. Cf. PERELMAN and OLBRECHTS-TYTECA, *Traité de l'argumentation*, 106. My suspicion is that the life   that should be chosen in Dt 30,19 is no mere concrete value of many days on the land but a wider, all-encompassing abstract value.

[5] PERELMAN and OLBRECHTS-TYTECA, *Traité de l'argumentation*, 100: "On y fait appel pour engager l'auditeur à faire certains choix plutôt que d'autres, et surtout pour justifier ceux-ci, de manière à les rendre acceptables et approuvés par autrui." English translation from CH. PERELMAN and L. OLBRECHTS-TYTECA *The New Rhetoric: A Treatise on Argumentation*, trans. John Wilkinson and Purcell Weaver (Notre Dame, Ind. 1969) 75.

[6] PERELMAN and OLBRECHTS-TYTECA, *Traité de l'argumentation*, 101.

It is more difficult to ascertain the *hierarchies* envisioned in the Third Discourse of Moses. One gets the impression that adult males have greater value or esteem than females or children (29,9-10); that "one's own" (family, resident aliens) have greater value than foreigners or enemies (29,7.10.13.17; 30,7.17-18); and that the god of the nation or clan is much more important than other gods (29,25).

At this point we will not pursue the final category of the *loci of the preferable,* since this brings us to our next section, that of *topics.*

4.2. Topics

Topics are places (τόποι; *loci*) where one can find something to say about a subject. Perelman and Olbrechts-Tyteca apply the term *loci* (*lieux*) to "des prémisses d'ordre très général permettant de fonder des valeurs et des hiérarchies...."[7] Thus premises and topics tend to blend.[8]

Aristotle discusses topics in both his *Rhetoric*[9] and his *Topics.* He divides *loci* into special topics (for particular kinds of discourse) and common topics (for any type of discourse). Quintilian also reflects on the topics, although he tends to identify them with *argumenta.*[10] Corbett summarizes this discussion by listing the following common topics with their subdivisions:[11] 1. Definition (Genus, Division); 2. Comparison (Similarity, Difference, Degree); 3. Relationship (Cause and Effect, Antecedent and Consequence, Contraries, Contradictions); 4. Circumstance (Possible and Impossible, Past Fact and Future Fact); 5. Testimony (Authority, Testimonial, Statistics, Maxims, Law, Precedents or Examples).

It's obvious that the authors of Dt never studied classical Greek and Roman rhetoric, which had its origins long after Dt's final text had been established. Yet one can easily find at least some of these topics within the text of Dt 28,69 – 30,20. What follows is a general listing of some of the common topics discernible in the Third Discourse of Moses. The specifics will be treated under the techniques of argumentation (4.5.2).

1. Definition: Although there are no precise definitions within the Third Discourse, there are moments when the sender feels the necessity of

---

[7] Ibid., 113.

[8] BURKE, *A Rhetoric of Motives,* 56, points out that ARISTOTLE's topics would probably be treated today as "attitudes" or "values."

[9] ARISTOTLE, *Rhetoric,* II.19.1392a-1393a.

[10] QUINTILIAN, *Institutio oratoria,* V.10.1-125.

[11] CORBETT, *Classical Rhetoric,* 110. A description and discussion of these categories can be found on pp. 110-145.

explaining or describing something more precisely. The opening words (אלה דברי הברית) let us know that what follows is a description of the covenant which God commanded Moses to make with the people (28,69). This covenant is defined more exactly with the words מלבד הברית אשר־כרת אתם בחרב (28,69).

The definitions in the rest of Dt 28,69–30,20 are largely in the subclass of *division*. The authors often divide things and concepts into smaller parts in order to explain or define what they mean. The audience has seen *all* that the Lord did in Egypt: המסות ... האתת והמפתים (29,1-2). In fact, these wonders in Egypt were performed against Pharaoh, all his servants, and all his land (29,1). The audience standing before the Lord is defined by its division into the heads of the tribes, the elders, the officers, all the men, the children, the women, and the resident aliens (29,9-10). Furthermore, the resident alien is identified as the one in the camp who gathers firewood and/or draws water (29,10).

In Dt 29,12 and 30,20 the sender isn't restricted to the mere mention of the ancestors; he also lists them. In 29,16 the detestable objects and idols are defined as those made of wood and stone, silver and gold. In 29,17 the prospective offender could be a man or a woman or a family or a tribe. In 29,25 the אלהים אחרים are defined as those which the people never knew and which had not been allotted to them. Dt 30,16 defines more precisely what it is that Moses has commanded: to love God, to walk in his ways, and to observe his law, which is divided into מצותיו וחקתו ומשפטיו.

2. Comparison: There are certainly comparisons within the Third Discourse of Moses, although these are mostly in the form of metaphors. Dt 29,17 compares the transgressor to שרש פרה ראש ולענה. Another metaphor appears in 29,18: ספות הרוה את־הצמאה. God's anger "smokes" and his curse "settles on" the sinner in 29,19. The punishment of the land is compared with the overthrow of Sodom and Gomorrah, Admah and Zeboiim in 29,22. In 30,5 there is a comparison with the blessing of the ancestors, while 30,6 presents us with the metaphor of the circumcision of the heart.

3. Relationship: A number of relationships occur within Dt 28,69–30,20. It's often difficult to ascertain whether the antecedent-consequent and cause-effect relationships are premises already accepted by the audience or theses the sender is attempting to persuade the audience to accept. Despite the audience's personal witness to the wonders performed in Egypt (antecedent), Moses accuses Israel of not understanding (consequence — 29,1-3). The consequence of forty years of privations in the desert should be the acknowledgment of Yahweh as "your God" (29,4-5). The faithful observance of the covenant regulations should also bring about the reward of prosperity (29,8).

This assembly has gathered for the express purpose of establishing a special relationship with God (29,9-12). In Dt 29,13-14 we have what seems to be a contradiction: those who are here are added to those who are not here. Since the audience has seen the idols of Egypt and other lands (antecedent), it should not be tempted to turn from the Lord to serve them (consequence — 29,16-17). But if some individual does forsake God (cause), Yahweh will not forgive but his anger will burn, curses will pounce on the fool, and that person's name will be wiped out (effects — 29,18-19). What is the cause of the land's punishments? The Lord did all this because Israel abandoned the covenant and worshiped other gods (29,21-27).

When the exiles (whom God banished) return to the Lord (antecedent), he will bring them back to their land and will bless them (consequence — 30,1-10). Once this happens (antecedent), God will then bring punishment upon their enemies (consequence — 30,7). The parallelism of 30,11-14 reveals certain contraries or antitheses built upon a near-far relationship. Contraries also occur with the pairs blessing and curse (30,1.19), life and death, good and evil (30,15). Again the consequence of obedience is life, increase in population, and blessing on the land (30,16). Whoever turns away and worships other gods (antecedent) will certainly perish (consequence — 30,17-18). Whoever chooses life (antecedent) will live a long life on the land promised to the ancestors (consequence — 30,19-20).

4. Circumstance: The subclassification of the possible and the impossible is evident in Dt 30,11-14, where the author attempts to convince the audience that it is possible to hear and do המצוה הזאת. Again the possible and the impossible is represented in 30,4. Here the line of argument may be: If one of a pair of similar things is possible, the other is possible as well. Thus if God can disperse his people, he can also gather them together. Past facts (regarding the audience's history) are presented in 29,1-2.4-5.6-7.15-16 and in the reference to the ancestors in 30,5. Future facts (especially in the form of examples projected into the future) occur in 29,13-14.18-20.21-27; 30,1-10).

5. Testimony: This group of topics contains a variety of external sources, some of which are also found in the Third Discourse of Moses. The fact that God commanded Moses to make a covenant and deliver these words (28,69) lends special authority to the entire address. Again, the fact that it is Moses who delivers this speech lends authority to what is said in it (29,1).

Moses appeals to the audience itself as a *witness* (29,1.2.16). Future generations and foreigners (29,21.24) and even heaven and earth will also provide testimony (30,19). The appeal to the ancestors (29,12; 30,5.20) may serve as a means of adding authoritative witnesses to the discourse as well.

There is a prolific use of legal terms in our text: ברית (28,69[2x];
29,8.11.13.20.24); אלה (29,13.18.19.20; 30,7); תורה (29,20.28; 30,10); מצוה
(30,8.10.11.16); חקות (30,10.16); משפט (30,16); as well as frequent use of
various forms of צוה, "command" (28,69; 30,2.8.11.16). The references to
ספר might also fall in line here (29,19.20.26; 30,10).

Examples can be found in both past facts and future facts, such as
the case of the individual who plots evil in his or her heart (29,17-20) and
the case of the devastated land (29,21-27). *Maxims* appear in 29,18.28.

In drawing from common themes and topics, then, the authors of the
Third Discourse of Moses seem to have a preference for history, juridical
and political language, nature (29,17.22; 30,9), and also parts of the body
and their functions (29,1-3.4.17.18; the word לב occurs twice while לבב
occurs nine times in the Third Discourse).

It is obvious that ancient Hebrew writers made use of many of the
same kinds of topics as ancient Greek and Roman rhetoricians. It is also
possible that Dt's authors drew from other topics that are as yet
unrecognized. In any case they had to find material in order to develop
their arguments. That material seems to coincide often with what the
ancient rhetoricians called *topics*. Of course they did so without the
conscious inventory of the ancient Greeks and Romans. But it seems that
they were just as adept at finding this material as those who had
theorized about *inventio*.

Perelman and Olbrechts-Tyteca also recognize various topics or
places, but they prefer to classify them under a few general headings: *loci*
of quantity, quality, order, the existing, essence, and the person.[12] Their
understanding of such *loci* concerns the superiority of one thing over
another and thus is narrower than the understanding of the ancient rhetoricians.[13] But they would see the place for the beginning of argumentation in the premises which the audience already accepts, as we saw
above. Thus premises and topics (and even the arguments drawn from
them) tend to become indistinguishable. Nevertheless Perelman and Olbrechts-Tyteca do insist that the *loci* have argumentative value and are
indispensable for arguments.

4.3 Ethos

Ethos is one of the three "modes" of argumentation. It involves the
credibility of the communicator and is somehow associated with his or her

---

[12] See chap. 2, n. 128.

[13] PERELMAN and OLBRECHTS-TYTECA, *Traité de l'argumentation*, 113-114; PERELMAN,
L'empire rhétorique, 43, tells us that "les lieux communs sont des affirmations très
générales concernant ce qui est présumé valoir plus, en quelque domaine que ce soit...."

character. Every speaker or writer must establish a relationship, a communion, with the audience. Such a relationship is created by the communication act itself (in oral discourse the delivery and appearance of the speaker also affect this relationship). Ethos involves the emotions, since the sender's own feelings about himself or herself and about the message being communicated will affect those of the audience.[14] Aristotle believes that ethos can be the most effective means of proof.[15]

Ethos also includes the relationship between sender and message, for the interaction between speaker and speech is important for argumentation. This is because an audience associates a speaker with his or her speech, a writer with his or her text.[16] The communicator is part of the context of the communication act, part of the rhetorical situation. The same words spoken by different people will be received differently by the same audience — for each new speaker introduces a new ethos, and thus a new context, into the communication act.[17]

Thus a speaker or writer will normally attempt to appeal to the audience by showing his or her solidarity with it, esteem for it, or confidence in it.[18] Perelman and Olbrechts-Tyteca tell us that this can be done particularly through the use of *figures of communion*, those literary devices which attempt to bring about or increase a sense of sharing in or participating with an audience. Often this is done through references to a common culture, tradition, or history.[19]

In Dt 28,69 – 30,20 (as in all Dt) the authors build their ethos upon Moses. He is the one who speaks, so it is his authority which the text appeals to. But even Moses' authority is strengthened by the allusions to God's authority behind his spokesman (28,69; 29,5).

---

[14] LANHAM, *Handlist*, 74; MARCHESE, *Dizionario di retorica e di stilistica*, 109.

[15] ARISTOTLE, *Rhetoric*, I.2.1356a. In II.1.1378a ARISTOTLE mentions that three traits inspire confidence in a speaker's character: good sense (φρόνησις), good moral character (ἀρετή), and good will or benevolence (εὔνοια). BARTHES, *L'ancienne rhétorique*, 146 (B.1.28), comments on these traits: "Pour Aristote, il y a trois 'airs', dont l'ensemble constitue l'autorité personnelle de l'orateur: 1. *phronèsis*: c'est la qualité de celui qui délibère bien, qui pèse bien le *pour* et le *contre*: c'est une sagesse objective, un bon sens affiché; 2. *arétè*: c'est l'affiche d'une franchise qui ne craint pas ses conséquences et s'exprime à l'aide de propos directs, empreints d'une loyauté théâtrale; 3. *eunoia*: il s'agit de ne pas choquer, de ne pas provoquer, d'être sympathique (et peut-être même: *sympa*), d'entrer dans une complicité complaisante à l'égard de l'auditoire. En somme pendant qu'il parle et déroule le protocole des preuves logiques, l'orateur doit également dire sans cesse: suivez-moi (*phronèsis*), estimez-moi (*arétè*) et aimez-moi (*eunoia*)."

[16] PERELMAN and OLBRECHTS-TYTECA, *Traité de l'argumentation*, 426.

[17] Ibid., 427, 429. Cf. T. TODOROV, "The Place of Style in the Structure of the Text," *Literary Style: A Symposium* (ed. S. CHATMAN; London 1971) 30.

[18] PERELMAN and OLBRECHTS-TYTECA, *Traité de l'argumentation*, 430-431.

[19] Ibid., 239.

The frequent references to Yahweh build up the authority of this text: God is the one who makes promises (29,12; 30,20), commands (28,69), punishes (29,19-20.23.26-27; 30,1.7), saves (29,1-2.24; 30,3-5.9), and is the partner of the covenant (28,69; 29,11-12). In fact, in these 49 verses the name יהוה is mentioned 38 times, 15 times by itself and 23 times with some form of יהוה אלהיך אלהים (17x); יהוה אלהינו (3x); יהוה אלהיכם (2x); and יהוה אלהי אבתם (1x). The word אלהים, when referring to Yahweh, occurs alone in this discourse only once, in the so-called *Bundesformular* (Dt 29,12).

Moses is mentioned by name only twice, and this occurs in reported speech (Dt 28,69; 29,1). But then he is the speaker of the Third Discourse. His relationship with his audience is explored above in 3.1.3.4. In general Moses keeps a certain distance from his audience by the use of the first person singular and the second person singular and plural. It seems that Moses has little need to ingratiate himself with his audience, since his authority is unchallenged. Yet there are those occasions when Moses deliberately identifies himself with his audience. These are figures of communion, for Moses refers to a common history (29,6-7.15.17), a common tradition, and a shared liturgical event in which the assembly recalls or renews its covenant relationship with Yahweh (29,14). The use of the second person plural in 29,14 is both a figure of communion and a figure of *presence*.[20]

There are still other possible (if hidden) voices of authority within the Third Address of Moses. For occasionally one perceives allusions to Isaiah, Jeremiah, and Ezekiel. Obviously Moses could not cite the words of his successors, but the authors could ensure that his words were in harmony with these exilic and pre-exilic prophets. In this way their authority could reinforce the ethos of the authors of Dt 28,69 – 30,20.

Thus it is possible (even likely) that the audience of the Third Discourse would have thought of Isa 6,9-10 when they heard the criticism of Dt 29,3.[21] Similarly listeners would recall Ezekiel when they heard the self-identification formula cited in Dt 29,5.[22] The occurrence of words such as שקוציהם and גלליהם (Dt 29,16) is frequent in both Jeremiah and

---

[20] Ibid., 235: "Les figures de la présence ont pour effet de rendre présent à la conscience l'objet du discours."

[21] DRIVER, *Deuteronomy*, 321; MAYES, *Deuteronomy*, 361; NTAGWARARA, "Alliance d'Israël," 36-37.

[22] BUIS and LECLERCQ, *Le Deutéronome*, 180; DRIVER, *Deuteronomy*, 321; NTAGWARARA, "Alliance d'Israël," 42-43; REITER, "Der Bundesschluß," 207; THOMPSON, *Deuteronomy*, 280; W. ZIMMERLI, "Erkenntnis Gottes nach dem Buch Ezechiel," *Gottes Offenbarung: Gesammelte Aufsätze zum Alten Testament* (TBü 19; München 1963), 41-119.

CHAPTER 4

Ezekiel,[23] while expressions such as שררות לב (29,18), נתש (29,27), and הדיח (30,1) are quite common in Jeremiah.[24] The question-and-answer scheme which appears in Dt 29,23-27 may have reminded the audience of similar schemes found in Jer 5,19; 9,11-15; 13,22; 16,10-13; and 22,8-9.[25] Likewise, references to return from exile, conversion, and an inner change brought about by God (Dt 30,1-10, especially vv. 1 and 6) may have recalled similar themes in Jeremiah and Ezekiel.[26] The poisonous and bitter fruit of Dt 29,17 may also have reminded the audience of Hosea and Amos (cf. Hos 10,4; Amos 5,7; 6,12).[27]

4.4 Pathos

The second mode of argumentation, pathos, concerns the emotions induced in an audience. When the audience begins to *feel* that the speaker is right, it is usually won over to his or her side.[28] The ancient rhetoricians recognized that logical argument is rarely sufficient to persuade an audience — there must also be an appeal to the emotions.[29] The two

---

[23] DRIVER, *Deuteronomy*, 324; HYATT, "Jeremiah and Deuteronomy," 170; MAYES, *Deuteronomy*, 364; NTAGWARARA, "Alliance d'Israël," 96; PENNA, *Deuteronomio*, 238; REITER, "Der Bundesschluß," 268.

[24] שררות לב occurs in Jer 3,17; 7,24; 9,13; 11,8; 13,10; 16,12; 18,12; 23,17. נתש occurs in Jer 1,10; 12,14[2X].15.17[2X]; 18,7; 24,6; 31,28; 42,10; 45,4 (cf. 18,14; 31,40). הדיח occurs in Jer 8,3; 16,15; 23,2.3.8; 24,9; 27,10.15; 29,14.18; 32,37; 46,28; 50,17. Cf. DRIVER, *Deuteronomy*, 325, 328-329; MAYES, *Deuteronomy*, 365; PENNA, *Deuteronomio*, 238; REITER, "Der Bundesschluß," 286-288; WOLFF, "Das Kerygma des deuteronomistischen Geschichtswerks," 181.

[25] BUIS and LECLERCQ, *Le Deutéronome*, 183-184; HYATT, "Jeremiah and Deuteronomy," 170; B. LONG, "Two Question and Answer Schemata in the Prophets," *JBL* 90 (1971) 129-139; NELSON, *Double Redaction*, 74-75; NTAGWARARA, "Alliance d'Israël," 214-215; D. SKWERES, "Das Motiv der Strafgrunderfragung in biblischen und neuassyrischen Texte," *BZ*, N.F. 14 (1970) 181-197; W. VOGELS, "The Literary Form of 'The Question of the Nations,'" *EgT* 11 (1980) 159-176.

[26] See, for exmple, Jer 4,4; 12,15; 23,3; 29,14; 30,3.18; 31,23.31-34; 32,39-41; Ezek 11,19; 29,14; 36,24-36; 37,23-28. Cf. BUIS, *Le Deutéronome*, 395-396; HYATT, "Jeremiah and Deuteronomy," 164-165; NTAGWARARA, "Alliance d'Israël," 146, 150-151, 156, 161; A. SCHENKER, "Unwiderrufliche Umkehr und neuer Bund: Vergleich zwischen der Wiederherstellung Israels in Dt 4,25-31; 30,1-14 und dem neuen Bund in Jer 31,31-34," *FZPhTh* 27 (1980), especially 94-95, 102-105; VON RAD, *Das fünfte Buch Mose*, 131. Here it may be good to note that such themes may also recall Deutero-Isaiah. See BUIS, *Le Deutéronome*, 394.

[27] BUIS and LECLERCQ, *Le Deutéronome*, 183; DRIVER, *Deuteronomy*, 325; LACONI, *Deuteronomio*, 199; MAYES, *Deuteronomy*, 364.

[28] DIXON, *Rhetoric*, 25.

[29] See ARISTOTLE, *Rhetoric*, I.2.1356a; in Book II, chaps. 1-11, ARISTOTLE describes various emotions. See also CICERO, *Brutus*, xlix.185; lxxx.279; *De oratore*, II.115; *Orator*, xxi.69. CICERO believes that without arousing the emotions a speaker cannot move

major techniques for producing emotions in an audience are lowering the level of abstraction (that is, becoming concrete) and the simulation in the communicator of the emotions he or she wishes to convey.[30]

4.4.1 Concreteness and Presence

Lowering the level of abstraction means presenting a subject in concrete terms. Thus one appeals to the imagination so that the listener or reader can "see" or "hear" the situation clearly.[31] The ancients called the vivid description of a person, thing, or event *demonstratio, illustratio, evidentia,* ἐνάργεια, or ὑποτύποσις. To stimulate anger, pity, or hatred in a judge or jury, for example, ancient rhetoricians might vividly describe the scene of the crime, the results of an action, or the life of the accused or his family.[32]

What stimulates the emotions is not the mere description of a person or an event but *contact* with them.[33] Perelman and Olbrechts-Tyteca have investigated at length the notion of *presence* in argumentation. Singling out or emphasizing something in a communication act draws the attention of the audience to it and prevents it from being neglected. Such presence acts directly on our sensibility, for what is foremost in our minds tends to become important to us, at least for the moment.[34]

So one of the tasks of any communicator is to make present what is absent, that is, to choose the elements which are important enough to offer to an audience, for by dwelling on a subject the sender makes it present and stimulates the emotions associated with it.[35] This means, of course, that the contrary is also true: deliberate suppression of certain aspects tends to minimize their importance by denying them presence.[36]

There are a number of techniques for drawing attention to something and thus creating a sense of presence. Perelman and Ol-

---

(*movere*) an audience. See also QUINTILIAN, *Institutio oratoria*, VI.2.1-36; AUGUSTINE, *De doctrina christiana*, IV.12.27.

[30] UEDING and STEINBRINK, *Grundriß*, 262. See 2.5.1.1, especially n. 113-115.

[31] BURKE, *A Rhetoric of Motives*, 81.

[32] *Rhetorica ad Herennium*, II.30.49; IV.55.68; QUINTILIAN, *Institutio oratoria*, VI.2.29-32; VIII.3.61; IX.2.40.

[33] "Excitat qui dicit spirito ipso, nec imagine rerum sed rebus incendit." QUINTILIAN, *Institutio oratoria*, X.1.16.

[34] PERELMAN and OLBRECHTS-TYTECA, Traité de l'argumentation, 155-156; PERELMAN, *L'empire rhétorique, 49-50.*

[35] PERELMAN and OLBRECHTS-TYTECA, *Traité de l'argumentation*, 156-157; PERELMAN, *L'empire rhétorique,* 51.

[36] PERELMAN and OLBRECHTS-TYTECA, *Traité de l'argumentation, 158.*

brechts-Tyteca call such devices *figures of presence*:[37] repetition[38] (e.g., *anaphora, epiphora* or *epistrophe, conduplicatio, adjunctio*), amplification (e.g., aggregation, *congeries,* synonymy, *interpretatio*), and accentuation (e.g., *onomatopoeia,* imaginary direct speech [*sermocinatio* or *dialogism*], *hypotyposis* or *demonstratio, enallage* of tense). All of the figures with Latin and Greek names were known to the ancient rhetoricians. But only in recent times has it been recognized that such devices are not merely ornamental but also contribute to argumentation. They accomplish this by making their objects present and concrete. To create the emotions which persuade, a communicator must be specific.[39]

The authors of Dt 28,69–30,20 certainly did not know the Greek and Latin figures, and yet they often made use of these or similar devices (perhaps unconsciously) to stimulate emotions. One gets the impression that the vocabulary and expressions of Dt were deliberately chosen to impart presence.

4.4.1.1 Repetition

As often noted, the Third Discourse of Moses (as well as most of Dt) is rather repetitious. In fact, repetition is a characteristic of ancient Hebrew literature. Although considered monotonous by some modern Western standards, Hebrew repetitiveness has also been seen as indicative of a certain "primitiveness," spontaneity, immediacy, and freshness.[40]

Repetition can be found especially in highly formalized discourse.[41] It is also a characteristic feature of oral communication. In fact, repetition may be a necessary aspect in conversation and speeches, since it aids the memory and helps the mind to organize for itself the information it is receiving. An oral communication act must make use of devices of

---

[37] Ibid., 235-239; PERELMAN, "The New Rhetoric," 289; *L'empire rhétorique,* 51-52.

[38] "La répétition est une condition de maintain, d'entretien, des charges affectives." OLÉRON, *L'argumentation,* 62. B. JOHNSTONE, "An Introduction," *Perspectives on Repetition, Text* 7 (1987) 208, confirms that repetition is a figure of presence. As a figure of presence, repetition tends to indicate a communicator's feelings (and thus can also stir the same feelings in an audience). See CORBETT, *Classical Rhetoric,* 475; and N. NORRICK, "Functions of Repetition in Conversation," *Text* 7 (1987) 254. J. MUILENBURG, "A Study in Hebrew Rhetoric: Repetition and Style," *VTS* 1 (1953) 101-102, describes what he calls "elemental or primitive iteration," spontaneous repetitions which are used in moments of excitement and urgency, that is, in moments when emotions are aroused. I. EITAN, "La répétition de la racine en hébreu," *JPOS* 2 (1921) 172, also refers to spontaneous and popular repetitions. On pp. 172-173 he describes various uses of repetition in ancient Hebrew: interjections, apostrophe, moments of pain, superlatives, and the expression of imperatives, differences, and emphasis. EITAN never mentions terms such as "emotional" or "affective," although these occurrences of repetition occur frequently when emotions run high.

[39] PERELMAN and OLBRECHTS-TYTECA, *Traité de l'argumentation,* 198.

[40] MUILENBURG, "A Study in Hebrew Rhetoric," 101, 103.

[41] B. JOHNSTONE, "An Introduction," *Perspectives on Repetition, Text* 7 (1987) 210.

repetition in order to recall wandering thoughts, to make transitions and summaries, and to give direction to the listener.[42] Repetition also supports argumentation and can be persuasive.[43]

There is something basic, spontaneous, and even "primitive" in repetition. Human beings experience a drive to imitate, and that imitation takes place also in speech patterns. Such a drive to imitate may be based, at least partly, on the pleasure associated with the familiar.[44] Understanding is also aided by repetition, since the new is comprehended only by integrating it into familiar and repeated patterns. Thus repetition is a cohesive factor in communication acts.[45] The underlying purpose of this drive to imitate is education, for repetition is one of the most fundamental and essential activities in the learning process.[46] The tendency to repeat in the Third Discourse, then, supports any instructional or persuasive aims on the part of the author(s).

The frequent repetitions of Dt, however, seldom result in the exact same words. Rather, there is variety within the repetitions: synonyms, antonyms, different word order, a selection of the various options available, and changes in person, number, and tense often occur.[47] Such variable similarity often indicates emphases, intensification, development, or even new information. Thus repetition can actually be creative.[48]

The Third Discourse of Moses actually has a rather limited vocabulary which is often repeated. There are 785 words in Dt 28,69 – 30,20.[49] Quite a few words and expressions are repeated again and again. These include:[50]

---

[42] BRANDT, *The Rhetoric of Argumentation,* 70-71; H.A. BRONGERS, "Merismus, Synekdoche und Hendiadys in der Bibel-Hebräischen Sprache," *OTS* 14 (1965) 111; ESLINGER, *Into the Hands of the Living God,* 4, n. 4; MUILENBURG, "Form Criticism and Beyond," 17; ONG, *Oralità e scrittura,* 68-69; TANNEN, "Repetition in Conversation," 226.

[43] NORRICK, "Functions of Repetition in Conversation," 258, mentions that studies of discourse in an adolescent group show that repetition can lead to greater persuasiveness and dominance in the group. JOHNSTONE, "An Introduction," 208, notes that anthropologists have shown that in some cultures repetition is seen as rhetorically powerful because words and thoughts in themselves are seen as having creative or controlling power.

[44] TANNEN, "Repetition in Conversation," 234-235.

[45] JOHNSTONE, "An Introduction," 212.

[46] TANNEN, "Repetition in Conversation," 235.

[47] BUIS, *Le Deutéronome,* 32-33.

[48] ALTER, *The Art of Biblical Narrative,* 97; GARAVELLI, *Manuale di retorica,* 189; JOHNSTONE, "An Introduction," 211; MUILENBURG, "A Study in Hebrew Rhetoric," 98; PLEBE and EMANUELE, *Manuale di retorica,* 68, 70; REBOUL, *La rhétorique,* 52.

[49] This figure represents MT: 28,69 — 20 words; chap. 29 — 439 words; chap. 30 — 326 words. In this counting *maqqephs* were ignored, so that each element before or after a *maqqeph* is considered an individual word.

[50] The following list does not include those words or expressons occuring only twice

word	*number of occurrences*
את (direct object marker)	42
(alone)	(36)
(with personal pronoun endings)	(6)
יהוה	38
אשר	33
אלהים	28
כל	26
demonstrative pronouns and adjectives	22
personal pronouns	20
לא	18
ארץ	15
היום	13
כי	12
לבב	9
(לב)	+(2)
עשׂה	9
שׁמע	9
אמר (including לאמר)	7
ברית	7
נתן	7
שׁוב	7

Occurring six times each are למען, דבר, אלה, and ראה. Occurring five times each are עבר, לפני, כרת, הלך, בוא, אף, אבות and צוה. Occurring four times each are כתובה, ירשׁ, ידע, חיים, גוים, גדול, בנים, אדמה (always plural), שׁבט, ספר, מצוה, לקח, and שׁמים. Occurring three times each are חיה, אחר, שׁמר, קללה, פרי, עבד, נפשׁ, נדח, מצרים, כאשר, ישראל, ישׁ (verb), and תורה.

There are also a few phrases which are repeated throughout this text;

expression	*number of occurrences*
אשר אנכי מצוך היום	4
הכתובה בספר הזה	4
שׁמע בקול	4
בכל־לבבך ובכל־נפשׁך	3
לאהבה את־יהוה אלהיך	3

The mere occurrence of repetitions within a text, however, does not imply the stirring of emotions or a sense of presence. Much depends on

---

in the text. These are numerous enough (e.g., משׁה, אברהם, יצחק, יעקב, etc.). It also makes no mention of the 68 prepositions in the text, 28 of which stand alone and 40 with personal pronoun endings. In this list I have also made no distinctions between the singular and the plural forms of nouns and the various verb forms. The list is meant only to give some idea of the limited vocabulary used in the text.

the proximity of the repetitions, their arrangement, and the emphases they produce. The ancient rhetoricians named as *figures of speech* or *schemes* only significant repetitions, that is, those occurring fairly close to one another, those occurring in a certain order, or those whose use draws attention to themselves. It is also possible that the ancient Hebrew speakers made use of repetitive patterns with which we are not familiar today.

The more obvious repetitions in the Third Discourse which seem to provoke a sense of presence are the following:

1. הברית אשר־ ... כרת את־ ... ב ... , which appears twice in Dt 28,69.

2. Various combinations of the verb ראה with the noun עינים occur three times in 29,1-3.

3. The word לא occurs four times in 29,4-5. In the first two of these occurrences the repetition extends to two other words as well:

$$\text{לא־בלו} \quad \text{שלמתיכם מעליכם}$$
$$\text{ונעלך לא־בלתה} \quad \text{מעל} \quad \text{רגלך} \qquad (29,4).$$

4. In Dt 29,14 we have two parallel clauses which express contrary situations:

(כי) את־אשר ישנו פה עמנו
ואת־אשר איננו פה עמנו (היום).

Since these parallels are speaking about the audience, it certainly should provoke presence.

5. Dt 29,15 appeals to the memory of the audience and establishes its members as witnesses. This sense of presence is reinforced by repetition. Moses tells them, For you have seen...

את אשר־ישבנו ב ...
ואת אשר־עברנו ב ... .

Except for the roots ישב and עבר, which are antonyms, the words and sounds are identical.

6. Dt 29,17 links the sinful individual or group with a root producing poison and wormwood or bitterness (certainly these are emotionally "loaded" terms) with the repetition of פן־יש בכם before each part of the comparison.

7. Dt 29,21.23.24 have what the ancient Greeks called *anaphora* (repetition at the beginning of successive clauses), using ואמר (v. 21) and ואמרו (vv. 23 and 24).

8. In Dt 29,22 we have the triple occurrence of לא, which aids the stark description of the land.

9. Dt 29,23-24 has a repetitive play in the questions and answers given here: על־מה (first question), מה (second question), and על־אשר (answer).

10. In Dt 30,1-10 there are a number of repetitive devices which tie together the whole section. To begin with, there is a seven-fold use of various forms of the verb שוב. The emphasis of the passage is on conversion. Of these occurrences of שוב, the two appearing in 30,3 are an *anaphora,* since the same form occurs at the beginning of each half of the verse (ושב). The last three occurrences of the verb appear in the *qal* imperfect: ואתה תשוב (v. 8); כי שוב (v. 9); and כי תשוב (v. 10).

11. A second word repeated throughout 30,1-10 is כל. It appears 13 times in this section. Six of these occur in the three-fold appearance of the phrase בכל־לבבך ובכל־נפשך (30,2.6.10).

12. Five relative clauses beginning with the word אשר occur in 30,1-5: three in v. 1, one in v. 3, and one in v. 5. Of these five, two are parallel and synonymous:

אשר הדיחך יהוה אלהיך שמה	(v. 1)
אשר הפיצך יהוה אלהיך שמה	(v. 3).

13. The phrase אשר אנכי מצוך היום appears four times in Moses' Third Discourse — all in chapter 30 (vv. 2.8.11.16). In this short phrase Moses calls upon his own authority by using the first person pronoun (an emphatic term here) and an emotional word ("command" — צוה). Then he makes that command present by referring to the audience ("you" singular) and the time (היום).

14. Dt 30,4 gives emphasis to the return from exile (thus making that possibility present to the audience) by the repetition of the word משם.

15. Dt 30,9 emphasizes the value of fertility through the triple use of פרי: בפרי בטנך ובפרי בהמתך ובפרי אדמתך. Such blessings are further made present by the occurrence of similar-sounding לטובה and לטוב.

16. Dt 30,9b.10a.10b all begin with כי. This *anaphora* is reinforced by the double use of שוב (ישוב in v. 9b, תשוב in v. 10b) and God's name in each half verse (יהוה in v. 9b, יהוה אלהיך in both 10a and 10b).

17. Dt 30,11-13 contains a four-fold לא הוא. The first two are found in short phrases in v. 11b. The second set is accompanied by longer parallel phrases and additional repetitions:

לא בשמים הוא לאמר מי יעלה־לנו השמימה	(v. 12)
ויקחה לנו וישמענו אתה ונעשׂנה:	
ולא מעבר לים הוא לאמר מי יעבר־לנו אל־עבר הים	(v. 13)
ויקחה לנו וישמענו אתה ונעשׂנה:	

The idea that obeying the word of God is possible is reinforced by these repetitions. A strong negation is given by a double negation and two rhetorical questions with almost identical wording. There is also a quadruple לנו. The last word of each rhetorical question is later taken up and contradicted by the last word in v. 14: לעשׂתו.

That these are *figures of presence* seems fairly certain. All of them help the audience to become aware of those factors crucial for the decision it needs to make. However, there is a difficulty in ascertaining the precise feelings which a particular repetition may stir up. Perhaps such emotions are guided by the "loaded" words which will be investigated later. Yet these various repetitions do emphasize the wonders of God, his threats, his commands, conversion, blessing, and the possibility of obeying his laws.

4.4.1.2 Amplification

What may seem monotonous and redundant to the modern Westerner often points to a specific rhetorical need in an audience. A communication act, especially oral discourse, cannot sufficiently inform, much less persuade and convince, an audience by announcement and simple demonstration. Listeners (and even readers) need time to integrate the communication with what they already know and accept. The sender must develop a subject by repeating, explaining, illustrating, and expanding its ideas. "All speech thus involves the 'working out' (*ergasia*) of its inventional topics."[51] In order to be accepted, the argumentation of a communication act needs a certain amount of "fullness' or "amplitude."

Amplification or accumulation is the process which gives the necessary "fullness" or "amplitude" to a discourse. It does this through the collecting or piling up of words, phrases, or longer sections of text with the aim of keeping the subject present in the thoughts of the audience.[52] It is the opposite of brevity or conciseness, since it seeks to add to what has already been communicated. Thus amplification may include descriptions, explanations, interpretations, synonyms, parentheses, and even digressions. These devices expand, develop, and extend an argument or an idea. Amplification, like repetition, gives presence to a communication act and serves to stimulate emotions.[53]

---

[51] KENNEDY, *New Testament Interpretation*, 22.

[52] The rhetorical device known as *amplificatio* was considered effective for stirring emotions. According to MESSER LEON, *Honeycomb's Flow*, II.11.10, it was especially good for provoking wrath and indignation. QUINTILIAN, *Institutio oratoria*, VIII.4.3, divided amplification into four parts: augmentation, comparison, deliberation (or enthymeme), and amalgamation: "Quattuor tamen maxime generibus video constare amplificationem, incremento, comparatione, ratiocinatione, congerie." Later rhetoricians listed up to 64 possible figures of amplification. Logically almost any figure could fit into this category except those which aim for brevity. See LANHAM, *Handlist*, 6; LAUSBERG, *Handbuch* I, 220-227 (§400-409); MARCHESE, *Dizionario di retorica e di stilistica*, 20; UEDING and STEINBRINK, *Grundriß*, 252-255. PERELMAN and OLBRECHTS-TYTECA, *Traité de l'argumentation*, 237, note that amplification in the form of division into parts recalls a quasi-logical argument.

[53] PERELMAN and OLBRECHTS-TYTECA, *Traité de l'argumentation*, 633; PERELMAN, *L'empire rhétorique*, 51-52, 158. What I have been calling *amplification* is called "parallelism" by CORBETT, *Classical Rhetoric*, 463.

Ancient Greek and Roman rhetoricians certainly recognized the necessity of developing a discourse and giving it fullness.[54] The term in Latin for such fullness was *copia*.[55] While fullness or amplitude is not often appreciated in Western oratory and literature, the ancients felt that it was necessary. It appears likely that the ancient Hebrews felt a similar need, for the Third Discourse of Moses seems to cater to it.

A number of amplifications may be found within the Third Discourse of Moses:

1. Dt 29,1-2 reminds the audience what they have witnessed in Egypt: את כל־אשר עשה יהוה. To whom do these things happen? The recipients are divided into three groups: לפרעה ולכל־עבדיו ולכל־ארצו. This is perhaps a type of *divisio* or *peristasis*. V. 2 then details the events themselves by dividing them into המסות הגדלת...האתת והמפתים הגדלים ההם (again a division into three groups). These three nouns are also synonyms.

2. In Dt 29,3 there is a lesson to be learned. But instead of simply saying that the audience did not understand, the author puts together three concrete expressons which together describe that lack of understanding. For God did not give them לב לדעת ועינים לראות ואזנים לשמע.

3. Dt 29,4-5 is not merely repetitive but also accumulative. It lists four non-occurrences during the forty years of wandering in the desert:

לא־בלו שלמתיכם מעליכם
ונעלך לא־בלתה מעל רגלך:
לחם לא אכלתם
ויין ושכר לא שתיתם.

Such wonders would certainly provoke amazement, wonder, awe, and perhaps desire (that it happen again).

4. The participant list, found in Dt 29,9-10 (which we discussed in chapter three), is also an aggregation or accumulation, since it is a division of the audience into its parts. The description of the גר is similarly an aggregation, since it describes in greater detail what the resident immigrant does: אשר בקרב מחניך מחטב עציך עד שאב מימיך. The accumulative effect is probably not very strong, since the terms are not very concrete. The *divisio* may be more of a logical rather than a pathetic figure. However, such a lengthy description of an audience which includes near relatives may have some effect on the emotions.

5. Dt 29,11 tells us that this audience is to enter בברית ובאלתו. It doesn't seem likely that they are about to participate in two separate

---

[54] *Rhetorica ad Alexandrum*, xxxv.1441b; QUINTILIAN, *Institutio oratoria*, VIII.4. Cf. MESSER LEON, *Honeycomb's Flow*, IV.55.1; CHAIGNET, *La rhétorique et son histoire*, 464; REBOUL, *La rhétorique*, 25.

[55] LAUSBERG, *Elemente*, 24.

events. Rather here are two synonyms for the same activity, an activity further described as אשר יהוה אלהיך כרת עמך היום. This phrase could be considered an *interpretatio*. The two synonyms are found again in v. 13.

6. In Dt 29,12 דבר and נשבע are really synonyms. Each is in an explanation-clause which begins with כאשר. Afterwards the ancestors are listed by name, which is another example of amplification.

7. Dt 29,14 contains an amplificaton as well, for it heaps up and repeats words in order to emphasize the membership of the audience. עמד is a synonym of נצבים in 29,9, while ישנו and איננו are antonyms. The jarring contrast between those present and those not present *makes present* to the audience their own participation in this communication act.

8. The description of the idols in 29,16 is also accumulative. First they are named through the use of two synonyms (שקוציהם and גלליהם). Then they are further described by listing the four materials of which they are made (עץ ואבן כסף וזהב).

9. Dt 29,17 divides possible sinners into four categories: איש או אשה או משפחה או־שבט.

10. Other synonyms are used frequently in Dt 28,69 – 30,20: אף and חמה, אף in 29,19; מכות and תחלאיה in 29,21; וישתחוו and ויעבדו in 29,25; קנאתו and קצף in 29,27; שנאיך and איביך in 30,4; יקחך and יקבצך in 30,7; המצוה in 30,11 is a synonym of הדבר in 30,14; ועבדתם and והשתחוית in 30,17; and חיים and ארך ימיך in 30,20.

11. In 29,21 הדור האחרון receives an explanation which is an aggregation:

בניכם אשר יקומו מאחריכם
והנכרי אשר יבא מארץ רחוקה.

It gives presence to a future event (which may be contemporary for a future audience!). There is also an explanation for the diseases: אשר־חלה יהוה בה.

12. The description of the afflicted land in Dt 29,22 is quite vivid. It is certainly an example of what the ancient rhetoricians called ἐνάργεια or *demonstratio*. The land is described in an accumulation of terms of destructive materials: גפרית ומלח שרפה כל־הארצה. Three synonymous phrases then proclaim the lack of vegetation: לא תזרע ולא תצמח ולא־יעלה בה כל־עשב. Then comes a comparison with four cities which God had previously destroyed with fire.

13. Dt 29,23-27 presents a conversation or question-and-answer scheme. V. 23 gives two questions which are quite similar. The answer which follows is lengthy. The people have abandoned the covenant which God made with their ancestors, the covenant אשר כרת עמם בהוציאו אתם מארץ מצרים (v. 24). Then the explanation becomes more detailed. How did they abandon the covenant? By the worship of other gods, אלהים אשר לא־ידעום ולא חלק להם (v. 25). Then the result of this abandonment is given:

the anger of God, the activation of the curses (v. 26), the uprooting of the people and their exile because of God's anger (v. 27). Expressions for God's anger (ויחר־אף in v. 26; באף ובחמה ובקצף in v. 27) are accumulated to make that anger seem very real and present.

14. In 30,1 the effect is continued by an aggregation of legal terms (כל־הדברים האלה הברכה והקללה) and an explanation (אשר נתתי לפניך).

15. Dt 30,1.3 contain the synonyms הגוים and העמים. Each is followed by an *interpretatio* (אשר הדיחך/הפיצך יהוה אלהיך שמה). V. 2 also accumulates phrases, for it insists that the audience must obey ככל אשר־אנכי מצוך היום and בכל־לבבך ובכל־נפשך.

16. Dt 30,5 gives a short description of the land as that אשר־ירשו אבתיך וירשתה.

17. Dt 30,9 indicates four ways in which God could make this audience prosper: בכל מעשה ידך בפרי בטנך ובפרי בהמתך ובפרי אדמתך.

18. In Dt 30,10 there are two words used as synonyms for the תורה which appears later in the verse: מצותיו and חקתיו. These commandments and stipulations are further described as those הכתובה בספר התורה הזה.

19. Again 30,11 describes this מצוה as the one אשר אנכי מצוך היום. Not only is הדבר in 30,14 its synonym, but each word has an adjective which builds up the notion that the law is possible: it is close (קרוב — v. 14) and not far (לא רחקה — v. 11). In fact, repetition is joined with accumulation to overwhelm the doubter: it is not too difficult, it is not too far, it is not in heaven, it is not over the sea. Here it is obvious that the law is very present and as such is also possible.

20. The choice offered in 30,15.19 is not limited to two possibilities. We have both synonyms and antonyms here: In v. 15 החיים is a synonym of הטוב; both of these are antonyms of the synonymous pair המות and הרע. In v. 19 החיים is a synonym of הברכה and an antonym of המות, while הקללה is a synonym of המות and an antonym of הברכה. Each of the two verses presents the choice in a different way. V. 15 lines up the equivalent "goods" first and then contrasts these with equivalent "evils," all of which follow the verb (נתתי לפניך). V. 19 gives two contrasts (good vs. good vs. bad) which are separated by נתתי לפניך.

21. Dt 30,20 gives an accumulation of three tasks that must be performed in order to choose life, all of which are synonymous:

לאהבה את־יהוה אלהיך
לשמע בקלו
ולדבקה־בו.

It also once again lists the names of the three ancestors.

What is made present through such amplification? The audience becomes aware of its history and its relationship with a powerful God. It also becomes aware of itself, for it is a widely inclusive group which is about to enter into a covenant. Idols and sinners too are made present, but these are associated with what is disgusting and with terrifying punishments. God's promises of blessings are brought to mind, as well as his covenant regulations and the choice that must be made. Generally speaking, the figures of presence represented by amplification or accumulation seem to establish negative feelings toward idols and sin and positive feelings toward Yahweh and his covenant.

4.4.1.3 Accentuation (Emphasis)

Various rhetorical devices also develop a sense of presence through accentuation or emphasis. These include *onomatopoeia,* imaginary direct speech, vivid description (ἐνάργεια, *demonstratio,* or *hypotyposis*), and *enallage* of tense. Certain emphatic words could also do this.

There is imaginary direct speech in Dt 29,18 which produces the thoughts of the sinner in the first person. The audience is reminded that not even their thoughts can escape the judgment of God. The imaginary case is made vivid and present by this citation. There is also an imaginary conversation, a question-and-answer scheme, in 29,23-27. The direct quote from God in 29,5 would also be emphatic and would heighten a sense of presence. An imagined citation of the audience also takes place in 30,12-13.

As already mentioned in the previous section, the description of the afflicted land in Dt 29,22 can be considered an example of ἐνάργεια or *demonstratio.* A land covered with sulphur, salt, and fire; where nothing can be planted or, if planted, nothing can grow; a land suffering an overthrow similar to that of the legendary Sodom, Gomorrah, Admah, and Zeboiim — such a land is an awful place indeed. One can visualize such a desolate and unproductive wilderness easily through this description. The description itself actually begins in v. 21 with the mention of מכות הארץ and the תחלאיה אשר־חלה יהוה בה.

Concreteness of expression also refers to individual words and phrases in a text. The authors of the Third Discourse of Moses do use general and abstract terms (e.g., אלה, אלהים אחרים, המפתים, האתת, המסות, החיים, הרע ,הטוב ,טובה ,ברכה, and המות). However, they also give some rather specific terms, some of which are metaphors: שכר, יין, לחם, נעלך, סיחן מלך־, שלמתיכם, ארץ מצרים, יצחק, אברהם, גרך, היום, מנשי, גדי, ראבני, עוג מלך־הבשן,חשבון, שרש פרה ראש ולענה, עץ ואבן כסף וזהב, יעקב (metaphor), יעשן (metaphor), מצרים, אדמה וצביים סדם ועמרה, שרפה, גפרית ומלח, בספר הזה, רבצה (metaphor), מל, לבבך (metaphor), וישלכם (metaphor), ויתשם, בהוציאו אתם מארץ מפיך, בפיך, and הירדן.

4.4.2 Emotional Words and Techniques

The second general method for producing emotions in an audience is the simulation of those emotions in the speaker. This technique was considered quite important in ancient rhetoric.[56] However, it is suitable only for oral discourse, since the reader cannot perceive the emotions of a writer so easily. But even in written discourse there are techniques for showing emotions.

Certainly one of the strongest means for provoking presence and emotions comes from the continual use of the second person, both singular and plural. Of the 785 words in the Third Discourse, 142 (or 18.1%) are marked with a second-person indicator (103 in the singular, 39 in the plural). Of these there are thirty verbs in the second person (16 in the singular, 14 in the plural). There are also 104 nouns, adjectives, and prepositions which have personal pronoun endings (82 in the singular, 22 in the plural). The most emphatic words, however, are those personal pronouns which are addressed directly to the audience. There are two direct object markers with second person plural endings (אתכם) in Dt 29,4.13. More importantly, three plural pronouns (אתם) occur as a subject or a vocative in 29,1.9.15. Similarly, five singular pronouns (אתה) occur in 30,2.8.16.18.19. These eight pronouns, indicating both the collective and individualistic nature of the audience, would certainly add a strong sense of presence to this text.

There are also various kinds of emotionally "loaded" words in the Third Discourse of Moses. Certainly one type comes in the form of the imperative or command, which appeals directly to an audience. Actually, there are not many imperatives or commands in the Third Discourse of Moses, so perhaps the occurrence of an imperative is to be noted. Imperatives promote presence, since they appeal directly to an audience and cannot be ignored. One must respond either positively or negatively to a command.

In Dt 28,69 God *commands* Moses to make a covenant with Israel. This is no imperative in itself, but we are informed that Moses himself receives and carries out an order. The fact that his discourse is the carrying out of this order gives Moses (and his words) a certain authority, an ethos. Thus when Moses himself gives a command, it's bound to be seen as a derivation of God's command.

In fact, the entire Third Discourse can be seen as one long command, since Moses mentions four times that he is giving the audience orders (אשר אנכי מצוך היום — Dt 30,2.8.11.16). In 30,2 this statement is a very general description of כל. It could refer to all the discourses of Moses. In v. 8 it modifies כל־מצותיו, The phrase in v. 11 refers more

---

[56] See especially CICERO, *Brutus*, lxxx.279.

specifically to *this* commandment, המצוה הזאת, but this commandment is not further defined. Thus it could also refer to everything that Moses has commanded. Only in v. 16 is there an object to the verb: לאהבה את־יהוה אלהיך ללכת בדרכיו ולשמר מצותיו וחקתיו ומשפטיו. This verse might be considered a summary of the Third Discourse or even of all of Dt: Moses commands the people to love God, to walk in his ways, and to observe his precepts.

The only word in Dt 28,69-30,20 with a specifically imperative form is רְאֵה which is found in 30,15. Actually this word can be considered an interjection, with a meaning similar to הנה. It is used as a means of drawing attention.[57] Having lost its real function as an imperative, it is still emphatic and attention-getting. The only command it really gives is to pay attention.

Only three of the 30 second-person verbs in Dt 28,69-30,20 can be considered as imperatives, and none of these has a normal imperative form. All three are *wᵉqataltís* (*waw*-consecutive perfects): ושמרתם and ועשיתם in 29,8 and ובחרת in 30,19. Because of the form, these verbs have not always been translated as imperatives,[58] but their context seems to insist on it, especially in 30,19. Although not a frequent occurrence, a perfect form with a *waw*-consecutive can be used to introduce a command or a wish.[59] It seems that ושמרתם and ועשיתם in 29,8 would be best translated by an imperative, although a future meaning would make sense here as well. But in 30,19 there is a choice offered between החיים and המות, between הברכה and הקללה, and the *qal* imperfect second-person singular verb ובחרת would almost certainly have to be translated "choose!" Even if we would translate the verb as a future here, the use of the *wᵉqatalti* would be an optimistic and emphatic prediction: "you *will* choose life!"

There are also a number of individual words and expressions in the Third Discourse which we might call "loaded," since they tend to arouse certain emotions when they are heard or read, and they may indicate the

---

[57] BROWN, DRIVER, and BRIGGS, *A Hebrew and English Lexicon of the Old Testament*, 907b; W. HOLLADAY, *A Concise Hebrew and Aramaic Lexicon of the Old Testament* (Leiden 1971) 328; GKC, §105b.

[58] The following translate one or both of the verbs ושמרתם and ועתשים (29,8) as imperatives: Vg, BJ, BUIS, CEI, EÜ, LACONI, NAB, REB, RSV (only ושמרתם, VON RAD; while the following do not: LXX (B), Targ. Onkelos, BLC, BUIS and LECLERCQ, CRAIGIE, LLS, NEB, PENNA and TOB. The following translate ובחרת (30,19) as an imperative: LXX (B) Vg, BJ, BLC (in the plural!), BUIS, BUIS and LECLERCQ, CEI, EÜ, LACONI, LLS, NAB, NEB, REB, RSV, and VON RAD; while the following do not: Targ. Onkelos, CRAIGIE, TOB. CRAIGIE, *Deuteronomy*, 366, translates ובחרת as "you shall choose," but he admits that Moses' "words are virtually a command." In many languages the future tense can substitute at times for the imperative.

[59] GKC, §112aa. Another example in Dt would be in 10,19.

author's feelings about the subject. Usually such terms are concrete rather than abstract.

First of all, there are those names and events associated with national or ethnic history. Most if not all social groups would seem to have a specific vocabulary that reminds them of their common bonds and common history. Israel could not have been an exception. Certainly some feelings would have been stirred up by words such as אדמה, אברהם, אבותך, מצרים, מדבר, לפני יהוה, ישראל, יצחק, יעקב, טפכם, חרב, זקניכם, גר, בניכם, ארץ, איביך, פרעה, עם, עוג, סחון, סדם ועמרה, נכרי, נחלה, and שבטיכם. Such words would certainly provoke memories, and with memories come feelings such as pride, a sense of bonding, fear or disgust. Such words would reinforce a sense of belonging as well as provoke emotions associated with a social group that has its own history.[60]

There are also those words which provoke certain kinds of feelings among most human beings: רע (fear, hatred, disgust); טוב (desire, satisfaction); מלחמה (fear, hatred, courage); מות (fear or horror, hatred); חיים or חיה or ארך ימיך (desire); and נשבע (fear, expectation). And what about the verb "love" (אהב), which appears three times in the Third Discourse of Moses (Dt 30,6.16.20)? Could the mention of such a feeling stir the same feeling?

The words אלה (29,11.13.18.19.20; 30,7) and קללה (29,26; 30,1.19) certainly cannot be neutral terms, for they carry with them a threatening or negative aspect.[61] In a similar manner their antonym, ברכה (30,1.19; see also the verb ברך in 29,18; 30,16), would carry with it a promising aspect or a positive feeling. One normally fears or at least respects an

---

[60] The presence of certain stock historical motifs (conventions) assures the audience that the history they hear is authentic. Historical references help a community to create and define its identity. Thus what is involved is not only facticity but also the audience's self-identity and its feelings about itself. "With history, especially of the corporate sort found in the Bible, the claim on the audience is much more profound. Rather than 'This is something which *might have* happened to someone *like you or me'*, the claim is, 'This *is* what happened to *us'*. It is our story and so has profound moral implications for how we see ourselves and how we live. As is the case with didactic fiction, or any discourse which makes some sort of truth-claim, this history also provides corroboration for its claim.... Insofar as the auditors find themselves responding with the warm glow of familiar recognition: 'Yes, this is who we are', the 'truth' of the story has been corroborated." PATRICK and SCULT, *Rhetoric and Biblical Interpretation,* 50. See also pp. 39 and 51. HEXTER, *Doing History,* 42-43, 68, reminds us that history is never pure facticity, since rhetoric also appears in its writing. The audience is important also for the historian, since an audience wants a kind of vicarious participation in the events of the past — especially the great moments of its own past.

[61] C.A. KELLER, "אלה," *THAT* I, 150, 152; "קלה," *THAT* II, 645-646; A. LEFÈVRE, "Malédiction et bénédiction," *SDB* V, 746; J. SCHARBERT, "'Fluchen' und 'Segnen' im Alten Testament," *Bib* 39 (1958) 2-4, 11-12.

oath or a curse, while blessings are generally desired or hoped for, for they have the power to transmit happiness.[62]

Similarly, words and expressions for anger[63] (especially *God's* anger) should touch feelings such as fear or horror. In Moses' Third Discourse such terms are found frequently in Dt 29,19-27: אף־יהוה וקנאתו (29,19); באף ובחמה (29,22); חרי האף (29,23); ויחר־אף יהוה (29,26); and באפו ובחמתו ובקצף (29,27). It is not only God's anger which is horrifying but also the terrible things which such anger threatens to accomplish: לא־יאבה יהוה סלח (29,20); והבדילו יהוה לרעה (29,19); ומחה יהוה את־שמו מתחת השמים לו (29,19); as well as the terrible ills inflicted on the land as a result of Israel's apostasy (29,21-22) and the fulfillment of the curses (29,20.26). In 30,18 comes the equally terrifying threat אבד תאבדון.

Metaphorical terms add to the concreteness and vividness of the language in the Third Discourse, especially in the description of God's threats and punishments. His anger and jealousy "smoke" (יעשׁן — 29,19), while the curse "couches" like an animal or "settles upon" the sinner (רבצה — 29,19). Such descriptions are certainly intended to stimulate fear, horror, or both. As a punishment the nation is "rooted up" or "plucked out" like a plant from the ground (ויתשם יהוה מעל אדמתם — 29,27) and "thrown" to another land (וישלכם אל־ארץ אחרת — 29,27). These are rather vivid and powerful images of punishment, and certainly they inspire fear, dread, or horror. It is possible if not likely that these are some of the emotions which the communicators themselves must have experienced.

There are still other words and expressions which are emotionally "loaded." These may include the use of וישתחוו in 29,25 and והשתחוית in 30,17. In each case some form of the verb עבד is also used, and the reference is to other gods. In the book of Dt the *hištafel* form of חוה occurs eight times, and only once does it refer to bowing down before Yahweh (Dt 26,10). Otherwise in Dt it always describes an act of worship of other gods.[64] Since it is used so often to describe reverence towards other gods, its emotional content could be rather negative. Certainly the authors of the Third Discourse of Moses felt horror and revulsion when such a word was applied to idols.

---

[62] C.A. KELLER and G. WEHMEIER, "ברך," *THAT* I, 365-367; LEFÈVRE, "Malédiction et bénédiction," 748.

[63] Terms for anger are found throughout Dt. אף is found in 6,15; 7,4; 9,19; 11,17; 13,18; 29,19.22.23.26.27; 31,17; 32,22; and 33,10. חמה is found in 9,19; 29,22.27; 32,24.33. קצף is found in 29,27. See PENNA, *Deuteronomio*, 32-33.

[64] Dt 4,19; 5,9; 8,19; 11,16; 17,3; 29,25; 30,17. The word עבד also occurs together with חוה in each of these passages. In fact, the use of the two words together is never associated with legitimate worship of Yahweh. See LOHFINK, *Das Hauptgebot*, 75; H.D. PREUSS, "הוה," *TWAT* II, 791-794, especially 793-794; H.-P. STÄHLI, "הוה," *THAT* I, 523-533.

Such feelings of horror and revulsion, as well as contempt and scorn, can be perceived in the use of the words שקוציהם and גלליהם in Dt 29,16. גלולים is a word of contempt used in the polemic against idols in the exilic period (and perhaps also previous to the exile). The word has even been associated with גלל, "ordure," "excrement," or "filth."[65] The term שקוצים was similarly a word of disdain and scorn.[66] Its very meaning — "abominable things," "detestable things," "detested things" — makes it evident that this was no neutral term.

In Dt 29,17 there is a metaphor which compares the sinner with a plant. The comparison is hardly complimentary, since the plant's root (or stock) produces ראש ולענה. ראש was some kind of poisonous plant, but the term eventually took on the general meaning "poison." לענה is usually translated as "wormwood." Both terms have been associated with specific plants, but the connections are tenuous.[67] In any case there is a sense of contempt, disdain, or even horor in the use of such terms for a person.

Another negative term is שררות לב which appears in Dt 29,18. It denotes obstinate thought or reflection and is a characteristic expression in Jeremiah.[68]

Finally, there are three strong statements issued by Moses near the end of his Third Discourse, statements phrased in what may be legal terminology. In Dt 30,18 Moses proclaims in the first person הגדתי ("I declare"); in 30,19 he asserts העידתי ("I call to witness"); in the same verse this is followed by נתתי ("I place" or "give"). The first two statements are threats, for with them Moses announces the destruction of the people if they make the wrong choice. Solemnly Moses declares the annihilation of those who err and calls upon heaven and earth as witnesses to the choice he now offers the people. Such declarations come in the first person

---

[65] DRIVER, *Deuteronomy*, 324; KNAPP, *Deuteronomium 4*, 147; H.D. PREUSS, *Verspottung fremder Religionen im Alten Testament* (BWANT 92; Stuttgart 1971) 156-157; "גלולים," *TWAT* II, 1-2; RASHI, in ROSENBAUM and SILBERMANN, *Pentateuch with Targum Onkelos, Haphtaroth and Rashi's Commentary*, 145; REITER, "Der Bundesschluß," 168.

[66] BREIT, *Die Predigt*, 52; DRIVER, *Deuteronomy*, 323-324; NTAGWARARA, "Alliance d'Israël," 91-92; PREUSS, *Verspottung fremder Religionen*, 156-157; RASHI, in ROSENBAUM and SILBERMANN, *Pentateuch with Targum Onkelos, Haphtaroth and Rashi's Commentary*, 145.

[67] W. McKANE, "Poison, Trial by Ordeal and the Cup of Wrath," *VT* 30 (1980) 478-479; PENNA, *Deuteronomio*, 238; WEINFELD, *Deuteronomy and the Deuteronomic School*, 91, n. 2; M. ZOHARY, *Plants of the Bible* (Cambridge 1982) 184, 186. H.L. GINSBERG, "'Roots Below and Fruit Above' and Related Matters," *Hebrew and Semitic Studies Presented to Godfrey Rolls Driver* (ed. D.W. THOMAS and W.D. McHARDY; Oxford 1963) 75, suggests that שרש actually means "stock" and פרה means "branch out." Thus the expression in Dt 29,17b means "a stock branching out into poison weed and wormwood."

[68] It occurs 10 times in the Hebrew Bible, of which 8 are in Jeremiah: Dt 29,18; Jer 3,17; 7,24; 9,13; 11,8; 13,10; 16,12; 18,12; 23,17; and Ps 81,13. See PENNA, *Deuteronomio*, 238; WEINFELD, *Deuteronomy and the Deuteronomic School*, 105-106, n. 105.

singular, in what seems to be legal or juridical language,[69] and with an ethos that has been built up throughout three discourses. So these statements must be powerful indeed. The listener or reader should feel fear and awe and should have the sense that this occasion and this decision are important.

4.4.3 Conclusion

Both ethos and pathos touch the affective life of the human person. *Pathos* is that mode of argumentation which induces emotions in an audience. The two major techniques for producing such emotions are lowering the level of abstraction and the simulation of emotions in the sender. Lowering the level of abstraction generally means presenting a subject in concrete terms, especially through figures of presence. These devices include repetition, amplification, and accentuation or emphasis. The Third Discourse of Moses makes use of numerous repetitions, descriptions, and emphatic words and phrases in order to make present the necessity of a choice between Yahweh and the other gods. This sense of presence provokes negative feelings towards the sinner and towards the worship of other gods and positive feelings towards Yahweh's covenant.

The second technique for producing emotions is their simulation in the sender. This is a powerful technique in oral discourse, but such emotions cannot be so readily perceived in a written text. However, through the use of various grammatical devices and emotionally "loaded" words, such feelings can still be expressd. The use of the second person; the emphasis on commands; and numerous words and phrases evoking national pride, hopes and fears, contempt and disgust all impart an affective message to the audience of the Third Discourse of Moses.

Which emotions would an audience of Dt 28,69–30,20 feel? These seem to be fear, horror, loathing or disgust, contempt, and perhaps hatred towards foreign gods and their worshippers. On the other hand there is evidence of ethnic or national pride, wonder or awe, admiration, and perhaps love, all in the service of Yahweh's covenant. There is no doubt, then, about the intent of the Third Discourse of Moses. In its argumentation, in its process of persuasion, it does not ignore the emotions of its audience but rather appeals to them.

4.5 Logos

The third mode of argumentation, logos, is the appeal to reason. The logic of rhetoric, however, is not identical to the logic of scientific

---

[69] At least in Dt 1,8 נתן לפני is considered legal language according to N. Lohfink, "Darstellungskunst und Theologie in Dtn 1,6-3,29," *Bib* 41 (1960) 125-126.

demonstration, since it deals with the probable rather than with what is necessarily and universally true. Nevertheless it is still a rational appeal, an appeal to reason.

For modern Westerners rational argumentation and logic depend on *proof* — "the presentation of evidence and arguments in a causal chain intended to pull the mind toward belief."[70]

> We claim that we know something when we are able to prove it. To prove [*apo-deiknumi*] means to *show* something to be something, on the basis of something. To have something through which something is shown and explained definitively is the foundation of our knowledge.[71]

Since its beginnings rhetoric has recognized that the proof required for oratory was probable rather than necessary. This link between persuasion and the probable was discovered and developed by Aristotle.[72] The function of rhetoric is to persuade, and in matters where truth is not self-evident, persuasion must be based on what is probable — that is, on the basis of what is reasonable, what usually happens, or what people believe can happen.[73]

The ancients looked upon proof differently than we do, since not only logos but also pathos and ethos were considered part of *internal* or *artificial* proof (*probationes artificiales* or πίστεις ἔντεχνοι). *External* or *nonartificial* proof (*probationes inartificiales* or πίστεις ἄτεχνοι) included laws, contracts, documents, confessions, acts, oaths, witnesses, and citations — what we today would normally call *evidence*.[74] Modern Westerners do not usually think of ethos and pathos as valid proofs. Rather they tend to give logos, especially the discipline which we call *logic*, a certain primacy in argumentation.[75] In doing so, of course, we tend to forget that any logic is a learned system and necessarily part of the culture in which it is learned.[76]

---

[70] BOOTH, *Now Don't Try to Reason with Me*, 6. Cf. CONDON and YOUSEF, *An Introduction to Intercultural Communication*, 213.

[71] GRASSI, *Rhetoric as Philosophy*, 19.

[72] ARISTOTLE, *Rhetoric*, I.2.1357a.

[73] BRANDT, *The Rhetoric of Argumentation*, 42-43; CORBETT, *Classical Rhetoric*, 73.

[74] ARISTOTLE, *Rhetoric*, I.2.1355b; in I.15.1375a-1377b, he discusses inartificial proof; *Rhetorica ad Herennium*, II.6.9-II.7.12; CICERO, *De oratore*, II.116; QUINTILIAN, *Institutio oratoria*, V.1.1-2 (he discusses inartificial proof in Book V, chaps. 1-7, and artificial proof in chap. 8); LANHAM, *Handlist*, 106-107; MARCHESE, *Dizionario di retorica e di stilistica*, 151; UEDING and STEINBRINK, *Grundriß*, 218. VICKERS, *In Defence of Rhetoric*, 69-70, points out that in Greco-Roman law probability (and the artificial proof based upon it) was more credible than witnesses or evidence.

[75] KANE, *Logic*, 5.

[76] CONDON and YOUSEF, *An Introduction to Intercultural Communication*, 212-213. They remind us that "there are many logics, each being a system with its own assumptions and consistent in itself, and different cultures will express different logics" (213).

It should be kept in mind that the Greek word λόγος is an ambiguous word, since it may be used both concretely (a word, words, an oration or speech) and abstractly (the meaning of a word, the power of thought, the rational principle of the universe, even the will of God). It involves human thought and reason, but also the power to create.[77] The appeals to reason of an ancient orator were not strict applications of logic but adaptations to it. For this reason the enthymeme and the example take on great importance in the logos of rhetoric.[78]

4.5.1 Enthymemes

The enthymeme, as we have already discovered,[79] is the rhetorical equivalent of the syllogism. Its function is to move from what is already accepted by an audience to the conclusion proposed by the communicator. It may be seen as a syllogism with one premise missing or simply as a statement supported by a reason.[80] Based on probability and a reserve of opinions, values, attitudes, and conventions, the enthymeme is nevertheless reasonable.

In the Third Discourse of Moses there are few obvious enthymemes. One gets the impression that the language and thought patterns of ancient Israel did not conform well to the pattern of syllogisms and enthymemes so well known in ancient Greece and Rome. However, the arguments presented in Dt 28,69–30,20 can often be drawn out in the form of enthymemes. The main premise can normally be surmised by ascertaining the presumptions of the text.

1. In Dt 29,1-8 there are listed a number of wonderful things which Yahweh has done for his people in the past (כל־אשר עשה יהוה: 29,1). This series of *examples* gives the impression of *inductive* reasoning. Its conclusion: Yahweh is wonderful, great, or powerful. An implied enthymeme can be built from this inductive process:

p¹: [All gods who do these things are powerful/great/wonderful.]
p²: Yahweh is a God who does these things.
c: Therefore, Yahweh is powerful/great/wonderful.

Here p¹ = major premise; p² = minor premise; and c = conclusion. The brackets [] indicate an unstated or presumed proposition.

2. The conclusion of the first implied enthymeme serves as the minor premise of another enthymeme which appears in Dt 29,8. It concerns the

---

[77] G. KENNEDY, *The Art of Persuasion in Greece* (Princeton, N.J. 1963) 8.
[78] CORBETT, *Classical Rhetoric,* 51.
[79] See 2.5.1.1.
[80] BRANDT, *The Rhetoric of Argumentation,* 32; KENNEDY, *New Testament Interpretation,* 7.

two verbs ושמרתם and ועשיתם, which have the force of an imperative. This enthymeme can be expressed in two different ways:

    p¹: [All powerful/wonderful gods should be obeyed.]
    p²: Yahweh is a powerful/wonderful God.
    c: Therefore, Yahweh should be obeyed.

Since, however, obedience to Yahweh is expressed through הברית הזאת, perhaps this enthymeme could be better stated in the following way:

    p¹: [Every powerful/wonderful god's covenant should be observed.]
    p²: Yahweh is a powerful/wonderful God.
    c: Therefore, Yahweh's covenant should be observed.

This is certainly the conclusion which the authors of Dt 29,1-8 wish to arrive at.

3. There is yet another enthymeme in Dt 29,8. This may be the closest in form to a true enthymeme in these eight verses. However, it must be expressed as a conditional proposition:

    p¹: [All who observe God's covenant will prosper.]
    p²: If you observe God's covenant,
    c: You will prosper.

4. Dt 29,1-5 (especially vv. 4-5) have another hidden enthymeme, since another conclusion can also be drawn from the examples. The presumption regards witness value and understanding or knowledge:

    p¹: [All who have seen something wonderful will understand.]
    p²: You have seen something wonderful.
    c: Therefore, you will understand (that I am Yahweh).

The words למען תדעו כי means "in order that you may know (or understand) that." Because this understanding is drawn from the examples, it seems one can be justified in translating it as "in order that you may conclude (or infer) that."

5. A similar inference occurs in Dt 29,16-17. The unstated presumption which forms the major premise regards what is detestable or disgusting:

    p¹: [All who have seen disgusting things should avoid them.]
    p²: You have seen disgusting things (v. 16).
    c: Therefore, you should avoid them.

Perhaps this enthymeme could be expressed better as a conditional proposition:

    p¹: [If you have seen disgusting things, you should avoid them.]
    p²: You have seen disgusting things.
    c: Therefore, you should avoid them.

6. Dt 29,17 contains another enthymeme which can also be stated conditionally. Once again the major premise is an unstated presumption:

p¹: [All who worship other gods turn away from Yahweh.]
p²: If you worship other gods,
c: (Then) you turn away from Yahweh.

7. There is certainly an enthymeme in Dt 29,18, but there is also a problem getting at it. The second half of the verse is considered a *crux interpretum*. It is necessary to investigate this verse more thoroughly.

V. 17 has already mentioned the possibility of apostasy by איש או־אשה או משפחה או־שבט. Such apostasy occurs when the heart turns from Yahweh to worship other gods. V. 18 now presents the case of the individual sinner who plots apostasy in his heart (והתברך בלבבו לאמר). What are his secret thoughts? שלום יהיה־לי כי בשררות לבי אלך: "I will be safe (literally: peace will be to me, that is, I will have peace) if/though I walk in the stubbornness of my heart." Then follows the difficult section: למען ספות הרוה את־הצמאה.

These words by themselves are not difficult: למען normally means "in order to," "in order that," "so that." ספה means "take away," "carry off," "snatch away"; however, other meanings have also been suggested.[81] רוה means "drenched," "wet," "well-watered," "saturated." And צמא means "thirsty," "arid," or "dry." But putting the words together into a meaningful whole has been problematic. For ספות is an infinitive, רוה and צמאה are feminine, and את could be either a direct-object marker or the preposition "with." Does למען express purpose or result? Is ספות transitive or intransitive?[82] The question is

---

[81] For example, Buis and Leclercq, *Le Deutéronome*, 182, mention that ספות could be explained by the Arabic word *shafâ*, "to quench or slake the thirst." J. Blau, "Über homonyme und angeblich homonyme Wurzeln II," *VT* 7 (1957) 99-100, also accepts this derivation and meaning. He translates: "damit die Sättigung den Durst stille d.h., um meine Gelüste zu befriedigen." He sees this as an allusion to sacred prostitution. Montet, *Le Deutéronome et la question de l'Hexateuque*, 562-563, suggests that in this case ספה is a synonym of יסף, "add." Rofé, "The Covenant in the Land of Moab," 313, suggests that the word is related to the Ugaritic word *s.p.'.*, "eat" or "feed." Thus he proposes a simile from drought and hunger: "the sated, irrigated land will feed the thirsty, dry land."

[82] Driver, *Deuteronomy*, 325; H. Ringgren, "סָפָה," *TWAT* V, 908. Here are some of the ways in which the phrase has been translated:

1. BJ: "si bien que l'abondance d'eau fera disparaître la soif."
2. BLC: "perché la pioggia metterà fine alla siccità."
3. CEI: "con il pensiero che il terreno irrigato faccia sparire quello arido..."
4. EÜ: "damit Wasserfülle die Dürre beendet."
5. NAB: "as though to sweep away both the watered soil and the parched ground."
6. NEB: "but this will bring everything to ruin."
7. REB: "but this will bring sweeping disaster."

whether the passage means "to carry away the wet with the dry" or "for the wet carries away the dry" or something similar. Even if one of these is the proper translation, what does it mean?

The early versions also seem to be uncertain about this phrase. LXX has ἵνα μὴ συναπολέσῃ ὁ ἁμαρτωλὸς τὸν ἀναμάρτητον (in order that the sinner not destroy the innocent). This may be an excellent interpretation of what the Hebrew means, but it is definitely *not* what the Hebrew says. Targ. Onkelos translates with בדיל לאוספא (לה) חטאי שלותא על זידנותא (in order to collect the sins of forgetfulness [that is, those committed unwittingly], along with those of willfulness).[83]

Another difficulty concerns the extent of the quotation signed by לאמר. Is v. 18b part of the sinner's thought or is it a comment on this apostasy by Moses? Where one ends the quotation would certainly affect the translation.[84]

Many commentators consider Dt 29,18b to be some sort of proverb or maxim.[85] And that is what in fact it seems to be. The proverb or maxim in many societies is considered an important source of proof. Its authority comes from experience, and one who can quote proverbs is normally considered wise, for they were often used with didactic purposes and moral persuasion in mind.[86] Maxims invite the listener or reader to participate in the thought processes of the communicator. They are also

---

8. RSV: "This would lead to the sweeping away of moist and dry alike."
9. TOB: "puisqu'il est vrai que terre arrosée n'a plus soif."
10. BDB: "to snatch away the moist with the dry."
11. BUIS: "je verrai arrosées mes terres les plus sèches"
12. BUIS and LECLERCQ: "en jouissant du mouillé comme du sec!"
13. CHOLEWINSKI: "affinché ciò che è irrigato faccia sparire ciò che è secco." Or: "per strappar via ciò che è irrigato insieme a ciò che è secco."
14. PENNA: "sì che il terreno irrigato faccia sparire quello asciutto."
15. RASHI: "to add drunkenness to the thirst."
16. RENNES: "de façon que ce qui est abreuvé supprime ce qui est assoiffé."
17. VON RAD: "und damit das Bewässerte samt dem Trockenen wegzuraffen!"

[83] NTAGWARARA, "Alliance d'Israël," 79, translates the Targum thus: "pour pouvoir ajouter les fautes de l'inadvertance aux fautes délibérées."

[84] Some translations (such as NEB, REB, and RSV) end the quote at אלך; thus the *crux interpretum* is an evaluation of the sinner's thoughts. Many if not most translations (e.g., BJ, BLC, CEI, EÜ, and TOB) include the entire verse within the sinner's thoughts. But others either translate as if there were no citation (NAB) or are ambiguous (VON RAD).

[85] CHOLEWINSKI, *Deuteronomio* II, 24; MONTET, *Le Deutéronome et la question de l'Hexateuque,* 562; NTAGWARARA, "Alliance d'Israël," 98; REITER, "Der Bundesschluß," 53-54.

[86] CONDON and YOUSEF, *An Introduction to Intercultural Communication,* 244; FRYE, *Anatomy of Criticism,* 298; A.R. JOHNSON, "מָשָׁל," *Wisdom in Israel and in the Ancient Near East* (ed. M. NOTH and D.W. THOMAS), *VTS* 3 (1960) 164.

general statements which command immediate assent.[87] They can serve as premises or conclusions in enthymemes.[88]

The maxim or proverb in Dt 29,18b also seems to form part of an enthymeme. Whether את is an object-marker or a preposition, whether הרוה has to be translated as a subject or a direct object, it is evident that the phrase is aiming at some description of totality. For it brings together two opposites or contraries, הרוה (wet, watered) and הצמאה (dry, thirsty). Somehow what is wet or watered will take away, feed, or add to what is dry or thirsty. The dry will be taken care of or provided for, no matter what it does. This seems to be the sense of the proverb.[89]

I suggest that this maxim or proverb is part of the thought process of the sinner. Thus the citation includes all of v. 18b. He thinks, "I will be safe, even if I walk in the stubbornness of my heart, since the wet carries away the dry (or: since the wet is carried away with the dry)." It fits the context, since v. 19 immediately describes the punishments for such a self-deceiving sinner. The enthymeme in the mind of the sinner would then run like this:

p^1: The wet provides for the dry.
p^2: [I am dry.]
c: Therefore, the wet provides for me.

If, as I suspect, the proverb refers to the safety of the individual sinner within the community, the implied enthymeme will then be something like this:

p^1: The community provides for all individual members.
p^2: (Although I am stubborn,) [I am an individual member.]
c: Therefore, the community provides for me (that is, I am safe).

Another way of constructing the enthymeme is as follows:

p^1: All individuals within the community are safe.
p^2: [I am an individual within the community.]
c: Therefore, I am safe.

8. In Dt 29,23 there is a question concerning the punishments inflicted upon the land: the nations ask why (על-מה) this is happening. The response begins in v. 24 (על-אשר) and continues until the end of v. 27. Within the answer there is an implied enthymeme, which might look like this:

---

[87] CORBETT, *Classical Rhetoric*, 142; DIXON, *Rhetoric*, 26; ONG, *Oralità e scrittura*, 73; PERELMAN and OLBRECHTS-TYTECA, *Traité de l'argumentation*, 224; T. POLK, "Paradigms, Parables, and *Měšālîm:* On Reading the *Māšāl* in Scripture," *CBQ* 45 (1983) 564-565.

[88] ARISTOTLE, *Rhetoric*, II.21.1394a; MESSER LEON, *Honeycomb's Flow*, III.19.1; cf. PERELMAN and OLBRECHTS-TYTECA, *Traité de l'argumentation*, 224.

[89] BUIS, *Le Deutéronome*, 391; CHOLEWINSKI, *Deuteronomio* II, 24-25; MAYES, *Deuteronomy*, 365. As a figure it would be a *merismus*.

p¹: [Yahweh punishes all who abandon his covenant.]
p²: They have abandoned his covenant.
c: Therefore, Yahweh is punishing them.

Or the enthymeme could be altered slightly to the following form:

p¹: [All who abandon Yahweh's covenant deserve punishment.]
p²: They have abandoned Yahweh's covenant.
c: Therefore, they deserve punishment.

9. In Dt 29,28 there is a second proverb or maxim. Many commentators recognize a wisdom motif here.[90] There are numerous interpretations of this verse, which is often seen as a gloss or a late addition.[91] Usually "the secret things"(הנסתרת) are interpreted as referring to the future, while "the revealed things" (הנגלת) are interpreted as referring to God's will made known through the *torah*.

This maxim contains contraries or antitheses, since what is hidden is the opposite of what is revealed. Since it signifies a totality, it is also a *merismus*. One part of this totality is in the divine sphere of activity, while the other part is in the human sphere. Unexpressed presumptions are contained in this maxim. It presupposes that things are either hidden or revealed and that human beings can do nothing about what is hidden.

---

[90] McCarthy, *Treaty and Covenant*, 201; Mayes, *Deuteronomy*, 368; Ntagwarara, "Alliance d'Israël," 125; Penna, *Deuteronomio*, 240; Phillips, *Deuteronomy*, 201; Preuss, *Deuteronomium*, 160; G. Ravasi, "Benedizione e maledizione nell'alleanza: Dt 27-30," *ParSpV* 21 (1990) 55, n. 6.

[91] Buis, *Le Deutéronome*, 392-393, calls the verse a traditional adage on the limits of human knowledge. Buis and Leclercq, *Le Deutéronome*, 185, say that this enigmatic sentence is meant to discourage speculation about the future. Cholewinski, *Deuteronomio* II, 30, adds that this future speculation concerns the length of the exile. R.A. Carlson, *David the Chosen King: A Traditio-Historical Approach to the Second Book of Samuel*, trans. Eric J. Sharpe (Stockholm 1964) 264, sees a hermeneutic rule here. J.G. Janzen, "The Yoke That Gives Rest," *Int* 61 (1987) 266, believes this verse is a counsel to Israel regarding covenant loyalty. Kearney, "The Role of the Gibeonites," 7, n. 23, sees Dt 29,28 as a balance to the lack of understanding in 29,3. In Dt 29 there is a subtle allusion to the failure of Israel's history, while v. 28 forms a contrast by means of hope in a hidden future. Labuschagne, "Divine Speech in Deuteronomy," 123, interprets the maxim to mean that the esoteric knowledge in the written text is for God's glory, while the law in its straight, plain language is for the benefit of the people. Levenson, "Who Inserted ... the Torah?," 208, calls this a late pious gloss — with which McCarthy, *Treaty and Covenant*, 201, n. 32, would agree. Ntagwarara, "Alliance d'Israël," 125; and Ravasi, "Benedizioni e maledizione nell'alleanza," 55, n. 6, call the verse a transition. Rennes, *Le Deutéronome*, 140, says that the verse really belongs to chapter 30, since Dt 30,11-14 are a development of its thought. Von Rad, *Das fünfte Buch Mose*, 129, says Dt 29,28 is the conclusion of a sermon. And Weinfeld, *Deuteronomy and the Deuteronomic Tradition*, 63-64, n. 5, refers to duplicate copies of the covenant, one hidden for the Deity and one open and revealed for the people.

V. 28 is divided into two parallel sections. The first half of the verse has only three words: הנסתרת ליהוה אלהינו. Its parallel also has three words: והנגלת לנו ולבנינו. But the second section doesn't end here. It adds two different notions. First it continues with עד־עולם. What "we" can deal with is revealed forever. It should be noted that no such limiting condition is placed upon God, who can reveal his secrets later if he wants. But then there is a second addition: לעשות את־כל־דברי התורה הזאת. One can somehow "manage," "do," or "act upon" what is revealed "for us" or "to us," since it is to be found in the words of the *torah*. There is no "doing" or "acting upon" what is hidden and therefore belongs to God. However, we can certainly act upon what is revealed to us.

An implied if somewhat truncated enthymeme thus appears in Dt 29,28:

p^1: [All things which belong to us can be done.]
p^2: Revealed things belong to us.
c: Therefore, revealed things can be done.

This would seem to imply a second enthymeme, one which has only the minor premise specifically stated within the text itself:

p^1: [All things which belong to God cannot be done.]
p^2: Hidden things belong to God.
c: [Therefore, hidden things cannot be done.]

The maxim in 29,28 then is a real transition between chapters 29 and 30. Dt 29 deals with witnessing, curse, and punishment; it is a warning to the audience. Dt 30 on the other hand concerns itself with conversion, the possibility of change, and observance of the law. Both chapters are about what has been revealed. The way is not hidden to *us,* since what is revealed and what we can do belong to *us* (that is, the audience).

10. Dt 30,1-3 contains another conditional proposition in an enthymeme. It presumes that there is an antecedent-consequent (or cause-effect) relationship between conversion/obedience and restoration:

p^1: [All who change/obey will be restored.]
p^2: If/when you change/obey,
c: You will be restored.

11. After the promise of the restoration of the exiles in v. 3 comes another enthymeme in Dt 30,4 which builds upon its predecessor. There is a presumption that Yahweh has great power, a presumption based perhaps on earlier descriptions of his wonders (e.g., Dt 29,1-7). Also evident here is the topic of the possible and the impossible, specifically the argument that if one of a pair of similar things is possible, the other is possible as well:

p^1: [If Yahweh has scattered you, he can also gather you.]
p^2: Yahweh has scattered you.
c: Therefore, he can also gather you.

12. In Dt 30,6b there is another implied enthymeme:

p¹: [All those who love God will live.]
p²: (If) you love God,
c: (Then) you will live.

13. Dt 30,8-9 contains an enthymeme similar to that of 30,1-3. It can also be expressed with a conditional proposition:

p¹: [All who repent/obey/observe the law will prosper.]
p²: (If) you repent/obey/observe the law,
c: (Then) you will prosper.

The minor premise is stated a second time in v. 10, so the enthymeme is actually repeated in reverse order: major premise (understood); minor premise (30,8); conclusion (30,9); minor premise (30,10).

14. Dt 30,11-14 is built upon the topic of the possible and the impossible. It also insists on the proximity of this commandment. There seems to be a presumption that that which is near is possible, that is, it can be done. In that case there is also an enthymeme implied in these verses:

p¹: [All that is near can be done.]
p²: The law is near.
c: Therefore, the law can be done.

15. The next enthymeme can be found in Dt 30,16, but it is complicated by a textual critical problem. MT begins the verse with אשר, which is normally a relative pronoun — and a rather strange way to begin a sentence.[92] LXX adds (καὶ) ἐὰν εἰσακούσῃς τὰς ἐντολὰς κυρίου τοῦ δεοῦ σου. The Syriac version agrees with LXX, but Tᴶ and Targ. Onkelos as well as Vg agree with MT. Modern translators are split about whether or not there was an original (ואם) תשמע אל מצות יהוה אלהיך in the text.[93]

MT remains the *lectio difficilior*, especially since it is easy to imagine the translator of LXX trying to correct the text. It is also possible to consider the relative pronoun in an absolute sense.[94] Another suggestion would be to see here an *ellipsis* in the text. In that case the missing words would automatically come to the mind of the reader or listener.[95]

---

[92] MERENDINO, "La via della vita," 42. DRIVER, *Deuteronomy*, 332, calls the Hebrew text here "imperfect."

[93] Those who emend the text in accordance with LXX include BJ, EÜ, LLS, NAB, NEB, REB, RSV; CRAIGIE, DRIVER, MAYES, and VON RAD (the emendation seems to be preferred by English translations). Those who translate according to MT include BLC, CEI, TOB; BUIS, BUIS and LECLERCQ, LACONI, and PENNA.

[94] NTAGWARARA, "Alliance d'Israël," 172.

[95] ALONSO SCHÖKEL, *A Manual of Hebrew Poetics*, 167; CORBETT, *Classical Rhetoric*, 468; MARCHESE, *Dizionario di retorica e di stilistica*, 89. GKC, §167a, suggests another figure: *aposiopesis*, which is "the concealment or suppression of entire sentences or

Whichever the case may be, we can still discern an implied enthymeme in the text as it stands:

p¹: [All who love God/walk in his ways/observe his
       commandments will live/multiply/be blessed.]
p²: (If) you love/walk/observe,
c: You will live/multiply/be blessed.

16. Dt 30,17-18 expresses a threat based on an enthymeme:

p¹: [All who disobey Yahweh and worship other gods will
       be destroyed and not live long.]
p²: (If) you disobey Yahweh and worship other gods,
c: You will be destroyed and not live long.

17. Finally, the choice offered in Dt 30,19 is based on an implied premise and an enthymeme:

p¹: [All who choose life will live.]
p²: (If) you choose life,
c: You will live.

This listing of enthymemes shows that the ancient Hebrews were no strangers to the reasoning process. Of course, these enthymemes may pose problems for modern Westerners, since they are usually based on unspoken premises which we may have trouble accepting. It is also difficult to be precise about the exact wording of many of these enthymemes, since they tend to be implied rather than directly expressed. The ancient Hebrews certainly did not conform their language to later Greek, Latin, and Western conceptions of what constitutes proper enthymemic or syllogistic form. It's possible that there are yet other enthymemes hidden in the text, but these suffice to demonstrate that even in this form the reasoning or logic of the communication act can be discovered.

Many of the enthymemes in the Third Discourse of Moses tend to be normative, that is, they suggest what is proper conduct and belief, what *should* be done: Yahweh should be obeyed, his covenant should be observed, disgusting things should be avoided. Or they suggest that obedience to God is reasonable, since turning from Yahweh is a punishable offense, that Yahweh is quick to punish, that conversion brings restoration, that his commandments are possible, and that Yahweh blesses the obedient. This may not be a logic that a universal audience would accept, but it could be quite effective with a wide audience of lay people from a relatively cohesive group which shares

---

clauses, which are of themselves necessary to complete the sense, and therefore must be supplied from the context."

certain values, presumptions, and conventions. The arguments begin to make sense while at the same time emotions are being provoked.

4.5.2 Techniques of Argumentation

Modern rhetoricians tend to downplay the enthymeme, since it is limited by its form in representing rational argumentation. In the Third Discourse of Moses, for example, most (if not all) of the enthymemes thus far discovered are implied and must be drawn out of the text. The reasoning process of Dt 28,69 – 30,20 is certainly not limited to these.

Perelman and Olbrechts-Tyteca point out that argumentation is the result of the *association* (*liaison*) or *dissociation* of ideas:

> Nous entendons par procédés de liaison des schèmes qui rapprochent des éléments distincts et permettent d'établir entre ces derniers une solidarité visant soit à les structurer, soit à les valoriser positivement ou néga-tivement l'un par l'autre. Nous entendons par procédés de dissociation des techniques de rupture ayant pour but de dissocier, de séparer, de dé-solidariser, des éléments considérés comme formant un tout ou du moins un ensemble solidaire au sein d'un même système de pensée: la dissociation aura pour effet de modifier pareil système en modifiant certaines des notions qui en constituent des pièces maîtresses.[96]

They list the various associative arguments under three main headings: quasi-logical arguments, arguments that are based on the structure of reality, and arguments which establish the structure of reality. First there will be an investigation of arguments of association, followed by an investigation of arguments of dissociation.

4.5.2.1 Quasi-Logical Arguments

Quasi-logical arguments are those which are similar to the formal reasoning processes of logic or mathematics. However, such arguments differ from logic and mathematics in that they presuppose adherence to nonformal, probable theses.[97] Such arguments include those involving incompatibility, identity and definition, reciprocity, the rule of justice, transitivity, inclusion of the part in the whole, division (including the dilemma and arguments *a pari* and *a contrario*), comparison, sacrifice, probabilities, and weights and measures.[98]

---

[96] PERELMAN and OLBRECHTS-TYTECA, *Traité de l'argumentation*, 255-256.

[97] Ibid., 259-260; PERELMAN, *L'empire rhétorique*, 65.

[98] PERELMAN and OLBRECHTS-TYTECA, *Traité de l'argumentation*, 262-350; PERELMAN, *L'empire rhétorique*, 70-94. An *incompatibility* resembles a contradiction and involves a choice between two assertions. It would include the ridiculous and irony in argumentation. The *rule of justice* demands identical treatment for beings or situations of

Perelman and Olbrechts-Tyteca consider enthymemes to be quasi-logical arguments, including them among arguments by transitivity.[99] So, with one or two exceptions, we will ignore enthymemes in the treatment of quasi-logical arguments in the Third Discourse of Moses, since they have already been discussed in the preceding section.

Under *topics* (4.2) were listed a number of definitions and divisions. It was admitted that in Dt 28,69–30,20 there occur no scientific definitions, but some of the descriptive definitions given might also be considered as arguments.

1. One important descriptive definition appears in Dt 28,69. Here the narrator announces the words of the covenant made בארץ מואב מלבד הברית אשר־כרת אתם בחרב. This distinction seems important, especially since this identity of a covenant made in Moab occurs nowhere else in the Pentateuch.[100] This identification may be significant for the audience of this text, especially if the original audience lived during the exilic period. For it would be consoling and reassuring to hear that another covenant was made with Yahweh after the one made at Horeb had been broken and thus abrogated.[101] Putting the two covenants together on a more or less equal basis also establishes a kind of equality between them. This would be one type of an argument by transitivity. This equality ensures that the covenant in Moab will be taken just as seriously as the one made at Horeb.[102] Thus perhaps there is also a kind of argument of reciprocity in this identification.

---

the same kind. Arguments of *reciprocity* are based on symmetry and aim at equal treatment in situations which are counterparts of one another. *Transitivity* makes it possible to infer from relations between *a* and *b* and between *b* and *c* that there is also a relationship between *a* and *c*. These could include the relations of equality, superiority, inclusion, and ancestry. The argument of *division* is based on the notion that a whole is the sum of its parts. It lies at the basis of dilemmas and arguments *a pari* and *a contrario*. These arguments appear similar to those used in mathematics. Underlying arguments of *comparison* is the idea of measurement. One of the most frequent arguments of comparison is based on the *sacrifice* one is willing to make to achieve a result.

[99] PERELMAN and OLBRECHTS-TYTECA, *Traité de l'argumentation*, 309.

[100] CHOLEWINSKI, *Deuteronomio* II, 7-8; KUTSCH, *Verheißung und Gesetz*, 151; VON RAD, *Das fünfte Buch Mose*, 128.

[101] Cf. CHOLEWINSKI, "Zur theologischen Deutung des Moabbundes," 96, 103; MERENDINO, "La via della vita," 38; MORAN, "Deuteronomy," 274.

[102] Cf. REITER, "Der Bundesschluß," 310. In 4.5.2.4 we will discover that there may also be a technique of dissociation here. An argument of transitivity claims an equality between the two covenants. Dissociation distinguishes between these particular manifestations of covenants and the notion of an eternal or permanent covenant (or relationship). Such dissociation means then that the breaking of one particular covenant, such as that of Mt. Horeb or that of Moab, would not lead to permanent estrangement from Yahweh. The dissociation, however, is not specifically stated but only implied.

2. An incompatibility is established in the relationship between Dt 29,1-2 and 29,16. These verses describe what the audience has personally witnessed. In 29,1-2 אתם ראיתם all the wonderful works of the Lord. In v. 16 the audience again sees (ותראו), but this time they witness the disgusting and filthy idols of the nations. An incompatibility involves a choice.[103] The audience in the Third Discourse is being set up to make a choice, and that begins almost immediately. For the choice will be between a God who can perform wonders (29,1-2) and disgusting, filthy idols made of עץ ואבן כסף וזהב (29,16). This description of idols in v. 16 follows two emotionally "loaded" words (שקוציהם and גלליהם) and is itself probably a form of ridicule, which is a strong argument against one possible choice or option.[104]

3. Within Dt 29,1-3 there is a second incompatibility expressed in a kind of tautology. It centers around seeing with the eyes. V. 1 affirms that the audience has seen God's wonders with its own eyes (...אתם ראיתם לעיניכם). This is reinforced in v. 2 (אשר ראו עיניך). But in v. 3 it is suddenly denied that the audience has eyes to see (ולא־נתן יהוה לכם ... ועינים לראות). The incompatibility makes sense only when we realize that the meaning of the third expression has changed, for here "eyes to see" refers to proper understanding of what has been witnessed. This is confirmed by the rest of v. 3, which also denies that God has given the audience לב לדעת ... ואזנים לשמע. The change in meaning gives rise to what Perelman and Olbrechts-Tyteca call an "apparent tautology."[105]

4. In Dt 29,11-13.17 we have yet another incompatibility. This one reinforces the choice that must be made between Yahweh and other gods. For it specifically contrasts two courses of action. First there is the entrance into the covenant with Yahweh (v. 11: לעברך בברית יהוה אלהיך ובאלתו; v. 13: אנכי כרת את־הברית הזאת) and the establishment of a relationship between Yahweh and his people (v. 12: למען הקים־אתך היום לו לעם והוא יהיה־לך לאלהים). But only a few verses later the danger of apostasy, the turning away from this relationship with Yahweh in order to worship other gods, is mentioned: אשר לבבו פנה היום מעם יהוה אלהינו ללכת לעבד את־ אלהי הגוים ההם (v. 17). The two activities are incompatible, for they conflict and demand differing loyalties. A choice must be made: either Yahweh or the other gods. Both activities are not possible.

5. Dt 29,19-22.26-27 contain a type of argument by comparison, for it is an effective threat. Threats can also form a type of argumentation or persuasion.[106] The threat in vv. 19-20 is against an individual who

---

[103] PERELMAN and OLBRECHTS-TYTECA, *Traité de l'argumentation*, 264.
[104] Ibid., 329.
[105] Ibid., 292.
[106] Ibid., 331.

harbors secret thoughts of apostasy. The threat in vv. 21-22 involves the punishment of the land, God's gift to his people. The threat in vv. 26-27 is that of exile, the loss of this gift of the land.

6. The incompatibility between the covenant with Yahweh and the worship of other gods returns in Dt 29,24-25. The worship of other gods (v. 25a) is specifically described as an abandonment of Yahweh's covenant (v. 24: עזבו את־ברית יהוה אלהי אבתם). In v. 25b these אלהים אחרים are described in different terms: אלהים אשר לא־ידעום ולא חלק להם. This is a kind of argument by definition or division, an argument which at the same time displays surprise or dismay: How could the people abandon their own God in favor of gods whom they don't know and who have nothing to do with them? It's possible that here the incompatibility exhibits ridicule.

7. In Dt 30,4 appears an argument *a pari*.[107] For it deduces that if God can scatter you to the ends of the heavens (אם־יהיה נדחך בקצה השמים), he can likewise gather you from the same places (משם יקבצך יהוה אלהיך ומשם יקחך).

8. If we have threats in Dt 29, we have promises of benefits in chapter 30. The promise of blessing in 30,5 is part of an argument of comparison, for it associates these promises with the golden past of the ancestors.[108] If the people convert and turn to God, he will not only bring them back to the land of their ancestors (אשר־ירשו אבתיך וירשתה), but they will have prosperity and numbers even greater than that of the ancestors (והיטבך והרבך מאבתיך).

9. This comparison with the ancestors appears a second time in Dt 30,9. For the promise is that the Lord will rejoice over his people in the future in the same way that he had in the past (כי ישוב יהוה לשוש עליך לטוב כאשר־שש על־אבתיך).

10. We have already noted that Dt 30,11-14 is founded upon the topic of the possible and the impossible. In terms of arguments which have developed from this topic, it seems that there is one of probability or measurement here. Why is obeying the law possible? Because it is *near*. The presumption is that what is near is possible, even probable. One does not have to go great distances (בשמים — v. 12; מעבר לים — v. 13) in order to *do* the commandment, for it is near (כי־קרוב אליך — v. 14). It is possible that this argument is a kind of refutation to an unstated objection that the law is impossible or inaccessible. It can also be considered an

---

[107] An argument *a pari* is a kind of identification, but it is based on the division of a whole into its parts. It deals with the application to another species of the same genus of what can be asserted about some particular species. See PERELMAN and OLBRECHTS-TYTECA, *Traité de l'argumentation*, 325.

[108] Ibid., 330.

argument of division. For God's commandment is either far away or near at hand. Since it is not far away, it must be near at hand!

11. Incompatibilities which require a choice appear again in Dt 30,15,19. In v. 15 the audience is presented with a choice between life and good (את־החיים ואת־הטוב) on the one hand and death and evil (ואת־המות ואת־הרע) on the other. The implication is that they cannot coexist; the audience must choose one or the other. This choice between incompatibilities is reaffirmed in v. 19. This time the choice is between life and death (החיים והמות), blessing and curse (הברכה והקללה).

12. Dt 30,16-18 presents us with another incompatibility, but this is a repetition of those we found in chapter 29. In 30,16 we have blessings which are the result of obedience. Vv. 17-18 present what is incompatible with such blessings: disobedience and its corresponding punishment. Thus the incompatibility between obedience and disobedience is seen also in their corresponding results: blessing (a promise) and destruction and punishment (a threat).

13. In Dt 30,19 Moses calls upon heaven and earth as witnesses to the audience's destruction if it refuses to obey: העידתי בכם היום את־השמים ואת־הארץ. This seems to be legal language connected with the treaty form.[109] "Heaven and earth," however, are also a kind of *merismus* or *divisio,* for it is one way of expressing totality by the opposition of contraries.[110] It's a bit more difficult to judge whether or not the ancient Hebrews would have recognized here the device of *personification,* since they may not have distinguished so precisely as we moderns the differences between living persons and natural elements.

4.5.2.2 Arguments Based on the Structure of Reality

This type of argument makes use of the structure of reality to establish a relationship between what is generally accepted about reality and the theses one wishes to promote.[111] Most arguments based on reality appeal to *liaisons of succession* (for example, cause and effect, ends and means; these will include pragmatic arguments and arguments of waste,

---

[109] M. Delcor, "Les attaches littéraires, l'origine et la signification de l'expression biblique 'prendre à témoin le ciel et la terre,'" *VT* 16 (1966) 8-25; H. Huffmon, "The Covenant Lawsuit in the Prophets," *JBL* 78 (1959) 285-295; McCarthy, *Treaty and Covenant,* 192-193; G.E. Wright, "The Lawsuit of God: A Form-Critical Study of Deuteronomy 32," *Israel's Prophetic Heritage: Essays in Honor of James Muilenburg* (ed. B.W. Anderson and W. Harrison; New York 1962) 44-48.

[110] P. Boccaccio, "I termini contrari come espressioni della totalità in ebraico," *Bib* 33 (1952) 177; Delcor, "'Prendre à témoin le ciel et la terre,'" 16; W.L. Moran, "Some Remarks on the Song of Moses," *Bib* 43 (1962) 318.

[111] Perelman and Olbrechts-Tyteca, *Traité de l'argumentation,* 351; Perelman, *L'empire rhétorique,* 95.

direction, and unlimited development, as well as *hyperbole*) or *liaisons of coexistence* (the relation between a person and his or her acts, the relation between an essence and its manifestations, the relation between a group and its members, as well as arguments of prestige and authority). But arguments based on the structure of reality can also include those characterized by the relation of participation (symbols, double hierarchy arguments, and *a fortiori* arguments).[112]

1. Arguments from *authority* are related to ethos, for both presume that a speaker is related to his or her acts, including the act of discourse.[113] Since ethos has already been discussed in 4.3, it is not necessary to mention those references here. However, it may be useful to recall that the entire Third Discourse of Moses is one which is delivered on the authority of God himself (28,69: אשר־צוה יהוה את־משה) as well as on the authority of Moses (29,1: ויקרא משה ... ויאמר אלהם). Yahweh is quoted only once in this discourse (29,5), but references to Yahweh and to God are numerous.[114] Perhaps an appeal to authority can also be seen in the frequent references to the ancestors (29,12.24; 30,5.20).

2. In Dt 29,1-5 there is an emphasis on כל־אשר עשה יהוה (29,1). The audience itself is a witness to these wondrous acts. It seems the author sees here a close relationship between a person and his acts, since through the acts of Yahweh one can recognize who he is. In fact, according to v. 5, the very purpose of all these marvelous occurrences is למען תדעו כי אני יהוה אלהיכם. But at the same time all these wonders seem to be a means to the end of recognizing Yahweh as "your God." It thus seems to be a combination of both a sequential relationship and a relationship of coexistence.

3. There is also a *hyperbole* in Dt 29,4. One can imagine easily enough a wandering which excluded bread, wine, and strong drink (v. 5). But v. 4 denies that the clothes and shoes worn by the people wore out despite forty years of wandering. This would be a miracle indeed! Perhaps there is hyperbole here in order to increase the sense of wonder and the acknowledgment of God's power.

4. The conclusion or consequence of Dt 29,1-7 comes in v. 8: ושמרתם את־דברי הברית הזאת. Here we note a fact-consequence or even an

---

[112] "Dans les liaisons de succession, ce sont des phénomènes de même niveau qui sont mis en relation, alors que, en se basant sur des liaisons de coexistence, l'argumentation prend appui sur des termes de niveau inégal...." PERELMAN, *L'empire rhétorique,* 95. For a discussion on arguments based on the structure of reality, see PERELMAN and OLBRECHTS-TYTECA, *Traité de l'argumentation,* 354-470; PERELMAN, *L'empire rhétorique,* 96-117.

[113] See PERELMAN and OLBRECHTS-TYTECA, *Traité de l'argumentation,* 429.

[114] יהוה appears 38 times and אלהים 25 times in these 49 verses.

end-means relationship: by reflecting on all these marvels one should conclude the necessity of observing the covenant. The performance of the wonders, then, is but God's means to get his people to obey, which is the proper end of these activities. But there is yet a consequence to the observance of the covenant — prosperity (v. 8: למען תשכילו את כל־אשר תעשׂון). Is this a cause-effect relationship? Modern Westerners, especially Christians, might feel uneasy accepting prosperity as a necessary effect of obedience, but the ancient Hebrews may not have been so hesitant in assuming such a relationship. Similar cause-effect relationships will appear again later.

5. In the participant list (29,9-10) there is a strong identification of the group with its members. Even those who are low on the social scale and/or who have no responsibilities in the cult community are acknowledged as members of this audience. In vv. 13-14 the group is extended to include those not present (especially future generations). The aim seems to be to ensure that all members identify themselves with the group, which has an obligation to enter into and obey the covenant. The implied argument could be paraphrased in these words: God's covenant includes those yet unborn and those not present; therefore even if you yourselves were not present, God's covenant includes you. After all, the very reason why אתם נצבים היום כלכם לפני יהוה אלהיכם (v. 9) is to enter the covenant and establish a relationship with Yahweh (vv. 11-12). Thus we also have a sequential relationship here (means-ends).

6. In Dt 29,15-17 there is a relationship of coexistence between the group and its members. What the audience has seen in Egypt and in the other lands through which it passed should prevent any part of it from straying from Yahweh to serve other gods. The fact is that *you* know (v. 15: ידעתם) and *you* saw (v. 16: ותראו). The consequence should be fidelity and not the apostasy of any group or individual within the audience (v. 17).

7. In Dt 29,18-20 a person is associated with his or her acts (evil thoughts leading to apostasy), and a cause-effect relationship is established (sin brings about punishment).

8. Dt 29,24-27 describes another cause-effect relationship in answer to the question raised by future generations and foreigners. The cause: they abandoned the covenant (v. 24: עזבו את־ברית) and worshipped other gods (v. 25: וילכו ויעבדו אלהים אחרים וישתחוו להם). The effect: God became angry and activated the curses (v. 26); he uprooted them from the land and exiled them (v. 27).

9. In Dt 29 the cause-effect relationships were those of sin bringing punishment. In 30,1-10 new sequential relationships are described: conversion (fact or cause) brings blessing (consequence or effect). This is seen for the first time in 30,1-3. For when the exiles call to mind the curse and the blessing (v. 1) and return to the Lord and obey him

(v. 2: וְשַׁבְתָּ עַד־יְהוָה אֱלֹהֶיךָ וְשָׁמַעְתָּ בְקֹלוֹ), the consequence will be return from exile (v. 3).

10. Similarly in Dt 30,6 Yahweh's circumcision of the heart (cause) will bring about love for God (effect), which becomes a new cause, since that assures life (לְמַעַן חַיֶּיךָ).

11. Dt 30,8-10 presents us with the cause-effect relationship in a chiastic pattern: if you convert, obey the Lord, and do his commandments (v. 8, cause), then God will make you prosper and rejoice over you (v. 9, effect), provided that you obey and convert (v. 10, cause).

12. In Dt 30,12-13 we see two examples of where this commandment is *not* to be found: in the skies and on the other side of the sea. These two examples have something of the *symbol* or of *hyperbole* in them, for both represent extreme distances. Perelman and Olbrechts-Tyteca[115] say that hyperbole is a form of an argument of unlimited development, which is classified as a sequential relation. (However, it is not always easy to distinguish a hyperbole from a metaphor.[116])

13. Another cause-effect relationship appears in 30,16. Whether or not there is an *ellipsis* here, and whether or not the text is emended, the cause appears in loving God, walking in his ways, and observing his precepts. The effect of these activities is life, increase, and blessing.

14. In Dt 30,17-18 we return to the threats of chapter 29 and the cause-effect relationship described there in terms of sin and punishment: if you turn away from Yahweh, refuse to obey, and worship other gods (v. 17, cause), you will perish and not live long on the land (v. 18, effect).

15. A final cause-effect relationship appears in Dt 30,19. The consequence of choosing life is life itself (לְמַעַן תִּחְיֶה).

Thus in terms of arguments based on the structure of reality, the Third Discourse of Moses especially favors the relationship of coexistence between a group and its members and the sequential relationship of cause and effect. Two cause-and-effect relationships appear frequently in our text: sin-punishment and conversion/obedience-blessing.

4.5.2.3 Arguments Which Establish the Structure of Reality

This type of argument establishes relations through particular cases (example, illustration, model) and through reasoning by analogy or metaphor. The example is the rhetorical equivalent of inductive reasoning, which proceeds from the particular to the general. However, the use of examples in argumentation often skips (or assumes) the generalization process and proceeds instead from the particular to the

---

[115] PERELMAN and OLBRECHTS-TYTECA, *Traité de l'argumentation*, 390-391.
[116] Ibid., 541.

particular. In this it is similar to reasoning by analogy.[117] Like the enthymeme, the example leads only to probability, but it has great persuasive value.[118] A metaphor is a condensed analogy, and analogies are important in argumentation because they aid the development and extension of thought.[119] We will now survey the Third Discourse of Moses in order to discover if any of these argumentative techniques occur there.

1. In Dt 29,4-5 we have examples — or better yet, *illustrations* — of Yahweh's power, illustrations coming from Israel's history. V. 2 had already referred vaguely to המסות הגדלת and הגדלים and האתת והמפתים. The illustrations in vv. 4-5 are more specific. In v. 4 it is recounted that neither their clothes nor their shoes wore out during forty years of wandering in the desert. V. 5 mentions the fact that during those forty years there was neither bread nor wine nor strong drink. Somehow from these historical examples members of the audience should conclude what kind of God Yahweh is.

2. Dt 29,17 presents a metaphor: שרש פרה ראש ולענה. The sinner or sinful group is compared with a plant, whose root or stock produces only poison and bitter fruit (or bitterness). We've already noted that ראש ולענה are probably emotionally "loaded" terms, since a person would naturally be afraid of poison and disgusted with the bitterness of certain plants. To compare apostates with such a root or stock would automatically identify them with what is dangerous and abhorrent.

3. A metaphor occurs within the maxim or proverb of Dt 29,18b. Here the communtity is compared with הרוה (the watered), while the individual is compared with הצמאה (the dry). The wet and the dry probably refer to the land or soil. The metaphor presents a powerful image of how the dry absorbs moisture from the wet, and thus it gives the maxim its force.

4. Dt 29,18-20 presents us with an illustration of the individual sinner who plots evil (and justifies that activity) in secret. This sinner serves as a kind of *anti-model,* that is, an example which one should *not* follow.[120]

---

[117] GARAVELLI, *Manuale di retorica*, 78; PERELMAN and OLBRECHTS-TYTECA, *Traité de l'argumentation*, 474; PERELMAN, *L'empire rhétorique*, 120.

[118] CORBETT, *Classical Rhetoric*, 82-83. MESSER LEON, *Honeycomb's Flow*, III.18.6, claims that the example is more persuasive than the enthymeme.

[119] PERELMAN and OLBRECHTS-TYTECA, *Traité de l'argumentation*, 517, 535. Metaphor is seen as capable of generating emotional intensity: see ARISTOTLE, *Rhetoric*, III.2.1405b; III.10.1410b; VICKERS, *In Defence of Rhetoric*, 320. However, it is also seen as a rational device and a positive contribution to communication. See P. COTTERRELL and M. TURNER, *Linguistics and Biblical Interpretation* (London 1989) 301; GRASSI, *Rhetoric as Philosophy*, 7, 95.

[120] For a description of anti-model, see PERELMAN and OLBRECHTS-TYTECA, *Traité de l'argumentation*, 492-495; PERELMAN, *L'empire rhétorique*, 125.

5. Dt 29,19 presents us with another metaphor, for it describes God's anger and jealousy as "smoking" (יֶעְשַׁן) against the individual sinner. It's possible that this term was already a "broken" metaphor, since anger in classical Hebrew was often expressed with words having to do with heat (e.g., חמה, חרה, הרי).[121] The verb עשן occurs six times in the Hebrew Bible (Exod 19,18; Dt 29,19; Ps 74,1; 80,5; 104,32; 144,5). Three of these occurrences associate smoking with mountains (Exod 19,18; Ps 104,32; 144,5). The other three occurrences associate the term with God's anger; in fact, in Ps 80,5 there is no other word expressing anger besides עשן. In any case the metaphor associates the anger of God toward the sinner as something powerful, violent, and threatening.

6. A second metaphor occurs in the same verse (29,19), for every curse written in the book "lies down on" or "settles on" the sinner (ורבצה). The verb רבץ occurs 24 times in the qal active in the Hebrew Bible.[122] In 20 of these occurrences the image is of an animal (or a human being described in terms of an animal) lying, usually at rest. The other occurrences are figurative, since sin (Gen 4,7), the deep (Gen 49,25; Dt 33,13), or a curse (here in Dt 29,19) can also lie down. Thus it seems the metaphor could be especially powerful here, for it shows the effectiveness of the curse, which is something alive and active.

7. In Dt 29,21 there are two metaphors used in the description of the land: מכות ("blows," "wounds," "plagues," or "miseries") and תחלאיה ("diseases"). The word מכה appears 45 times in the Hebrew Bible, but only here does it refer to the land.[123] תחלאים occurs five times, but this is

---

[121] These words, plus אף (anger), are probably "broken" or "dormant" metaphors. See PERELMAN and OLBRECHTS-TYTECA, Traité de l'argumentation, 542-543. See also n. 43 of this chapter for the listing of words for anger in Dt.

[122] Gen 4,7; 29,2; 49,9.14.25; Exod 23,5; Num 22,27; Dt 22,6; 29,19; 33,13; Isa 11,6.7; 13,21; 14,30; 17,2; 27,10; Ezek 19,2; 29,3; 34,14; Zeph 2,7.14; 3,13; Ps 104,22; Job 11,19.

[123] מכה occurs in Lev 26,21; Num 11,33; Dt 25,3; 28,59(3X).61; 29,21; Josh 10,10.20; Judg 11,33; 15,8; 1 Sam 4,8.10; 6,19; 14,14.30; 19,8; 23,5; 1 Kgs 20,21; 22,35; Is 1,6; 10,26; 14,6; 27,7; 30,26; Jer 6,7; 10,19; 14,17; 15,18; 19,8; 30,12.14.17; 49,17; 50,13; Mic 1,90; Nah 3,19; Zech 13,6; Ps 64,8; Prov 20,30; Est 9,5; 2 Chr 13,17; 28,5. There are references, however, in Jeremiah and later prophets to the blows or wounds suffered by a city, a people, or a nation: Jer 6,7 (Jerusalem); 10,19 (Jerusalem or Israel); 14,17 (the virgin daughter of my people); 19,8 (Jerusalem) 30,12 (Israel); 30,14 (Israel); 49,17 (Edom); 50,13 (Babylon); Mic 1,9 (Jerusalem); Nah 3,19 (Assyria). Actually there is some disagreement as to the number of occurrences of מכה in the Bible. F.I. ANDERSEN and A.D. FORBES, The Vocabulary of the Old Testament (Rome 1989) 146, say that there are 45 occurrences, but they list only the first 40 of these (they limit themselves to 40 references for all words). On p. 358 they indicate three occurrences in 2 Chr. EVEN-SHOSHAN, 654, gives only 44 occurrences, of which only two appear in 2 Chr. MANDELKERN I, 747, lists 45 occurrences plus a reference to 2 Chr 2,9, which he places with the verb אכל. He also includes occurrences from 2 Kgs 8,29; 9,15; which neither The Vocabulary of the Old Testament

also the only reference to the land.[124] These metaphors emphasize the extent of the punishment and the seriousness of the sin which brought them about.

8. Probably all of 29,21-22 could be considered an illustration of the punishments which apostasy brings about. Such an illustration would correspond with the ἐνάργεια or *demonstratio* of the ancient rhetoricians. One part of this illustration is the comparison with the overthrow of Sodom and Gomorrah, Admah and Zeboiim in v. 22. A comparison is also considered an illustration when it is not an evaluative argument.[125]

9. Two other metaphors appear in Dt 29,27, where God is said to "uproot" or "tear out" (וִיתְּשֵׁם) the people from the land and to "throw" them (וַיַּשְׁלִכֵם) to another land. The image is one of a plant or an object which is uprooted and then thrown away.[126] The metaphors again emphasize the power of God and the severity of the punishment — and thus the seriousness of the sin which provoked such punishments.

10. Another metaphor appears in Dt 30,6: God will circumcize the heart (וּמָל יהוה אלהיך את־לבבך ואת־לבב זרעך). The image of the heart's circumcision was perhaps the product of the exilic period; it expresses an interior renewal of the people made possible by the power of God.[127] This metaphor emphasizes the need for change, especially an interior change.

11. Dt 30,9 contains yet another metaphor. God's blessings include fertility of the womb, of one's flocks, and of the land. The same word (פרי: fruit) is used for each of these categories: בפרי בטנך ובפרי בהמתך ובפרי אדמתך. It's possible that these are "dormant" metaphors, since their use may have been common. פרי אדמתך could possibly be a normal use of the term, but the other two examples are definitely metaphors.

---

nor EVEN-SHOSHAN mention. MANDELKERN also gives only two instead of three occurrences in Dt 28,59.

[124] תחלאים occurs in Dt 29,21; Jer 14,18; 16,4; Ps 103,3; and 2 Chr 21,19.

[125] PERELMAN and OLBRECHTS-TYTECA, *Traité de l'argumentation*, 486.

[126] HOLLADAY, *Lexicon*, 251, specifically calls the use of נתש with people as its object a metaphor. However, it is a common metaphor, to say the least. Of 16 occurrences of נתש in the Hebrew Bible (11 of which are in the book of Jeremiah: Dt 29,27; 1 Kgs 14,15; Jer 1,10; 12,14[2X].15.17[2X]; 18,7; 24,6; 31,28; 42,10; 45,4; Mic 5,13; Ps 9,7; 2 Chr 7,20), only one does not refer to the uprooting or plucking out of a people, nation, or city. That one appears in Mic 5,13, where the *asherim* will be pulled out.

[127] The metaphor of a circumcized heart also appears in Dt 10,16; Jer 4,4; 9,24-25; Ezek 44,7.9; cf. Lev 26,41. See BUIS, *Le Deutéronome*, 179; "La nouvelle alliance," *VT* 18 (1968) 4; H. CAZELLES, "Jérémie et le Deutéronome," *RSR* 38 (1951) 13; LE DÉAUT, "Le thème de la circoncision du coeur," 180-181; S. LYONNET, "'La circoncision du coeur, celle qui relève de l'Esprit et non de la lettre' (Rom 2:29)," *L'évangile hier et aujourd'hui: Mélanges offerts au Professeur Franz-J. Leenhardt* (Genève 1968) 93-94.

4.5.2.4 Dissociation

Besides techniques of association or liaison in argumentation, there are also techniques of *dissociation* or severance. As already mentioned, this involves the separation of elements normally considered as belonging together. This type of technique is especially important in philosophical thought, since it attempts to overcome incompatibilities by establishing a new vision of reality through the dissociation of current ideas.[128] Thus dissociation brings about a profound change in the conceptions upon which argumentation is based.[129]

There are not many dissociations in the Third Discourse of Moses, but one or the other can be discerned in the text:

1. Dt 28,69 may contain a dissociation, although it's difficult to judge in this case. It is noteworthy that God commands Moses to make a covenant with Israel in the land of Moab מלבד הברית אשר־כרת אתם בחרב. The accent is on a distinction: this covenant is different from the original one made at Horeb. If a covenant was considered permanent, an incompatibility arises: With the breaking of the covenant, is the relationship with Yahweh ended? But one can dissociate the failure to observe a particular covenant from the permanent relationship with God. In such a case one can construct the philosophical pair thus: particular covenant/everlasting covenant. This dissociation is reinforced by 29,13-14, which grants membership in this covenant (audience) to future generations. Somehow, it seems, the covenant can even survive the sins of one's parents.

2. We have already noticed the incompatibility between seeing and not seeing in Dt 29,1-3 (see 4.5.2.1, no. 3). We're now in a position to discover here a technique of dissociation, for it's obvious that there's a difference between seeing and seeing! Perelman and Olbrechts-Tyteca note that an "apparent tautology" is a dissociative technique.[130] A quasi-logical argument and dissociation thus work hand in hand here. The philosophical pair probably would be described as seeing/under-standing, for what one sees physically with the eyes differs from what one understands.

3. Dt 29,15-17 sets up a strong dissociation between God (Yahweh) and the other gods. Not only is there an incompatibility between the worship of Yahweh and the worship of other gods (v. 17: פנה היום מעם יהוה אלהינו ללכת לעבד את־אלהי הגוים ההם), but the text even seems to

---

[128] PERELMAN, *L'empire rhétorique*, 139-140, 147; for a longer discussion see PERELMAN and OLBRECHTS-TYTECA, *Traité de l'argumentation*, 415-436.

[129] PERELMAN and OLBRECHTS-TYTECA, *Traité de l'argumentation*, 551.

[130] Ibid., 588; PERELMAN, *L'empire rhétorique*, 149.

suppose a great distinction between Yahweh and all others. Vv. 15 and 16 do not even call them gods. Rather, they receive ridicule and an insulting description: שקוציהם, גלליהם, and עץ ואבן כסף וזהב (v. 16). The authors here are dissociating Yahweh from these abominations. Perhaps a philosophical pair can be constructed in these ways: abominations/God or other (false) gods/Yahweh. Yahweh is not of the same caliber as these other disgusting things, and thus the worship of other gods can only be opposed to and incompatible with the worship of Yahweh.

4. We find the same dissociation between Yahweh and the other gods in Dt 29,25. This time it's presented in terms of a relationship. Whoever worships other gods abandons Yahweh (v. 24). And who are these gods? They are אלהים אשר לא־דעום ולא חלק להם. Again we can construct a philosophical pair something like this: other gods/God (Yahweh).

5. The maxim in Dt 29,28 may also be a kind of dissociation. The presumption, which we have previously noted in an enthymeme, is that what belongs to God can't be done. How then can one observe the covenant, which comes from God? A dissociation between what is revealed and what is hidden serves to separate the various things that come from God. The philosophical pair could be constructed thus: hidden/revealed. What is revealed thus belongs to us and can be accomplished. Such a dissociation is reinforced by Dt 30,11-14.

4.5.3 Conclusion

In this section on logos we have investigated five different ways of pursuing rational argumentation, all of which can be found in the Third Discourse of Moses. Enthymemes (and examples) are associated with the traditional approach of rhetoric, while processes of association and dissociation have been proposed by contemporary rhetoricians. The two approaches overlap, since both are attempting to describe what is rational in the communication act. Both indicate that within Dt 28,69 – 30,20 there is an attempt to show that 1) the worship of other gods means the abandonment of Yahweh; 2) sin brings punishment; 3) obedience and observance of the covenant bring reward; 4) observance of Yahweh's covenant is possible; and 5) a choice must be made between Yahweh and the other gods.

1. Enthymemes draw from the examples of God's power and the contemporary presumptions about divine power the conclusion that Yahweh's covenant must be observed. From the examples of disgusting things one should conclude that such things should be avoided. Worship of other gods is a turning away from Yahweh, which leads to punishment. Obedience to Yahweh and the observance of his covenant

bring blessing and prosperity. Conversion also brings restoration and blessing. The covenant regulations are within the realm of the possible.

2. Quasi-logical arguments use descriptions and divisions to provide facts and establish incompatibilities. Such incompatibilities require a choice between a God who can perform wonders and filthy idols; between good and evil, blessing and curse, life and death. Threats of punishment and promises of blessings reinforce the necessity of a choice.

3. Arguments based on the structure of reality include appeals to the authority of Yahweh and hyperbole. They also draw on the relationship between a person and his or her acts to identify Yahweh with the wonders which he has accomplished. The audience is called upon to identify with this group gathered in order to enter into a covenant with Yahweh. Perhaps the strongest arguments here are those based on cause-and-effect relationships: abandoning the covenant and worshipping other gods (= sin) bring punishment, while obedience and conversion bring prosperity.

4. Arguments which establish the structure of reality use illustrations of Yahweh's power, his anger when provoked, and his punishments. There are also illustrations of blessings, although these are not as vivid as the images of wrath and punishment. Metaphors also occur which identify sinners with what is detestable and God's anger with what is powerful and alive.

5. Dissociation occurs in the distinction between the covenants of Moab and Horeb, between seeing and understanding, between Yahweh and the other gods, and between what is hidden and what is revealed. Such dissociations confirm the possibility of a covenant renewal, the possibility of obeying the covenant stipulations, and the necessity of choosing a God who is totally different from other so-called divine beings.

In the following chapter we will take a closer look at the structure of the text and the arrangement of these arguments in the Third Discourse of Moses.

CHAPTER 5

DISPOSITIO

In the previous chapter we examined the premises and argumentation discernible in Dt 28,69 – 30,20. In this chapter the investigation will focus on the arrangement or order of those argumentative techniques and processes.

5.1 Rhetorical Unit

Before one can describe the arrangement of arguments in a
particular discourse, the *rhetorical unit* must be determined, that is, the
limits of the discourse must be defined.[1] It can be difficult to distinguish
between a rhetorical unit and a literary unit, but a rhetorical unit must be
a convincing or persuasive unit.[2] It certainly must make some sense by
itself, having a beginning, a middle, and an end.[3]
    What are the limits of the Third Discourse of Moses? They appear to
be fairly obvious. The reported speech of this discourse appears in Dt
29,1b – 30,20. Dt 28,69 – 29,1a and 31,1-2a are reporting speech, where
the narrator interrupts the actual words of Moses. The reporting speech
of 31,1-2a appears to be an introduction to another (brief) discourse of
Moses (which is followed by more reporting speech): ־וילך משה וידבר את
הדברים האלה אל־כל־ישראל: ויאמר אלהם. Thus   the   Third   Discourse   of
Moses comes to an end with Dt 30,20.
    Establishing the beginning of the Third Discourse is a bit more
problematic. Obviously the reported speech begins in 29,1b (after ויאמר
אלהם, the same words as in 31,2a). But does the introduction to the
speech begin with 29,1a or with 28,69? This has been the subject of much

---

[1] GREENWOOD, "Rhetorical Criticism and Formgeschichte," 423. Indeed the rhetorical
unit must be defined before one can work on a text. KENNEDY, *New Testament
Interpretation,* 33-34, proposes that the delimitation of the rhetorical unit be the first step
in rhetorical criticism. Since this paper has attempted to follow the traditional parts of
rhetoric more closely, however, the rhetorical unit has been associated with that part to
which it most naturally belongs: *dispositio.*
[2] WUELLNER, "Where Is Rhetorical Criticism Taking Us?" 455.
[3] KENNEDY, *New Testament Interpretation,* 33-34.

debate among scholars in recent years, for some would see 28,69 as the close or "subscript" of the Second Discourse while others would see it as the opening or "superscript" of what follows.[4]

Dt 28,69 functions as a transition between the Second and the Third Discourses of Moses.[5] Some scholars consider it to be a later addition to the text.[6] If we take the semantic field of דברי הברית into consideration, it is evident that the stipulations and curses they normally signify are found in Dt 12–28 and not in chapters 29–30.[7] At the same time 28,69 may be considered a summary of or inclusion with Dt 1,1-5.[8] However, a good case can be made that the verse is one of a series of superscripts found in Dt and has greater literary and terminological contacts with what follows.[9] The dissociation between the covenant of Horeb and that made in Moab also tends to link the verse with what follows rather than what precedes it.[10]

Therefore I believe it is justified to include 28,69 in the rhetorical unit we know as the Third Discourse of Moses. This verse, like 29,1a, is reporting speech; thus it is not part of the actual oration of Moses. However, Dt 28,69–29,1a are part of the immediate context of chapters 29–30 and are important for the rhetorical situation. Nevertheless, it

---

[4] Those who consider Dt 28,69 a *subscript* to what precedes it include: Buis, *Le Deutéronome*, 387; Buis and Leclercq, *Le Deutéronome*, 181; Driver, *Deuteronomy*, 319; Lundbom, *Jeremiah*, 141, n. 155; Mitchell, "The Use of the Second Person in Deuteronomy," 105; Montet, *Le Deutéronome et la question de l'Hexateuque*, 556; Penna, *Deuteronomio*, 236; H.F. Van Rooy, "Deuteronomy 28,69 - Superscript or Subscript?" *JNWS* 14 (1988) 215-222. MT also seems to favor this division. Among those who consider 28,69 to be a *superscript* to what follows are Cholewinski, *Deuteronomio* II, 7; "Zur theologischen Deutung des Moabbundes," 96, n. 2; Lohfink, "Der Bundesschluß im Land Moab," 32-35, 45; McCarthy, *Treaty and Covenant*, 202; Mayes, *Deuteronomy*, 360; Ntagwarara, "Alliance d'Israël," 7-9, 11-12; Reiter, "Der Bundesschluß," 33; Rennes, *Le Deutéronome*, 136; Rofé, "The Covenant in the Land of Moab," 310-311; Seitz, *Redaktionsgeschichtliche Studien zum Deuteronomium*, 33, 35; and Von Rad, *Das fünfte Buch Mose*, 128. LXX and Vg seem to favor this division. L.J. De Regt, *A Parametric Model for Syntactic Studies of a Textual Corpus, Demonstrated on the Hebrew of Deuteronomy 1-30* (Studia Semitica Neerlandica 24; Assen/Maastricht 1988) I, 8, denies that the question will ever be resolved on grammatical grounds alone. Rather interpretation will always influence one's decision here.

[5] Mayes, *Deuteronomy*, 44; Seitz, *Redaktionsgeschichtliche Studien zum Deuteronomium*, 25. Cf. Buis, *Le Deutéronome*, 387.

[6] Ntagwarara, "Alliance d'Israël," 218.

[7] Van Rooy, "Dt 28,69 - Superscript or Subscript?" 220-221.

[8] Ibid., 222; Lundbom, *Jeremiah*, 141, n. 155.

[9] Cholewinski, *Deuteronomio* II, 7; Lohfink, "Der Bundesschluß im Land Moab," 32, n. 4; Ntagwarara, "Alliance d'Israël, 8-9; and Rofé, "The Covenant in the Land of Moab," 310-311.

[10] Cf. 4.5.2.4, no. 1. Also see Cholewinski, *Deuteronomio* II, 7-8; Rofé, "The Covenant in the Land of Moab," 310.

should not be forgotten that 28,69 still remains a link with the Second Discourse.

Thus we can consider Dt 28,69 – 30,20 a rhetorical unit.[11]

5.2 Literary Structure

The literary structure of a text is not identical with the arrangement of its arguments. The literary structure is "the network of relations among the parts of an object or a unit,"[12] a network which can be discovered by an examination of the patterns of a text. Such patterns may include the techniques of alternation, chiasm, inclusion, keywords, motifs, and symmetry. An investigation of the literary structure of a text is not without value for rhetoric, however. For the structure of a discourse has rhetorical value, since it is one of the factors which affects an audience and which can affect the meaning.[13] Moreover, the arguments of a discourse are woven into its literary structure.

The Third Discourse of Moses has the following literary structure:

I.   Reporting speech (28,69 – 29,1a)
II. Reported speech (29,1b – 30,20)
    A. Establishing the incompatibility (29,1b-28)
        1. The lessons of history (29,1b-8)
        2. The audience and its relationship with Yahweh (29,9-14)
        3. Disobedience brings punishment (29,15-28)
            a. Warning (29,15-17)
            b. Example of the individual sinner (29,18-20)
            c. Example of the punishment of the land (29,21-27)
            d. Transitional maxim (29,28)
    B. Resolving the incompatibility/making a choice (30,1-20)
        1. Future conversion and blessing (30,1-10)
        2. Exhortation: the law is possible (30,11-14)
        3. The offer of a choice (30,15-20)

5.2.1 Dt 28,69 – 29,1a

The reporting speech in this small section is that of the narrator, who gives the circumstances of the Third Discourse. There seems to be an

---

[11] LOHFINK, "Der Bundesschluß im Land Moab," 45, says that Dt 28,69 has to be the superscript for at least chaps. 29 and 30 (although he prefers to see it as the superscript for all Dt 29-32). He admits on p. 48 that "Dt 29.30 ist eine einzige, zwei Kapitel umspannende 'Rede.'"

[12] S. BAR-EFRAT, "Some Observations on the Analysis of Structure in Biblical Narrative," *VT* 30 (1980) 155.

[13] Ibid., 172.

inclusion which links 28,69 with 29,8, since both verses mention the דברי
הברית. For this reason some scholars consider 28,69 – 29,8 to be a single
unit.[14] Because of the differences between reporting speech and reported
speech, however, they have been separated in this analysis.

5.2.2 Dt 29,1b-28

The Third Discourse of Moses is a single literary unit with a rather
obvious beginning and end. But there is a subtle shift in Dt 29,28. Before
this point the discourse builds up the incompatibilities and is rather
negative, since it describes the threats which are carried out when an
individual or the community sins (29,15-27). Chapter 30 takes on a more
positive tone, since it emphasizes conversion, blessing, the possibility of
obedience, and the necessity of a choice.

Dt 29,1b-28 is also marked by a three-part division, each begun by
the word אתם, an emphatic personal pronoun. This can be found in
vv. 1b, 9, and 15.

5.2.2.1 Dt 29,1b-8

This section is tied together by an inclusion, for the phrase את
כל־אשר עשה appears in vv. 1b and 8 (in v. 8b the verb form is תעשׂון).[15] At
the same time the inclusion is a kind of contrast; in v. 1b it is what the
Lord will do, while v. 8 refers to what the audience will do. A further
contrast is found in time references: God's activity is in the past, the
audience's is in the future.

Dt 29,1b-8 can be divided into three balanced subsections (vv. 1b-3,
4-5, 6-8). Each subsection describes events (wonders, wanderings, and
battles) in a different place (v. 1b: בארץ מצרים; v. 4a: במדבר; v. 6a: המקום
הזה) with a reflection or lesson for each (v. 3b: God didn't give you the
ability to understand; v. 5b: that you might know that I am the Lord
your God; v. 8: that you might observe the words of the covenant and
prosper).[16]

5.2.2.2 Dt 29,9-14

This section, which describes the audience of the Third Discourse (cf.
3.1, especially 3.1.3.2 and 3.1.3.3), is compact and well bonded together.
The keyword היום appears five times (vv. 9.11.12.14[2x]) and there is an
inclusion: נצבים/עמד היום לפני יהוה אליהיכם/אלהינו (vv. 9 and 14). Many also

---

[14] Cf. Ntagwarara, "Alliance d'Israël," 25.

[15] Reiter, "Der Bundesschluß," 94.

[16] See Cholewinski, "Zur theologischen Deutung des Moabbundes," 106; Lohfink,
"Der Bundesschluß im Land Moab," 37.

see a chiasm in this section, one which can be described in two different ways. First, one can see here a very general *ABB'A'* (or *ABA'*) pattern.[17] Here *A* = vv. 9-10, which list various participants in the audience; *B* = v.11, which gives the purpose of the gathering, the establishment of a covenant; *B'* = v.12, which reiterates the making of a covenant in different words, for it is a special relationship which is in focus here. Finally *A'* = v.14, which again describes the participants or audience.

The second way of describing the chiasm in vv. 9-14 is by seeing a more complex *ABCB'A'* pattern in the text. This way of describing the structure usually sees the inclusion as the extremes (*AA'*) and focuses on v. 12 (= *C*):

A	(v. 9)	(נצבים) היום לפני יהוה אלהיכם
B	(v. 11)	בברית ~~ ובאלתו ~~ כרת
C	(v. 12)	*die Bundesformel*
B'	(v. 13)	כרת ~~ הברית ~~ האלה
A'	(v. 14)	(עמד) היום לפני יהוה אלהינו .[18]

5.2.2.3 Dt 29,15-28

Vv. 15-28 are harder to categorize than the rest of Moses' Third Discourse. Yet there are certain indications that it can be subdivided into vv. 15-17, 18-20, 21-27, and 28. The maxim found in v. 28 has already been discussed above in 4.5.1, no. 9. The other subdivisions are based primarily on sense, although והיה in v. 18 and ואמר in v. 21 may be minor

---

[17] There is some confusion over terms. BAR-EFRAT, "Analysis of Structure in Biblical Narrative," 170, prefers to call the *AXA'* structure a "ring pattern," the *ABXB'A'* structure a "concentric pattern," and the *ABB'A'* structure a "chiastic pattern." W.G.E. WATSON, *Classical Hebrew Poetry: A Guide to Its Techniques* (JSOTSS 26; Sheffield 1986) 201-202, also defines chiasm in terms of a,b,c//c,b,a. J. BRECK, "Biblical Chiasmus: Exploring Structure for Meaning," *BTB* 17 (1987) 71, insists that authentic chiasm is inverted or antithetical parallelism built symmetrically around a central idea (*ABCB'A'*). CHOLEWINSKI, *Deuteronomio* II, 21, describes the structure in Dt 29,9-14 as chiastic, even when it has only three terms: *A* (vv. 9-10), *B* (vv. 11-12), *A'* (vv. 13-14). MEYNET, *Initiation à la rhétorique biblique*, 28; and STOCK, "Chiastic Awareness and Education in Antiquity," 23, would agree. KESSLER, "Inclusio in the Hebrew Bible," 44, prefers to call this an "introversion."

[18] See LOHFINK, "Der Bundesschluß im Land Moab," 38-39. Similar schemata can be found in BUIS and LECLERCQ, *Le Deutéronome*, 182; A. DI MARCO, *Il chiasmo nella Bibbia: Contributi di stilistica strutturale* (Collana ricerche e proposte; Torino 1980) 32; GARCÍA LÓPEZ, *Le Deutéronome*, 56; REITER, "Der Bundesschluß," 87, prefers to organize the chiasm along the following lines:

V. 9-10	Teilnehmer
11	Abschluß von Bund und Fluch
12	Bundesverhältnis gemäß Zusage
13(b)	Abchluß von Bund und Fluch
(13a).14	Teilnehmer

introductory formulas. Vv. 15-17 contain the warning or hypothesis which binds together the whole: you know what disgusting things other nations worship, and you are not to follow their example. Vv. 18-20 give the example of the individual who secretly disobeys and is punished, while vv. 21-27 vividly describe the punishments inflicted on the land as a result of the community's abandonment of the covenant relationship with Yahweh.[19]

An important keyword in 29,15-27 is ארץ, which appears eight times (vv. 15.21[2x].22.23.24.26.27). The same word appears once in 28,69; three times in 29,1-9, and three times in Dt 30. Not all of these references, however, are to the land of Israel, since ארץ in 29,15.24 refers to Egypt and in 29,21.27 to some unknown faraway land. But the large number of occurrences in this section, plus the vivid description of the land's suffering in v. 22 and the synonym אדמתם in v. 27, shows how important this *Leitmotiv* is here.

The words (הזה) הכתובה בספר appear in vv. 19a, 20b, and 26b. Two of these three occurrences are in the example of the individual sinner, that is, in the subsection which includes vv. 18-20. Also in this small section the word אלה occurs three times and ברית once. So this subsection is bound together by a juridical semantic field which includes written oaths/curses and the notion of covenant. Similar juridical language appears in vv. 24 (ברית)and 26 (כל־הקללה הכתובה בספר הזה).[20]

The description of the punishments in vv. 18-27 is bound together by frequent references to God's anger or wrath. Several different terms are employed. The most important of these is אף, which appears five times in

---

[19] NTAGWARARA, "Alliance d'Israël," 88, sees 29,15-20 as one unit based on the following structure: 29,15-16: constat; 29,17: loi; 29,18-20: illustration.

[20] Vv. 18-28 seem to be linked by a series of juridical or legal expressions which use different words but approximate the same idea. There are five such expressions scattered unevenly throughout the text (plus the single word ברית, which appears in v. 24). They appear in two groups, one in the beginning (vv. 18-20) and one at the end (vv. 26.28) of these eleven verses. One could almost claim that they form an inclusion for this section, but I believe that would be stretching them beyond what is reasonable. Another interesting but probably accidental fact is that the five expressions *by themselves* form a kind of chiasm:

A	הזאת		דברי האלה	את־	v. 18
B	הזה	הכתובה בספר	האלה	כל־	v. 19
C	התורה הזה	אלות הברית הכתובה בספר		ככל־	v. 20
B'	הזה	הכתובה בספר	הקללה	את־כל־	v. 26
A'	התורה הזאת		את־כל־דברי		v. 28.

The chiasm, if we can call it that, is probably coincidental. After all, the expressions are not exactly the same — in fact, no two are alike. There is great variety and freedom in the use of these terms. But they add a juridical element to this part of Dt 29, an element concerned with the words or oaths/curses from the written covenant/torah.

these verses (vv. 19.22.23.26.27).[21] In v. 19 both God's anger and his "jealousy" or "zeal" (וקנאתו) "smoke" against the sinner. In v. 22 אף is joined by חמה, in v. 23 by חרי, and in v. 27 by both חמה and קצף. V. 26 joins אף with the verb ויחר.

So the main themes or motifs of Dt 29,15-28 are the land, God's anger, and the curses of the covenant. Vv. 18-20 center around the individual who does not obey; while vv. 21-27 focus on the land, its punishment, and its loss. Vv. 21-27 are not only vivid, but they are set within a question-and-answer scheme. Future generations and strangers will see the afflictions of the land and ask "why?" (vv. 21-23). The answer lies in the people's abandonment of the covenant in order to worship other gods (vv. 24-27).

5.2.3 Dt 30

A number of factors bind the chapter together as a whole. To begin with, there is an inclusion in vv. 1 and 19: הברכה והקללה plus נתתי לפניך. The word נתן, in fact, may even be considered a keyword here, since it appears five times throughout the chapter (vv. 1.7.15.19.20). Even if נתן would not be a keyword, the expression נתתי לפניך, which appears at the beginning (v. 1), the middle (v. 15), and the end (v. 19), undoubtedly would have to be considered so.

Other words and expressions which appear throughout chapter 30 include: היום (7 times: vv. 2.8.11.15.16.18.19); אשר אנכי מצוך היום (vv. 2.8.11.16); and לאהבה את־יהוה אלהיך (vv. 6.16.20).

5.2.3.1 Dt 30,1-10

This section is joined together by a number of keywords and key expressions. The word כל appears 13 times in these ten verses (Dt 30,1[2x].2[3x].3.6[2x].7.8.9.10[2x]) — it fails to appear at all in the rest of the chapter. Again the root שוב occurs in various forms seven times in these ten verses (vv. 1.2.3[2x].8.9.10).[22] A word with a similar sound and perhaps related meaning (שבותך) also appears in v. 3. The expression בכל־לבבך ובכל־נפשך occurs three times (vv. 2.6.10). Although this is a deuteronomic phrase, it does not occur elsewhere in Dt 29–30.[23] The expression שמע בקול also occurs three times here (vv. 2.8.10).

---

[21] REITER, "Der Bundesschluß," 291, calls אף a *Leitwort* in 29,21-27.

[22] The *qal* actually appears only six times, since the first appearance of the root in v. 1 is actually *hiphil*. The theme "return" is important for the Deuteronomistic History. Cf. MAYES, *Deuteronomy*, 368-369; WOLFF, "Das Kerygma des deuteronomistischen Geschichtswerks," 171-186.

[23] It also occurs in Dt 4,29; 6,5; 10,12; 11,13; 13,4; 26,16.

Interestingly enough, the majority of these keywords and key expressions are found within two blocks of this text: vv. 1-3 and 8-10, that is, at the beginning and the end. Only three occurrences of the word כל plus one corresponding phrase בכל־לבבך ובכל־נפשך can be found within vv. 4-7. The two extremes are especially interested in the corresponding activities of God and the audience. If *A* = if you (audience) repent/obey/listen (that is, the audience's activity) and *B* = God will bless/gather from exile, then there is one *AB* pattern (vv. 1-2 = *A*; v. 3 = *B*) and one chiastic pattern (v. 8 = *A*; v. 9 = *B*; v. 10 = *A'*). The chiasm can also be viewed in the following way:

A   תשוב
  B   ושמעת בקול יהוה
    C   vv. 8b-9: if you do all these commandments, the Lord will bless you and rejoice over you
  B'   תשמע בקול יהוה
A'   תשוב. [24]

5.2.3.2 Dt 30,11-14

This small section is so well balanced that it almost seems like poetry. To begin with, there is an inclusion here if one recognizes that מצוה (v. 11) and דבר (v. 14) are synonyms. A second inclusion is apparent in the contrast between רחקה in v. 11 and קרוב in v. 14.[25]

Then there is the fourfold repetition of לא ... הוא, which describes what the commandment is *not*. Two of these continue with parallel phrasing with only a few changes (vv. 12-13):

(v. 12)   לא בשמים הוא לאמר מי יעלה־לנו השמימה
             ויקחה לנו   וישמענו אתה ונעשׂנה :
(v. 13)   ולא־מעבר לים הוא לאמר מי יעבר־לנו אל־עבר הים
             ויקחה לנו.   וישמענו אתה ונעשׂנה :

---

[24] CHOLEWINSKI, *Deuteronomio* II, 31, sees a three-part structure in Dt 30,1-10, based on the threefold repetition of בכל־לבבך ובכל־נפשך: I. vv. 1-2 (the subject is Yahweh); II. vv. 3-6 (the subject is again Yahweh); and III. vv. 7-10 (the subject alternates: Yahweh - Israel - Yahweh - Israel). DI MARCO, *Il chiasmo nella Bibbia,* 32, follows LOHFINK, "Der Bundesschluß im Land Moab," 41, who sees a chiasm throughout Dt 30,1-10:

A   30,1-2   antecedent clause
  B   3-6   consequence
    C   7   consequence
      D   8   antecedent clause
    C'   9a   consequence
  B'   9b   consequence
A'   10   antecedent clause.

[25] CHOLEWINSKI, *Deuteronomio* II, 37.

Each of these two parallel sentences contains a similar question followed by a purpose clause to explain the question. Inclusion plus parallelism combine to produce a chiasm here:

A   The commandment is not... (v. 11)
  B   It is not in heaven... (v. 12)
  B'   It is not over the sea... (v. 13)
A'   The word is... (v. 14).

5.2.3.3 Dt 30,15-20

This final section of the Third Discourse of Moses begins with ראה, an imperative-turned-interjection which sets off the passage and attracts attention. An important semantic concept which joins the paragraph together is that of *life*: the noun חיים occurs four times (vv. 15.19[2X].20), while the verb חיה appears twice (vv. 16.19). But "length of days"(ארך ימיך) also appears in v. 20 and "you will lengthen days" = "you will live a long life" in v. 18. At the same time life's opposite, death (מות), occurs in vv. 15 and 19, while the threat in v. 18 (אבד תאבדן) is certainly in contrast with life.

This section is also tied together by an inclusion between vv. 15 and 19, for life and death are offered not once but twice to the audience. Between the two parallel offers appear parallel solemn declarations(הגדתי לכם היום in v. 18; העידתי בכם היום in v. 19). Thus another chiastic pattern appears here:[26]

A	נתתי לפניך ...את־החיים ... ואת המות	(v. 15)
B	הגדתי לכם היום	(v. 18)
B'	העידתי בכם היום	(v. 19aα)
A'	החיים והמות נתתי לפניך	(v. 19aβ).

In both A and A' a second choice is also offered, although they are different in each case: a choice between good and evil in v. 15 and between blessing and curse in v. 19a.

There is also a certain amount of *pairing* in vv. 15 and 19. V. 15 puts together synonyms: life and good (את־החיים ואת־הטוב) and death and evil (ואת־המות ואת־הרע). Of course life and death are antonyms, while good and evil are also antonyms. Similarly in v. 19 there is the pairing of contrasting terms or antonyms: life or death, blessing or curse. A further pair is found in the first part of v. 19, where heaven and earth are joined together as witnesses.

---

[26] NTAGWARARA, "Alliance d'Israël," 179, calls this a "double parallelism."

5.3 Rhetorical Arrangement

Rhetorical arrangement (*dispositio* or τάξις) deals with the order and disposition of ideas and arguments.[27] Thus there may be a difference between the rhetorical arrangement of a discourse and its literary structure. The two, however, will be related and will influence one another, since argumentation is embedded within the literary structure, while literary structure and style will contribute to the force of the argumentation.

Despite the efforts of ancient rhetoricians to define the various parts of an oration,[28] the arrangement of arguments does not really depend on a fixed form. The order of arguments depends largely on the desire to bring forward new premises, to make present certain ideas, and to get one's opponent to admit certain premises or conclusions.[29] Since argumentation is conditioned by the audience, the order of arguments will also depend on that audience. Thus elements which effect the order of a discourse include the rhetorical situation, the conditioning of the audience by the speech itself, and the reactions of the audience during the discourse.[30] The only important rule in *dispositio* is that arguments should be arranged in that order which gives them the greatest strength — and this depends to a great extent on the audience.[31]

5.3.1 Dt 28,69-29,1a

As already mentioned, this short section is reporting speech, that is, it is the voice of the narrator. As such it introduces and sets the scene for the Third Discourse of Moses. It introduces the two authoritative voices in the discourse, that of Moses (the actual sender in this communication act) and that of God. Neither has to prove or establish his authority; the fact that two discourses have already been given and that the Third Discourse is probably delivered in a liturgical context eliminates the need to spend time establishing an ethos. Yahweh simply commands Moses to perform a legal act (28,69), which Moses immediately does (29,1a). The entire following oration is dominated by the ethos and personality not only of Moses (the speaker) but also of Yahweh.

The Third Discourse is described as דברי הברית. This covenant is immediately given a descriptive definition (a quasi-logical argument),

---

[27] Corbett, *Classical Rhetoric*, 299; Marchese, *Dizionario di retorica e di stilistica*, 83.
[28] See 2.5.2, especially n. 149.
[29] Perelman and Olbrechts-Tyteca, *Traité de l'argumentation*, 651.
[30] Ibid.
[31] Ibid., 661; Perelman, *L'empire rhétorique*, 166.

which includes a historical fact (it was to be concluded with Israel in the land of Moab) and a distinction from a previous covenant on Horeb. The repetition of ברית and its accompanying descriptive legal language (ב ... כרת את־ ... אשר) certainly give a sense of presence to the notion of covenant. At the same time an underlying dissociation between particular covenants and a permanent relationship with God establishes the validity of this new ברית, which is equal to that made on Horeb. Since the establishment of a covenant (Dt 29,11-12) and the choice to follow its obligations (30,19) are the main subjects of the following discourse, this reporting speech briefly but forcefully introduces what will follow.

In these one and one-half verses the audience is mentioned twice. In 28,69 the בני־ישראל are the object of God's command to Moses, for they will be partners in a covenant. Dt 29,1a further defines this audience in a wide sense: כל־ישראל. Those who are listening must have perked up their ears immediately, for in a few words they have been mentioned twice and have heard of their involvement in a legal relationship which carries the authority of their "founder" and their God.

5.3.2 Dt 29,1b

The very first word of the discourse is personal and emphatic: אתם. What follows is the beginning of several ideas which will be developed in later verses. The first statement by Moses is an appeal to the audience's memory and to their own authority as witnesses. Moses calls upon the members of the audience to be his first witnesses, which means that they have to involve themselves from the very beginning. This personal testimony is reinforced by the threefold repetition of various forms of ראה and עינים in this half-verse and the next two verses.

The object of the audience's testimony is כל־אשר עשה יהוה. The audience will be reminded of certain historical facts that they themselves have witnessed. The first group of historical facts took place in Egypt and will extend into v. 2. The description of all these (historical) deeds of God will continue until a conclusion is drawn in v. 8. The list of God's deeds which follows is acceptable because a relationship is assumed between a person and his or her acts. These acts lead to certain lessons or conclusions in vv. 5 and 8, and thus a means-end sequential relationship may also be involved. Thus personal witness, historical facts, and arguments based on the structure of reality are already at work in the first verse of this discourse.

V. 1b also contains an amplification, since Yahweh's acts in Egypt were accomplished לפרעה ולכל־עבדיו ולכל־ארצו. Whatever feelings may be aroused by national or ethnic pride in the past are reinforced by a description of Yahweh's power: it affected not only the hated ruler but also his servants and his entire land. A sense of wonder must have begun already in this first verse, and it should grow throughout the next few verses.

5.3.3 Dt 29,2-3

In these two verses the appeal to historical facts and to the personal witness and memory of the audience continues. The repetition of ראה and עינים emphasizes what the audience has personally witnessed, although the final occurrence in v. 3 abruptly changes the idea and seems to be a kind of reproach. Despite their own eyes seeing all these wonderful deeds of the Lord, God has not given them eyes to see: an incompatibility appears. Dissociation here explains the apparent tautology, for "seeing" in this final sense refers to understanding. This is amplified by a *divisio,* for it is not only seeing eyes which the audience lacks. God has also not given them an understanding heart and listening ears. Such a rebuke might remind the audience of Isa 6,9-10.

V. 2 is basically an amplification of what the Lord has done, for it lists three synonyms describing such deeds: המסות הגדלת האתת והמפתים הגדלים ההם. It is thus building upon and developing the historical facts used as premises in this discourse, although they remain vague and abstract descriptions of Yahweh's deeds. Considering that a person is associated with his or her acts, the ethos of Yahweh can only develop positively. The audience must know these facts and thus needs only allusions to them.

Dt 29,1b-3 thus begins the Third Discourse of Moses by references to historical facts, by appeal to the personal memory and testimony of the audience, and by building up a feeling of wonder or awe before the deeds of Yahweh. V. 3 ends all this with the first negative judgment: there is a lack, a problem, a failure, for the audience fails to understand the significance of these wonderful deeds of God. V. 3 thus gives the exigence for the discourse and is important for understanding its rhetorical situation. This lack of understanding is something which has lasted עד היום הזה, a figure of presence which extends the problem to those who hear or read the discourse even now. The audience might be taken aback by this, for it is being provoked to pay close attention to what follows.

The rebuke in Dt 29,3 is especially effective because of repetition and contrast. Various forms of ראה and עינים occur three times in vv. 1b-3. In vv. 1b-2 there are two complimentary appeals to the witness authority of the audience. But these are followed by the negative evaluation of this testimony. Vv. 4-7 then contain specific reminders of some of the audience's experiences. Thus the rebuke is in the form of an ironic twist and is sandwiched between two sets of historical reminiscences.

5.3.4 Dt 29,4-5

In vv. 4-5 the recounting of historical facts continues. Now they recall the forty years of wandering in the wilderness. Again there is a sense of wonder at what the Lord has done, a sense of wonder brought out by the fourfold repetition of לא and the twofold occurrence of בלה and מעל. These illustrations of Yahweh's power are in the form of amplification, since four sets of "non-occurrences" are listed: their clothes didn't wear out, their shoes didn't wear out (v. 4), they had no bread to eat, no wine or other alcohol to drink (v. 5). The description of the clothes and shoes in v. 4 is probably hyperbole, used to elicit wonder from the audience. God's power (and authority) have been reaffirmed by these illustrations. Since illustrations help to "establish reality," a firm basis is being built for the decision to conclude and live out the covenant relationship, toward which the Third Discourse of Moses is leading. The illustrations are also associated with relations of co-existence (a person and his or her acts).

V. 5b is a kind of conclusion or lesson to be drawn from all these illustrations. Again it is also a shock to the audience, since Moses' voice changes to that of God (and just as quickly reverts to that of Moses). There is the authority of a citation or quotation of God's words here, which emphasizes God's authority and perhaps puts a bit of "the fear of God" into the audience, since God's voice suddenly and mysteriously enters and again disappears.[32]

The illustrations or historical facts which serve as premises in the opening section of the Third Discourse have led to a conclusion in v. 5. They help the audience to recognize and acknowledge Yahweh, who will later be involved with an important choice on their part. In v. 3b we learned that Yahweh had not yet made it possible to understand the meaning of his powerful acts in history, and thus an exigence was

---

[32] A question arises: Where does God actually begin speaking, that is, where does the quotation begin? LXX may have felt that the citation was out of place and thus translated ὅτι οὗτος κύριος ὁ θεὸς ὑμῶν. BLC follows LXX and translates the quotation in the third person. Most translations and commentaries avoid quotation marks and thus make no judgment about where the citation may begin. One or the other, including NAB, begin the citation with v. 4. Thus all vv. 4-5 would be Yahweh speaking. This is certainly a good possibility, since God himself could be said to have led the people for forty years in the wilderness. But there is no formal indication of a break here, and only when the identity formula occurs (אני יהוה אלהיכם) is one aware that God is speaking. However, the ancient audience may have been able to distinguish the citation at the beginning of v. 4 with the word ואולך. For the only other occurrences of הלך *hiphil* in Dt can be found in 8,2.15; 28,36 (all in the Second Discourse). In all of these instances Yahweh is the one who leads, and nowhere in Dt does Moses lead the people using this word. The two appearances in chap. 8 specifically refer to God leading the audience. However, none of these examples is in the first person. Thus only ואולך in Dt 29,4 could possibly begin a citation.

revealed. Now in v. 5b that meaning seems to be hinted at. Yahweh
identifies himself through his deeds, and the audience should marvel and
should fear this powerful God. It's important that they get to know him.
Yahweh is powerful, he has authority, and somehow he is tied to the
collective memory of this nation, its history.

5.3.5 Dt 29,6-7

Vv. 6-7 continue the illustrations of God's wonderful deeds which
come from Israel's national history. But now it is the people (together
with their leader Moses) who act; there is no miracle or wonder involved,
even if Yahweh is behind the events of this history. With sentiments of
pride and wonder the audience is reminded of its victories over two kings,
victories associated with the audience's present location (ותבאו אל־המקום
הזה). In this history of battles and taking possession of the land Moses
identifies strongly with his audience (ונכם ,לקראתנו [v. 6]; ונתנה ,ונקח [v. 7]).
Here an individual member of the audience can easily identify with the
group which has accomplished these great deeds.

5.3.6 Dt 29,8

All the indications are that this verse is a conclusion or an inference
to what precedes it. The דברי הברית in the reporting speech of 28,69, which
announced the beginning of this discourse, resounds again here. The
demonstrative adjective זאת also seems to make the covenant very present.
At the same time the expression את כל־אשר תעשון (referring to what the
audience will do in the future) sounds very much like the את כל־אשר עשה
(referring to what Yahweh did in the past) of 29,1b.

Dt 29,8 contains two *weqataltí* verbs which have imperatival force
(ושמרתם and ועשיתם) The historical facts presented and the emotions
raised seem to insist that the listeners observe the covenant. Whether one
considers the sequential relations in vv. 1b-8 as fact-consequence or
means-end, the conclusion is that such wonders should result in
observance of the covenant. If one prefers to think in terms of
enthymemes, the logical process may proceed in this manner:

p^1: [Every wonderful god's covenant should be observed.]
p^2: Yahweh is a wonderful God.
c: Therefore, Yahweh's covenant should should be observed.

But the conclusion does not end with the necessity of observing the
covenant stipulations. It quickly adds a promise: למען תשכילו את כל־אשר
תעשון. There is a reward for obedience. The repetition of עשה also seems
to hint at its possibility, since there is ambiguity here. ועשיתם is imperatival
and refers to the keeping of the covenant regulations; תעשון may refer

to the covenant regulations, but it can also concern anything the audience is successful at in the future. This last promise exhibits another cause-effect relationship, for it claims that prosperity is the result of the observance of the covenant.

5.3.7 Dt 29,9-10

Another emphatic personal pronoun begins v. 9, drawing attention to the audience's presence. Other figures of presence in this verse are the time indicator היום and the place indicator לפני יהוה אלהיכם. Both seem to indicate a liturgical event. Similar terms are repeated in v. 14.

The participant list of vv. 9-10, as noted in chapter 3, is widely inclusive. Most individuals and groups within the community would identify with one or more of the participants listed. It presumes a common social identity. The list might serve as a *divisio,* a descriptive definition, or an amplification. The group and its members are identified, and various sentiments may be associated with these participants. Certainly a sense of familiarity and the common bond found in such a socially cohesive group would promote a sense of belonging, a sense of "we are all in this together." The only participant who receives a brief description or definition is the resident alien (v. 10).

5.3.8 Dt 29,11-12

Vv. 11 and 12 are similar in that both express the purpose of this gathering, and each verse can be generally considered as synonymous with the other. This audience is standing before Yahweh today in order to make a covenant with him (v. 11), to establish a special relationship with him (v. 12). Both verses also express the second part of a means-end relationship begun in vv. 9-10: by means of the gathering of this audience a covenant relationship will be established.

V. 11 uses legal terminology: ברית (already found in 28,69; 29,1.8), אלה (its first occurrence both in the Third Discourse as well as in Dt as a whole), כרת עמך, and עבר ב. ברית and אלה are synonyms here. In fact, the relative clause which begins with אשר and describes the אלה is an amplification (the figure may be specifically an *interpretatio*).

V. 12 is also an amplification, since it says the same thing as v. 11, but in different words. It accumulates other phrases as well, for כאשר דבר־לך and כאשר נשבע לאבתיך are synonymous, and the ancestors' names are specifically given. This may add a certain authority or ethos to the covenant, which had not only been promised to the audience but had also been sworn on oath to their ancestors.

Finally, both vv. 11 and 12 repeat the היום of v. 9. The covenant relationship is very present, for it is being established *today*.

These two verses emphasize a particular (covenant) relationship with God. It is this relationship with which Dt 29,8 is concerned and from which the regulations flow which must be observed. Thus vv. 11-12 help to define and amplify the issue raised in 29,8.

5.3.9 Dt 29,13-14

In v. 13 the accumulation of synonyms and legal terms found in v. 11 (כרת, אלה, ברית) is repeated. But now the subject is different. Instead of Yahweh, it is the speaker (in the first person singular, that is, אנכי = Moses) who establishes the covenant.

V. 14 is full of repetitions, amplification, and parallelism. In it appears twice the word היום, which is a strong figure of presence (the twofold occurrence of פה is also a figure of presence). The verse also repeats in slightly different words the formula (found in v. 9) which seems to indicate a liturgical context: עמד היום לפני יהוה אלהינו. The two phrases in the verse which are separated by this formula are parallel amplifications which are likewise repetitions, since they differ only by one word:

את־אשר ישנו פה עמנו
ואת אשר איננו פה עמנו.

The words which are different (ישנו and איננו) are antonyms. They are *contraries* but not really incompatibilities, since together they announce a widely-inclusive audience. The phrases form a kind of *divisio* or description which probably touches on both pathos and logos. As figures of presence the phrases bring to mind those present and absent and all the sentiments associated with such an audience; as a quasi-logical argument they help to define and identify the audience.

This amplification and definition is tied to a means-end relationship in reverse: you are standing here (v. 14: means) in order to enter into a covenant (vv. 11-12: end). This repeats and inverts the same means-end relationship found in vv. 9-12. In fact, vv. 13a.14 are essentially an amplification and repetition of vv. 9-10, while v. 13b largely repeats v. 11.

The ethos of v. 14 is in contrast with that of v. 13. In v. 13 there is a sharp distinction between the speaker (אנכי) and the audience (אתכם). But in v. 14 that distinction is eliminated by three first-person plural pronoun endings (עמנו [2x] and אלהינו). These identify the speaker with the audience and are thus figures of communion.

5.3.10 Dt 29,9-14

This section is a tightly-bound unity which describes the audience of the Third Discourse and the purpose of the assembly in which they are participating. The speaker identifies the audience and establishes a relationship with it, especially by means of figures of presence and communion, by repetition and amplification. This audience has a common social identity with a recognizable hierarchy and with links to the past (v. 12: ancestors) and to the future (v. 10: children; v. 14: those not here).

There is a strong sense of presence from adverbs of time and place: היום (5x: vv. 9a.11b.12a.14a.14b), פה (vv. 14a.14b), and לפני אלהיכם ינו (vv. 9.14). A sense of communion between the speaker and audience is minimal at first: from the first word in v. 9 (אתם) until the אתכם of v. 13a all the references are to the second person, either singular (vv. 10-12) or plural (vv. 9.13a). This separation between speaker and audience is emphasized by the אנכי of v. 13b. This אנכי identifies the speaker with God's authority, since both make the covenant with the people. Then v. 14 establishes communion between sender and receiver by the threefold use of the first-person plural ending and a total lack of second-person references.

There is a sequential means-end relationship here as well, since the audience has gathered with an end in view: the establishment of a covenant with Yahweh. This relationship rests on the authority of God's promises and the audience's relationship to their ancestors (v. 12). Dt 29,9-14 follows up on the issue expressed in v. 8 by defining the relationship between Yahweh and the audience and by describing that audience. The use of legal language marks the serious or "official" nature of this occasion and this relationship. The accent in this section, however, seems to be on pathos and ethos.

5.3.11 Dt 29,15-16

V. 15 returns to historical facts and to the personal witness of the audience. In very general terms the speaker makes reference to the sojourn in Egypt and to the period of wandering in the desert. The verse begins with an emphatic second person plural pronoun (אתם) followed by a verb in the second person plural (ידעתם). Here personal testimony is invoked, testimony based on the memories of Egypt and of other lands. The verse also ends with a verb in the second person plural (עברתם).

However, what comes between the two verbs is phrased in the first person plural — thus the speaker shares with the audience these common memories. What they witnessed is emphasized and made present also by a repetition:

אַת אשר־ישבנו ב ...
.ואת אשר־עברנו ב ...

The two roots which are not repeated are antonyms.

This personal witness continues in v. 16, for the verb (ותראו) is an amplification (perhaps even a synonym) of ידעתם in v. 15. Now what the audience can testify to is given in specific terms: את־שקוציהם ואת גלליהם עץ ואבן כסף וזהב אשר עמהם.There is amplification here, since the idols of the nations are first described by means of two emotionally "loaded" synonyms (שקוציהם and גלליהם) and then a *divisio* or descriptive definition is given of the materials used to make them — wood and stone, silver and gold. The terms and the description are meant to ridicule these idols and to raise emotions such as disgust, abhorrence, or even hatred. Such terms may also contribute to ethos here if they remind the audience of the prophets Jeremiah and Ezekiel.[33]

The witness of such disgusting things recalls the witness of God's wonders in the very same localities (Egypt, the nations). An incompatibility is raised, for there is a great difference between the wonders of Yahweh and these disgusting idols. In fact, a dissociation underlies the incompatibility: the false gods or abominations cannot be compared with our God Yahweh. The gods of the nations (29,17) are just not in the same class as יהוה אלהינו. It is in these verses that for the first time the process begins of establishing an incompatibility which will result finally in the choice demanded in Dt 30,19.

5.3.12 Dt 29,17

V. 17 is meant to be a conclusion to vv. 15-16. From what they have witnessed, the audience should be able to draw a lesson.[34] Thus the disgusting things of the nations are illustrations of their depravity, just as the wonders in Egypt and in the desert were illustrations of the power of Yahweh. the contrast (and therefore incompatibility) between Yahweh and the other gods continues. This incompatibility is brought out in v. 17 by the mention of the danger of abandoning Yahweh (פנה ... מעם יהוה אלהינו) in order to serve the gods of the nations (ללכת לעבד את־אלהי)

---

[33] Cf. 4.3.

[34] A similar reasoning process occurs in Dt 29,1-8. Vv. 3, 5, and 8 all seem to be conclusions or inferences of what precedes them. The lesson in v. 3 is an apparent tautology which can be resolved by dissociation. The play on words links it strongly to vv. 1-2. The lessons or conclusions in vv. 5 and 8 seem to be more like that in 29,17. Seeing or witnessing certain events or knowing certain facts can produce a conclusion, perhaps in a form of inductive reasoning. Modern logic sometimes uses the formula "if *p*, then *q*." The ancient Hebrews may have sensed something similar when the perceptions were involved. The eyes (and perhaps other sense as well) seem to serve as witnesses or intermediaries in the thinking process: if (the eyes see) *p*, then *q*. LOHFINK, *Das Hauptgebot*, 125-128 (especially 127-128), sees a deuteronomic "Schema der Beweisführung" in Dt 29,1b-8 (as well as in Dt 1,29-31; 4,32-40; 7,6-11; 8,2-6; 9,4-7; 10,20-22; 11,1-7). However, his schema is built upon historical facts plus the use of the terms ידע and שמר.

הגוים ההם). Such action is incompatible with Dt 29,11-12, which proclaims a special relationship between Yahweh and the audience. In fact, Yahweh is described here as *our* God (אלהינו), a figure of communion between speaker and audience. What the sender and receiver share is a special relationship with Yahweh. Serving other gods is incompatible with this relationship. Such activity would also set up a barrier between speaker and audience.

A relation of co-existence also appears here between a group and its members. Since any man, woman, or group in the audience could become similar to poison and bitterness, there is a sense of danger here for the entire community. This sense is emphasized and made present by the amplification (*divisio*) in the first part of the verse, where a list of possible apostates is given: a man, a woman, a family or clan, a tribe. This list is an *incrementum* or *auxesis,* for the words are placed in a kind of increasing order.

The feeling of horror or fear is reinforced by the repetition at the beginning and end of the verse (פן־יש בכם), by the chiastic structure,[35] by emotionally "loaded" terms (ראש ולענה), and by the use of metaphor. For the sinful individual or group is compared with a plant which produces dangerous poison and disgusting bitterness. Such vivid language provokes emotions such as horror, fear, or hatred, for these sinners are described in a way that associates them with what is dangerous and abhorrent.

5.3.13 Dt 29,15-17

This section returns to personal witness and to historical facts as illustrations which draw a conclusion. The viewpoint is different from that of vv. 1-8. There the personal witness of God's wonders led to the acknowledgment of his identity and the observance of his covenant. Here the personal witness of the disgusting idols of the nations should lead to the avoidance of a dangerous situation. An enthymeme may best describe the logical process here:

p¹: [If you have seen disgusting things, you should avoid them.]
p²: You have seen disgusting things.
c: Therefore, you should avoid them.

---

[35] Dt 29,17 seems to have a chiastic pattern:

A	...פן־יש בכם
B	אשר לבבו פנה היום מעם יהוה אלהינו
B'	ללכת לעבד את־אלהי הגוים ההם
A'	.פן־יש בכם...

A and *A'* are not only repetitious but describe the sinner in real (*A*) or figurative (*A'*) terms. *B* and *B'* are synonymous phrases for apostasy. Thus they would be amplification.

At the same time v. 17 builds on the incompatibility between the worship of other gods and the worship of Yahweh:

p¹: [All who worship other gods turn away from Yahweh.]
p²: If you worship other gods,
c: You turn away from Yahweh.

Up to v. 15 the Third Discourse testified to the (historical) wonders and marvels of Yahweh and focused on an audience with a special relationship with him. Figures of presence and communion, pathos, and ethos are the chief means to highlight this special relationship. But logical argumentation is also being used to infer the necessity of observing the covenant. With vv. 15-17 a negative aspect enters the argumentative process. There is a dissociation between Yahweh and other gods. Therefore the service of other gods is not only dangerous but disgusting. Any individual or group within the community which worships other gods — even secretly (בללבו) — is making a grave mistake.

5.3.14 Dt 29,18

V. 18 now gives an illustration of a mistaken individual who plots evil or defection in his heart (בלבבו). He thus serves as an *anti-model*, someone who is cited as an example of what *not* to do. This individual has heard the words of the אלה — note here that the term ברית is avoided and the more negative word is used. Despite his hearing the curse, the anti-model does not draw the proper conclusions. Instead he rebels secretly. The presumption is that the heart is the seat of thought and decision-making.

There is an appeal to pathos in this verse. Not only is אלה an emotionally "loaded" term, but so is בשררות לבי (the use of this expression may also remind the audience of the prophet Jeremiah, thus appealing to his authority). How could even the most foolish sinner so readily admit his own stubbornness? Through imaginary direct speech the sinner's thoughts are not only revealed but also accentuated. The listener or reader should be horrified by these foolish thoughts accentuated by loaded terms. Since a person is associated with his or her acts (which include thoughts), one can quickly imagine some horrifying consequences (which appear in the next two verses).

The sinner tries to justify himself by means of a maxim and an enthymeme. The maxim, based on a metaphor associating the wet with the community and the dry with the individual, fools the sinner into believing that he will be safe despite his sinfulness. It is an example of fallacious reasoning.[36]

---

[36] Cf. 4.5.1, no. 7.

5.3.15 Dt 29,19-20

These two verses give the results of the individual's sinfulness. The punishments inflicted upon him are threats to the audience, which should be drawing the proper conclusions from this illustration of the anti-model. Various emotionally "loaded" terms are used here: רעה (v. 20); אלה (twice, once in each verse; in v. 20 the plural form אלות appears); and terms for anger (אף־יהוה וקנאתו in v. 19). Legal terminology also appears in a kind of parallel and repetitive amplification:

(v. 19b)	כל־האלה	הכתובה בספר	הזה
(v. 20b).	ככל אלות הברית הכתובה בספר התורה הזה		

Metaphors in v. 19 add vivid imagery to make the punishments seem present and abhorrent: God's anger and jealousy "smoke" (יעשן), while the curse "lies down on" or "settles on" (רבצה) the sinner. To "wipe out" or "blot out" a name (ומחה...את־שמו), a vivid image, is probably also a metaphor. This kind of vivid imagery certainly raises emotions such as fear, dread, or abhorrence.

Arguments in these two verses are represented by threats and a cause-effect relationship. In v. 19 four different threats are given: God will not forgive, his anger will burn, curses will settle on the sinner, and the individual's name will be wiped out. To these v. 20 adds the threat of separating the individual from the community and consigning him to evil (a kind of excommunication?). Interestingly enough, despite the vivid imagery, the punishments envisioned by these threats are rather vague and abstract. The cause-effect relationship here begins in v. 18 (or even in v. 17): sin brings about punishment.

5.3.16 Dt 29,18-20

In this section an anti-model is presented as an illustration of the danger given in v. 17. The illustration flows naturally from the list of possible sinners in that verse. The language in vv. 18-20 is strongly emotional, with an emphasis on anger, punishment, threats, and legal terminology. So pathos is quite evident here. The sinner has only to *think* about apostasy (בלבבו) in order to be punished, and not even membership in the community will save him. For the first time in the Third Discourse threats appear and one of the principal cause-effect relationships in the oration (sin brings about punishment) has been raised. The curse or oath has been mentioned before this (29,11.13 — as a synonym for ברית), but here it is negative and threatening.

5.3.17 Dt 29,21-22

With v. 21 begins a long section on the land which ends in v. 27. This section is an illustration of the punishment of the sinful community. V. 21 also introduces an imaginary conversation which extends as well to v. 27. The conversation is divided into three parts by the use of the verb אמר at the beginning of vv. 21, 23, and 24.

Numerous commentators have remarked that the transition between vv. 20 and 21 is not a smooth one, and some have even seen a major break at this point.[37] The change from the punishment of the individual sinner to the following generation's questions on the punishment of the land is indeed abrupt. (The change from individual to group sinfulness, however, flows naturally from v. 17, which mentions both dangers.) The authors seem so concerned about including the consequences of both individual and group defection from Yahweh within the discourse that they neglected a smooth transition from the one to the other. If the question-and-answer scheme is conventional and stereotyped — which it seems to be[38] — the authors' unwillingness to change the form may explain the rough transition.

Certainly the rhetorical effect is to attract attention and to lead the audience into accepting the notions of both individual and communal punishment. For the ambiguity here forces the audience to contemplate the prospect that the punishment of the land was associated with the lone individual who had sinned. The entire nation's guilt is not mentioned until v. 24. Thus the abruptness is a bit of a shock while at the same time it leads to the conclusion that the cause-effect relationship between sin and punishment includes both individual and nation.

V. 21 contains two metaphors which are at the same time synonyms (מכות and תחלאיה). The land itself exhibits wounds and illnesses, metaphors which emphasize the extent of the punishment and the seriousness of the sin involved. The subject of ואמר is the future generation, but two different groups are meant. They will speak in the future after they have personally witnessed (וראו) these punishments. These groups are the audience's own children plus "the foreigner" — emotionally "loaded" terms whose contrast is emphasized by the following descriptive amplifications (בניכם אשר יקומו מאחריכם והנכרי אשר יבא מארץ רחוקה). The repetition of ארץ in this verse also contrasts a far-away land with *this* afflicted land.

---

[37] For example, Buis, *Le Deutéronome,* 391; Buis and Leclercq, *Le Deutéronome,* 183; Driver, *Deuteronomy,* 326; Mayes, *Deuteronomy,* 365; Reiter, "Der Bundesschluß," 33-35; Rofé, "The Covenant in the Land of Moab," 313.

[38] Cf. Hillers, *Treaty-Curses,* 65, n. 60; B. Long, "Two Question and Answer Schemata," 129-139; Skweres, "Strafgrunderfragung," 181-197; Vogels, "The Question of the Nations," 159-176.

V. 22 is certainly the most descriptive scene in the entire Third Discourse of Moses. It amplifies and describes the wounds and ills mentioned in v. 21. This is the ἐνάργεια or *demonstratio* so often mentioned by the ancient rhetoricians, a device which provokes emotions through concrete and vivid images. The picture of a devastated land is produced by the accumulation of destructive materials (sulphur, salt, burning), the accumulation of three synonymous phrases for the lack of vegetation (which includes a threefold repetition of לא), and the comparison of this scene with the overthrow of the legendary sinful cities Sodom and Gomorrah, Admah and Zeboiim. This overthrow is further amplified by the comment that Yahweh was responsibile for it. Two synonyms for God's anger are also given (באפו ובחמתו).

Despite the ואמר at the beginning of v. 21, the future generations do not say anything in these two verses. That's left for v. 23.

5.3.18 Dt 29,23-24

With the ואמרו at the beginning of this verse the imaginary conversation finally begins. It consists of two questions (both found in v. 23) followed by a long answer (vv. 24-27). The children of the audience and the distant foreigner, the subjects of ואמר in v. 21, do not actually speak. Rather they are replaced by כל־הגוים,[39] nations who do not know Yahweh but worship disgusting idols. The questions begin in a similar fashion: the first with על־מה, the second with מה. Since the answer in v. 24 begins with על־אשר, one gets the impression that there is a play on words here which links the questions with the answer. The first question asks why God has done this to the land; the second asks about God's anger. To some extent the questions are synonymous, and yet there is a difference in emphasis. The presumption in both is that Yahweh's anger leads to punishments and disasters, which is a cause-effect relation.

V. 24 presumes the historical facts of a covenant made with the audience's ancestors and of an exodus from Egypt. Once again it uses legal language (ברית and כרת), and the reference to the ברית יהוה אלהי אבתם seems to draw on the authority or ethos of both God and the ancestors. The second half of the verse is an amplification, for it further describes the covenant.

It is possible that the accusation here (עזבו) is a rather strong term. In any case this answer begins to describe an incompatibility that continues in v. 25: the covenant relationship with Yahweh excludes the worship of

---

[39] This may be more in line with the conventions of the so-called type A question and answer schemata. Cf. B. LONG, "Two Question and Answer Schemata," 130; VOGELS, "The Question of the Nations," *EgT* 90 (1980) 161-164, 167. The rhetorical device here is *anacoluthon*. Cf. GKC, §167b.

other gods. The same statement completes the cause-effect relationship begun in v. 23 but expressed in reversed order: abandoning the covenant brings about Yahweh's anger which brings about punishment.

5.3.19 Dt 29,25-27

These three verses continue and complete the answer to the question raised by the nations. In fact, vv. 24-27 can be considered as one long thought, seeing that the four main verbs in vv. 25-27 are all *wayyiqtols* (converted imperfects).

V. 25 completes the accusation against the community, which had abandoned Yahweh's covenant (v. 24) and served other gods. Here two synonyms (ויעבדו and וישתחוו) are used to describe that service, while אלהים אחרים are further defined as אלהים אשר לא־ידעום ולא חלק להם. This amplification (plus repetition) may be ridicule, and it confirms the incompatibility between these gods and Yahweh (which began in v. 24). At the same time v. 25 continues the cause-effect relationship begun in v. 24 (abandoning the covenant and serving other gods brings about God's anger and subsequent punishment).

V. 26 continues the explanation begun in v. 25 by answering the second question on God's anger. It repeats a phrase used in v. 19 (כל־האלה הכתובה בספר הזה), except that it substitutes קללה for אלה. קללה is the contrary or antonym of ברכה in the choice offered in Dt 30,19; it seems also to have a stronger emotional impact here than אלה would have, since it is associated more with anger.[40] The cause-effect relation (abandoning the covenant causes God's anger and punishment) continues here from vv. 24-25.

In v. 27 we note the end of the cause-effect relation under consideration since v. 24 (abandoning the covenant and serving other gods causes God's anger and punishment). The punishments mentioned here are loss of the land and exile. Both of these punishments are described through metaphors: uprooting or tearing out (ויתשם) the people from the ground and throwing them (וישלכם) to another land. These metaphors may recall the plant metaphor of 29,17. They certainly are vivid, giving a sense of presence to the punishment. They also emphasize the severity of the sin with its corresponding punishment as well as the power of God.

V. 27 also makes use of amplification, since three synonyms are used to describe God's anger (באף ובחמה ובקצף). Two other synonyms occur in אדמתם and ארץ. However, these two synonyms are contrasted, for they are

---

[40] LEFÈVRE, "Malédiction et bénédiction," 746-747; SCHARBERT, "'Fluchen' und 'Segnen' im Alten Testament," 11-13.

described as *their* ground but *another* land. The verse ends with a strong figure of presence: כיום הזה.

5.3.20 Dt 29,21-27

This entire section then is an imaginary conversation (questions followed by answers). Questions tend to attract the attention of an audience, since they demand an answer or response of some kind. This conversation is full of pathos, since it makes use of vivid scenes (ἐνάργεια or *demonstratio*), emotionally "loaded" terms (especially those of anger), repetition, and amplification. There are two major themes or semantic fields in this section. The first is the land, which suffers punishment and is lost to the sinful community (ארץ appears seven times in these seven verses, and four of these refer to the promised land; אדמה appears once in v. 27). The second is God's anger, expressed by eight nouns and one verb (in four different combinations of words, none of which is the same; however, the word אף appears in all of them: vv. 22b.23b.26a.27a).

The main logical argument in this section extends from v. 24 to v. 27. It expresses a cause-effect relation: the abandonment of the covenant brings about God's anger, which brings about punishment. This cause-effect relation is a reasonable one — even the idol-worshipping nations (v. 23: כל־הגוים) can see that!

5.3.21 Dt 29,28

This verse serves as a transition between chapters 29 and 30. It ends the emphasis on punishment that we have seen in 29,15-27 and leads to that of conversion in 30,1-10. Dt 29,28 ends with לעשות את־כל־דברי התורה הזאת. The legal term תורה occurs only once before this in 29,20 and once afterwards in 30,10. It may be considered parallel with or synonymous to ברית. The expression דברי הברית occurs in 28,69; 29,8; while דברי האלה occurs in 29,18. כל־הדברים האלה also appears in the following verse (30,1).

Whether the words are those of הברית or those of תורה, an important element in this verse is לעשות. It seems to refer back to 29,8, where the conclusion was that the audience should observe the words of the covenant and *do* them. In fact, in 29,8 the root עשה appears twice. This word also appears four times in chapter 30 (vv. 8.12.13.14), and each time it refers to obedience and to commandments. The word does not appear in the choice required of the audience in 30,15-20. However, considering the emphasis in Dt 30 on obedience which brings blessing, the same idea is present in the choice for blessing and life. Dt 30,20a may even be considered a paraphrase or *interpretatio* of לעשות את־כל־דברי התורה הזאת.

As noted above in 4.5.1, no. 9, there is a maxim in Dt 29,28 which serves as part of a hidden enthymeme:

p¹: [All things which belong to us can be done.]
p²: Revealed things belong to us.
c: Therefore, revealed things can be done.

Thus the maxim reinforces the idea that the *torah* can be done, since it is revealed by God. This will be taken up again in Dt 30,11-14.

The maxim suggests a dissociation: what is hidden is dissociated from what is revealed. The antonyms הנסתרת and הנגלת are also an expression of totality or *merismus*. The three words ולבנינו, לנו, אלהינו and are figures of communion which bind the speaker to the audience. At the same time they serve as figures of presence, since what is revealed belongs to us and to our children (who are also present). This sense of presence is reinforced and emphasized by עד־עולם (forever). The audience at this point, especially after hearing about the dire consequences of apostasy, can only recognize that it cannot escape the responsibilities demanded of it by the תורה or ברית revealed by *our* God.

5.3.22 Dt 30,1-3

V. 1 accumulates emotional terms (הברכה והקללה and perhaps גוים), legal terms (נתתי לפניך and perhaps כל־הדברים האלה), and two explanations or descriptions which are relative clauses beginning with אשר. It presumes that the blessing and curse have already been activated and that a new phase is about to begin. V. 1 also begins a long section of second person singular references.

V. 2 emphasizes the individual member of the audience through the use of the second person singular pronoun (אתה). Another figure of presence follows immediately with the reference to ובניך. The separation between speaker and audience is established by אשר אנכי מצוך היום: the first person singular pronoun focuses on the one who is giving commands, and a sense of presence is reaffirmed by היום. V. 2 is actually one long amplification of its first four words, for returning to the Lord is accomplished by obedience to his commands with all one's heart and soul (which is a *merismus* expressing the totality of the individual human being in his or her inner life); לבבך and נפשך in this expresson are metonymies (or perhaps synecdoches).

V. 3 contains references to and amplifications of v. 1: כל־העמים is synonymous with כל־הגוים in v. 1, and the explanatory clause which follows כל־העמים is parallel to the clause which follows כל־הגוים. In fact, the only difference between the two clauses in wording is in the verbs (הדיחך in v. 1; הפיצך in v. 3), which are also synonyms.

Taken as a whole, Dt 30,1-3 reveals a number of repetitive devices and amplifications. The root שוב, which is a keyword throughout 30,1-10, appears four times in these first three verses (vv. 1b.2a.3a.3b). The first occurrence is *hiphil,* the others are *qal.* The word כל appears six times, while there are four explanatory relative clauses beginning with אשר. Two of these are the parallel *interpretationes* found in vv. 1 and 3.[41]

The three verses together also develop a fact-consequence or (better) cause-effect relationship: conversion and obedience bring about restoration. As an enthymeme, it might be expressed in this way:

p¹: [All who change/obey will be restored.]
p²: If you change/obey,
c: You will be restored.

5.3.23 Dt 30,4-7

V. 4 is a short conditional proposition with an antecedent clause (protasis) and two synonymous consequences (apodosis). Within each apodosis there is repetition (משם: an *anaphora*) and a synonym (יקבצך and יקחך). The apodosis contains hyperbole (בקצה השמים), which emphasizes God's power and the wonder of this return from exile. The reasoning is *a pari* (which is a quasi-logical argument): if God can scatter you, he can likewise gather you. V. 5 contains repetitions of the verb ירש and of the word אבתיך. The promises made to the audience's ancestors, presumed historical and serving as a common bond, remind those present of a glorious past. The promise now is that they can enjoy a prosperity and an increase greater than that of their ancestors. The relative clause beginning with אשר which defines or explains הארץ is amplification. It links this entire section with 30,1-3, since it is the last of five such relative clauses.

Dt 30,6 also has a link with what precedes this section, since it repeats בכל-לבבך ובכל-נפשך, found in v. 2 (as well as in v. 10). The word לבב is found three times in this verse. The first two occurrences are objects of ומל and are not only repetition but part of an amplification. There are emotional links here with the audience's children and with future generations, who are included within this special action of Yahweh. In v. 6 cause-effect relations are also described: circumcision of the heart brings about love for God which brings about life. God's circumcision of the heart is a metaphor for interior change.

V. 7 contains a promise: God will transfer the curses to the audience's enemies. The objects of these curses are synonyms: איביך and שנאיך. These, plus the term האלות, are emotionally "loaded" terms with negative connotations: one naturally fears or hates one's enemies, and fear may also be associated with oaths or curses.

---

[41] The indications are that Dt 30,1-3 has a chiastic structure:

A	vv. 1-2aα:	שוב (2X) + בכל-הגוים אשר הדיחך יהוה אלהיך שמה
B	v. 2αβ.b:	ושמעת בקלו ככל אשר-אנכי מצוך היום
A'	v. 3:	שוב (2X) + מכל-העמים אשר הפיצך יהוה אלהיך שמה.

Dt 30,4-7 then is essentially a description of promised blessings: return from exile, prosperity, increase, inner renewal, and the punishment of one's enemies. The emphasis here is on what יהוה אלהיך will do, since he is the subject of all the main clauses and the object of one of the purpose/result clauses (v. 6b: לאהבה את־יהוה אלהיך). Rational arguments are built upon cause and effect, promises, and comparisons with the past and the future. The whole section revolves around the very first (provocative) word: אם.

5.3.24 Dt 30,8-10

V. 8 begins with an emphatic figure of presence (ואתה). It contains three short conditional clauses (protasis), whose consequence (apodosis) appears in v. 9. Again we find here the relative clause אשר אנכי מצוך היום, with its separation of speaker from audience and its sharp sense of presence. This clause also occurs in v. 2; here, however, it specifically modifies or amplifies כל־מצותיו.

V. 9 continues the conditional clause by supplying the consequence or apodosis: conversion, obedience, and practice of the law bring about prosperity (and the pleasing of God). This of course is a cause-effect relation. There is also repetition (פרי appears three times; a double use of לטובה ;שוש and לטוב) and amplification (four areas in which God will make his people abundant), plus a comparison with the golden age of the past. Of the three occurrences of פרי, at least two are metaphoric.

V. 10 contains a number of repetitions, most of which connect it with the previous two verses or even with all of 30,1-10. There is *anaphora* in this verse, since each half-verse begins with כי. These two actually repeat the כי found in v. 9b. תשמע בקול is a variation of the same expression found in vv. 2 and 8. תשוב is an exact repetition of the same root in v. 8a, and both rhyme with ישוב in v. 9b. V. 10 ends with בכל־לבבך ובכל־נפשך, an expression also found in 30,2.6. (הכתובה בספר התורה הזה is an expression not otherwise found in Dt 30,1-10, but it can be found in 29,20; while similar expressions occur in 29,19.26.)

V. 10 also contains legal terms (מצותיו, התורה, and חקתיו), the last two of which are synonyms. The cause-effect relation of vv. 8-9 is also found in vv. 9-10, but in reverse order: prosperity and the pleasing of God (v. 9) are brought about by obedience, observance of the law, and conversion (v. 10).

Dt 30,8-10 emphasizes conversion (שוב occurs three times), obedience, and observance of the commandments. In fact, by means of a chiastic conditional proposition, it emphasizes a cause-effect relationship: conversion, obedience, and observance of the commandments bring about blessing and prosperity. The structure could be described in this way:

A (v. 8 protasis: if you convert, obey, and do the commandments
 B (v. 9) apodosis: God will make you prosper
 A' (v. 10) protasis: if you obey, observe the commandments, and convert.

There seems to be an extraordinary amount of repetition and amplification in these three verses in order to get across this simple message (which summarizes chapter 30).

5.3.25 Dt 30,1-10

Dt 30,1-10 is characterized by the cause-effect relation of conversion and obedience bringing about blessing and prosperity. Its general chiastic structure reveals this emphasis: *A* (vv. 1-3): conversion and obedience; *B* (vv. 4-7): blessings; *A'* (vv. 8-10): conversion and obedience. Other features reinforce this relationship: the presumption that the curse has already been activated, the keyword שוב (7x: vv. 1.2.3[2x].8.9.10), the expression שמע בקול (vv. 2.8.10), and the keyword לבב (6x: vv. 1.2.6[3x].10).

There are other repetitions which bind this section together: בכל-לבבך ובכל-נפשך (vv. 2.6.10); אשר אנכי מצוך היום (vv. 2.8); and the keyword כל (13x). An interesting feature is the repetition of יהוה אלהיך (12x in these ten verses; also the name יהוה appears alone in vv. 8 and 9[42]). In the Third Discourse of Moses יהוה אלהיך appears before this only in 29,11. Otherwise יהוה occurs alone or with אלהיכם or אלהינו. Although the rest of Dt 30 also makes use of יהוה אלהיך, it is found only four times in vv. 16-20, and not at all in vv. 11-15. The emphasis in vv. 1-10 then is on a relationship with *your* (singular) God, who acts and intervenes in this conversion process of the audience.[43]

It is to be noted that the promises and blessings here are not given in such vivid and descriptive language as the threats and punishments of Dt 29,15-27. The emotions raised in this section would certainly include hope and desire for benefits or blessings.

5.3.26 Dt 30,11-14

In this section Dt's prose comes very close to poetry, for it is replete with repetition, amplification, and parallelism. There is a fourfold occurrence of לא ... הוא (vv. 11-13), each of which encloses an

---

[42] BHS notes that a few manuscripts in Hebrew as well as Sam, LXX, Syr, and Vg all add אלהיך in Dt 30,8. No similar comments are made for v. 9.

[43] In eight of twelve occurrences in Dt 30,1-10, יהוה אלהיך is the subject of the verb: vv. 1b.3a.3b.4b.5a.6a.7a.9a. In v. 9b the single name יהוה also acts as a subject.

amplification, since בשמים, רחקה, נפלאת, and מעבר לים are practically synonyms. Each phrase can be paraphrased "it is not far" or "it is not beyond our reach." The last two of these four phrases add further repetitions and amplifications to create close parallels. Thus לאמר מי occurs twice, לנו four times, and a large part of the imaginary citation twice: ויקחה ... וישמענו אתה ונעשׂנה.

These verses also contain synonyms (v. 11: המצוה; v. 14: הדבר) and antonyms (v. 11: רחקה; v. 14: קרוב; since רחקה is negated, the two descriptions or expressions are actually synonymous). המצוה (v. 11) is defined by the amplification אשׁר אנכי מצוך היום. This is a repetition of 30,2.8 (with its emphasis on the separation of speaker and audience and with figures of presence in היום and in the command). The word עשׂה appears three times in this section (vv. 12.13.14), each time concluding the verse. The focus then is on *doing* the law and defending its possibility (the topic of the possible and the impossible enters here). This repetition of עשׂה may be a reference to Dt 29,8.28. The double mention of "heaven" (v. 12) and "across the sea" (v. 13) is both hyperbole (expressing what is very distant) and *merismus* (expressing a totality).[44] There is also accentuation in the imagined citation of the audience in vv. 12-13.

An enthymeme probably best clarifies the logical thought of this section:

p^1:   [All that is near can be done.]
p^2:   The law is near.
c: Therefore, the law can be done.

We may recall that Dt 29,28 contained a vaguely similar enthymeme, for it also refers to what is possible, to what can be done. Another way to view the logic of Dt 30,11-14 is in terms of an argument of division: The law may be either far away or near; since it is not far away, it must be near! Such an argument, of course, offers no proof other than its relationship with 29,28 (and perhaps also with Dt 4,7-8). Like much religious rhetoric, Moses chooses to proclaim or announce this fact without attempting to prove it.[45] But the very fact that he has just proclaimed a law code in the Second Discourse gives him the ethos to do so.

Dt 30,11-14 has its own logos, but it seems much more directed by pathos. It is appealing to the audience's emotions while proclaiming the nearness of the law. More than anything else it seems to be answering an objection, perhaps one expressed by the double and parallel questions. There is no need to send someone to fetch the law for us — it is on your

---

[44] Cf. KRAŠOVEC, *Der Merismus*, 38.

[45] Cf. FRYE, *The Great Code*, 29; GRASSI, *Rhetoric as Philosophy*, 103-104; KENNEDY, *New Testament Interpretation*, 6, 158.

lips and in your heart. That is, it can be proclaimed, pondered over, and accomplished.

5.3.27 Dt 30,15-18

V. 15 begins with ראה, which demands the attention of the audience. It is an interjection whose original form is that of an imperative. It signals that what follows is important. And what follows is legal language (נתתי לפניך) plus a figure of presence (היום) folllowed by incompatibilities requiring a choice. Two synonyms (החיים and הטוב) are followed by two other synonyms (המות and הרע), which are antonyms of the first pair. The choice is being described even if no demand is yet made to choose. That will come only after another quick summary of all that has been said in Dt 29, 15 – 30,10.

V. 16 summarizes the promise of blessings which result from obedience. With or without an ellipsis, the verse expresses a cause-effect relation: love for God and observance of his commandments brings about life, increase, and blessing. Repetition, amplification, and accentuation all appear in this verse to reinforce this idea.

The verse begins with אשר אנכי מצוך היום, a repetition of Dt 30,2.8.11. Once again it distinguishes between speaker and audience while adding figures of presence (היום and "command"). This separation between sender and receiver will continue and will even be emphasized in the remainder of the Third Discourse. Dt 30,15-20 has no first-person plural forms which could provide communion between speaker and audience. Instead there are first-person singular (v. 15: נתתי; v. 16: אנכי; v. 18: הגדתי; v. 19: העידתי and נתתי) and second-person (all singular except for vv. 18-19aα) forms. In fact, the emphatic second-person singular pronoun (אתה) appears three times in these verses (vv. 16.18.19). It is up to every individual in the audience to make this choice.

Another repetition in v. 16 is לאהבה את־יהוה אלהיך, which also occurs in 30,6.20. Amplification is prolific in this verse: there are three tasks (love God, walk in his ways, observe his commands), three synonyms for laws (מצותיו וחקתיו ומשפטיו), and three results or blessings (וחיית ורבית וברכך יהוה אלהיך). The land is further defined as that which *you* are about to enter and inherit.

Vv. 17-18 reminds the audience of the punishments for disobedience. V. 17 presents the protasis (ואם). This verse is largely amplification, for it presents the sin of apostasy with five brief but synonymous expressions: יפנה לבבך, ולא תשמע, ונדחת, והשתחוית, and ועבדתם. V. 18 completes the conditional proposition with its consequence or apodosis: the threat of destruction and death. It does this through a solemn legal proclamation on the part of the speaker (הגדתי לכם היום), through emphatic and synonymous expressions (אבד תאבדון and לא־תאריכן ימים), and through an

amplified description of האדמה which recalls and parallels a similar
description of ארץ (a synonym) in v. 16.

Dt 30,16-18 sets up an incompatibility to clarify the options before
the final command to choose. Those options: the promise of blessings in
the case of loyalty and the threat of doom in the case of infidelity. The
cause-effect relations here are therefore two: obedience and loyalty bring
about blessings (v. 16), while disobedience and infidelity bring about
punishments (vv. 17-18). These three verses summarize the Third Address
of Moses by presenting the two choices and their consequences.

5.3.28 Dt 30,19-20

V. 19 begins with a solemn legal declaration parallel to that in v. 18
(העידתי בכם היום). Moses himself, with all his authority and ethos,
solemnly calls on heaven and earth (*merismus* and personification) to
witness the choice presented to the audience. The language is both similar
to and different from v. 15. For the speaker presents (נתתי לפניך, the same
words as v. 15) a choice between two antonyms (החיים והמות) followed by
two other antonyms (הברכה והקללה), each of which is synonymous with
one of the words in the first pair of antonyms. The pairing of antonyms
reinforces their incompatibility: a choice must be made between them, for
both are not possible.

After this comes the imperative (or near-imperative): ובחרת בחיים.
There's no doubt about which choice the speaker wants the audience to
make. Choosing life has a result which is a cause-effect relation: choose
life that you may live. This "you" (אתה) is emphatic, and it is joined by
וזרעך; this choice affects not only the audience but its descendants. The
appeal is not only rational but also emotional.

V. 20 ends the Third Discourse with a final description of what
choosing life means. This description could be seen as an expanded version
of Dt 29,8. For the third and final time in Dt 30 (see also vv. 6 and 16) the
expression לאהבה את־יהוה אלהיך appears. Choosing life consists of three
synonymous tasks: loving God, obeying him, and "sticking" to him (this
last expression is a strong image of fidelity and may be a metaphor).

Other synonyms in v. 20 are חייך and ארך ימיך. There is also
amplification in the description of the ground and the naming of the
three ancestors. The very last things mentioned in the Third Discourse
are positive and "upbeat": love, obedience, fidelity; life, land, and the
promise to the ancestors. These are the natural results of choosing life.

5.3.29 Dt 30,15-20

This final section of the Third Discourse is the culmination of the
entire speech. Making use of the incompatibilities and cause-effect

relations expressed throughout Dt 29–30, this final section calls attention to itself (v. 15: ראה) and then twice proceeds to offer a choice to the audience (vv. 15.20: נתתי לפניך). Between the two offers there is a final description or summary of the results of fidelity and of infidelity. The covenant (ברית), so important for Dt 29, is not even mentioned in chapter 30. Instead there is a focus on the difference between promise and threat, blessing and curse, life and death. In fact, *life* is the keyword in these verses: the noun חיים occurs four times (vv. 15.19[2x].20), the verb חיה twice (vv. 16.19), and other expressions for long life twice (v. 18: תאריכן ימים; v. 20: וארך ימיך).

Dt 29, 8 introduced the notion of observing and doing the covenant regulations. In Dt 30,15-10 שמר appears only once (v. 16), but neither ברית nor עשה (other important words in 29,8) appear at all. And yet twice this final part of the Third Discourse summarizes neatly what observing or doing the covenant is all about: לאהבה את־יהוה אלהיך ללכת בדרכיו ולשמר מצותיו וחקתיו ומשפטיו (v. 16a); and לאהבה את־יהוה אלהיך לשמע בקלו ולדבקה־בו (v. 20a). Each of these summaries appears immediately after the choice offered to the audience.

The call to choose between life and death, blessing and curse, good and evil, is hardly impartial. There is no doubt that Moses wants his audience to choose rightly, and that means to choose life. That choice will result in the observance of God's laws but also in an attitude that affects the emotions, for it includes the love of God, obedience, and fidelity. The Third Discourse of Moses concludes without any indication of what the audience has chosen. But somehow that indication is not necessary. We can presume what choice the audience will make. After all, that is the aim of the author's rhetoric.

5.4 Summary

The Third Discourse of Moses is a persuasive speech designed to induce its audience to make a choice to observe the stipulations of a covenant. Its rhetorical arrangement or *dispositio* can be summarized in the following fashion:

I. Dt 28,69–29,1a: Reporting speech. This brief introduction to the discourse appeals to the authority of both God and Moses. It also mentions the audience (all Israel) and the main subject (a covenant relationship).

II. Dt 29,1b–30,20: The discourse itself. This can be divided into the following parts:

A. Dt 29,1b-7: Narration or statement of facts (*narratio*). Beginning with illustrations of historical facts and the appeal to the personal testimony of the audience, this section builds up a sense of wonder (pathos) and connects a person with his acts (Yahweh and his marvelous deeds). The problem or exigence is presented: the audience does not understand. The result of such personal witness should be the recognition of who Yahweh is (v. 5) and the observance of his covenant (v. 8).

B. Dt 29,8: Proposition (*propositio* or *expositio*). This verse is the logical conclusion of the narration and it states the issue of the discourse: the audience should observe the covenant. The emphasis is on doing, and imperatival force is attached to this doing. A promise of blessing is also attached to the doing. For the first time in this discourse the cause-effect relation of obedience bringing about blessing is presented. This verse then is basically what the Third Discourse is about, and the rest of the speech will be dedicated to persuading and convincing the audience to make a choice to observe the covenant.

C. Dt 29,9-14: The identification of the audience and the reinforcement of the proposition. This section appeals to the audience by defining it widely and by establishing a strong sense of presence. Vv. 11-12 are related to the proposition in v. 8 and may be said to reaffirm it or amplify it. The observance of the covenant is tied to a legal relationship established between God and the audience. Those who will be called upon to choose to follow this covenant relationship are defined and given an identity. The covenant relationship is linked to the authority and ethos of both God and the ancestors. Thus the accent is on pathos, ethos, a sense of presence, and the identity of the audience.

D. Dt 29,15–30,10: Proof or argumentation (πίστις, *confirmatio, argumentatio* or *amplificatio*). This section can be divided and subdivided into different parts.

D.1 Dt 29,15-27: The negative consequences of disobedience: punishment. There are three subsections:

D.1.a Dt 29,15-17: The discourse returns to illustrations of historical facts and to personal witness. Repetition, amplification, and emotionally "loaded" terms are used to inspire horror and/or fear. At the same time an incompatibility appears between the wonders of Yahweh and the disgusting things seen among the nations. A dissociation is also made between Yahweh and the other gods. Differences and incompatibilities are being established which will make it clear that a choice must be made. At this point a negative aspect (disobedience, punishment, other gods) is introduced which will continue until the end of chapter 29. Both individuals and groups could be involved in this defection from Yahweh.

D.1.b Dt 29,18-20: This is an illustration of the individual sinner or anti-model. This sinner makes use of fallacious reasoning in order to justify himself. For the first time in the Third Discourse there appear threats and the cause-effect relation (disobedience and infidelity bring about punishment) which will characterize one side of the choice. Pathos reigns supreme, for the language is highly emotional, and vivid metaphors reinforce those emotions (fear and horror). The emphasis is on anger, threats, punishment, and legal language.

D.1.c Dt 29,21-27: This section revolves around an imaginary future conversation or question-and-answer scheme. Questions attract the attention of the audience (as does the imaginary situation), while ἐνάργεια and vivid metaphors produce pathos (once again fear and horror are provoked). At the same time the incompatibility between a covenant relationship with Yahweh and the worship of other gods is developed. The cause-effect relation (disobedience and infidelity bring about punishment) continues. The themes here are the land and God's anger.

D.2 Dt 29,28: This verse is a transition which links the negative and positive aspects of the choice. Dt 29,28 refers back to the proposition in 29,8 and looks forward to 30,11-14. The maxim which is quoted teaches that what is possible can be done. Figures of presence remind the audience of its responsibilities.

D.3 Dt 30,1-10: Here the positive aspect of the choice is described. Repetition and amplification are numerous. The keyword is שוב, so the emphasis is on conversion. The cause-effect relation here demonstrates that conversion and obedience bring about restoration and blessing. Promises are made, but only with a condition: *if* there is conversion and obedience. The incompatibility between a relationship with Yahweh and the worship of other gods has now been completely described. There is a great difference between obedience and disobedience, between reward and punishment.

E. Dt 30,11-14: Refutation of a possible objection (*confutatio, refutatio,* or *reprehensio*). Before the offer of the choice can be made, an important objection must be anticipated and refuted. Is the observance of the law even possible? This section argues that it is. The use of an enthymeme and of an argument of division makes observance of the law seem reasonable. With authority, but also in communion with his audience, Moses proclaims that the law is near — and thus able to be put into practice. The use of repetition, amplification, and parallelism (with imaginary conversation, hyperbole, and *merismus*) gives this section a strong emotional thrust (desire and hope) as well.

F. Dt 30,15-20: Conclusion: the call for a choice (*peroratio, conclusio*). In this concluding section, which can be called a peroration,[46] there is a strong sense of presence, and the audience's attention is once

---

[46] BUIS and LECLERCQ, *Le Deutéronome,* 187, also call this section a peroration.

again demanded. Twice a choice is offered — no, demanded or commanded. The speaker separates himself from the audience and makes a solemn, legal declaration. This declaration is reinforced by the authority of Moses and the testimony of all creation. The incompatibility between Yahweh and the other gods is reiterated a final time through pairs of antonyms and a summary of the cause-effect relations which have appeared throughout the *confirmatio* (disobedience brings about punishment, fidelity brings blessing). There is no doubt about which choice is expected — it is even commanded. The discourse ends on a positive note: love, obedience, fidelity; life, land, and the promise to the ancestors all receive a final mention. Then all is silent. No record of the audience's response is given. Obviously it was not needed.

In this summary there are references to ancient Greek and Latin rhetorical terminology. This does not imply that ancient Hebrew discourses followed exactly the same arrangement. Even Greek and Roman rhetoricians recognized that particular speeches could deviate from the general pattern. The terminology is given, however, to show that various sections of Moses' Third Discourse at least approximate some of the various parts of an ancient Latin or Greek oration. Of course, there are also some differences.

Perhaps the greatest difference is that there is no real *exordium* in the Third Discourse of Moses. Dt 28,69 – 29,14 does perform some of the functions of an *exordium,* and yet it is probably more accurate to describe these introductory verses in other terms. The basic function of an *exordium* or introduction is to lead the audience into the discourse, to prepare it for what follows by making its members attentive, benevolent, and docile.[47] However, an *exordium* could be omitted in a speech (and often was). Considering that the Third Discourse of Moses is preceded by two other discourses, which have already established the authority of Moses, it is easy to understand why an *exordium* is not necessary here.

Otherwise it is to be noted that, at least in the case of the Third Discourse of Moses, some of the rhetorical terms for the arrangement of a speech can be applied to Hebrew discourse. It is probably wise not to overidentify the *dispositio* of a Hebrew oration with Greek and Roman concepts. At the same time it is evident that even the ancient Hebrews had to order their ideas and their arguments in a manner which would be effective. They too thought in terms of a beginning, a middle, and an end

---

[47] ARISTOTLE, *Rhetoric,* III.14.1415a; *Rhetorica ad Alexandrum,* XXIX.1436a; *Rhetorica ad Herennium,* I.iv.7-8; QUINTILIAN, *Institutio oratoria,* IV.1.5; CORBETT, *Classical Rhetoric,* 303, 311; PERELMAN and OLBRECHTS-TYTECA, *Traité de l'argumentation,* 656; PERELMAN, *L'empire rhétorique,* 161-162.

(even if they did not express it this way). They too attempted to persuade and convince their audiences with rational and emotional arguments. A discourse such as that of Dt 28,69 – 30,20 was organized to make sense and to make an impression on those who heard (or read) it.

In chapter six there will be an investigation of the third and final part of rhetoric: *elocutio* or style.

CHAPTER 6

ELOCUTIO

Chapter four concentrated on invention, which is the discovery of arguments. Chapter five investigated the arrangement of those arguments. This chapter will focus on style (*elocutio*, λέξις). Once arguments have been discovered or selected, once they have an arrangement or order, they need to be formulated in words. Greek and Roman rhetoricians generally considered style that part of rhetoric which actually puts into words the arguments which a speaker or writer wants to express.[1]

Style may be defined as the personal expression of an author or as the formal aspect or appearance of a work.[2] It is especially in the area of style that rhetoric meets poetics.[3]

In ancient rhetoric four qualities were associated with style: 1) *purity* or the correctness of language (*puritas* or *latinitas*; καθαρότης or ἑλληνισμός); 2) *clarity* or intelligibility (*perspicuitas*, σαφήνεια); 3) *decorum* or appropriateness (*aptum*, τὸ πρέπον); and 4) *ornament* or the decorative aspects of style (*ornatus*, κατασκευή).[4] Increasing attention was paid to the ornamental aspects of style, so that finally in the Renaissance period rhetoric became almost exclusively associated with style as decoration or ornamentation.[5]

---

[1] CORBETT, *Classical Rhetoric*, 414; GARAVELLI, *Manuale di retorica*, 111; LAUSBERG, *Elemente*, 42-43.

[2] MARCHESE, *Dizionario di retorica e di stilistica*, 305, 307. Cf. chap. 2, n. 148. Actually there is wide disagreement over the meaning of style (which MARCHESE, 305-309, acknowledges), but the focal points of the discussion on style are the author and the work. Cf. BARTHES, "Style and Its Image," 3-10; S. CHATMAN, ed., *Literary Style: A Symposium* (London/New York 1971); see especially his "Introduction," xi-xiii; DUCROT and TODOROV, ed., *Dictionnaire encyclopédique des sciences du langage*, 383-388; Groupe μ, *Rhétorique générale*, 147-148; G. MOLINÉE, *La stylistique*, 2nd ed., (Que sais-je? 646; Paris 1989) 23-27; T. TODOROV, "The Place of Style in the Structure of the Text," *Literary Style: A Symposium* (ed. S. CHATMAN, 1971) 30; S. ULLMANN, "Stylistics and Semantics," *Literary Style: A Symposium* (ed. S. CHATMAN, 1971) 133; WELLEK and WARREN, *Theory of Literature*, 184.

[3] GARAVELLI, *Manuale di retorica*, 112.

[4] DIXON, *Rhetoric*, 34; GARAVELLI, *Manuale di retorica*, 115-116; LANHAM, *Handlist*, 115; LAUSBERG, *Elemente*, 44, 50, 59, 153.

[5] A. FOUQUELIN, a disciple and co-worker of RAMUS, defined rethoric as "un art de bien et élégamment parler" and limited it to two parts, elocution and pronunciation. His

Style, however, is not merely an ornament of thought. It is also a means of persuasion, a way of arousing emotional responses in an audience.[6] For it can delight, excite, surprise, and demand attention. Even if style were considered only for itself, its beauty, or its delight, it would be difficult to separate this from the other parts of rhetoric. For it is unlikely that there is such a thing as "pure" poetry or "pure" literature, where rhetoric is totally uninvolved. Rather, literature may even be defined or described as "the rhetorical organization of grammar and logic,"[7] whose stylistic features are also rhetorical schemes.

Following the lead of Perelman and Olbrechts-Tyteca, this work views rhetorical devices chiefly in functional terms, that is, as participating in the persuasive or argumentative process. However, unlike Perelman and Olbrechts-Tyteca, attention will be given to *elocutio* as a separate and legitimate feature of rhetoric. *Elocutio* was one of the principal parts of ancient rhetoric, and modern rhetoricians and experts in stylistics are beginning to recognize that some reconciliation is possible between its argumentative and stylistic functions.[8] This chapter then will attempt to examine more systematically that which is appropriate to style in the Third Discourse of Moses. However, it will not repeat what has already been discussed about rhetorical devices in chapters four and five.

6.1 Stylistic Patterns and Features

Style is revealed through the use of vocabulary, grammar, repetition, figures, and sounds. Most writers and speakers follow definite patterns which they employ again and again. What are some of the patterns which the author or authors use in the Third Discourse of Moses?

---

definition of elocution: "Élocution n'est autre chose que l'ornement et enrichissement de la parole et oraison...." A. FOUQUELIN, *La rhétorique française* (1555), in *Traités de poétique et de rhétorique de la Renaissance* (ed. Francis GOYET; Paris 1990), 351, 353.

[6] CORBETT, *Classical Rhetoric,* 415; KENNEDY, *New Testament Interpretation,* 25; PERELMAN and OLBRECHTS-TYTECA, *Traité de l'argumentation,* 200-207. On p. 200 they insist that "le choix des termes, pour exprimer sa pensée, est rarement sans portée argumentative."

[7] FRYE, *Anatomy of Criticism,* 245. Cf. BOOTH, *The Rhetoric of Fiction,* 100; *A Rhetoric of Irony,* 41; "Rhetoric," *Synopticon* II, 651.

[8] Cf. chap. 2, n. 93. See also CORBETT, *Classical Rhetoric,* 33-39; GARAVELLI, *Manuale di retorica,* 57-60; M. FUMAROLI, "Conclusion: Rhétorique persuasive et littérature," *Figures et conflits rhétoriques* (ed. M. MEYER and A. LEMPEREUR, 1990) 159-161; J.-M. KLINKENBERG, "Rhétorique de l'argumentation et rhétorique des figures," *Figures et conflits rhétoriques* (ed. M. MEYER and A. LEMPEREUR, 1990) 115-137; A. LEMPEREUR, "Les restrictions de deux néo-rhétoriques," *Figures et conflits rhétoriques* (ed. M. MEYER and A. LEMPEREUR, 1990) 139-157. *Figures et conflits rhétoriques* is the product of a colloquium between those who see rhetoric as argumentative and those who identify it with literature and stylistics.

6.1.1 Groups of Two (Pairs)

One of the features of Dt 28,69–30,20 is its tendency to link words, phrases, and clauses into pairs. It is not satisfied with a statement or a description; often it adds a synonym, parallel phrase, explanation, or repetition. There are numerous examples of this pattern or habit.

In Dt 28,69 there is the linking of two different covenants, one in the land of Moab and one on Horeb. In 29,4b two articles of dress do not wear out: the people's clothing (שלמתיכם) and their shoes. V. 5a speaks of two important human functions which were limited in the desert, for the people ate no bread and drank no alcohol. The statement on drinking can likewise be divided into two, for the objects of drinking are יין and שכר. Dt 29,6 reports that two kings, Sihon and Og, came out to do battle with Israel. In 29,8 two results are expected after all the previous examples: observance of the covenant (ושמרתם) and doing it (ועשיתם).

Dt 29,10b describes the resident alien in terms of two tasks: gathering wood and drawing water. This is actually a *merismus* which stands for the totality of all their work. The relationship which the audience is establishing is described in terms of two synonyms in 29,11: ברית and אלה. The following verse (v. 12) emphasizes that this relationship comes from a past promise which is mentioned twice in different terms (כאשר דבר־לך and וכאשר נשבע לאבתיך). V. 13 again uses two synonyms to describe the covenant relationship (את־הברית הזאת ואת־האלה הזאת).

Dt 29,15 lists two objects of knowing: that which they experienced while living in Egypt and that which they experienced while passing through the nations. (The two different localities should also be noted.) V. 16 lists two objects of seeing, the synonyms שקוציהם and גלליהם. The materials from which such disgusting idols are made are *four,* but one can easily distinguish two pairs here (each pair joined by־ו): two are natural, nonprecious materials (wood and stone), while two are precious metals (silver and gold).

In Dt 29,17a we have a listing of *four* possible sinners, but again two pairs are distinguishable. In the first pair there are individuals (man or woman), while the second pair mentions groups (family or tribe). In v. 17b the plant produces two fruits — poison and wormwood. V. 18 gives a contrast between the antonyms wet and dry. There are two synonyms which smoke in Dt 29,19a (אף and קנאתו). In general we can say that 29,19 lists *four* punishments which fall upon the individual sinner. However, one pair is brought about by forces somewhat exterior to God (his *anger* and his *jealousy* smoke, while every *curse* settles on the sinner). The other pair is accomplished by Yahweh himself (he blots out the sinner's name and separates that individual for evil).

Dt 29,21a presents us with two different questioners who belong to the future generation (your children and the stranger), while v. 21b mentions two general afflictions of the land (מכות and תחלאיה: these are synonyms). Synonyms also appear in v. 22, where the anger of Yahweh is given under two different terms (אף and חמה). In v. 22 we also hear of a group of *four* cities which were destroyed; however, they are divided into two pairs by the use of the copulative (סדם ועמרה אדמה וצביים). In Dt 29,23 two similar questions are asked.

Dt 29,25 describes the sin of Israel by means of two synonyms (ויעבדו and וישתחוו). The other gods worshipped by Israel are characterized in the same verse by two non-relationships with this audience: they weren't known by nor were they allotted to Israel. Dt 29,27 describes the exile in terms of two metaphors: God uprooted the people and threw them to another land. V. 28 contains an antithesis, for what is hidden is an antonym of what is revealed.

Dt 30,1 contains two antonyms, blessing and curse. It also mentions the nations (הגוים) and includes an explanatory clause describing them. This is taken up again in v. 3, where a synonym (העמים) is followed by a parallel explanatory clause. Two subjects of conversion (אתה ובניך) are listed in 30,2; the same verse locates the place of conversion (heart and soul — the same pair also appears in 30,6.10). Dt 30,3 makes use of *four* verbs for the actions/responses of God, two of which are the same (ושב). But these four actions can be subdivided into two groups, each of which begins with ושב.

Dt 30,4 describes Yahweh's gathering of the exiles in two synonymous expresss (משם יקבצך and ומשם יקחך). In v. 6 God's circumcision will be performed on *your* heart and also on *your offspring's* heart. Two synonyms (איביך and שנאיך) name the recipients of God's punishments in 30,7. Dt 30,10 lists two synonyms of laws (מצותיו וחקתיו) and two conditions for receiving blessings (obedience, conversion).

Dt 30,11-14 describes the law in *four* negative terms, but once again this is easily divisible into two pairs. In v. 11 the law is *not* too difficult and *not* far; in vv. 12-13 we have a spatial dimension — it is not in the skies, it is not across the sea. Also in vv. 11-13 there are two rhetorical questions phrased in almost the same words. Each rhetorical question lists two tasks for the messenger (יעבר/יעלה — synonyms of movement; and יקחה) and two tasks for the receivers (וישמענו אתה ונעשנה). Vv. 11 and 14 have a pair of antonyms (near and far), while v. 14 mentions the two places where the word can be found (in the mouth and in the heart).

In Dt 30,15 there are two pairs of synonyms (each word is an antonym of a word in the other pair): life and good, death and evil. Dt 30,17 contains one of the few groupings of five in the Third Discourse. Of the five verbs listing the sins committed, the first has the heart as a subject and the other four are in the second person singular. These four verbs can be subdivided into two pairs of synonyms: 1) you do not obey, you go astray and 2) you worship other gods, you serve them.

Dt 30,18-19 contains two first-person declarations. In v. 18 the first declaration specifies two punishments which are synonyms (you will perish, you will not live long). V. 18 also lists two infinitives which follow the participle עבר (לבא and לרשתה). In 30,19 there are a number of pairs: two witnesses (heaven and earth — this is probably a *merismus*); two pairs of antonyms (life and death, blessing and curse); and two indications of those who must choose life (אתה וזרעך). Dt 30,20 contains two synonyms (חייך and ארך ימיך).

It is apparent that an important stylistic feature of the Third Discourse of Moses is pairing. This discourse has a tendency to pattern its material in groups of two. Such pairing aids the argumentative process, since almost by instinct the audience adapts itself to accepting groups of two. Thus when an incompatibility between two ideas or practices occurs, a choice becomes necessary. So this habit of pairing may help an audience accept its obligation to choose.

A tendency to form pairs is a natural (and one could even say "primitive") habit. Conventional and stereotyped pairs (husband and wife, sun and moon, beginning and end, up and down, left and right) and rhyming couplets demonstrate this habit also in English. The ancient Greek's preference for antitheses and the modern structuralist's fascination with binomial relationships reflect this tendency. It seems that the ancient Hebrew also easily developed a habit of thinking and associating in pairs.

6.1.2 Parallels and Contrasts

It has alredy been noted that many of these pairs appear in the form of parallels and contrasts/antitheses.[9] Such patterns especially reinforce the notion of a choice between two incompatibilities, since the audience becomes used to the appearance of pairs and the differentiation that must be made between each of its members. The previous two chapters have already noted various parallels in the Third Discourse of Moses. Often such parallels contain repetitions; sometimes they are contrasted.

1. The three subsections or panels of Dt 29,1b-8 can be seen in terms of three contrasts. As mentioned in 5.2.2.1, each subsection (vv. 1b-3, 4-5, 6-8) describes different events in a different place, followed

---

[9] CORBETT, *Classical Rhetoric*, 464, defines *antithesis* as "the juxtaposition of contrasting ideas, often in parallel structure." RICE and SCHOFER, "Tropes and Figures," 107, define antithesis as "a syntagmatic relationship involving opposition *without* incompatibility." ALONSO SCHÖKEL, *A Manual of Hebrew Poetics,* 85, points out that antithesis is a fundamental form of thought and expression which became one of the most important stylistic techniques in Hebrew poetry.

by a reflection or lesson. The lessons can be contrasted with the events in the first two panels; the third subsection contrasts the intentions of the kings with the results of their efforts: 1. (vv. 1b-3): you saw wonders ... *but* God did not give you understanding. 2. (vv. 4-5): I led you forty years in the wilderness, *but* (this word does not actually appear in Hebrew) your clothes did not wear out, etc. 3. (vv. 6-7): kings came out to do battle, *but* we defeated them and took their land.

2. Dt 29,4-5 contains four parallel clauses divided into two pairs. All four clauses are united by the fourfold occurrence of לא and by the fact that they describe what happened in the wilderness:

לא־בלו   שלמתיכם מעליכם
ונעלך לא־בלתה   מעל   רגלך:
לחם לא אכלתם
.ויין ושכר לא שתיתם

3. There is a contrast between two actions which are expressed by antonyms in Dt 29,6: "You (plural) come in" (ותבאו) to this place, while Sihon as well as Og "went out"(ויצא) to meet you in battle.

4. Another set of parallels occurs in Dt 29,9.14. This parallel is an inclusion which unites all of vv. 9-14:

(v. 9)   אתם נצבים היום לפני יהוה אלהיכם
(v. 14).   עמד. היום לפני יהוה   אלהינו

The wording is basically the same, yet there are also differences: the verb for "standing" is different in each case (although they are synonyms); in v. 9 the second-person plural is used, whereas in v. 14 it is the third-person singular; v. 9 adds the emphatic pronoun אתם; and where v. 9 has אלהיכם (second person plural ending), v. 14 has אלהינו (first-person plural ending).

5. Another parallel appears in Dt 29,14. Here the wording is almost exactly the same. The change from positive to negative, however, produces an *antithesis* or contrast:

כי את־אשר ישנו פה עמנו ...
ואת אשר איננו פה עמנו היום:

6. The objects of knowing in Dt 29,15 are formed in two parallel clauses. These are not contrasted, but the verbs used are antonyms, since ישב indicates rest or immobility, while עבר is a verb of motion. The locations also differ:

את אשר־ישבנו בארץ מצרים
.ואת אשר־עברנו בקרב הגוים אשר עברתם

7. The double פן־יש בכם of Dt 29,17 establishes a parallel between the sinner and the poisonous plant.

8. Dt 29,28 also shows a parallel structure in antithesis or contrast. What is hidden is an antonym of what is revealed; each is assigned to a different sphere of influence:

הנסתרת ליהוה אלהינו...

והנגלת לנו ולבנינו.

9. In Dt 30,1.3 appear two parallel expressions which are separated by v. 2. Each describes the nations; many of the words are the same in both:

(v. 1)   בכל־הגוים אשר הדיחך יהוה אלהיך שמה:

(v. 3).   מכל־העמים אשר הפיצך יהוה אלהיך שמה:

10. The most extensive parallels of the Third Discourse occur in Dt 30,11-14. Here we have the synonyms המצוה (v. 11) and הדבר (v. 14); the antonyms רחקה (v. 11) and קרוב (v. 14); a fourfold use of לא...הוא; and the double occurrence of nearly identical rhetorical questions. This passage has been discussed extensively above.[10]

11. Dt 30,15 makes use of a parallel structure for the objects of the choice. Here there is little repetition. Rather one pair of synonyms is contrasted with a second pair of synonyms:

את־החיים ואת־הטוב

ואת־המות ואת־הרע:

12. Dt 30,16b.18b have parallel descriptions of the land. Synonyms are used for the land as well as for the act of entering. There is also some repetition in this parallel:

בא־שמה לרשתה: בארץ אשר־אתה   (v. 16b)

האדמה אשר אתה עבר את־הירדן לבא שמה לרשתה: (v. 18b).

13. There is a brief but emphatic parallelism in the two declarations of Dt 30,18.19:

(v. 18)   הגדתי לכם היום

(v. 19).   העידתי בכם היום

14. Finally, Dt 30,19 repeats in a different way the choice offered in 30,15. This verse may be seen as a parallel to v. 15. It also sets forth two pairs of antonyms, one before and one after the verb offering the choice:

החיים והמות   נתתי לפניך

הברכה והקללה.

Such parallelism no doubt was pleasant to the Hebrew ear. It helped to create a certain receptivity in the audience. At the same time it establishes a pattern of pairs which are often synonymous and sometimes

---

[10] Cf. 4.4.1.1, no. 17; 5.2.3.2; and 5.3.26.

contrasting. Such parallels thus seem to prepare the mind for the necessity of resolving the incompatibilities presented by making a choice between opposing options. It is probably no accident that the options themselves are presented in 30,15.19 in a kind of parallel structure.

6.1.3 Groups of Three (Triads)

The patterns in the Third Discourse of Moses are not limited to groups of two (and four). In a number of instances groups of three (triads) occur.

Dt 29,1b lists three recipients of God's punitive actions in Egypt (Pharaoh, his servants, and his land). V. 2 gives three synonyms for God's wonders (המסות, האתת, and המפתים). In v. 3 we find three parts of the body associated with their perceptual or communicative functions (eyes see, ears hear, and the heart knows or understands). Perhaps this can be considered a kind of *commoratio* (emphasizing a strong point by repeating it several times in different words).

The wonders in the wilderness which are found in Dt 29,4-5 can also be divided into three groups: 1) clothes and shoes do not wear out; 2) no bread is eaten; 3) nothing alcoholic is drunk. Dt 29,6-7 lists three progressive actions accomplished regarding the kings Sihon and Og: we defeat them, we take their land, and we distribute it. V. 7b also lists three tribes (actually 2 and 1/2) who are the recipients of the land — the Reubenites, the Gadites, and half the tribe of the Manassites. Here we may also recall the three panels or subsections of actions and contrasts found in 29,1b-8 (cf. 5.2.2.1 and 6.1.2, n. 1).

The participant list of Dt 29,9-10 may be divided into two sets of three, if ראשיכם שבטיכם actually represents one group: 1) your heads of your tribes, your elders, and your officers; 2) your children, your wives, and your resident alien. Dt 29,12 lists three ancestors (Abraham, Isaac, and Jacob).

There are three materials or elements afflicting the land in Dt 29,22 (sulphur, salt, and burning). In the same verse there are three things which plants cannot do in this ravaged land: be sown, sprout up, and grow. Dt 29,27 lists three synonyms for God's anger (אף, חמה, and קצף).

In Dt 30,1-2 there are three elements or actions in the process of conversion (calling to mind, turning to the Lord, obeying). V. 5 lists three rewards or actions which Yahweh will accomplish: he will bring you to the land, he will treat you kindly (or: make you prosper), and he will increase your number. There are three conditions for blessing in 30,8 (conversion, obedience, and doing the commandments); while 30,9 promises blessings in three products or fruit (of the womb, of animals, and of the soil).

Dt 30,16 contains three sets of three items. There are three synonymous tasks to perform: love God, walk in his ways, and observe his commandments. Then there are three consequences or results of performing such tasks, that is, three blessings: you will live, you will increase, and God will bless you. There are also three synonyms for commandments or laws here. (מצותיו וחקתיו ומשפטיו).

Dt 30,20 again lists three tasks which are synonymous: love God, obey, and adhere to him. The same verse again lists the three ancestors (Abraham, Isaac, and Jacob).

Groups of three do not occur with the frequency of groups of two within the Third Discourse of Moses. But it is obvious that this pattern is also present. They appear especially in Dt 29,1b-12 and 30,1-9. There are only a few other occurrences scattered in the remaining sections of our text.

Triads also seem to be natural groupings. It is probably no accident that there are three rhetorical genres (judicial, deliberative, and epideictic), three propositions in a syllogism (major premise, minor premise, and conclusion), and three moments in dialectic (thesis, antithesis, synthesis).[11] Some cultures tend to be characterized by tripartite patterns in their rhetoric.[12] Perhaps the ancient Hebrews were among them. Unlike the groups of two, triads do not seem to prepare the mind for the necessity of making a choice. But perhaps their use gives variety to discourse, especially where parallelism and pairing dominate.

6.1.4 Other Stylistic Features

Many of the other characteristic stylistic features of the Third Discourse of Moses have also been presented in chapters four and five from the viewpoints of invention and arrangement. But it may be good to remember that such features are not usually perceived consciously as developing the argumentation of a work. Rather they are appreciated for themselves, since they may be pleasing, delightful, or beautiful. Or they may simply call forth the attention of the audience.

6.1.4.1 Direct Address

One obvious stylistic feature of the Third Discourse of Moses is its form as a discourse, that is, it directly addresses an audience. Only Dt 28,69 – 29,1a is reporting speech; the rest is reported speech. This direct address is represented and reinforced by an accumulation of second-person forms, both singular and plural. We may recall that 142 (18.1%) of the 785 words in the Third Discourse are marked with a second-person indicator.[13] The plural forms predominate in Dt 29, the singular in Dt 30.

---

[11] CHAIGNET, *La rhétorique et son histoire,* 437-438.
[12] CONDON and YOUSEF, *An Introduction to Intercultural Communication,* 233, note that American speech tends to follow a pattern of three in descriptions.
[13] Cf. 4.4.2.

Second-person forms, however, are not scattered evenly throughout the text. In Dt 29,18-28, for example, only two occurrences can be found (in the second-person plural). Other sections of the text carry greater concentrations of these second-person markers. Of the 101 words in Dt 29,1b-8, 16 (15.8%) are in the second-person plural while 3 (3.0%) are in the second-person singular. The highest concentration of such forms is to be found in 29,9-10aα. These 14 words include 9 (56.3%) which have second-person plural markers. Immediately afterwards come the 39 words of Dt 29,10aβ-12. Among these occur 12 words (30.8%) in the second-person singular. Dt 30,1-10 also has a rather large concentration of second-person singular markers: 60 (36.4%) of the 165 words in this section. Considering that eight of these are verbs and two are independent personal pronouns, this means that 50 words (30.3% of the total) carry the -ka sound of the second-person singular ending.

Thus Dt's audience could not escape noticing how strongly they were personally being addressed.[14] Its members were constantly barraged with references in both the singular and the plural. These references were reinforced by emphatic personal pronouns: אתם in Dt 29,1.9.15 and אתה in Dt 30,2.8.16.18.19.

There are places where the direct address switches suddenly and unaccountably from plural to singular or from singular to plural. After the plural forms in Dt 29,1b appears a lone singular form in v. 2. V. 3 then switches back to plural forms, but v. 4b adds two more in the singular. Again the plural occurs until 29,10aβ, when — in the middle of a list and in the middle of a sentence — the discourse switches to the singular. This continues until v. 13, when the plural returns for the rest of the chapter. However, fewer and fewer second-person markers occur after this until they disappear entirely after v. 21.

The singular forms appear en masse in Dt 30,1-10, but they also continue throughout chapter 30, with the exception of three plural forms in v. 18 and one in v. 19. Dt 30,12-13 has no second-person forms, but it does contain eight first-person plural forms (27.6% of the 29 words in these two verses). The effect of such changes in form is that the audience is sometimes appealed to as a group, sometimes as individuals, and on rare occasions in solidarity with the speaker and with one another. Although singular and plural forms are mixed throughout the Third Discourse, the emphasis in chapter 29 is on the group, on plurality; then more and more attention is given to the individual, who must make a decision for or against life.

---

[14] It is to be noted, however, that there are no vocatives in the Third Address of Moses.

6.1.4.2 Imperatives and Questions (Modality)

It has already been noted that the entire Third Discourse can be seen both as one long command and as the fulfillment of a command.[15] Although only one imperative form occurs in Dt 28,69 – 30,20 (ראה in 30,15; this is actually used as an interjection), three imperatival weqataltís appear in 29,8 and 30,19. All three are associated with the *issue* to which the Third Discourse addresses itself, namely obedience to covenantal law.

The verbs ושמרתם and ועשׂיתם in Dt 29,8 are in the second-person plural. They give the main message of this discourse: obey the law! This is a command which the entire audience must perform. In 30,19 the verb used is in the singular: ובחרת. The entire Third Discourse is directed to this moment. The concern is that every individual choose to do that which is necessary to live long and receive blessings: observe and do the covenantal stipulations.

Such imperatives insist on audience participation and involvement. One must either do it or not do it — there is no other option. Since the issue is one of life and death, curse and blessing for the whole community, every individual must become personally involved.[16]

The Third Discourse of Moses also makes use of the interrogative modality. There are two parallel questions expressed by the nations concerning the afflictions of the land in Dt 29,23. There are also two very similar rhetorical questions in 30,12-13. According to Perelman and Olbrechts-Tyteca, questions are quite important in the rhetorical process.[17]

The imaginary question-and-answer scheme of Dt 29,23-27 is a kind of instruction which is both forceful and enlightening. The fact that the גוים can both ask and answer the question indicates their own ability to see clearly what is at issue in Israel's relationship with Yahweh. The question not only asks the reason for the affliction of the land but also presumes that Yahweh is responsible for it. The supposed ignorance of

---

[15] Cf. 4.4.2.

[16] It is worth noting that 21.4% of the clauses in Dt 1-30 are positive or negative commands of some kind. However, this rather high figure is to be explained by the nature of Dt, which is both legislative and hortatory. See DE REGT, *A Parametric Model*, I, 74. It is also worth noting that PERELMAN and OLBRECHTS-TYTECA, *Traité de l'argumentation*, 213, do not ascribe persuasive force to imperatives. Rather, they see imperatives as figures of presence.

[17] PERELMAN and OLBRECHTS-TYTECA, *Traité de l'argumentation*, 214. Cf. BRAULIK, *Die Mittel*, 141. C. CONROY, *Absalom, Absalom!* (AnBib 81; Rome 1978) 139, notes that both real and rhetorical questions add dramatic force to a *narrative* by involving the hearer more actively than an affirmation. Questions can also be used to stimulate an audience's interest. Cf. W. ISER, *The Implied Reader: Patterns of Communication in Prose Fiction from Bunyan to Beckett* (Baltimore/London 1974) 278-279.

the nations gives rise to the question. But they seem to know the answer better than the audience! The question-and-answer scheme is much more effective at involving the audience and presenting the result of disobedience than a mere statement would be.

Dt 30,12-13 contains two parallel rhetorical questions. The rhetorical question is an effective way to affirm or emphasize some idea so that it will be accepted. This is because the audience does not merely listen to the question but also participates in it. In fact, a rhetorical question is not a true question, for it does not elicit information nor evoke a reply. It is actually an emphatic affirmation or negation, one which is stronger than a direct statement. It is a literary technique used to promote audience contact (presence). However, the rhetorical question still teaches. Even if the audience already knows the answer, it is invited to reflect deeper and to make that answer its own.[18]

The rhetorical questions in Dt 30,12-13 emphasize a negative expectation. Of course no one will do this! They reaffirm the statements made previously: this law is not in the skies, it is not across the sea. What is enticing about these questions is that they are phrased in such a way as though the audience itself were asking them. The audience participates in these questions automatically, for the speaker imagines that the audience is formulating them. "Who will go up to heaven/across the sea for *us* and take it for *us* in order that he may announce it to *us* and *we* may do it?" No one will actually attempt such voyages, since it is obvious that the law is neither in heaven nor across the sea.

The speaker's further assertion that this law is very near to *you*, on *your* mouth and in *your* heart, is but an amplification of what has already been affirmed by these two rhetorical questions. Repeatedly, in different forms, it is proclaimed that the law is possible, since it is near. The audience is practically coerced into agreeing with these statements, for they are involved in them. If, as I suspect, all Dt 30,11-14 is a refutation of some unspoken objection on the part of the audience,[19] then the rhetorical questions are important in making that refutation effective and successful.

6.1.4.3 Appeal to the Imagination

Dt 28,69 – 30,20 is not a strongly imaginative text: it is neither poetry nor narrative. But it does include some sections which appeal to

---

[18] ALONSO SCHÖKEL, *A Manual of Hebrew Poetics,* 150; CORBETT, *Classical Rhetoric,* 488-489; GITAY, "Deutero-Isaiah," 196-197; "A Study of Amos's Art of Speech," 302; KENNEDY, *New Testament Interpretation,* 57; VOGELS, "The Question of the Nations," 168; WATSON, *Classical Hebrew Poetry,* 338-342.

[19] See 4.5.2.1, no. 10; 5.3.26; and 5.4, E.

the imagination. This is especially true of Dt 29,15-27. The sender calls upon the receivers to remember (imagine) the various disgusting idols they had seen in Egypt and among the nations, idols made of wood and stone, silver and gold (v. 16). The sinner is compared to some unknown plant which produces poison and wormwood (v. 17). Then there is the illustration of the anti-model (vv. 18-20), followed by a description of the afflictions of the land (vv. 21-22, especially v. 22). Finally there is the imaginary future conversation or question-and-answer scheme (vv. 23-27). Each of these appeals to the imagination to picture the scene for itself. Sufficient description is given to tease or entice the imagination into providing further details.

Another section of the Third Discourse which invites the imagination to let itself go is the nearly poetic 30,11-14. An abundance of synonyms and antonyms, parallelism and rhetorical questions, hyperbole and imaginary conversation aid the fantasies of the audience.

Metaphors are especially suitable for stimulating the imagination and other mental processes. A number of metaphors appear in the Third Discourse of Moses. These will be listed later in this chapter.

6.2 Figures and Tropes

Rhetoricians, especially ancient rhetoricians, consider the use of figures and tropes an important part of *elocutio*. These rhetorical devices and patterns are related to all three modes of argumentation (ethos, pathos, logos), even if they have usually been associated solely with ornamentation and emotions. Figures can aid the communicator in making thoughts clear and concrete, in stirring emotions, and in eliciting admiration for the speaker.[20] Their functions include emphasis, division, comparison, definition — as well as delight and surprise.[21]

Previous works which have concentrated their attention on rhetorical figures have tended to neglect the Third Discourse of Moses.[22] Bullinger[23] lists the following figures of speech in Dt 29-30:

---

[20] CORBETT, *Classical Rhetoric,* 459.

[21] BRANDT, *The Rhetoric of Argumentation,* 101; KENNEDY, *New Testament Interpretation,* 29. Cf. the discussion in 2.5.3.

[22] W. BÜHLMANN and K. SCHERER, *Stilfiguren der Bibel: Ein kleines Nachschlagewerk* (BibB 10; Fribourg 1973), do not list a single example from the Third Discourse of Moses.

[23] BULLINGER, *Figures of Speech Used in the Bible.* The examples can be found on the following pages: 29,19 (821); 30,3 (309); 30,4 (598); 30,9 (882); 30,15 (564); 30,19 (941).

29,19:   *anthropopatheia* (the attributing of human emotions or pas-
              sions to gods or natural objects): God is spoken of in terms of
              a fire.

30,3:   *paronomasia*: וּשָׁבֹתָי[24] and שְׁבוּתְךָ.

30,4:   *metonymy*: from the end of heaven.

30,9:   *anthropopatheia*: rejoicing is attributed to God.

30,15:   *metonymy* (here: the effect for the thing or action causing it):
              good things which end in life; evil things which end in death.

30,19:   *deasis* or *adjuration* (an expression of feeling by oath or
              asseveration); also called *obsecratio* (beseeching) and *obtestatio*
              (calling God to witness).

König[25] lists the following rhetorical devices in this part of Dt:

29,1b: *synecdoche.* König believes that אתם is a type of *"totum pro
              parte,"* but I have some doubts about this.

29,15b: *palindrome* (a word, sentence, verse, etc. that is the same read
              forward or backward): With this definition, at least, the repeti-
              tion of עברתם is not a real palindrome. Perhaps König's notion
              of palindrome is wider.[26]

29,16:   *metonymy*: "stone" and "wood" both give the material for the
              product.

29,17:   *metaphor*: a root which produces poison and bitterness.

29,22a: He calls גפרית ומלח a "half" polysyndeton, although one con-
              junction hardly establishes *poly*syndeton.

29,22b: *brachyology* (brevity in speech or writing; abbreviated con-
              struction): כמהפכה.

30,1-3:   *annomination* (= paronomasia)[27]: He considers annomination
              a stronger form of alliteration because it is built upon etymo-
              logically related terms.

---

[24] BHS gives וְשׁב and lists no variants.

[25] König, *Stilistik, Rhetorik, Poetik.* The examples can be found on the following
pages: 29,1b (62); 29,15b (172); 29,16 (20); 29,17 (97); 29,22a (159); 29,22b (204); 30,1-2
(291); 30,6 (108); 30,15.19 (58); 30,20b (21).

[26] Perhaps König's *palindrome* is related to S. McEvenue's *palistrophe.* McEvenue
describes this device in *The Narrative Style of the Priestly Writer* (AnBib 50; Rome 1971)
29, n. 18. *Palistrophe* is formed from the Greek words πάλιν and στροφή and has often
been misnamed "concentric inclusion," "chiastic structure" or "concentric structure," and
"complex inclusion." Its essential feature is return. *Palistrophe* is a thought which
stretches outward over a series of elements and then retraces its steps over the same
elements. The elements are not repetitions but correspondences; thus they can even be
contrasts.

[27] I. Casanowicz, "Paronomasia in the Old Testament," *JBL* 12 (1893) 159, also
considers Dt 30,1-3 to contain paronomasia. On p. 105 he tells us that "the charm and
effect of paronomasia lie ... in the union of similarity of sound with dissimilarity of sense.
Hence it does not include the reiteration of the same words or word-stems in the same
meaning."

30,6:   *metaphor*: circumcision of the heart.
30,15.19:   *synecdoche*: life and death. Here König describes the device as
               a "Synekdoche mehrerer Hauptrepräsentanten." It's possible
               that he wanted to describe a *merismus* but lacked the term.
30,20b: *metonymy*: *life* as the condition and source of life.

Gesenius-Kautsch[28] lists one more figure:

29,21ff.:   *anacolouthon* (the change from a construction already begun to
               one of a different kind).

There now follows a more developed listing of rhetorical devices
(figures and tropes) found within the Third Discourse of Moses. Not
included below are those devices of parallelism and antithesis already
explored elsewhere in this chapter (6.1.1, 6.1.2, and 6.1.3). Such a bare
list, of course, fails to reveal the argumentative functions of these figures
and tropes. These functions must be sought in context; many have
already been suggested above in chapters four and five.

Alliteration: repetition of initial or medial consonants in two or more
adjacent words.[29]

29,1:   l-sound in לפרעה ולכל ... ולכל ...
29,4b-5a: extensive use of the l-sound (ל).
29,6b: m-sound in למלחמה ונכם.
29,7:   l-sound in לנחלה לראובני ולגדי ולחצי.
29,12:   l-sound in לאבתיך לאברהם ליצחק וליעקב.
29,17:   š-sound (שׁ).
29,21a: r-sound (ר).
30,2.6.10:   l- and b-sounds in בכל־לבבך ובכל־נפשך.
30,4:   m- and š-sounds in השמים משם.
30,5:   r- ans š-sounds in אשר־ירשו ... וירשתה.
30,7:   l-sound in כל־האלות האלה על ...
30,20:   l-sound in לאבתיך לאברהם ליצחק וליעקב לתת להם.

Anacoluthon: ending a sentence with a different construction from that
with which it began.

29,21-23

Anaphora: repetition of the same word or group of words at the beginnings of successive clauses.

---

[28] GKC, §167b.
[29] O. RANKIN, "Alliteration in Hebrew Poetry," *JTS* 31 (1930) 289, points out that
alliteration is used to express taunting, sorrow, threat, and invective.

29,12:   כאשר דבר־לך וכאשר נשבע
29,14:   כי את־אשר ... ואת־אשר
29,15:   את אשר ... ואת־אשר
29,17:   (2x) פן יש בכם
29,23:   על־מה ... מה
29,23-24:   (2X) ואמרו
29,25:   (2X) אלהים
30,1.3:   here the clauses are not actually successive, but each begins
              with אשר. They also end with the same words (epistrophe).
30,3:   (2x) ושב
30,4:   משם ... ומשם ...
30,8-10?:   תשוב (v. 8); ישוב (v. 9); תשוב (v. 10); actually, this doesn't quite
              qualify as an anaphora, since the clauses are not adjacent, the
              words are not exactly the same, and all three words are in the
              second position in their clauses.
30,10:   כי heads each half verse.
30,11-13:   (4x) לא ... הוא
30,12-13?:   (2x) לאמר מי

Anastrophe: inversion of natural or usual word order (also called *hyper-baton*).

29,4-5:   Here there are four clauses: the first begins with לא and then is
              followed by a verb and the subject (לא־בלו שלמתיכם); this is fol-
              lowed by three clauses with an inverted order: subject
              + לא + verb: ...ונעלך לא־בלתה   (v. 4b)
                                  לחם לא אכלתם   (v. 5a)
                                  ויין ושכר לא שתיתם.
30,19:   Two direct objects are followed by a verb, which is followed by
              two more direct objects:
              החיים והמות נתתי לפניך הברכה והקללה.
              (A more usual order appears in 30,15.)

Antonym: a word that is the opposite of another in meaning.

29,6:   ויצא and ותבאו
29,14:   איננו and ישנו
29,15:   עברנו and ישבנו
29,18:   הצמאה and הרוה
29,21?:   הנכרי and בניכם
29,28:   הנגלת and הנסתרת
30,1:   הקללה and הברכה
30,11.14:   קרוב and רחקה
30,15:   המות and החיים
30,15:   הרע and הטוב
30,18:   תאריכן ימים and תאבדון
30,19:   המות and החיים
30,19:   הקללה and הברכה

Apposition: placing side by side two co-ordinate elements, the second of which serves as an explanation or modification of the first. An apposition is thus often an *interpretatio,* a repetition or amplification in other words.

29,2:   האתת והמפתים הגדלים ההם is in apposition to המסות הגדלת אשר ראו עיניך.

29,6:   מלך־חשבון is in apposition to סיחן, while מלך־הבשן is in apposition to עוג.

29,9-10:   The entire participant list is in apposition to כלכם.

29,10:   מחטב עציך עד שאב מימיך is in apposition to גרך.

29,12:   The names Abraham, Isaac, and Jacob are in apposition to לאבתיך.

29,14?:   עמד היום לפני יהוה אלהינו may be considered to be in apposition to the previous clause; however, it may also be considered a *parenthesis*: the two figures are practically indistinguishable here.

29,16?:   עץ ואבן כסף וזהב אשר עמהם may be considered to be in apposition to גלליהם; and שקוציהם; however, this may also be considered a parenthesis.

29,21:   בניכם and והנכרי with their successive relative clauses are in apposition to הדור האחרן.

29,24:   אלהי אבתם is in apposition to יהוה.

29,25?:   אלהים אשר לא־ידעום ולא חלק להם may be considered as an apposition to אלהים אחרים; it may also be considered a parenthesis.

30,1:   הברכה והקללה is in apposition to כל־הדברים האלה.

30,20:   The names Abraham, Isaac, and Jacob are in apposition to לאבתיך.

Assonance: the repetition of similar vowel sounds.

29,2:   o-sound: המסות הגדלת ... האתת והמפתים הגדלים
29,7:   i-sound: לראובני ולגדי ולחצי ... המנשי
29,19:   o-sound: לא־יאבה יהוה סלח לו
29,27:   short e: אל־ארץ אחרת

Asyndeton: deliberate omission of conjunctions between a series of related words or clauses.

29,9?:   The three (or four) types of leadership positions in this part of the participant list are joined together by only one conjunction (ושטריכם); however, this may actually be a *normal* use in Hebrew. Nevertheless, the phrase כל איש ישראל appears without a conjunction and is thus a real asyndeton.

29,10?:   The second listing of three once again has a conjunction only with the last item (וגרך). It would be impossible to say if the omission of a conjunction in the previous word is deliberate or normative.

29,12?:   To Abraham, to Isaac, and to Jacob
30,20?:   To Abraham, to Isaac, and to Jacob

Thus, except for כל איש ישראל, it's difficult to say if there are any real asyndetons in this text. A similar situation occurs with *polysyndeton*.

Auxesis or *climax* or *incrementum*: words or clauses placed in an order of increasing importance.

29,9-10:   heads of tribes, elders, officers (diminishing importance?); children, women, resident alien (diminishing importance?).
29,17:   איש או־אשה או משפחה או־שבט.
29,22:   Plants cannot be sown, nor will they sprout, nor will they grow (a chronological order).

Chiasm: Cf. 5.2.2.2, 5.2.3.1, 5.2.3.2, 5.2.3.3, 5.3.24, and 5.3.25.

Conduplicatio: repetition of a word or words in succeeding clauses. This definition is wide enough to cover most of the repetitions in the Third Discourse! Therefore it may not be too useful. However, it does name those occasions when repetition takes place which does not occur at the beginning or end of a verse. It may cover the following examples:

28,69:   הברית אשר ... כרת את occurs twice.
29,4-5:   a fourfold occurrence of לא
29,22:   a triple occurrence of לא
30,9:   a triple occurrence of בפרי

There are also those repeated phrases which are difficult to classify according to traditional rhetorical patterns, since they occur at irregular intervals: בכל־לבבך ובכל־נפשך,הכתובה בספר הזה ,אשר אנכי מצוך היום, and לאהבה את־יהוה אלהיך.

Demonstratio or *descriptio* or *hypotyposis* or ἐνάργεια: vivid description.

29,19?:   description of the threat against the individual
29,22:   description of the afflicted land

Divisio: division into kinds or classes (synonyms not listed here).

29,1b: to Pharaoh, his servants, and his land
29,3:   a heart to understand, eyes to see, and ears to hear
29,4-5?:   clothing, shoes, bread, wine and strong drink
29,7:   to the Reubenites, the Gadites, and half the tribe of the Manassites
29,9-10:   participant list
29,12:   to Abraham, Isaac, and Jacob

29,14:   those who are here with us and those who are not here with us
29,16:   wood and stone, silver and gold
29,17:   man or woman or family or tribe
29,22:   Sodom and Gomorrah, Admah and Zeboiim
30,9:   fruit of the womb, of animals, and of the soil
30,16?:   to love God, to walk in his ways, and to observe his command-
            ments
30,20?:   to love God, to obey him, and to stick to him
30,20:   to Abraham, Isaac, and Jacob

Ellipsis: deliberate omission of a word or words which are readily implied by the context. Another term perhaps would be *aposiopesis*.

30,16:   (If you obey the commandments of the Lord your God...:
            LXX)

Epanalepsis: repetition at the end of a clause of the word or group of words that occurred at the beginning of the clause.

29,14:   כי את־אשר ישנו פה עמנו ...
            ואת אשר איננו פה עמנו ...

Epistrophe or *epiphora*: repetition of the same word or group of words at the ends of successive clauses.

29,13:   את־הברית הזאת ואת־האלה הזאת

30,1.3:   אשר ... יהוה אלהיך שמה closes these two verses.
30,11-13:   הוא comes at the end of four clauses.
30,12-13?: לנו appears at or near the end of four clauses.
30,12-13:   ויקחה לנו וישמענו אתה ונעשׂנה

Homoioptoton: the use of various words in a sentence or verse with similar case endings. This is often identified with *homoioteleuton,* which is the use of similar endings in a clause. Both are often simply rhyming patterns, especially at the end of words or clauses.

29,1:   אתם ראיתם
29,9-10aα: כם ־ used as an ending for eight words
29,10b: מחטב עציך...
             עד שׁאב מימיך (5-syllable rhyming pattern)
29,13:   אתכם לבדכם
29,15:   אתם ידעתם
30,16:   מצותיו וחקתיו ומשׁפטיו

Hyperbole: the use of exaggerated terms for the purpose of emphasis or heightened effect.

29,4:   Your clothes and your shoes didn't wear out (despite forty
            years of wandering).

30,4:   Even if the Lord has scattered you to the end of the heavens...
30,12:   Who will go up to the skies for us...?
30,13:   Who will cross to the other side of the sea for us...?

Isocolon: similarity not only of structure but also of length.

29,10b: ...מחטב עציך עד שאב מימיך
30,1.19:   הברכה והקללה
30,12-13?:   These two parallel verses are not true isocola, since the number
             of syllables is not exactly the same. Yet they are very close in
             length and rhythm.
30,15:   ואת־החיים ואת־הטוב
             ואת־המות ואת־הרע
30,19?:   את־השמים ואת־הארץ
             החיים והמות ... הברכה והקללה

Maxim: short pithy statement of a general truth.

29,18:   למען ספות הרוה את־הצמאה
29,28:   הנסתרת ליהוה אלהינו
             והנגלת לנו ולבנינו (עד־עולם)

Merismus: a figure which reduces a complete series to (usually) two of its
constituent elements. Thus it represents a whole or totality through the
detailing of some of its parts (and thus may be a species of *synecdoche*).
When two named species exhaust the whole genus, the merismus assumes
the form of a *polar expression*.[30]

29,9?:   ראשיכם שבטיכם זקניכם ושטריכם   (the totality of leadership in
             Israel?)
29,10:   מחטב עציך עד שאב מימיך   (the totality of services performed by
             resident aliens)
29,14?:   ואת אשר איננו פה עמנו and את־אשר ישנו פה עמנו (these two phrases
             include everyone, but they express two "halves" rather than
             two extreme parts; thus this may not be a true merismus).
29,16:   עץ ואבן (the totality of all natural materials from which idols
             are fashioned)
29,16:   כסף וזהב (the totality of precious metals from which idols are
             made)

---

[30] KRAŠOVEC, *Der Merismus,* does not list the examples in 29,9.10.14.16 (he includes
עץ ואבן but not כסף וזהב). 17 (he lists איש או אשה but not שבט או משפחה). 28; 30,2.6.10. But he
does include as merismus עץ and אבן and also ראה and שמע in 29,3 plus אכל and שתה in 29,5.
He does not examine or explain any of these examples; he is satisfied with merely listing
them. BRONGERS, "Merismus, Synekdoche und Hendiadys," 104, calls a merismus the
three words for anger in 29,27 (אף, חמה and קצף). SCHENKER, "Unwiderrufliche Umkehr,"
99, calls the combination פי and לבב in 30,14 a merismus.

29,17:	איש או אשה (every individual human being)
29,17:	משפחה או שבט (all social groups within Israel)
29,18:	הרוה את-הצמאה (wet and dry: the totality of all plants, growing things, or soil; here it refers to all individuals within Israel as a society)
29,28:	הנסתרת and הנגלת (the totality of knowledge or of all things)
30,1.19:	הברכה והקללה (all possible results/effects of the covenant relationship)
30,2.6.10:	בכל-לבבך ובכל-נפשך (the totality of a human being's inner life)
30,12-13:	שמים and ים (the totality of the created universe)
30,15.19:	המות and החיים (all the possibilities one can expect in the future)
30,15:	הטוב and הרע (all that is)
30,19:	השמים and הארץ (the totality of the created universe)

Metaphor: implied comparison between two things of unlike nature.

29,17:	stock/root producing poison and bitterness (both שרש and לענה are metaphors)
29,18:	the wet and the dry (land)
29,19:	anger and jealousy "smoke"
29,19:	the curse "settles on" the sinner
29,19:	God "wipes out" or "blots out" the sinner's name
29,21:	afflictions/ blows (מכות) and diseases (תחלאיה) of the land
29,27:	God "pulls out" or "roots out" the people from the ground and "throws them" to another land
30,9:	the "fruit" of the womb and of one's animals (a dormant metaphor?)
30,20:	"cling," "adhere," or "stick" to God

It is to be noted that all these metaphors, except the last two, are concentrated in Dt 29,17-27, the most vivid and descriptive section of the Third Discourse of Moses. The metaphors thus help to give a sense of reality and presence to the punishments which are the consequences of disobedience.

Metonymy: substitution of some attributive or suggestive word for what is actually meant. This often associates causes and effects, the abstract and the concrete, and also moral qualities with the physical. Unfortunately, metonymy and synecdoche have no clear boundaries and are sometimes confused.[31]

29,23:	all the *nations* will say (place for inhabitants)
30,2.6.10?:	love with all the *heart* and all the *soul* (physical for moral attributes; it's also possible that this is a synecdoche, since a part represents the whole)

---

[31] GARAVELLI, *Manuale di retorica*, 151, 155.

30,14:   בפיך ובלבבך (physical for moral attributes, since the mouth
                       represents one's speech and the heart one's thoughts)

Parenthesis: a word, phrase, or sentence inserted as an aside in a sentence
complete in itself.

29,16?:   עץ ואבן כסף וזהב אשר עמהם
29,22:   entire verse
29,25:   אלהים אשר לא־ידעום ולא חלק להם

Paronomasia or *punning*: use of words alike in sound but different in
meaning; playing on the sound and meanings of words.

29,6?:   הבשן and חשבון
30,3:   ושב ... את־שבותך
30,7:   כל־האלות האלה על ...

Personification or *prosopopoeia*: an animal or inanimate object is
represented as having human attributes or addressed as if it were human.

30,19:   heaven and earth called upon as witnesses

Polyptoton: repetition of words derived from the same root; this seems to
be an important technique in Hebrew.

29,8:   ועשׂיתם ... תעשׂון
29,15:   עברנו ... עברתם
30,1-3.8-10?:   the sevenfold occurrence of various forms of שׁוב (*qal* and
                 hiphil)
30,5:   ירשׁו ... וירשׁתה
30,9:   לטובה ... לטוב
30,9:   לשׂושׂ ... שׂשׂ
30,18:   אבד תאבדון

Polysyndeton: deliberate use of many conjunctions.

29,22?:   לא ... ולא ... ולא
29,27?:   באף ובחמה ובקצף
30,9?:   בפרי ... ובפרי ... ובפרי
30,15:   את־החיים ואת־הטוב ואת־המות ואת־הרע
30,16?:   מצותיו וחקתיו ומשפטיו

It is difficult to ascertain both asyndeton and polysyndeton in
classical Hebrew, since the conjunction ו played such an important role
in syntax. Hebrew made extensive use of parataxis and thus used the
copulative frequently. Can one call the frequent verb sequences using the
waw-conversive polysyndeton? (see, for example, 30,16: וחיית ורבית וברכך

יהוה אלהיך). In any case, sometimes a conjunction is used in biblical Hebrew with every member of a series, sometimes only with the final member.

Rhetorical Question: asking a question, not for the purpose of eliciting an answer but for the purpose of indirectly asserting or denying something.

30,12:   מי יעלה־לנו השמימה ויקחה לנו וישמענו אתה ונעשׂנה

30,13:   מי יעבר־לנו אל־עבר הים ויקחה לנו וישמענו אתה ונעשׂנה

Simile: explicit comparison between two things of unlike nature.

29,22:   like the overthrow of Sodom and Gomorrah, Admah and Zeboiim

Synecdoche: figure of speech in which a part stands for the whole.

29,1b: לעיניכם: this term emphasizes that the members of the audience are themselves witnesses to such marvels; however, more than just their eyes were present at the time!

29,3:   a heart to understand, eyes to see, and ears to hear (part for the whole)

29,17:   lest his *heart* turn away from God (part for the whole)

29,21:   הנכרי: the stranger (singular for plural)

30,1:   והשבת אל־לבבך (part for the whole)

30,9:   מעשׂה ידך (part for the whole)

30,17:   if your *heart* turns (part for the whole)

Synonym: a word having the same or almost the same meaning as some other.

29,2:   המסות, האתת, and המפתים

29,5:   שׁכר and יין

29,8:   ושׁמרתם and ועשׂיתם

29,9.14:   עמד and נצבים

29,11:   אלה and ברית

29,12:   נשׁבע and דבר

29,13:   האלה and הברית

29,16:   גלליהם and שׁקוציהם

29,17?:   ראשׁ and לענה

29,19:   קנאתו and אף

29,21:   תחלאיה and מכות

29,22:   בחמתו and באפו

29,25:   וישׁתחוו and ויעבדו

29,26:   קללה appears for the first time as a synonym of אלה, which occurs in 29,11.13.18.19.20.

29,27:   חמה, אף, and קצף

29,27:	ארץ and אדמה
30,1.3:	העמים and הגוים
30,1.3:	הפיצך and הדיחך
30,4:	יקחך and יקבצך
30,7:	שנאיך and איביך
30,10:	חקתיו and מצותיו
30,11.14:	הדבר and המצוה
30,11:	רחקה and נפלאת
30,12.13:	יעבר and יעלה
30,15:	הטוב and החיים
30,15:	הרע and המות
30,16:	חקתיו, and משפטיו, מצותיו
30,16.18:	אדמה and ארץ,
30,17:	ונדחת and ולא תשמע
30,17:	עבדתם and השתחוית
30,18:	לא־תאריכן ימים and אבד תאבדון
30,19:	הברכה and החיים
30,19:	הקללה and המות
30,20:	ארך ימיך and חייך

Synonyms are scattered throughout the Third Discourse of Moses, although they seem to be especially frequent in Dt 30,10-20.

CHAPTER 7

CONCLUSION

7.1 Summary

This essay seeks to explore the Third Discourse of Moses (Dt 28,69 – 30,20) from a rhetorical-critical point of view. Rhetorical exegesis, despite roots which reach back to ancient Greece and Rome, is in its infancy, since it has still no definitive method or procedure. This work, based on both ancient and modern notions of rhetoric, is one attempt at discovering a methodology for such a rhetorical exegesis.

Chapter one provides the background and context of the Third Discourse of Moses. It does not try to examine all the questions and problems associated with the book of Dt. Rather it establishes that exegetes have long seen in the fifth book of the Pentateuch traits which characterize it as rhetorical. For Dt is a series of valedictory addresses or discourses by Moses directed to an audience of all Israel gathered together on the plains of Moab prior to the conquest of the promised land. These speeches have been described as didactic, homiletic, urgent, and parenetic. Dt's roots in ancient Israelite liturgy, jurisprudence, political diplomacy, and wisdom traditions contribute to its distinctive style, its personal appeal to every member of the community, and its urgent call for reform. The nature of Dt then is rhetorical or argumentative.

Chapter two defines and describes rhetoric and rhetorical criticism. In the past thirty years there has been a resurgence of interest in these areas. Rhetorical-critical studies of the Old Testament have usually emphasized stylistics or literary analysis. Thus rhetorical criticism to date has often neglected the argumentative or persuasive aspects of the Hebrew text.

This essay opts for a rhetorical criticism which concentrates on the argumentation of a written or spoken discourse. (This does not exclude some consideration of style, however.) Chapter two reviews the fundamental concepts of both ancient and modern rhetoric. The methodology used in this work follows the ancient divisions of rhetoric (*inventio, dispositio, elocutio*) but adapts itself to the "New Rhetoric" of Perelman and Olbrechts-Tyteca.

Chapter three examines the audience and the rhetorical situation of the Third Discourse of Moses. In Dt 28,69 – 30,20 Moses addresses "all Israel," an audience further delineated by participant lists and other audience indicators. This audience is a widely inclusive lay community of individuals and general classes, both those with privileges and obligations in the cult community (officials and adult male citizens) and those without (children, women, and resident aliens). Moses identifies with his audience when he recalls their common history, but otherwise he tends to separate himself from his listeners.

The rhetorical situation includes an exigence, a need which gives rise to a communication act. In the Third Discourse of Moses that exigence seems to be expressed in Dt 29,3, where Moses accuses the audience of lacking insight and understanding. That lack leads to the necessity of making a decision, a decision to accept or renew the covenant with God. The *issue* of the Third Discourse then centers on Dt 29,8; 30,15.19: observance of the covenant and its obligations, and a conscious choice to accomplish that observance. The rhetorical situation of a discourse also includes its context or the circumstances in which it is read or proclaimed. Dt 28,69 – 30,20 is affected by its position after two other speeches, one of which is rather long.

Chapter four investigates *inventio,* the finding of arguments. There are three basic types of arguments, based on the modes of ethos, pathos, and logos. In the Third Discourse of Moses pathos is revealed by figures of presence (especially devices of repetition, amplification, and accentuation) and the use of emotional words and techniques. These provoke negative feelings towards the sinner and towards the worship of other gods (such as fear, horror, loathing or disgust, contempt, and hatred) and positive feelings towards Yahweh and his covenant (national pride, admiration, wonder or awe, and love). The ethos of this discourse is dominated by the authority of both Moses and Yahweh.

Chapter four also investigates rational argumentation in two different ways. First it attempts to discover the enthymemes implicit within Dt 28,69 – 30,20. Then it searches for arguments of association (quasi-logical arguments, arguments based on the structure of reality, and arguments which establish the structure of reality) and dissociation in the text. Rational argumentation within the Third Discourse attempts to prove that 1) the worship of other gods means the abandonment of Yahweh; that is, the worship of other gods is incompatible with the worship of Yahweh; 2) infidelity to God's covenant brings punishment; 3) observance of God's covenant brings reward; 4) observance of God's covenant is possible; and 5) a choice must be made between Yahweh and the other gods.

The establishment of incompatibilities requires a choice between Yahweh (who can perform wonders) and filthy idols; between good and evil, blessing and curse, life and death. The individuals within the audience are called upon to identify with "all Israel." Illustrations of Yahweh's power, anger, blessings, and punishments reinforce the cause-effect relationships established between sin and punishment, fidelity and blessing.

Chapter five determines the rhetorical unit (Dt 28,69–30,20) and then establishes the literary structure of the Third Discourse of Moses. However, the literary structure is not identical with rhetorical arrangement or *dispositio*. So chapter five produces a continuous commentary on the argumentation of each verse and subsection of this text. It then summarizes this arrangement by means of classical Greek and Latin terminology.

Finally chapter six investigates the *elocutio* or style of Dt 28,69–30,20. The Third Discourse of Moses has a tendency to link words, phrases, and clauses into groups of two (pairs) and three (triads). Many of the pairs appear in the form of parallels or contrasts. These pairs, parallels, and contrasts support the incompatibilities which the rational argumentation seeks to establish. They also, together with the triads, constitute most of the numerous repetitions and amplifications in this text. Other stylistic features include direct address, imperative and interrogative modality, appeal to the imagination, and the use of a large variety of figures and tropes.

This essay demonstrates that the ancient Hebrews also practiced rhetoric, whether or not they theorized about it. They too wanted to influence and persuade, to arouse feelings and change minds, to effect and convince. The Third Discourse of Moses is an attempt to convince a widely inclusive audience to resolve the incompatibility of relationships with both Yahweh and other gods, an incompatibility that could lead to the destruction of the nation. The author(s) of this discourse did not hesitate to use whatever means they could find — emotional, logical, authoritative, stylistic, etc. — to convince their audience to make the right choice: *for* Yahweh, *for* his covenant, and *for* the observance of the covenant regulations.

The argumentation of Dt 28,69–30,20 is not merely rational. This discourse also provokes emotions, especially through the lowering of abstraction, vivid imagery, "loaded" terms, repetition, and accumulation. Moses (and through him the communicator) wants to touch not only the mind but also the heart and soul. The fact that this text still speaks to us may indicate that such appeals to emotion still have a place in rhetoric. Our modern world may need to rediscover that God's message may not be properly understood through rational analysis alone.

Contemporary science and philosophy may have difficulty with many of the premises and common opinions of ancient Hebrew reasoning. Moses' audience accepted the Exodus, the wandering in the wilderness, and the destruction of Sodom and Gomorrah, Admah and Zeboiim as historical facts. They lived in a world of clans and tribes, of powerful blessings and curses, and of concrete values (many children, land, one's name) which may not affect us so profoundly. The ancient Israelites may have accepted certain cause-effect relationships (e.g., fidelity brings blessing) which are uncomfortable for us. However, such understandings were important for ancient Hebrew rhetoric. Without them perhaps the Third Discourse would have lost much of its power and effectiveness — perhaps it would never even have survived.

7.2 Rhetorical Genre

Ancient rhetoricians recognized three categories or genres of persuasive discourse: deliberative, forensic, and epideictic.[1] These categories originally described the classes of oratory in the ancient Greek city-state: *deliberative* oratory was used in public meetings to settle questions of civic policy; *forensic* oratory was used in law courts to settle private disputes and carry out justice; while *epideictic* oratory was used on ceremonial occasions and included funeral addresses, congratulatory speeches, and oratorical exhibitions. These genres, however, came to be applied to all discourse: deliberative rhetoric is that in which a speaker attempts to persuade another to do something in the future; forensic rhetoric is that used in any kind of judgment made about the past; and epideictic rhetoric is that used to persuade someone to hold or reaffirm some point of view or value (thus it is often associated with education).[2] The three genres tend to blend into one another, so identifying a particular discourse with one of them can be problematic.[3] Nevertheless, this division is still often retained, since it is traditional and can be useful.

Does the Third Discourse of Moses fall into one of these categories? By itself, Dt 28,69–30,20 appears to be *deliberative,* for it displays many of the features of this genre. It concerns a future choice, makes use of exhortation (parenesis), and often refers to the special topics of the expedient/inexpedient, advantageous/injurious, and happiness/unhappiness. Its concern is what course of action should be chosen, its audience is an assembly, and it does make use of some inductive arguments based on past examples. The Third Discourse also appeals to the common topic of

---

[1] Cf. 2.4.

[2] KENNEDY, *New Testament Interpretation,* 19.

[3] Cf. BRANDT, *The Rhetoric of Argumentation,* 13-14; CORBETT, *Classical Rhetoric,* 152; KENNEDY, *New Testament Interpretation,* 74; PERELMAN, "The New Rhetoric," 279; *L'empire rhétorique,* 33.

the possible and the impossible and stirs up emotions such as hope, fear, desire, and animosity. All of these features are typical of the deliberative genre.[4]

However, there are also some features of epideictic rhetoric present in Dt 28,69–30,20. One gets the impression that this valedictory address of Moses is reinforcing certain values, especially in what concerns virtue and vice, the noble and the base. Although examples and illustrations do appear, these are minor features in comparison with amplification, which is characteristic of epideictic. Other emotions, such as loathing or disgust, contempt, hatred, national pride, admiration, wonder or awe, and love are all indicative of the epideictic genre.[5] This impression is confirmed by the fact that no decision is actually reported, that this address is preceded by two others, and that it is meant to be read before the assembly on a regular basis (Dt 31,10-13).

Thus the Third Discourse of Moses has both deliberative and epideictic features. Taken by itself, it is strongly deliberative; but in the context of all Dt, it also reveals itself as epideictic.

7.3 Theological Considerations

The theology of the book of Dt has often been summarized as: one God, one sanctuary, one people, one land, one law.[6] Israel, which is one united people, must worship Yahweh (and no other god) at the sanctuary in Jerusalem. Israel is a community of brothers and sisters, a community held together by the common worship of Yahweh, a community which can even be addressed as though it were a single person.[7] Yahweh is unique, for only he has a special relationship with Israel. It is he who gave Israel the gift of the land, where the law is to be obeyed.[8] Yahweh loves Israel and demands a faithful love and obedience in return. Thus Dt

---

[4] CORBETT, *Classical Rhetoric*, 26, 146-149; KENNEDY, *New Testament Interpretation*, 19-20, 36-37.

[5] CORBETT, *Classical Rhetoric*, 40, 152; DIXON, *Rhetoric*, 23; KENNEDY, *New Testament Interpretation*, 73-75; PERELMAN and OLBRECHTS-TYTECA, *Traité de l'argumentation*, 62-68; ROSENFIELD, "The Practical Celebration of Epideictic," 133-135.

[6] See especially GARCÍA LÓPEZ, *Le Deutéronome*, 19-28; HERRMANN, "Die konstruktive Restauration," 158-162, who uses the terms "Kultuseinheit," "Kultusreinheit," and "ganz Israel"; MAYES, *Deuteronomy*, 57-58; VON RAD, *Theologie des Alten Testaments*, I, 242 (he also adds "one prophet"); and WATTS, "The Deuteronomic Theology," 325-330.

[7] BUIS, *Le Deutéronome*, 210-211; BUIS and LECLERCQ, *Le Deutéronome*, 20; MAYES, *Deuteronomy*, 55.

[8] MAYES, *Deuteronomy*, 78-81; PENNA, *Deuteronomio*, 40-42; VON RAD, *Theologie des Alten Testaments*, I, 242; WATTS, *"The Deuteronomic Theology,"* 328-329; WRIGHT, *Deuteronomy*, 327.

invitation to renew and observe the covenant.[9] One could even say that Dt's theology centers around the idea of covenant.[10]

The Third Discourse of Moses has little to say about the sanctuary. That the audience has been gathered לפני יהוה אלהיכם/אלהינו (29,9.14) may indicate that this discourse takes place in a sanctuary or in a liturgical context. (That liturgical context would probably be the reading of the *torah* before the congregation every seventh year.) However, the other theological themes of Dt — one God, one people, one land, and one law (the covenant) — are all certainly present in Dt 28,69 – 30,20.

7.3.1 One God

Yahweh is no stranger to the audience of the Third Discourse. The history of God's intervention in Egypt and in the wilderness (29,1-5) is a premise rather than a conclusion — that is, the audience accepts this history as true and important. Yahweh is also associated with the audience's ancestors (29,12; 30,20). That Yahweh can command with authority (28,69), lending weight to the ethos of the work, similarly indicates that the audience acknowledges his authority, at least to some extent. However, this recognition of Yahweh is impaired or imperfect, for the audience can be accused of lacking in understanding (29,3). In the only place where God himself speaks (or is cited) there is a demand that he be truly recognized for who he is (29,5). In fact, a personal experience of Yahweh should lead to confessing or acknowledging his identity.

What is that identity? For the most part the Third Discourse of Moses does not need to establish it, since it is included among the presumptions, truths, and values presented within the text. Yahweh is powerful (29,1-2.4-5) and capable of either punishing (29,18-27) or blessing (30,5.7.9.16). In fact, there is great emphasis on his anger (29,19.22.23.26.27) and jealousy (29,19). But God is also capable of showing kindness and mercy, since he will bring back those whom he has exiled (30,3-5) and renews his blessings (30,5-7.9). Yahweh wants a special relationship with the audience (29,11-12) and will even effect an inner change within its individual members (30,6).

Above all, Yahweh demands that his relationship with Israel be an exclusive one. Serving or worshipping other gods is incompatible with this relationship (29,17.18.25; 30,17). These other gods are ridiculed and dissociated from Yahweh, for they are disgusting material objects (29,15-16). The mere thought of serving such abominations will bring doom to that foolish individual who does so (29,18-20). For every

---

[9] WATTS, "The Deuteronomic Theology," 329; WRIGHT, *Deuteronomy,* 312.
[10] BUIS, *Le Deutéronome,* 193; WATTS, "The Deuteronomic Theology," 325, 327.

relationship with another god is incompatible with the covenant which Yahweh makes with Israel (29,17.19.20.24.26). This covenant demands an exclusive love for Yahweh, a love with all one's heart and soul (30,6.16.20).

The emphasis then in the Third Discourse is on a God who demands an exclusive relationship and will admit no rivals. That demand is presented in terms of an incompatibility between Yahweh and other gods and by means of a dissociation between Yahweh and other gods. It is for this reason that Dt 28,69 – 30,20 revolves around the issue of observance of Yahweh's covenant laws and regulations. The sender makes use of both rational and emotional arguments to emphasize the incompatibility and to draw the conclusion that only Yahweh must be worshipped and his covenant laws must be obeyed.

7.3.2 One people: Israel

Within the Third Discourse of Moses the audience is named Israel in Dt 28,69; 29,1a.9.21. Of these, only the two occurrences in reporting speech (28,69; 29,1a) actually define the audience. The audience is never addressed as Israel in the vocative, which contrasts with other parts of Dt.[11] And yet the use of the second person, both singular and plural, demonstrates that the audience is addressed directly and constantly, both as individuals and in solidarity with the entire community. Argumentation must appeal both to the individual conscience and to social groups. One gets the impression that the members of this audience still identify strongly with the group; yet they are also beginning to experience themselves as individuals within the community.

All Israel is involved in a covenant relationship with Yahweh (28,69). In the Third Discourse of Moses there is no reference to the common brotherhood of individual Israelites. Rather it addresses a widely inclusive lay audience which has gathered in an assembly to enter into or renew the covenant with its God (29,9-14). This audience includes women children, and alien residents (29,10); even future generations (29,14) are somehow within this group. Yet there is no mention of any priestly or prophetic class. It is unlikely that this is a radical move to remove priests, levites, and prophets from authoritative postions within the community. Rather it seems to emphasize that *each* and *every* Israelite — even those without political or religious obligations and those who remain on the margins of the community — is intimately involved in this covenant relationship with Yahweh.

---

[11] See Dt 4,1; 5,1; 6,3.4; 9,1; 10,12; 27,9. The vocative also appears in 20,3 and 32,29, but these are special occurrences.

Israel's experiences of God's wonders in Egypt and his providential care in the wilderness (29,1-2.4-5) make it a primary witness in the argumentation of the Third Discourse. It should be able to draw the proper conclusions about the identity of Yahweh as well as that of disgusting idols (29,5.15-16). However, this audience is lacking in understanding (29,3) and quite capable of sin and infidelity (29,17-18). Yet Israel is also capable of repentance and observance of the covenant regulations (30,1-3.8-10.11-14). Its proper response to Yahweh is wholehearted love and faithful observance of the covenant obligations (29,8.28; 30,6.16.20). The Third Discourse of Moses is both threat and promise to the audience, for it seeks to convince Israel to observe the covenant regulations. This can be done if each individual member of the audience personally chooses the life-giving laws and regulations of Yahweh's covenant.

So the emphasis in Dt 28,69–30,20 is on an Israel which is free to choose. The author or authors do not merely demonstrate the incompatibility of serving both Yahweh and other gods and the dissociation between Yahweh and disgusting idols. They also use every means possible to convince Israel that there is only one reasonable and viable choice. Israel is free to choose, but it would be foolish and self-destructive to choose other gods — even secretly. We are not given Israel's response, which gives the impression that such a decision is ever constant in the making.

7.3.3 The land

The land, taken from others, is a gift or inheritance from God (29,6-7; 30,16-18). The results of Israel's infidelity to Yahweh's covenant include the loss of the land (29,27; 30,18) and even punishment of the land itself (29,21-22.26). Return from exile to the land is the result of conversion (30,3-5); prosperity and long life in the land are the rewards for faithful observance of Yahweh's covenant (30,9.16.20).

Thus the land plays an important role in the covenant relationship with Yahweh, in Israel's theology, and in the argumentation of the Third Discourse. The threat of the land's loss is a powerful one, while restoration of the land is a motivation for conversion and observance of the covenant regulations. Within Dt 28,69–30,20 the cause-effect relationships (arguments based on the structure of reality) involving the land are among the most frequent and powerful of rational arguments: infidelity brings punishment (especially loss of the land and punishment of the land), while fidelity and conversion bring blessings (restoration of the land and prosperity in the land). The importance given to this concrete value reflects a materialistic notion of salvation found within Dt.[12]

---

[12] Buis, *Le Deutéronome*, 206; Von Rad, *Theologie des Alten Testaments*, I, 242.

7.3.4 Covenant

The Third Discourse of Moses recognizes more than one covenant between Yahweh and Israel, since Dt 28,69 distinguishes the covenant made in Moab from that made on Horeb. In both cases it is Yahweh who initiates the special relationship which a covenant symbolizes (28,69). This special relationship is clear: Yahweh is Israel's God, Israel is Yahweh's people (29,12).

The issue of the Third Discourse is precisely the observance of this covenant (29,8.28; 30,2.8.10.16.20). In fact, the choice which this discourse culminates in (30,15.19) is not only one between Yahweh and other gods, but more specifically between the observance and non-observance of the covenant regulations. For the covenant demands an exclusive worship of Yahweh (30,2.6.10.16.20) which tolerates no worship of any other god (29,17.18.24-25). Any activity which serves or favors another god automatically severs Israel's special relaitonship with Yahweh. Even thoughts of betrayal in the mind of an individual are subject to severe punishment (29,18-20).

The strong cause-effect relationships within the Third Discourse give the notion of covenant a rather conditional character. This is reinforced by the association of the covenant with an oath (29,11.13.18.19.20; 30,7) and a curse (29,26; 30,1.19). However, the possibility of repentance and its resulting restoration and prosperity (30,1-10), which includes an inner renewal effected by God himself (30,6), transcends the threat of a final and permanent break in the covenant relationship. The double mention of God's promise to the ancestors (29,12; 30,20) also seems to contribute to the notion of covenant an unconditional element.

The Third Discourse of Moses also associates the covenant with תורה (29,20.28; 30,10). Written down in a book (29,19.20.26; 30,10), this *torah*-covenant can be learned and handed down to future generations. Thus it becomes a kind of manual or instruction for a way of life. As such it is something within the realm of possibility for this audience (29,28; 30,11-14).

7.3.5 Conclusion

This brief description of the major features of the theology of the Third Discourse of Moses differs little from those of other contemporary commentators on Dt. A rhetorical-critical approach is distinguished not so much by its results concerning the *content* of a text as by its *manner* of viewing that text. Many, if not all, biblical texts can be examined from an argumentative point of view. Such an investigation reveals what is important in getting the text's message across.

This examination of Dt 28,69 – 30,20 reveals the issue of the discourse: observance of the covenant regulations. It is important that Israel makes a decision, and that it chooses freely. However, it should also choose well. Worship of other gods is incompatible with the worship of Yahweh. The senders make use of various rational and emotional appeals to convince the receivers (a widely inclusive lay audience) to choose Yahweh and his covenant. We may never know the response of the first audience which heard this discourse. But we do know that Israel eventually did choose to follow this highly recommended course of action.

ABBREVIATIONS

AJSL	*American Journal of Semitic Languages*
AnBib	Analecta biblica
ANET	*Ancient Near Eastern Texts Relating to the Old Testament,* ed. J. PRITCHARD. 3rd ed. with Supplement. Princeton, N.J.: Princeton University Press, 1969.
AS	*Assemblées du Seigneur*
ATANT	Abhandlungen zur Theologie des Alten und Neuen Testaments
ATD	Das Alte Testament Deutsch
B	Codex Vaticanus
BA	*Biblical Archaeologist*
BASOR	*Bulletin of the American Schools of Oriental Research*
BBB	Bonner biblische Beiträge
B.C.E.	Before Common Era
BDB	BROWN, DRIVER, and BRIGGS (ed.), *A Hebrew and English Lexicon of the Old Testament*
BETL	Bibliotheca ephemeridum theologicarum lovaniensium
BHS	*Biblia Hebraica Stuttgartensia* (1977)
Bib	*Biblica*
BibB	Biblische Beiträge
BibLeb	*Bibel und Leben*
BibOr	Biblica et Orientalia
BJ	La Bible de Jérusalem (1975)
BLC	La Bibbia in Lingua Corrente (1985)
BLS	Bible and Literature Series
BLtg	*Bibel und Liturgie*
BN	*Biblische Notizen*
BR	*Biblical Research*
BTB	*Biblical Theology Bulletin*
BTFT	*Bijdragen: Tijdschrift voor Filosofie en Theologie*
BWANT	Beiträge zur Wissenschaft vom Alten und Neuen Testament
BZ	*Biblische Zeitschrift*
BZAW	Beihefte zur Zeitschrift für die alttestamentliche Wissenschaft
c:	conclusion (in enthymemes)
CBQ	*Catholic Biblical Quarterly*
C.E.	Common Era
CEI	*La Bibbia* approvata dalla Conferenza Episcopale Italiana (ed. Pietro VANETTI; 3rd ed. 1983)
cf.	confer
chap(s)	chapter(s)
ColT	*Collectanea Theologica*

Diss.	Dissertation
DRev	*The Downside Review*
Dt	Deuteronomy
Dtr	Deuteronomistic History

ed.	editor(s); edited by; edition
e.g.	for example
EgT	*Église et théologie*
EKL	*Evangelisches Kirchenlexikon* (ed. Erwin FAHLBUSCH; 3rd ed.) Göttingen: Vandenhoeck & Ruprecht, 1986. 2 Vols.
ETL	*Ephemerides theologicae lovanienses*
EÜ	*Einheitsübersetzung der Heiligen Schrift* (2nd ed., 1983)
EvT	*Evangelische Theologie*
ExpTim	*Expository Times*

FRLANT	Forschungen zur Religion und Literatur des Alten und Neuen Testaments
FS.	Festschrift
FZPhTh	*Freiburger Zeitschrift für Philosophie und Theologie*

GBS	Guides to Biblical Scholarship
GBWW	*Great Books of the Western World.* Robert M. HUTCHINS, ed. Chicago: Encyclopaedia Britannica, 1952.
GKC	W. GESENIUS, *Hebrew Grammar* (edited and enlarged by E. KAUTZSCH, translated by A.E. COWLEY.
GTA	Göttinger theologische Arbeiten

Hen	*Henoch*
HeyJ	*The Heythrop Journal*
Hrsg.	Herausgeber (editor)
HSM	Harvard Semitic Monographs
HTR	*Harvard Theological Review*
HUCA	*Hebrew Union College Annual*

IB	*Interpreter's Bible*
ICC	International Critical Commentary
IDB	*Interpreter's Dictionary of the Bible*
IDBSup	*Interpreter's Dictionary of the Bible, Supplementary Volume*
i.e.	that is
IEJ	*Israel Exploration Journal*
Int	*Interpretation*
IsrOrSt	*Israel Oriental Studies*

JAAR	*Journal of the American Academy of Religion*
JAOS	*Journal of the American Oriental Society*
JBL	*Journal of Biblical Literature*
JNES	*Journal of Near Eastern Studies*

JNWS	*Journal of Northwest Semitic Languages*
JPOS	*Journal of the Palestine Oriental Society*
JQR	*Jewish Quarterly Review*
JSOT	*Journal for the Study of the Old Testament*
JSOTSS	Journal for the Study of the Old Testament Supplement Series
JSS	*Journal of Semitic Studies*
JTS	*Journal of Theological Studies*

LCL	Loeb Classical Library
LD	Lectio divina
LLS	Los Libros Sagrados
LXX	Septuagint

MT	Masoretic Text

n.	note
NAB	*New American Bible* (1st ed., 1970)
NEB	*New English Bible* (1973)
N.F.	Neue Folge
no.	number
N.S.	New Series

OBO	Orbis Biblicus et Orientalis
OTS	*Oudtestamentische Studiën*

p^1:	major premise (enthymemes)
p^2:	minor premise (enthymemes)
ParSpV	*Parola spirito e vita*
PEGLBS	*Proceedings, Eastern Great Lakes Biblical Society*
PIBA	*Proceedings of the Irish Biblical Association*
plur.	plural
PTMS	Pittsburgh Theological Monograph Series

RB	*Revue biblique*
REB	*Revised English Bible*, 1989
RechBib	Recherches bibliques
RevExp	*Review and Expositor*
RHR	*Revue de l'histoire des religions*
RIP	*Revue internationale de philosophie*
RivB	*Rivista biblica*
RivStoLR	*Rivista di storia e letteratura religiosa*
RSR	*Recherches de science religieuse*
RSV	Revised Standard Version (Catholic Edition, 1966)

Sam	Samaritan Pentateuch
SBAB	Stuttgarter biblische Aufsatzbände
SBLDS	Society of Biblical Literature Dissertation Series
SBLMS	Society of Biblical Literature Monograph Series
SBLSS	Society of Biblical Literature Semeia Supplements

SBT	Studies in Biblical Theology
ScEs	*Science et esprit*
SDB	*Supplément au Dictionnaire de la Bible* (L. PIROT, A. ROBERT, and H. CAZELLES, ed.). Paris: Librairie Letouzey et Ané, 1928-1988 (11 volumes to date).
SJT	*Scottish Journal of Theology*
SR	*Studies in Religion*
SSCJ	*The Southern Speech Communication Journal*
Syr	Syriac

Targ.	Targum(s)
TBT	*The Bible Today*
TBü	Theologische Bücherei
TF	*Theologische Forschung*
THAT	*Theologisches Handwörterbuch zum Alten Testament*, 2 vols. E. JENNI and C. WESTERMANN, ed.
Them	*Themelios*
T^J	Targum Pseudo-Jonathan
TLZ	*Theologische Literaturzeitung*
TOB	Traduction Oecuménique de la Bible (2nd ed., 1975)
TP	*Theologie und Philosophie*
TQ	*Theologische Quartalschrift*
trans.	translator, translated by
TRE	*Theologische Realenzyklopädie*
TRu	*Theologische Rundschau*
TS	*Theological Studies*
TSK	*Theologische Studien und Kritiken*
TThZ	*Trierer theologische Zeitschrift*
TToday	*Theology Today*
TWAT	*Theologisches Wörterbuch zum Alten Testament*. G.J. BOTTERWECK, H. RINGGREN, and H.-J. FABRY, ed.

| Univ. | University, Universität, Université |

v.	verse
Vg	Vulgate
VT	*Vetus Testamentum*
VTS	*Vetus Testamentum Supplements*
vv.	verses

| WMANT | Wissenschaftliche Monographien zum Alten und Neuen Testament |
| WUNT | Wissenschaftliche Untersuchungen zum Neuen Testament |

| *ZAW* | *Zeitschrift für die alttestamentliche Wissenschaft* |
| *ZKT* | *Zeitschrift für katholische Theologie* |

BIBLIOGRAPHY

ACHTEMEIER, Elizabeth, "Plumbing the Riches: Deuteronomy for the Preacher," *Int* 61 (1987) 269-281.

ADAM, Jean-Michel, "Une rhétorique de la description," *Figures et conflits rhétoriques* (ed. M. MEYER and A. LEMPEREUR, 1990). Pp. 165-192.

AHARONI, Yohanan, *The Archaeology of the Land of Israel: From the Prehistoric Beginnings to the End of the First Temple Period* (ed. Miriam AHARONI). Translated by Anson F. Rainey. Philadelphia: The Westminster Press, 1978, 1982.

AIROLDI, Norberto, "Le 'Sezioni-noi' nel Deuteronomio," *RivB* 16 (1968) 143-157.

ALBRIGHT, William Foxwell, *From the Stone Age to Christianity*. 2nd ed. Garden City, N.Y.: Doubleday, 1957.

ALONSO SCHÖKEL, Luis, "Hermeneutical Problems of a Literary Study of the Bible," *VTS* 28 (1975) 1-15.

———, "Hermeneutics in the Light of Language and Literature," *CBQ* 25 (1963) 371-386.

———, *A Manual of Hebrew Poetics* (Subsidia Biblica 11). Translated by Adrian Graffy. Rome: Pontifical Biblical Institute, 1988.

———, "Of Methods and Models," *VTS* 36 (1985) 3-13.

ALONSO SCHÖKEL, Luis; MATEOS, Juan; and VALVERDE, José María, *Pentateuco* (LLS). I: *Genesis - Exodo*. II: *Levitico - Numeros - Deuteronomio*. Madrid: Ediciones Cristiandad, 1970. The introduction and notes to *Deuteronomio* are authored by Alonso Schökel.

ALTER, Robert, *The Art of Biblical Narrative*. New York: Basic Books, 1981.

AMSLER, Samuel, "Loi orale et loi écrite dans le Deutéronome," *Das Deuteronomium* (ed. N. LOHFINK, 1985). Pp. 51-54.

———, "עמד," *THAT* II, 328-332.

ANBAR, Moshe, "The Story about the Building of an Altar on Mount Ebal: The History of Its Composition and the Question of the Centralization of the Cult," *Das Deuteronomium* (ed. N. LOHFINK, 1985). Pp. 304-309.

ANDERSEN, Francis I., "Chiastic Sentences," *The Sentence in Biblical Hebrew* (Janua Linguarum, Series Practica, 231). The Hague/Paris: Mouton, 1974. Pp. 119-140.

ANDERSEN, Francis I., and FORBES, A. Dean, *The Vocabulary of the Old Testament*. Rome: Biblical Institute Press, 1989.

ANDERSON, Bernhard W., "Martin Noth's Traditio-Historical Approach in the Context of Twentieth-Century Biblical Research." Introduction to *A History of Pentateuchal Traditions*, by Martin NOTH. Chico, California: Scholars Press, 1981. Pp. xiii-xxxii.

———, "The New Frontier of Rhetorical Criticism: A Tribute to James Muilenburg." Introduction to *Rhetorical Criticism: Essays in Honor of James Muilenburg* (PTMS 1; ed. J.J. JACKSON and M. KESSLER). Pittsburgh: Pickwick, 1974. Pp. ix-xviii.

ANDREWS, James R., "'Charting Cultural Paths': Toward a Method for Investigating Rhetorical-Cultural Interaction," *Rhetoric in Transition* (ed. E. WHITE, 1980). Pp. 101-114.

ANSCOMBRE, Jean-Claude and DUCROT, Oswald, "Argumentativité et informativité," *De la métaphysique à la rhétorique* (ed. Michel MEYER, 1986). Pp. 79-94.

APOSTEL, Leo, "What Is the Force of an Argument? Some Problems and Suggestions," *RIP* 33 (1979) 99-109.

ARISTOTLE, *Poetics* (ed. Friedrich SOLMSEN). Translated by Ingram Bywater. New York: The Modern Library, 1954.

———, *Rhetoric* (ed. Friedrich SOLMSEN). Translated by W. Rhys Roberts. New York: The Modern Library, 1954. Greek text: *Rhétorique,* Tome premier (Livre I). Texte établi et traduit par Médéric Dufour. Paris: Société d'édition "Les Belles Lettres," 1932.

———, *Topics* (*GBWW* 8). Translated by W.A. Pickard-Cambridge. Chicago: Encyclopaedia Britannica, 1952. Pp. 139-223.

ARNOLD, Carroll C., Introduction to *The Realm of Rhetoric* by Chaim PERELMAN. Notre Dame/London: University of Notre Dame Press, 1982. Pp. vii-xx.

———, "Oral Rhetoric, Rhetoric, and Literature," *Rhetoric in Transition* (ed. E. WHITE, 1980). Pp. 157-173. Originally published in *Philosophy and Rhetoric* (Fall, 1968).

ARNOLD, Carroll C., and FRANDSEN, Kenneth D., "Conceptions of Rhetoric and Communication," *Handbook of Rhetorical and Communication Theory* (ed. Carroll C. ARNOLD and John Waite BOWERS). Boston: Allyn and Bacon, 1984. Pp. 3-50.

AUGUSTINE, *De doctrina christiana* (ed. Henr. Jos. VOGELS) (Florilegium patristicum tam veteris quam medii aevi auctores complectens 24). Bonnae: Sumptibus Petri Hanstein, 1930. English translation: *On Christian Doctrine* (GBBW 18). Translated by J.F. Shaw. Chicago: Encyclopaedia Britannica, 1952. Pp. 619-698.

BALL, Ivan Jay, Jr., *A Rhetorical Study of Zephaniah.* Berkeley, Calif.: BIBAL Press, 1988. Reprint of 1973 dissertation.

BALTZER, Klaus, *Das Bundesformular* (WMANT 4). Neukirchen: Neukirchener Verlag, 1960.

BAR-EFRAT, S., "Some Observations on the Analysis of Structure in Biblical Narrative," *VT* 30 (1980) 154-173.

BARILLI, Renato, "Rhétorique et culture," *RIP* 33 (1979) 69-80.

BARR, James, "Childs' *Introduction to the Old Testament as Scripture,*" *JSOT* 16 (1980) 12-23.

BARRETT, Cyril, "The Language of Ecstasy and the Ecstasy of Language," *The Bible as Rhetoric* (ed. Martin WARNER, 1990), pp. 205-221.

BARTHÉLEMY, Dominique, *Critique textuelle de l'Ancien Testament. 1. Josué, Juges, Ruth, Samuel, Rois, Chroniques, Esdras, Néhémie, Esther* (OBO 50/1). Fribourg, Suisse: Éditions Universitaires, 1982.

BARTHES, Roland, *L'ancienne rhétorique: Aide-mémoire, Communications* 4 (1964). Reprinted in: *L'aventure sémiologique.* Paris: Éditions du Seuil, 1985.

———, "Style and Its Image," *Literary Style: A Symposium* (ed. S. CHATMAN, 1971). Pp. 3-10.

BARTON, John, "History and Rhetoric in the Prophets," *The Bible as Rhetoric* (ed. Martin WARNER, 1990), pp. 51-64.

————, *Reading the Old Testament: Method in Biblical Study*. London: Darton Longman and Todd, 1984.

BEAUJOUR, Michel, "Rhétorique et littérature," *De la métaphysique à la rhétorique* (ed. Michel MEYER, 1986), pp. 157-174.

BEE, Ronald, "A Study of Deuteronomy Based on Statistical Properties of the Text," *VT* 29 (1979) 1-22.

BEGG, Christopher T., "'Bread, Wine and Strong Drink' in Deut 29:5a," *BTFT* 41 (1980) 266-275.

————, "The Destruction of the Calf (Exod. 32,20/Deut 9,21)," *Das Deuteronomium* (ed. N. LOHFINK, 1985). Pp. 208-251.

————, "The Literary Criticism of Deut 4,1-40: Contributions to a Continuing Discussion," *ETL* 56 (1980) 10-55.

————, "The Reading *šbṭy(km)* in Deut 29,9 and 2 Sam 7,7," *ETL* 58 (1982) 87-105.

————, "The Reading in 2 Sam 7,7: Some Remarks," *RB* 95 (1988) 551-558.

————, "The Significance of the *Numeruswechsel* in Deuteronomy: The 'Pre-History' of the Question," *ETL* 55 (1979) 116-124.

————, "The Tables (Deut X) and the Lawbook (Deut XXXI)," *VT* 33 (1983) 96-97.

BERGMAN, J.; RINGGREN, H.; and HAAG, H., "בֵּן," *TWAT* I, 668-682.

BERTHOLET, Alfred, Review of *Das Deuteronomium*, by Carl STEUERNAGEL, *TLZ* 24 (1899) 482-486.

BESTERS, André, "'Israël' et 'fils d'Israël' dans les livres historiques (Genèse — II Rois)," *RB* 74 (1967) 5-23.

BETTENZOLI, Giuseppe, "I Leviti e la riforma deuteronomica," *RivStoLR* 22 (1986) 3-23.

BEYERLIN, Walter, "Die Paränese im Bundesbuch und ihre Herkunft," *Gottes Wort und Gottes Land* (FS. H.W. Hertzberg; ed. Henning Graf REVENTLOW). Göttingen: Vandenhoeck & Ruprecht, 1965. Pp. 9-29.

BILLIG, Michael, "Rhétorique et idéologie," *Figures et conflits rhétoriques* (ed. M. MEYER and A. LEMPEREUR, 1990). Pp. 209-225.

BITZER, Lloyd F., "Functional Communication: A Situational Perspective," *Rhetoric in Transition* (ed. E. WHITE, 1980). Pp. 21-38.

BITZER, Lloyd F. and BLACK, Edwin, *The Prospect of Rhetoric*. Englewood Cliffs, N.J.: Prentice-Hall, 1971.

BLACK, C. Clifton, "Rhetorical Criticism and Biblical Interpretation," *ExpTim* 100 (1988-89) 252-258.

————, "The Rhetorical Form of the Hellenistic Jewish and Early Christian Sermon: A Response to Lawrence Wills," *HTR* 81 (1988) 1-18.

BLACK, Edwin, "The Mutability of Rhetoric," *Rhetoric in Transition* (ed. E. WHITE, 1980). Pp. 71-85.

————, *Rhetorical Criticism: A Study in Method*. Madison: University of Wisconsin Press, 1979.

BLAIR, Edward P., "An Appeal to Remembrance: The Memory Motif in Deuteronomy," *Int* 15 (1961) 41-47.

BLAU, Josua, "Über homonyme und angeblich homonyme Wurzeln II," *VT* 7 (1957) 98-102.

BLENKINSOPP, Joseph, "Are There Traces of the Gibeonite Covenant in Deuteronomy?" *CBQ* 28 (1966) 207-219.

――――, "A New Kind of Introduction: Professor Childs' *Introduction to the Old Testament as Scripture*," *JSOT* 16 (1980) 24-27.

BOCCACCIO, P., "I termini contrari come espressioni della totalità in ebraico," *Bib* 33 (1952) 173-190.

BONORA, Antonio, "La libertà di scelta: Dt 11,22-28 e 30,15-20," *ParSpV* 23 (1991) 49-60.

BOORER, Suzanne, "The Importance of a Diachronic Approach: The Case of Genesis-Kings," *CBQ* 51 (1989) 195-208.

BOOTH, Wayne C., *Now Don't Try to Reason with Me: Essays and Ironies for a Credulous Age*. Chicago/London: University of Chicago Press, 1970.

――――, *The Rhetoric of Fiction*. 2nd ed. Chicago: University of Chicago Press, 1983.

――――, *A Rhetoric of Irony*. Chicago/London: University of Chicago Press, 1974.

BOSTON, James R., "The Wisdom Influence upon the Song of Moses," *JBL* 87 (1968) 198-202.

BOTTERWECK, G. Johannes (Bände 1-5); RINGGREN, Helmer; and FABRY, Heinz-Josef (Bände 4-6), ed., *Theologisches Wörterbuch zum Alten Testament*, 6 vols. to date. Stuttgart: W. Kohlhammer, 1973-1989.

BRANDT, William J., *The Rhetoric of Argumentation*. Indianapolis/New York: Bobbs-Merrill, 1970.

BRAULIK, Georg, "Die Abfolge der Gesetze in Deuteronomium 12-26 und der Dekalog," *Das Deuteronomium* (ed. N. LOHFINK, 1985). Pp. 252-272. Reprinted in: *Studien zur Theologie des Deuteronomiums* (ed. G. BRAULIK, 1988). Pp. 231-255.

――――, "Die Ausdrücke für 'Gesetz' im Buch Deuteronomium," *Bib* 51 (1970) 39-66. Reprinted in: *Studien zur Theologie des Deuteronomiums* (ed. G. BRAULIK, 1988). Pp. 11-38.

――――, *Deuteronomio: Il testamento di Mosè* (Bibbia per tutti). Assisi: Cittadella editrice, 1987.

――――, *Deuteronomium 1-16,17* (Die Neue Echter Bibel). Würzburg: Echter Verlag, 1986.

――――, "Das Deuteronomium und die Geburt des Monotheismus," *Gott, der einzige: Zur Entstehung des Monotheismus in Israel* (ed. E. HAAG; Quaestiones Disputatae 104). Freiburg i.B.: Herder, 1985. Pp. 115-159. Reprinted in: *Studien zur Theologie des Deuteronomiums* (ed. G. BRAULIK, 1988). Pp. 257-300.

――――, "Das Deuteronomium und die Menschenrechte," *TQ* 166 (1986) 8-24. Reprinted in: *Studien zur Theologie des Deuteronomiums* (ed. G. BRAULIK, 1988). Pp. 301-323.

――――, "Die Freude des Festes: Das Kultverständnis des Deuteronomium — die älteste biblische Festtheorie," *Theologisches Jahrbuch 1983* (ed. W. ERNST *et al.*) Leipzig: St. Benno-Verlag, 1983. Pp. 13-54. Reprinted in: *Studien zur Theologie des Deuteronomiums* (ed. G. BRAULIK, 1988). Pp. 161-218.

――――, "Gesetz als Evangelium: Rechtfertigung und Begnadigung nach der deuteronomischen Tora," *Gesetz und Freiheit* (ed. J. REIKERSTORFER, 1983).

Reprinted in: *Studien zur Theologie des Deuteronomiums* (ed. G. BRAULIK, 1988). Pp. 123-160.

————, "Law as Gospel: Justification and Pardon According to the Deuteronomic Torah," *Int* 38 (1984) 5-14.

————, "Leidensgedächtnisfeier und Freudenfest: 'Volksliturgie' nach dem deuteronomischen Festkalendar (Dtn 16,1-17), " *TP* 56 (1981) 335-357. Reprinted in: *Studien zur Theologie des Deuteronomiums* (ed. G. BRAULIK, 1988). Pp. 95-121.

————, "Literarkritik und archäologische Stratigraphie zu S. Mittmanns Analyse von Deuteronomium 4,1-40," *Bib* 59 (1978) 351-383.

————, *Die Mittel deuteronomischer Rhetorik* (AnBib 68). Rome: Biblical Institute Press, 1978.

————, Review of *Deuteronomium 4: Literarische Analyse und theologische Interpretation*, by Dietrich KNAPP. In *RB* 96 (1989) 266-286.

————, (ed.) *Studien zur Theologie des Deuteronomiums* (SBAB 2). Stuttgart: Katholisches Bibelwerk, 1988.

————, "Weisheit, Gottesnähe und Gesetz — Zum Kerygma von Deuteronomium 4,5-8," *Studien zum Pentateuch: Walter Kornfeld zum 60. Geburtstag* (ed. G. BRAULIK). Wien: Herder, 1977. Pp. 165-195. Reprinted in: *Studien zur Theologie des Deuteronomiums* (ed. G. BRAULIK, 1988). Pp. 53-93.

————, "Zur Abfolge der Gesetze in Deuteronomium 16,18-21,23: Weitere Beobachtungen," *Bib* 69 (1988) 63-92.

————, "Zur deuteronomistischen Konzeption von Freiheit und Frieden" *VTS* 36 (1985) 29-39. Reprinted in: *Studien zur Theologie des Deuteronomiums* (ed. G. BRAULIK, 1988). Pp. 219-230.

BRECK, John, "Biblical Chiasmus: Exploring Structure for Meaning," *BTB* 17 (1987) 70-74.

BREIT, Herbert, *Die Predigt des Deuteronomisten*. München: Chr. Kaiser Verlag, 1933.

BREKELMANS, Chr., "Deuteronomy 5: Its Place and Function," *Das Deuteronomium* (ed. N. LOHFINK, 1985). Pp. 164-173.

————, "Wisdom Influence in Deuteronomy," *La Sagesse de l'Ancien Testament* (BETL 51; ed. M. GILBERT). Leuven: 1979 (1st ed.). Pp. 28-38. 2nd ed. 1990.

BRINTON, Alan, "Situation in the Theory of Rhetoric," *Philosophy and Rhetoric* 14 (1981) 234-248.

BRONGERS, H.A., "Merismus, Synekdoche und Hendiadys in der Bibel-Hebräischen Sprache," *OTS* 14 (1965) 100-114.

————, "Die Partikel לְמַעַן in der biblisch-hebräischen Sprache," *Syntax and Meaning: Studies in Hebrew Syntax and Biblical Exegesis, OTS* 18 (1973) 84-96.

BROWN, Francis; DRIVER, S.R.: and BRIGGS, Charles A. (ed.), *A Hebrew and English Lexicon of the Old Testament with an Appendix Containing the Biblical Aramaic* (Based on the Lexicon of William Gesenius as Translated by Edward Robinson). Oxford: Clarendon Press, 1972. 1st edition in 1907.

BROWN, Richard Harvey, *Society as Text: Essays on Rhetoric, Reason, and Reality*. Chicago/London: University of Chicago Press, 1987.

BROWN, Schuyler, "Biblical Philology, Linguistics and the Problem of Method,"
     HeyJ 20 (1979) 295-298.
BRUEGGEMANN, Walter, "The Kerygma of the Deuteronomistic Historian," *Int*
     22 (1968) 387-402.
BRYANT, Donald C., "Uses of Rhetoric in Criticism," *Papers in Rhetoric and
     Poetic* (ed. Donald C. BRYANT). Iowa City: University of Iowa Press, 1965.
     Pp. 1-14.
BUCHHOLZ, Joachim, *Die Ältesten Israels im Deuteronomium* (GTA 36).
     Göttingen: Vandenhoeck & Ruprecht, 1988.
BÜHLMANN, Walter and SCHERER, Karl, *Stilfiguren der Bibel: Ein kleines
     Nachschlagewerk* (BibB 10). Fribourg: Schweizerisches Katholisches
     Bibelwerk, 1973.
BUIS, Pierre, *Le Deutéronome* (Verbum Salutis, Ancien Testament, 4). Paris:
     Beauchesne, 1969.
———, "La nouvelle alliance," *VT* 18 (1968) 1-15.
BUIS, Pierre and LECLERCQ, Jacques, *Le Deutéronome* (Sources Bibliques). Paris:
     Librairie Lecoffre, 1963.
BULLINGER, Ernest W., *Figures of Speech Used in the Bible Explained and
     Illustrated.* London: 1898; reprint: Grand Rapids: Baker Book House, 1968.
BURKE, Kenneth, *A Rhetoric of Motives.* Berkeley: University of California Press,
     1969.
———, *The Rhetoric of Religion: Studies in Logology.* Berkeley, Calif.: Uni-
     versity of California Press, 1970.
BUSS, Martin J., "The Idea of Sitz im Leben — History and Critique," *ZAW* 90
     (1978) 157-170.
———, Review of *Bundestheologie im Alten Testament,* by Lothar PERLITT, *JBL*
     90 (1971) 210-212.
CAMPBELL, A.F., "An Historical Prologue in a Seventh-Century Treaty," *Bib* 50
     (1969) 534-535.
CARLSON, R.A., *David the Chosen King: A Traditio-Historical Approach to the
     Second Book of Samuel.* Translated by Eric J. Sharpe and Stanley Rudman
     (notes). Stockholm: Almqvist & Wiksell, 1964.
CASANOWICZ, Immanuel M., "Paronomasia in the Old Testament," *JBL* 12
     (1983) 105-167.
CASSIN, Barbara, "Bonnes et mauvaises rhétoriques: De Platon à Perelman,"
     Figures et conflits rhétoriques (ed. M. MEYER and A. LEMPEREUR).
     Bruxelles: Univ. de Bruxelles, 1990. Pp. 17-37.
CAZELLES, Henri, "The Canonical Approach to Torah and Prophets," *JSOT* 16
     (1980) 28-31.
———, "Droit public dans le Deutéronome," *Das Deuteronomium* (ed. N.
     LOHFINK, 1985). Pp. 99-106.
———, "Jérémie et le Deutéronome," *RSR* 38 (1951) 5-36.
———, "Passages in the Singular within Discourse in the Plural of Dt 1-4,"
     CBQ 29 (1967) 207-219.
———, "Pentateuque: Deutéronome," *SDB* VII, 813-822.
CERESKO, Anthony R., "The Chiastic Word Pattern in Hebrew," *CBQ* 38 (1976)
     303-311.
———, "The Function of Chiasmus in Hebrew Poetry," *CBQ* 40 (1978) 1-10.

————, "A Rhetorical Analysis of David's 'Boast' (1 Samuel 17:34-37): Some Reflections on Method," *CBQ* 47 (1985) 58-74.

CHAIGNET, Antoine-Edouard, *La rhétorique et son histoire*. Paris: 1888. Unchanged reprint: Frankfurt/Main: Minerva, 1982.

CHATMAN, Seymour, ed. *Literary Style: A Symposium*. London/New York: Oxford Univ. Press, 1971.

CHILDS, Brevard S., *Introduction to the Old Testament as Scripture*. 2nd ed. London: SCM, 1979.

————, *Memory and Tradition in Israel* (SBT 37). London: SCM, 1962.

————, "Response to Reviewers of *Introduction to the OT as Scripture*," *JSOT* 16 (1980) 52-60.

————, "A Study of the Formula, 'Until This Day,'" *JBL* 82 (1963) 279-292.

CHOLEWINSKI, Alfred, *Deuteronomio, II* (Lecture Notes). Rome: Pontifical Biblical Institute, 1982.

————, "Zur theologischen Deutung des Moabbundes," *Bib* 66 (1985) 96-111.

CHRISTENSEN, Duane L., "Form and Structure in Deuteronomy 1-11,' *Das Deuteronomium* (ed. N. LOHFINK, 1985). Pp. 135-144.

CICERO, *Brutus* (LCL 342). Latin text with English translation by G.L. Hendrickson. Cambridge, Mass.: Harvard University Press, 1971.

————, *De oratore*. Latin text with German traslation by Harald Merklin. Stuttgart: Philipp Reclam Jun., 1976.

————, *Orator* (LCL 342). Latin text with English translation by H.M. Hubbell. Cambridge, Mass.: Harvard University Press, 1971.

CLABURN, William Eugene, "Deuteronomy and Collective Behavior," Diss. Princeton University, 1968. Published on demand by University Microfilms, Inc., Ann Arbor, Mich.

CLARK, W.P., "Ancient Reading," *The Classical Journal* 26 (1930-31) 698-700.

CLEMENTS, R.E., *Deuteronomy* (Old Testament Guides). Sheffield: JSOT Press, 1989.

————, *God's Chosen People: A Theological Interpretation of the Book of Deuteronomy*. London: SCM, 1968.

————, *Old Testament Theology: A Fresh Approach* (Marshalls Theological Library). Basingstoke, Hants (England): Marshall Morgan & Scott, 1978. Paperback ed. 1985.

CLINES, David J.A., "The Arguments of Job's Three Friends," *Art and Meaning* (ed. D.J.A. CLINES, D.M. GUNN, and A. HAUSER, 1982). Pp. 199-214.

————, "Deconstructing the Book of Job," *The Bible as Rhetoric* (ed. Martin WARNER, 1990), pp. 65-80.

CLINES, David J.A.; GUNN, David M.; and HAUSER, Alan J., ed., *Art and Meaning: Rhetoric in Biblical Literature* (JSOTSS 19). Sheffield: JSOT Press, 1982.

COATS, George W., "Another Form-Critical Problem of the Pentateuch," *Semeia* 46 (1989) 65-73.

————, "Humility and Honor: A Moses Legend in Numbers 12," *Art and Meaning* (ed. D.J.A. CLINES, D.M. GUNN, and A. HAUSER, 1982). Pp. 97-107.

COGAN, Morton, *Imperialism and Religion: Assyria, Judah and Israel in the Eighth and Seventh Centuries B.C.E.* (SBLMS 19). Missoula: Scholars Press, 1974.

COHEN, Matty, "Le 'ger' biblique et son statut socio-religieux," *RHR* 207 (1990) 131-158.

COLLINS, John J., "The 'Historical Character' of the Old Testament in Recent Biblical Theology," *CBQ* 41 (1979) 185-204.

CONDON, John C. and YOUSEF, Fathi S., *An Introduction to Intercultural Communication* (The Bobbs-Merrill Series in Speech Communication). Indianapolis: Bobbs-Merrill, 1975.

CONRAD, J.,"פלא," *TWAT* VI, 569-583.

CONROY, Charles, *Absalom, Absalom!* (AnBib 81). Rome: Biblical Institute Press, 1978.

——, "Reflections on the Exegetical Task: Apropos of Recent Studies on 2 Kg 22-23," *Pentateuchal and Deuteronomistic Studies* (BETL 94; ed. C. BREKELMANS and J. LUST). Leuven: University Press, 1990. Pp. 255-268.

CORBETT, Edward P.J., *Classical Rhetoric for the Modern Student*. 2nd ed. New York: Oxford University Press, 1971.

COTTERRELL, Peter and TURNER, Max, *Linguistics and Biblical Interpretation*. London: SPCK, 1989.

CRAIGIE, Peter C., *The Book of Deuteronomy* (The New International Commentary on the Old Testament). Grand Rapids: William B. Eerdmans, 1976.

CROSS, Frank Moore, *Canaanite Myth and Hebrew Epic*. Cambridge, Mass.: Harvard, 1973.

CROSSAN, John Dominic, "Perspectives and Methods in Contemporary Biblical Criticism," *BR* 22 (1977) 39-49.

——, "Waking the Bible: Biblical Hermeneutic and Literary Imagination," *Int* 32 (1978) 269-285.

CRÜSEMANN, Frank, "Fremdenliebe und Identitätssicherung: Zum Verständnis der 'Fremden' - Gesetze im Alten Testament," *Wort und Dienst* N.F. 19 (1987) 11-24.

CULLEY, Robert C., "An Approach to the Problem of Oral Tradition," *VT* 13 (1963) 113-125.

——, "Oral Transmission of Prose," *Studies in the Structure of Hebrew Narrative*. Philadelphia/Missoula: Fortress and Scholars Press, 1976. Pp. 1-32.

——, "Some Comments on Structural Analysis and Biblical Studies," *VTS* 22 (1971) 129-142.

CUNNINGHAM, David S., "Theology as Rhetoric," *TS* 52 (1991) 407-430.

DAHOOD, Mitchell, "Additional Pairs of Parallel Words in the Psalter and in Ugaritic," *Wort, Lied und Gottesspruch* (FS. für Joseph Ziegler; FzB 2: Beiträge zu Psalmen und Propheten; ed. Joseph SCHREINER). Würzburg: Echter Verlag, 1972. Pp. 35-40.

——, "Chiasmus," *IDBSup* 145.

DAUBE, David, "The Extension of a Simile," *Interpreting the Hebrew Bible: Essays in Honour of E.I.J. Rosenthal* (ed. J.A. EMERTON and Stefan C. REIF). Cambridge: Cambridge University Press, 1982. Pp. 57-59.

DEARIN, Ray D., "The Philosophical Basis of Chaim Perelman's Theory of Rhetoric," *The Quarterly Journal of Speech* 55 (1969) 213-224.

DELCOR, M., "Les attaches littéraires, l'origine et la signification de l'expression biblique 'prendre à témoin le ciel et la terre,'" *VT* 16 (1966) 8-25.

DEMSKY, Aaron, Response to "An Assessment of the Evidence for Writing in Ancient Israel," by Alan R. MILLARD, in *Biblical Archaeology Today: Proceedings of the International Congress on Biblical Archaeology. Jerusalem, April, 1984* (ed. Avraham BIRAN et al.). Jerusalem: Israel Exploration Society, 1985. Pp. 349-353.

DE REGT, L.J., *A Parametric Model for Syntactic Studies of a Textual Corpus, Demonstrated on the Hebrew of Deuteronomy 1-30* (Studia Semitica Neerlandica 24). Assen/Maastricht: Van Gorcum, 1988. 2 vols.

DEROCHE, Michael, "Structure, Rhetoric, and Meaning in Hosea IV 4-10," *VT* 33 (1983) 185-198.

DE VRIES, Simon J., "The Development of the Deuteronomic Promulgation Formula," *Bib* 55 (1974) 301-316.

DE WETTE, Wilhelm M.L., *Dissertatio critico-exegetica qua Deuteronomium a prioribus Pentateuchi libris diversum, alius cuiusdam recentioris auctoris opus esse monstratur.* Jena: Etzdorf, 1805.

DIETRICH, Walter, *Prophetie und Geschichte* (FRLANT 108). Göttingen: Vandenhoeck & Ruprecht, 1972.

DI MARCO, Angelico, *Il chiasmo nella Bibbia: Contributi di stilistica strutturale* (Collana Ricerche e Proposte). Torino : Marietti, 1980.

DION, Paul-Eugène, "Quelques aspects de l'interaction entre religion et politique dans le Deutéronome," *ScEs* 30 (1978) 39-55.

DIXON, Peter, *Rhetoric* (The Critical Idiom 19). London/New York: Methuen, 1971.

DOMMERSHAUSEN, Werner, "Der Wein im Urteil und Bild des Alten Testaments," *TThZ* 84 (1975) 253-260.

DONNER, Herbert, *Geschichte des Volkes Israel und seiner Nachbarn in Grundzügen*, 2 vols. (Grundrisse zum Alten Testament: Das Alte Testament Deutsch — Ergänzungsreihe 4/1 & 4/2). Göttingen: Vandenhoeck & Ruprecht, 1984-1986.

DOTY, William G., "Fundamental Questions about Literary-Critical Methodology: A Review Article," *JAAR* 40 (1972) 521-527.

———, "Linguistics and Biblical Criticism," *JAAR* 41 (1973) 114-121.

DOUAY, Françoise, "'Mettre dans le jour d'apercevoir ce qui est': Tropologie et argumentation chez Dumarsais," *Figures et conflits rhétoriques* (ed. M. MEYER and A. LEMPEREUR, 1990). Pp. 83-101.

DOZEMAN, Thomas B., "Inner-Biblical Interpretation of Yahweh's Gracious and Compassionate Character," *JBL* 108 (1989) 207-223.

DRIVER, G.R., *Semitic Writing: From Pictograph to Alphabet.* London: Oxford University Press, 1948.

DRIVER, S.R., *A Critical and Exegetical Commentary on Deuteronomy,* 3rd ed. (ICC). Edinburgh: T. & T. Clark, 1895; reprint 1973.

DUCROT, Oswald and TODOROV, Tzvetan, ed. *Dictionnaire encyclopédique des sciences du langage* (Points 110). Paris: Éditions du Seuil, 1972.

DUKE, Rodney K., *The Persuasive Appeal of the Chronicler: A Rhetorical Analysis* (JSOTSS 88; BLS 25). Sheffield: Almond Press, 1990.

DUMORTIER, Francis, "Une loi, principe de vie: Dt 30,10-14," *AS* 46 (1974) 52-56.

EDWARDS, Michael, "The World Could Not Contain the Books," *The Bible as Rhetoric* (ed. M. WARNER, 1990), pp. 178-194.

EHNINGER, Douglas, "Toward a Taxonomy of Prescriptive Discourse," *Rhetoric in Transition* (ed. E. White, 1980). Pp. 89-100.

EICHRODT, Walther, *Theologie des Alten Testaments*. Teil I: *Gott und Volk*. 7th ed. Stuttgart/Göttingen: Ehrenfried Klotz/Vandenhoeck & Ruprecht, 1962 (1st ed. 1933).

EINHORN, Lois, "Oral and Written Style: An Examination of Differences," *SSCJ* 43 (1978) 302-311.

EISING, H.,"זָכַר," *TWAT* I, 571-593.

EITAN, Israel, "La répétition de la racine en hébreu," *JPOS* 2 (1921) 171-186.

ESLINGER, Lyle M., "Hosea 5:12a and Genesis 32:29: A Study in Inner Biblical Exegesis," *JSOT* 18 (1980) 91-99.

——, "Inner-Biblical Exegesis and Inner-Biblical Allusion: The Question of Category," *VT* 42 (1992) 47-58.

——, *Into the Hands of the Living God* (JSOTSS 84; BLS 24). Sheffield: Almond Press, 1989.

EVEN-SHOSHAN, Avraham, קוֹנְקוֹרְדַנְצִיָה חֲדָשָׁה לְתוֹרָה נְבִיאִים וּכְתוּבִים. Jerusalem: Kiryath-Sepher, 1981.

FENSHAM, F. Charles, "Father and Son as Terminology for Treaty and Covenant," *Near Eastern Studies in Honor of William Foxwell Albright* (ed. Hans GOEDICKE). Baltimore/London: Johns Hopkins Press, 1971. Pp. 121-135.

——, "The Treaty between Israel and the Gibeonites," *BA* 27 (1964) 96-100.

FERGUSON, Duncan S., *Biblical Hermeneutics: An Introduction*. London: SCM, 1987.

FICHMAN, Jacob, *'Arugot*. Jerusalem: Bialik Institute, 1954.

FINEGAN, Jack, *Light from the Ancient Past: The Archeological Background of Judaism and Christianity*, 2 vols. Princeton: Princeton University Press, 1959.

FISCHEL, Henry A., "Story and History: Observations on Greco-Roman Rhetoric and Pharisaism," *American Oriental Society, Middle West Branch, Semi-Centennial Volume*. Bloomington, Indiana: Indiana University Press, 1969. Pp. 59-88. Reprinted in: FISCHEL, Henry A. (ed.). *Essays in Greco-Roman and Related Talmudic Literature*. New York: Ktav, 1977. Pp. 443-472.

FISHBANE, Michael, *Biblical Interpretation in Ancient Israel*. Oxford: Clarendon Press, 1988 (paperback ed.). 1st ed. 1985.

——, "Inner Biblical Exegesis: Types and Strategies of Interpretation in Ancient Israel," *Midrash and Literature* (ed. G. HARTMAN and S. BUDICK). New Haven/London: Yale University Press, 1986. Pp. 19-37. Reprinted in: *The Garment of the Torah: Essays in Biblical Hermeneutics* (Indiana Studies in Biblical Literature). Bloomington/Indianapolis: Indiana University Press, 1989. Pp. 3-18.

——, *Text and Texture: Close Readings of Selected Biblical Texts*. New York: Schocken, 1979.

——, "Varia Deuteronomica," *ZAW* 84 (1972) 349-352.

FLANAGAN, James W., "The Deuteronomic Meaning of the Phrase *'kol yiśrā'ēl*,'" *SR* 6 (1976/77) 159-168.

FONTANIER, Pierre, *Les figures du discours*. Paris: Flammarion, 1977. First published 1821-1830.

FOUQUELIN, Antoine, *La rhétorique française* (1555), in *Traités de poétique et de rhétorique de la Renaissance* (ed. Francis GOYET). Paris: Librairie Générale Française, 1990. Pp. 345-464.

FOWLER, Henry T., *A History of the Literature of Ancient Israel.* New York: Macmillan, 1927.

FOWLER, Robert M., "Who Is 'The Reader' in Reader Response Criticism?" *Semeia* 31 (1985) 5-23.

FOX, Michael V., "The Rhetoric of Ezekiel's Vision of the Valley of the Bones," *HUCA* 51 (1980) 1-15.

———, "*Ṭôb* as Covenant Terminology," *BASOR* 209 (1973) 41-42.

FRANKENA, R., "The Vassal-Treaties of Esarhaddon and the Dating of Deuteronomy," *OTS* 14 (1965) 122-154.

FREEDMAN, David Noel, "The Deuteronomic History," *IDBSup* 226-228.

———, "Pentateuch," *IDB* III, 711-727.

———, "Pottery, Poetry, and Prophecy: An Essay on Biblical Poetry," *JBL* 96 (1977) 5-26.

FRIEDMAN, Richard Elliott, *The Exile and Biblical Narrative: The Formation of the Deuteronomistic and Priestly Works* (HSM 22). Chico, Calif.: Scholars Press, 1981.

———, *Who Wrote the Bible?* New York: Summit Books, 1987.

FRYE, Northrop, *Anatomy of Criticism: Four Essays.* Princeton, N.J.: Princeton University Press, 1957.

———, *The Great Code: The Bible and Literature.* San Diego: Harvest/Harcourt Brace Jovanovich, 1982.

FUMAROLI, Marc, "Conclusion: Rhétorique persuasive et littérature," *Figures et conflits rhétoriques* (ed. M. MEYER and A. LEMPEREUR, 1990). Pp. 159-161.

GABEL, John B., and WHEELER, Charles B., *The Bible as Literature: An Introduction.* New York/Oxford: Oxford University Press, 1986.

GADAMER, Hans-Georg, "Hermeneutik als theoretische und praktische Aufgabe," *RIP* 33 (1979) 239-259.

GARAVELLI, Bice Mortara, *Manuale di retorica* (Studi Bompiani). Milano: Bompiani, 1988.

GARCÍA LÓPEZ, Felix, *Le Deutéronome: Une loi prêchée* (Cahiers Evangile 63). Paris: Éditions du Cerf, 1988.

———, "Le Roi d'Israël: Dt 17,14-20," *Das Deuteronomium* (ed. N. LOHFINK, 1985). Pp. 177-197.

GEMSER, B., "*Be'ēber hajjardēn*: In Jordan's Borderland," *VT* 2 (1952) 349-355.

———, "The Importance of the Motive Clause in Old Testament Law," *VTS* 1 (1953) 50-66.

GENETTE, Gérard, *Figures I* (Points 74). Paris: Éditions du Seuil, 1966.

———, *Figures II* (Points 106). Paris: Éditions du Seuil, 1969.

———, *Noveau discours du récit* (Collection poétique). Paris: Éditions du Seuil, 1983.

GERLEMAN, G., "ישראל," *THAT* I, 782-785.

GERSTENBERGER, Erhard, "Covenant and Commandment," *JBL* 84 (1965) 38-51.

GESENIUS, W., Cf. KAUTZSCH, E. and COWLEY, A. E.

GEVIRTZ, Stanley, "On Canaanite Rhetoric: The Evidence of the Amarna Letters from Tyre," *Orientalia* N.S. 42 (1973) 162-177.

———, "On Hebrew *šēbeṭ* = 'Judge,'" *The Bible World: Essays in Honor of Cyrus H. Gordon* (ed. Gary RENDSBURG et al.). New York: Katv, 1980. Pp. 61-66.

GINSBERG, H. Louis, *The Israelian Heritage of Judaism* (Texts and Studies of the Jewish Theological Seminary of America 24). New York: The Jewish Theological Seminary of America, 1982.

———, "'Roots Below and Fruit Above' and Related Matters," *Hebrew and Semitic Studies Presented to Godfrey Rolles Driver* (ed. D. Winton THOMAS and W.D. McHARDY). Oxford: Clarendon Press, 1963. Pp. 72-76.

GITAY, Yehoshua, "Deutero-Isaiah: Oral or Written?" *JBL* 99 (1980) 185-197.

———, "The Effectiveness of Isaiah's Speech," *JQR* 75 (1984) 162-172.

———, "Isaiah and His Audience," *Prooftexts* 3 (1983) 223-230.

———, "Reflections on the Study of the Prophetic Discourse: The Question of Isaiah I 2-20," *VT* 33 (1983) 207-221.

———, "A Study of Amos's Art of Speech: A Rhetorical Analysis of Amos 3:1-15," *CBQ* 42 (1980) 293-309.

GOLDINGAY, John, *Theological Diversity and the Authority of the Old Testament*. Grand Rapids: Eerdmans, 1987.

GONÇALVES, Francolino J., Review of *The Double Redaction of the Deuteronomistic History*, by Richard D. NELSON. In *RB* 96 (1989) 131-133.

GOOD, Edwin M., *Irony in the Old Testament*. Philadelphia: Westminster, 1965.

GORDIS, Robert, "A Rhetorical Use of Interrogative Sentences in Biblical Hebrew," *AJSL* 49 (1932-1933) 212-217.

GORDON, Cyrus H., *The Common Background of Greek and Hebrew Civilizations*. New York: W.W. Norton, 1965.

GOTTWALD, Norman K., *The Hebrew Bible: A Socio-Literary Introduction*. Philadelphia: Fortress, 1985.

GOWAN, Donald E., "Wealth and Poverty in the Old Testament: The Case of the Widow, the Orphan, and the Sojourner," *Int* 41 (1987) 341-353.

GRANT, Robert and TRACY, David, *A Short History of the Interpretation of the Bible*. 2nd ed. London: SCM, 1984.

GRASSI, Ernesto, *Rhetoric as Philosophy: The Humanist Tradition*. University Park/London: The Pennsylvania State University Press, 1980.

GRAY, J. Patrick, "Structural Analysis of Folktales: Techniques and Methodology," *Asian Folklore Studies* 37 (1978) 77-95.

GREENWOOD, David, "The Origins of the Deuteronomic Literature," *Proceedings of the Sixth World Congress of Jewish Studies*, I, (ed. A. SHINAN). Jerusalem: World Union of Jewish Studies 1977. Pp. 91-199..

———, "Rhetorical Criticism and Formgeschichte: Some Methodological Considerations," *JBL* 89 (1970) 418-426.

GRIFFIN-COLLART, Evelyne, "L'argumentation et le raisonnable dans une philosophie du sens commun," *RIP* 33 (1979) 202-215.

GRIMES, J.E., *The Thread of Discourse*. The Hague: Mouton, 1975.

GROSS, Heinrich, "Zur Wurzel *zkr*," *BZ*, N.F. 4 (1960) 227-237.

GROUPE μ (J. DUBOIS, F. EDELINE, J.-M. KLINKENBERG, P. MINGUET, F. PIRE, H. TRINON), *Rhétorique générale* (Points 146). Paris: Éditions du Seuil, 1982. 1st ed.: Librairie Larousse, 1970.

GUILLAUME, A., "Paronomasia in the Old Testament," *JSS* 9 (1964) 282-290.

HAARSCHER, Guy, "La rhétorique de la raison pratique: Réflexions sur l'argumentation et la violence," *RIP* 33 (1979) 110-128.

HABEL, Norman C., *Literary Criticism of the Old Testament* (GBS, Old Testament Series). Philadelphia: Fortress, 1971.

HALBE, Jorn, "'Gemeinschaft, die Welt unterbricht': Grundfragen und -inhalte deuteronomischer Theologie und Überlieferungsbildung im Lichte der Ursprungsbedingungen alttestamentlichen Rechts," *Das Deuteronomium* (ed. N. LOHFINK, 1985). Pp. 55-75.

HALPERN, Baruch, "The Centralization Formula in Deuteronomy," *VT* 31 (1981) 20-38.

HARL, Marguerite, "Le péché irrémissible de l'idolâtre arrogant: Dt 29,19-20 dans la Septante et chez d'autres témoins," *Tradition of the Text: Studies Offered to Dominique Barthélémy in Celebration of His 70th Birthday* (ed. Gerard J. NORTON and Stephen PISANO; OBO 109). Freiburg, Switzerland/Göttingen: Universitätsverlag/Vandenhoeck & Ruprecht, 1991. Pp. 63-78.

HENDRICKSON, G.L., "Ancient Reading," *The Classical Journal* 25 (1929-30) 182-196.

HERRMANN, Siegfried, "Die konstruktive Restauration: Das Deuteronomium als Mitte biblischer Theologie," *Probleme biblischer Theologie* (FS. Gerhard von Rad; ed. Hans Walter WOLFF). München: Chr. Kaiser Verlag. 1971. Pp. 155-170.

HESTER, James D., "The Rhetorical Structure of Galatians 1:11-2:14," *JBL* 103 (1984) 223-233.

HEXTER, Jack, *Doing History*. Bloomington, Ind./London: Indiana University Press, 1971.

HILLERS, Delbert R., *Treaty-Curses and the Old Testament Prophets* (BibOr 16). Rome: Pontifical Biblical Institute, 1964.

HÖFFKEN, Peter, "Eine Bemerkung zum religionsgeschichtlichen Hintergrund von Dtn 6,4," *BZ, N.F.* 28 (1984) 88-93.

HOLLADAY, William L., *A Concise Hebrew and Aramaic Lexicon of the Old Testament* (Based upon the Lexical Work of Ludwig Koehler and Walter Baumgartner). Leiden: E.J. Brill, 1971.

———, "Form and Word-Play in David's Lament over Saul and Jonathan," *VT* 20 (1970) 153-189.

———, "A Proposal for Reflections in the Book of Jeremiah of the Seven-Year Recitation of the Law in Deuteronomy," *Das Deuteronomium* (ed. N. LOHFINK, 1985). Pp. 326-328.

———, *The Root Šûbh in the Old Testament: With Particular Reference to Its Usages in Covenantal Contexts*. Leiden: E.J. Brill, 1958.

HONEYMAN, A.M., "*Merismus* in Biblical Hebrew," *JBL* 71 (1952) 11-18.

HOPPE, LESLIE J., "Deuteronomy and the Poor," *TBT* 24 (1986) 371-375.

———, "Deuteronomy on Political Power," *TBT* 26 (1988) 261-266.

———, "Elders and Deuteronomy: A Proposal," *EgT* 14 (1983) 259-272.

———, "Jerusalem in the Deuteronomistic History," *Das Deuteronomium* (ed. N. LOHFINK, 1985). Pp. 107-110.

———, "The Meaning of Deuteronomy," *BTB* 10 (1980) 111-117.

HORST, Friedrich, "Der Eid im Alten Testament," *Gottes Recht: Gesammelte Studien zum Recht im Alten Testament* (TBü 12; ed. H.W. WOLFF). München: Chr. Kaiser Verlag, 1961. Pp. 292-314. First published in *EvT* 17 (1957) 366-384.

HOWELL, Wilbur Samuel, *Poetics, Rhetoric and Logic: Studies in the Basic Disciplines of Criticism*. Ithaca, N.Y.: Cornell University Press, 1975.

HUFFMON, Herbert B., "The Covenant Lawsuit in the Prophets," *JBL* 78 (1959) 285-295.

——, Review of *Das Hauptgebot: Eine Untersuchung literarischer Einleitungsfragen zu Dtn 5-11*, by Norbert LOHFINK, *JBL* 83 (1964) 197-198.

HULST, A.R., "Der Name 'Israel' im Deuteronomium," *OTS* 9 (1951) 65-106.

HURVITZ, Avi, "The Evidence of Language in Dating the Priestly Code," *RB* 81 (1974) 24-45.

HYATT, J. Philip, "Jeremiah and Deuteronomy," *JNES* 1 (1942) 156-173.

ISER, Wolfgang, *The Implied Reader: Patterns of Communication in Prose Fiction from Bunyan to Beckett*. Baltimore/London: John Hopkins University Press, 1974.

JACKSON, Jared Judd, "Rhetorical Criticism and the Problem of Subjectivity," *PEGLBS* 2 (1982) 34-45.

JACKSON, J.J., and KESSLER, Martin, ed., *Rhetorical Criticism: Essays in Honor of James Muilenburg* (PTMS 1). Pittsburgh: Pickwick, 1974.

JACOBSON, Richard, "The Structuralists and the Bible," *Int* 28 (1974) 146-164. Reprinted in: *A Guide to Contemporary Hermeneutics* (ed. D. McKAY, 1986). Pp. 280-296.

JACQUES, Francis, "Logique ou rhétorique de l'argumentation?" *RIP* 33 (1979) 47-68.

JANZEN, J. Gerald, "The Yoke That Gives Rest," *Int* 61 (1987) 256-268.

JASPER, David, "'In the Sermon Which I Have Just Completed, Wherever I Said Aristotle, I Meant Saint Paul,'" *The Bible as Rhetoric* (ed. Martin WARNER, 1990), pp. 133-152.

JASTROW, Marcus, *A Dictionary of the Targumim, the Talmud Babli and Yerushalmi, and the Midrashic Literature*, 2 vols. New York: Judaica Press, 1982. First published 1903.

JENNI, Ernst, "למד," *THAT* I, 872-875.

JENNI, Ernst and WESTERMANN, Claus, ed., *Theologisches Handwörterbuch zum Alten Testament*, 2 vols. München/Zürich: Chr. Kaiser/ Theologischer Verlag, 1984 (1st ed. 1971).

JOHAG, Ingeborg, "טוב - Terminus Technicus in Vertrags- und Bündnisformularen des alten Orients und des Alten Testaments," *Bausteine biblischer Theologie* (FS. G. Johannes Botterweck; ed. Heinz-Josef FABRY) (BBB 50). Köln/ Bonn: Peter Hanstein, 1977. Pp. 3-23.

JOHNSON, A.R., "מָשָׁל," *Wisdom in Israel and in the Ancient Near East* (ed. M. NOTH and D. Winton THOMAS), *VTS* 3 (1960) 162-169.

JOHNSTONE, Barbara, "An Introduction," *Perspectives on Repetition, Text* 7 (1987) 205-214.

——, (ed.), *Perspectives on Repetition, Text* 7-3. Berlin/New York: De Gruyter, 1987.

JOHNSTONE, Henry W., Jr, "Rhetoric and Death," *Rhetoric in Transition* (ed. E. WHITE, 1980). Pp. 61-70.

JoÜon, Paul, *Grammaire de l'hébreu biblique*. Rome: Biblical Institute Press, 1923. Corrected edition 1965; reprinted 1987.

KAISER, Otto, *Einleitung in das Alte Testament: Eine Einführung in ihre Ergebnisse und Probleme*, 5th ed. Gütersloh: Gerd Mohn, 1984. (1st ed.: 1969).

KALKBRENNER, Anton, "Schon tot vor dem Sterben?" *BLit* 58 (1985) 154-155.

KALLUVEETTIL, Paul, *Declaration and Covenant: A Comprehensive Review of Covenant Formulae from the Old Testament and the Ancient Near East* (AnBib 88). Rome: Biblical Institute Press, 1982.

KANE, Dennis C., *Logic: The Art of Inference and Predication*. New York: Sheed and Ward, 1969.

KAPELRUD, A.S., "למד," *TWAT* IV, 576-582.

KAUFER, David, "Irony and Rhetorical Strategy," *Philosophy and Rhetoric* 10 (1977) 90-110.

KAUFMAN, Stephen A., "Deuteronomy 15 and Recent Research on the Dating of P," *Das Deuteronomium* (ed. N. LOHFINK, 1985). Pp. 273-276.

KAUTZSCH, E., and COWLEY, A.E. (ed.), *Gesenius' Hebrew Grammar*, 2nd ed. Oxford: Clarendon Press, 1910 (based on the 28th German edition, 1909). Reprinted 1982.

KEARNEY, Peter J., "The Role of the Gibeonites in the Deuteronomic History," *CBQ* 35 (1973) 1-19.

KEEGAN, Terence J., *Interpreting the Bible: A Popular Introduction to Biblical Hermeneutics*. New York/Mahwah, N.J.: Paulist, 1985.

KEIL, Carl Friedrich, *Leviticus, Numeri und Deuteronomium* (Biblischer Kommentar über das Alte Testament). Giesen/ Basel: Brunnen Verlag, 1987. Reprint of 3rd ed., 1870.

KELLER, C.A., "אלה," *THAT* I, 149-152.

————, "קלל," *THAT* II, 641-647.

KELLER, C.A., and WEHMEIER, G., "ברך," *THAT* I, 353-376.

KELLERMANN, D., "גּוּר," *TWAT* I, 979-991.

KENNEDY, George A., *The Art of Persuasion in Greece*. Princeton, N.J.: Princeton University Press, 1963.

————, *New Testament Interpretation through Rhetorical Criticism*. Chapel Hill: University of North Carolina Press, 1984.

————, "'Truth' and 'Rhetoric' in the Pauline Epistles," *The Bible as Rhetoric* (ed. Martin WARNER, 1990), pp. 195-202.

KENYON, Frederic C., *Books and Readers in Ancient Greece and Rome*, 2nd ed. Oxford: Clarendon, 1951. 1st ed. 1932.

KESSLER, Martin, "Inclusio in the Hebrew Bible," *Semitics* 6 (1978) 44-49.

————, "An Introduction to Rhetorical Criticism of the Bible: Prolegomena," *Semitics* 7 (1980) 1-27.

————, "A Methodological Setting for Rhetorical Criticism," *Semitics* 4 (1974) 22-36. Reprinted in *Art and Meaning* (ed. D.J.A. CLINES, D.M. GUNN, and A. HAUSER, 1982), pp. 1-19.

KIBEDI-VARGA, Aaron, "Une rhétorique aléatoire: Agir par l'image," *Figures et conflits rhétoriques* (ed. M. MEYER and A. LEMPEREUR, 1990). Pp. 193-200.

KIKAWADA, Isaac M., "Some Proposals for the Definition of Rhetorical Criticism," *Semitics* 5 (1977) 67-91.

KITTEL, Bonnie, "Brevard Childs' Development of the Canonical Approach," *JSOT* 16 (1980) 2-11.

KLINKENBERG, Jean-Marie, "Rhétorique de l'argumentation et rhétorique des figures," *Figures et conflits rhétoriques* (ed. M. MEYER and A. LEMPEREUR, 1990). Pp. 115-137.

KLOSTERMANN, August, "Das Lied Moses (Deut 32) und das Deuteronomium: Ein Beitrag zur Entstehungsgeschichte des Pentateuchs," *TSK* 44 (1871) 249-294.

————, *Der Pentateuch. Beiträge zu seinem Verständnis und seiner Entstehungsgeschichte,* II, Neue Folge. Leipzig: Georg Böhme, 1907.

KLUBACK, William and BECKER, Mortimer, "The Significance of Chaim Perelman's Philosophy of Rhetoric," *RIP* 33 (1979) 33-46.

KNAPP, Dietrich, *Deuteronomium 4: Literarische Analyse und theologische Interpretation* (GTA 35). Göttingen: Vandenhoeck und Ruprecht, 1987.

KNIERIM, Rolf, "Old Testament Form Criticism Reconsidered," *Int* 27 (1973) 435-468.

KÖNIG, Ed., *Stilistik, Rhetorik, Poetik in Bezug auf die biblische Litteratur.* Leipzig: Theodor Weicher, 1900.

————, "The Unity of Deuteronomy," *ExpTim* 10 (1898-99) 16-18, 124-126, 227-230.

KRAŠOVEC, Jože, *Der Merismus im Biblisch-Hebräischen und Nordwestsemitischen* (BibOr 33). Rome: Biblical Institute Press, 1977.

KRENTZ, Edgar, *The Historical-Critical Method* (GBS). Philadelphia: Fortress, 1975.

KSELMAN, John S., "Semantic-Sonant Chiasmus in Biblical Poetry," *Bib* 58 (1977) 219-223.

KUGEL, James, "On the Bible and Literary Criticism," *Prooftexts* 1 (1981) 217-236.

KUHL, Curt, "Die 'Wiederaufnahme' — ein literarkritisches Prinzip?" *ZAW* 64 (1952) 1-11.

KUTSCH, Ernst, *Verheissung und Gesetz: Untersuchungen zum sogenannten "Bund" im Alten Testament* (BZAW 131). Berlin: Walter de Gruyter, 1973.

————,"בְּרִית,"*THAT* I, 339-352.

LABERGE, Leo, "La Septante de Dt 1-11: Pour une étude du 'texte,'" *Das Deuteronomium* (ed. N. LOHFINK, 1985). Pp. 129-134.

LABUSCHAGNE, C.J., "Divine Speech in Deuteronomy," *Das Deuteronomium* (ed. N. LOHFINK, 1985). Pp. 111-126.

————,"קרא," *THAT* II, 666-674.

LACONI, Mauro, *Deuteronomio.* Roma: Edizioni Paoline, 1981.

LAHURD, Carol Schersten, "Rhetorical Criticism, Biblical Criticism and Literary Criticism: Issues of Methodological Pluralism," *PEGLBS* 5 (1985) 87-101.

LANDES, George M., "The Canonical Approach to Introducing the Old Testament: Prodigy and Problems," *JSOT* 16 (1980) 32-39.

LANGLAMET, F., Review of *Deuteronomy and the Deuteronomic School,* by Moshe WEINFELD. In *RB* 79 (1972) 605-609.

LANHAM, Richard A., *A Handlist of Rhetorical Terms: A Guide for Students of English Literature.* Berkeley: University of California Press, 1968.

LAPOINTE, Roger, "The New Status of Language," *CBQ* 36 (1974) 233-236.

LARSON, James E., "The Dynamics of Enga Persuasive Speech," *Exploring Enga Culture: Studies in Missionary Anthropology* (ed. Paul W. BRENNAN). Second Anthropological Conference of New Guinea Lutheran Mission—1970. Wapenamanda, Papua New Guinea: Kristen Pres, 1970. Pp. 1-16.

LAUSBERG, Heinrich, *Elemente der literarischen Rhetorik: Eine Einführung für Studierende der klassischen, romanischen, englischen und deutschen Philologie.* München: Hueber, 1963.

——, *Handbuch der literarischen Rhetorik: Eine Grundlegung der Literaturwissenschaft.* 2 vols. München: Max Hueber Verlag, 1960.

LEACH, Edmund, "Structuralism," *The Encyclopedia of Religion* (ed. Mircea ELIADE) XIV, 54-63. New York/London: Macmillan/Collier Macmillan, 1987.

LE DÉAUT, ROGER, "Le thème de la circoncision du cœur (Dt. XXX 6; Jér. IV 4) dans les versions anciennes (LXX et Targum) et à Qumran," *VTS* 32 (1981) 178-205.

LEFÈVRE, A., "Malédiction et bénédiction," *SDB* V, 746-751.

LEMAIRE, André, *Les écoles et la formation de la Bible dans l'Ancien Israël* (OBO 39). Fribourg/Göttingen: Éditions Univesitaires/Vandenhoeck & Ruprecht, 1981.

——, "Sagesse et écoles," *VT* 34 (1984) 270-281.

LEMPEREUR, Alain, "Les restrictions de deux néo-rhétoriques," *Figures et conflits rhétoriques* (ed. M. MEYER and A. LEMPEREUR, 1990). Pp. 139-157.

LEVENSON, Jon D., "The Theologies of Commandment in Biblical Israel," *HTR* 73 (1980) 17-33.

——, "Who Inserted the Book of the Torah?" *HTR* 68 (1975) 203-233.

LEVIN, Christoph, *Die Verheißung des neuen Bundes in ihrem theologie-geschichtlichen Zusammenhang* (FRLANT 137). Göttingen: Vandenhoeck & Ruprecht, 1985.

L'HOUR, Jean, "Formes littéraires, structure et unité de Deutéronome 5-11," *Bib* 45 (1964) 551-555.

——, "Une législation criminelle dans le Deutéronome," *Bib* 44 (1963) 1-28.

LIEDKE, G., and PETERSEN, C., "תּוֹרָה," *THAT* II, 1032-1043.

LINDARS, Barnabas, "Torah in Deuteronomy," *Words and Meanings* (FS. D.W. Thomas; ed. P.R. ACKROYD and B. LINDARS). Cambridge: Cambridge University Press, 1968. Pp. 117-136.

LIWAK, Rüdiger, "Literary Individuality as a Problem of Hermeneutics in the Hebrew Bible," *Creative Biblical Exegesis: Christian and Jewish Hermeneutics through the Centuries* (ed. Benjamin UFFENHEIMER and Henning Graf REVENTLOW; JSOTSS 59). Sheffield: JSOT Press, 1988.

——, *Der Prophet und die Geschichte: Eine literar-historische Untersuchung zum Jeremiabuch* (BWANT 121). Stuttgart: W. Kohlhammer, 1987.

LOCHER, Clemens, "Deuteronomium 22,13-21: Vom Prozessprotokoll zum kasuistischen Gesetz," *Das Deuteronomium* (ed. N. LOHFINK, 1985). Pp. 298-303.

LOERSCH, Sigrid, *Das Deuteronomium und seine Deutungen: Ein forschungs-geschichtlicher Überblick* (Stuttgarter Bibelstudien 22). Stuttgart: Verlag katholisches Bibelwerk, 1967.

LOHFINK, Norbert, "Botschaft vom Bund: Das Deuteronomium," *Wort und Botschaft des Alten Testaments,* 2nd ed. (ed. Josef SCHREINER). Würzburg: Echter-Verlag, 1969. Pp. 179-193.

———, "Der Bundesschluß im Land Moab: Redaktionsgeschichtliches zu Dt 28,69-32,47," *BZ,* N.F. 6 (1962) 32-56. Reprinted in: *Studien zum Deuteronomium und zur deuteronomistischen Literatur* I (ed. N. LOHFINK, 1990), pp. 53-82.

———, "Die Bundesurkunde des Königs Josias (Eine Frage an die Deuteronomiumsforschung)," *Bib* 44 (1963) 261-288, 461-498. Reprinted in: *Studien zum Deuteronomium und zur deuteronomistischen Literatur* I (ed. N. LOHFINK, 1990), pp. 99-165.

———, "Culture Shock and Theology," *BTB* 7 (1977) 12-22. Translated by Richard Kugelman.

———, "Darstellungskunst und Theologie in Dtn 1,6-3,29," *Bib* 41 (1960) 105-134. Reprinted in: *Studien zum Deuteronomium und zur deuteronomistischen Literatur* I (ed. N. LOHFINK, 1990), pp. 15-44.

———, "Die deuteronomistische Darstellung des Übergangs der Führung Israels von Moses auf Josue: Ein Beitrag zur alttestamentlichen Theologie des Amtes," *Scholastik* 37 (1962) 32-44. Reprinted in: *Studien zum Deuteronomium und zur deuteronomistischen Literatur* I (ed. N. LOHFINK, 1990), pp. 83-97.

———, (ed.) *Das Deuteronomium: Entstehung, Gestalt und Botschaft* (BETL 68). Leuven: University Press, 1985.

———, "Dtn 26,6-9: Ein Beispiel altisraelitischer Geschichtstheologie," *Geschichte, Zeugnis und Theologie* (ed. F. THEUNIS; *TF* 58). Hamburg/Bergstedt: Herbert Reich/Evangelischer Verlag, 1976. Pp. 100-107. Reprinted in: *Studien zum Deuteronomium und zur deuteronomistischen Literatur* I (ed. N. LOHFINK, 1990), pp. 291-303.

———, "Dt 26,17-19 und die 'Bundesformel,'" *ZKT* 91 (1969) 517-553. Reprinted in: *Studien zum Deuteronomium und zur deuteronomistischen Literatur* I (ed. N. LOHFINK), pp. 211-262.

———, "Deuteronomy," *IDBSup* 229-232.

———, "Der Glaube und die nächste Generation: Das Gottesvolk der Bibel als Lerngemeinschaft," *Das Jüdische am Christentum: Die verlorene Dimension.* Freiburg/Basel/Wien: Herder, 1987. Pp. 144-166.

———, "Glauben lernen in Israel," *Katechetische Blätter* 108 (1983) 84-99.

———, "Gott im Buch Deuteronomium," *La notion biblique de Dieu: Le Dieu de la Bible et le Dieu des philosophes* (BETL 41; ed. J. COPPENS). Leuven: University Press, 1976. Pp. 101-126.

———, *Das Hauptgebot: Eine Untersuchung literarischer Einleitungsfragen zu Dtn. 5-11* (AnBib 20). Rome: Biblical Institute Press, 1963.

———, *Höre, Israel! Auslegung von Texten aus dem Buch Deuteronomium* (Die Welt der Bibel 18). Düsseldorf: Patmos Verlag, 1965.

———, "Die ḥuqqîm ûmišpaṭîm im Buch Deuteronomium und ihre Neubegrenzung durch Dtn 12,1," *Bib* 70 (1989) 1-29.

———, "Kerygmata des deuteronomistischen Geschichtswerks," *Die Botschaft und die Boten* (FS. Hans Walter Wolff; ed. Jorg JEREMIAS and Lothar PERLITT). Neukirchen/Vluyn: Neukirchener Verlag, 1981. Pp. 87-100.

————, Review of *Das Bundesformular*, by Klaus BALTZER. In *Scholastik* 36 (1961) 419-425.

————, Review of *Deuteronomy and Tradition*, by E.W. NICHOLSON. In *Bib* 49 (1968) 106-110.

————, Review of *Literarkritik, formgeschichtliche und stilkritische Untersuchungen zum Deuteronomium*, by Josef G. PLÖGER. In *Bib* 49 (1968) 110-115.

————, Review of *Deuteronomium*, by Horst Dietrich PREUSS. In *TLZ* 108 (1983) 349-353.

————, *Rückblick im Zorn auf den Staat: Vorlesungen zu ausgewählten Schlüsseltexten der Bücher Samuel und Könige*. Frankfurt am Main: Hochschule Sankt Georgen, 1984.

————, "Die Sicherung der Wirksamkeit des Gotteswortes durch das Prinzip der Schriftlichkeit der Tora und durch das Prinzip der Gewaltenteilung nach den Ämtergesetzen des Buches Deuteronomium (Dt 16,18-18,22)," *Studien zum Deuteronomium und zur deuteronomistischen Literatur* I (ed. N. LOHFINK, 1990). Pp. 305-323. First printed in: *Testimonium Veritati* (FS. Wilhelm Kempf; ed. H. WOLTER) (Frankfurter Theologische Studien 7). Frankfurt: Knecht, 1971. P. 143-155.

————, (ed.) *Studien zum Deuteronomium und zur deuteronomistischen Literatur* I (SBAB 8). Stuttgart: Katholisches Bibelwerk, 1990.

————, "Verkündigung des Hauptgebots in der jüngsten Schicht des Deuteronomiums (Dt 4,1-40)," *BibLeb* 5 (1964) 247-256. Revised in: *Höre, Israel! Auslegung von Texten aus dem Buch Deuteronomium*, pp. 87-120. Reprinted in: *Studien zum Deuteronomium und zur deuteronomistischen Literatur* I (ed. N. LOHFINK, 1990), pp. 167-191.

————, "Die Wandlung des Bundesbegriffs im Buch Deuteronomium," *Gott in Welt* (FS. Karl Rahner; Hrsg. Herbert VORGRIMLER), I. Freiburg: Herder, 1964. Pp. 423-444.

————, "Wie stellt sich das Problem Individuum - Gemeinschaft in Deuteronomium 1,6-3,29?" *Scholastik* 35 (1960) 403-407. Reprinted in: *Studien zum Deuteronomium und zur deuteronomistischen Literatur* I (ed. N. LOHFINK, 1990), pp. 45-51.

————, "Zum 'kleinen geschichtlichen Credo' Dtn 26,5-9," *TP* 46 (1971) 19-39. Reprinted in: *Studien zum Deuteronomium und zur deuteronomistischen Literatur* I (ed. N. LOHFINK, 1990), pp. 263-290.

————, "Zum 'Numeruswechsel' in Dtn 3,21f.," *BN* 49 (1989) 39-52.

————, "Zur Dekalogfassung von Dt 5," *BZ*, N.F. 9 (1965) 15-32. Reprinted in: *Studien zum Deuteronomium und zur deuteronomistischen Literatur* I (ed. N. LOHFINK, 1990), pp. 193-209.

————, "Zur deuteronomischen Zentralisationsformel," *Bib* 65 (1984) 297-329.

————, "Zur neueren Diskussion über 2 Kön 22-23," *Das Deuteronomium* (ed. N. LOHFINK, 1985). Pp. 24-48.

LONG, Burke O., "Recent Field Studies in Oral Literature and the Question of *Sitz im Leben*," *Semeia* 5 (1976) 35-49.

————, "Two Question and Answer Schemata in the Prophets," *JBL* 90 (1971) 129-139.

LONG, Thomas G., "Committing Hermeneutical Heresy," *TToday* 44 (1987) 165-169.

Loza, José, "Les catéchèses étiologiques dans l'Ancien Testament," *RB* 78 (1971) 481-500.

Lundbom, Jack R., *Jeremiah: A Study in Ancient Hebrew Rhetoric* (SBLDS 18). Missoula, Mont.: Scholars Press, 1975.

——, "The Lawbook of the Josianic Reform," *CBQ* 38 (1976) 293-302.

Lust, J., "A. Van Hoonacker and Deuteronomy," *Das Deuteronomium* (ed. N. Lohfink, 1985). Pp. 13-23.

Lyonnet, Stanislaus, " 'La Circoncision du cœur, celle qui relève de l'Esprit et non de la lettre' (Rom 2:29)," *L'Évangile hier et aujourd'hui: Mélanges offerts au Professeur Franz-J. Leenhardt*. Genève: Labor et Fides, 1968. Pp. 87-97.

——, "De Modo Argumentandi ex Deut 30,11-14," *Quaestiones in Epistolam ad Romanos*. Series altera, editio tertia cum supplemento. Rome: Pontifical Biblical Institute, 1975. Pp. 94-106.

Lyons, John, *Language and Linguistics: An Introduction*. Cambridge: Cambridge University Press, 1981.

McBride, S. Dean, Jr., "Deuteronomium," *TRE* 8 (1981) 530-543.

——, "Polity of the Covenant People: The Book of Deuteronomy," *Int* 61 (1987) 229-244.

McCarthy, Dennis J., "$b^e r\hat{\imath}t$ in Old Testament History and Theology," *Bib* 53 (1972) 110-121.

——, *Old Testament Covenant: A Survey of Current Opinions*. Richmond, Virginia: John Knox Press, 1972.

——, Review of *Deuteronomy and the Deuteronomic School*, by Moshe Weinfeld. In *Bib* 54 (1973) 448-452.

——, *Treaty and Covenant*, 2nd ed. (AnBib 21A). Rome: Biblical Institute Press, 1981. 1st ed. 1963.

——, "II Samuel 7 and the Structure of the Deuteronomic History," *JBL* 84 (1965) 131-138.

——, "The Wrath of Yahweh and the Structural Unity of the Deuteronomistic History," *Essays in Old Testament Ethics: P.J. Hyatt Memorial* (ed. J.L. Crenshaw and J.T. Willis). New York: Ktav, 1974. Pp. 99-110.

McConville, J.G., *Law and Theology in Deuteronomy* (JSOTSS 33). Sheffield: JSOT Press, 1984.

McEvenue, Sean E., *The Narrative Style of the Priestly Writer* (AnBib 50). Rome: Biblical Institute Press, 1971.

Mack, Burton L., *Rhetoric and the New Testament* (GBS, New Testament Series). Minneapolis: Fortress, 1990.

McKane, W., "Poison, Trial by Ordeal and the Cup of Wrath," *VT* 30 (1980) 474-492.

McKay, J.W., "Man's Love for God in Deuteronomy and the Father/Teacher-Son/Pupil Relationship," *VT* 22 (1972) 426-435.

McKim, Donald K., ed., *A Guide to Contemporary Hermeneutics: Major Trends in Biblical Interpretation*. Grand Rapids, Mich.: Eerdmans, 1986.

Macky, Peter W., "The Coming Revolution: The New Literary Approach to New Testament Interpretation," *A Guide to Contemporary Hermeneutics* (ed. D. McKim, 1986). Pp. 263-269. Reprinted from: *The Theological Educator* 9 (Spring, 1979) 32-46.

McNamara, Martin, *The New Testament and the Palestinian Targum to the Pentateuch* (AnBib 27A). Rome: Biblical Institute Press, 1978.

Malfroy, Jean, "Sagesse et loi dans le Deutéronome," *VT* 15 (1965) 49-65.

Malina, Bruce J., "The Social Sciences and Biblical Interpretation," *Int* 36 (1982) 229-242.

Mandelkern, Solomon, *Veteris Testamenti Concordantiae Hebraicae atque Chaldaicae* (Editio altera locupletissime aucta et emendata cura F. Margolin). Graz: Akademische Druck- und Verlagsanstalt, 1955 (unchanged from the 1937 edition). 2 vols.

Maneli, Mieczyslaw, "The New Rhetoric and Dialectics," *RIP* 33 (1979) 216-238.

Manetti, Giovanni, *Le teorie del segno nell'antichità classica* (Strumenti Bompiani). Milano: Bompiani, 1987.

Marchese, Angelo, *Dizionario di retorica e di stilistica: Arte e artificio nell'uso delle parole: retorica, stilistica, metrica, teoria della letteratura,* 5th ed. Milano: Arnoldo Mondadori, 1989. 1st ed. 1978.

Martin-Achard, R., "גור," *THAT* I, 409-412.

Mason, Rex, "Some Echoes of the Preaching in the Second Temple? Tradition Elements in Zechariah 1-8," *ZAW* 96 (1984) 221-235.

Mathias, Dietmar, "'Levitische Predigt' und Deuteronomismus," *ZAW* 96 (1984) 23-49.

Mayes, A.D.H., *Deuteronomy* (New Century Bible Commentary). Grand Rapids: Wm. B. Eerdmans, 1979.

———, "Deuteronomy 4 and the Literary Criticism of Deuteronomy," *JBL* 100 (1981) 23-51.

———, "Deuteronomy: Law of Moses or Law of God?" *PIBA* 5 (1981) 36-54.

———, "Deuteronomy 29, Joshua 9, and the Place of the Gibeonites in Israel," *Das Deuteronomium* (ed. N. Lohfink, 1985). Pp. 321-325.

———, *The Story of Israel between Settlement and Exile: A Redactional Study of the Deuteronomistic History.* London: SCM, 1983.

Mejia, Jorge, "The Aim of the Deuteronomic Historian: A Reappraisal," *Proceedings of the Sixth World Congress of Jewish Studies,* I (Ed. A. Shinan). Jerusalem: World Union of Jewish Studies, 1977. Pp. 291-298.

Melugin, Roy F., "Muilenburg, Form Criticism, and Theological Exegesis," *Encounter with the Text: Form and History in the Hebrew Bible* (ed. M.J. Buss; SBLSS 8). Philadelphia/Missoula: Fortress/Scholars, 1979. Pp. 91-100.

Mendecki, Norbert, "Dtn 30,3-4 — nachexilisch?" *BZ,* N.F. 29 (1985) 267-271.

Merendino, Rosario P., "La via della vita (Dt 30, 15-20)," *ParSpV* 5 (1982) 35-51.

Merriam, Thomas, "Dissociation and the Literal Interpretation of the Bible," *DRev* 96 (1978) 79-84.

Messer Leon, Judah, *The Book of the Honeycomb's Flow: Sēpher Nōpheth Ṣūphīm.* Edited and translated by Isaac Rabinowitz. Ithaca, N.Y./ London: Cornell University Press, 1983.

Meyer, Michel (ed.), *De la métaphysique à la rhétorique: Essais à la mémoire de Chaïm Perelman.* Bruxelles: Éditions de l'Université de Bruxelles, 1986.

———, "Dialectique, rhétorique, herméneutique et questionnement: Les fondements du langage," *RIP* 33 (1979) 145-177.

MEYER, Michel and LEMPEREUR, Alain (ed.), *Figures et conflits rhétoriques.* Bruxelles: Éditions de l'Université de Bruxelles, 1990.

MEYNET, Roland, "Analyse rhétorique du prologue de Jean," *RB* 96 (1989) 481-510.

———, *L'analyse rhétorique: Une nouvelle méthode pour comprendre la Bible: Textes fondateurs et exposé systématique.* Paris: Éditions du Cerf (Initiations), 1989.

———, *Initiation à la rhétorique biblique: "Qui donc est le plus grand?"* Paris: Les Éditions du Cerf, 1982.

MILGROM, J., "The Alleged 'Demythologization and Secularization' in Deuteronomy," *IEJ* 23 (1973) 156-161.

MILLARD, Alan R., "An Assessment of the Evidence for Writing in Ancient Israel," *Biblical Archaeology Today: Proceedings of the International Congress on Biblical Archaeology: Jerusalem, April 1984* (ed. Avraham BIRAN et al.). Jerusalem: Israel Exploration Society, 1985. Pp. 301-312.

———, "The Question of Israelite Literacy," *Bible Review* 3 (3, 1987) 22-31.

MILLER, Patrick D., Jr., "'Moses My Servant': The Deuteronomic Portrait of Moses," *Int* 61 (1987) 245-255.

MINETTE DE TILLESSE, Georges, "Martin Noth et la Redaktionsgeschichte des livres historiques," *Aux grands carrefours de la révélation et de l'exégèse de l'Ancien Testament* (RechBib 8; ed. Ch. HAURET). Louvain: Desclée du Brouwer, 1967. Pp. 51-76.

———, "Sections 'tu' et sections 'vous' dans le Deutéronome," *VT* 12 (1962) 29-87.

MIRSKY, Aharon, "Stylistic Device for Conclusion in Hebrew," *Semitics* 5 (1977) 9-23.

MITCHELL, H.G., "The Use of the Second Person in Deuteronomy," *JBL* 18 (1899) 61-109.

MOLINIÉ, Georges, *La stylistique* (Que sais-je? 646), 2nd ed. Paris: Presses Universitaires de France, 1989.

MONTET, Ferdinand, *Le Deutéronome et la question de l'Hexateuque: étude critique et exégétique.* Paris: Fischbacher, 1891.

MORAN, William L., "The Ancient Near Eastern Background of the Love of God in Deuteronomy," *CBQ* 25 (1963) 77-87.

———, "Deuteronomy," *A New Catholic Commentary on Sacred Scripture* (ed. Reginald C. FULLER, Leonard JOHNSTON, & Conleth KEARNS). London: Nelson, 1969 (1st ed. 1953). Pp. 256-276.

———, Review of *Das Bundesformular,* by Klaus BALTZER. In *Bib* 43 (1962) 100-106.

———, Review of *Israel und die Völker: Eine Studie zum Deuteronomium,* by Otto BÄCHLI. In *Bib* 44 (1963) 375-377.

———, "Some Remarks on the Song of Moses," *Bib* 43 (1962) 317-327.

MORGAN, Robert and BARTON, John, *Biblical Interpretation* (Oxford Bible Series). Oxford: Oxford University Press, 1988.

MOULTON, Richard G., *The Literary Study of the Bible: An Account of the Leading Forms Represented in the Sacred Writings Intended for English Readers.* London: Isbister & Company, 1896.

MUILENBURG, James, "The Form and Structure of the Covenantal For-
mulations," *VT* 9 (1959) 347-365.
———, "Form Criticism and Beyond," *JBL* 88 (1969) 1-18.
———, "The Gains of Form Criticism in Old Testament Studies," *ExpTim* 71
(1960) 229-233.
———, "The Linguistic and Rhetorical Usages of the Particle in the Old
Testament," *HUCA* 32 (1961) 135-160.
———, "A Study in Hebrew Rhetoric: Repetition and Style," *VTS* 1 (1953)
97-111.
MULDER, M.J., "סְדֹם; עֲמֹרָה," *TWAT* V, 756-769.
MURPHY, Roland E., "Deuteronomy — A Document of Revival," *Concilium* 9
(1973) 26-36.
———, "The Old Testament as Scripture," *JSOT* 16 (1980) 40-44.
MURRAY, Donald, "Once Again *'t 'ḥd šbṭy yśr'l* in II Samuel 7:7," *RB* 94 (1987)
389-396.
MYERS, Jacob M., "The Requisites for Response: On the Theology of
Deuteronomy," *Int* 15 (1961) 14-31.
NATIONS, Archie L., "Historical Criticism and the Current Methodological
Crisis," *SJT* 36 (1983) 59-71.
NAVEH, Joseph, Response to "An Assessment of the Evidence for Writing in
Ancient Israel," by Alan R. MILLARD. In *Biblical Archaeology Today:
Proceedings of the International Congress on Biblical Archaeology:
Jerusalem, April 1984* (ed. Avraham BIRAN et al.). Jerusalem: Israel
Exploration Society, 1985. P. 354.
NELSON, Richard D., *The Double Redaction of the Deuteronomistic History*
(JSOTSS 18). Sheffield: JSOT Press, 1981.
NICHOLSON, E.W., *Deuteronomy and Tradition*. Oxford: Basil Blackwell, 1967.
———, "Deuteronomy's Vision of Israel," *Storia e tradizioni di Israele: Scritti
in onore di J. Alberto Soggin* (ed. Daniele GARRONE and Felice ISRAEL).
Brescia: Paideia, 1991. Pp. 191-203.
———, *Preaching to the Exiles: A Study of the Prose Tradition in the Book of
Jeremiah*. Oxford: Basil Blackwell, 1970.
NIDA, Eugene A., and REYBURN, William D., *Meaning across Cultures* (American
Society of Missiology Series 4). Maryknoll, N.Y.: Orbis, 1981.
NORRICK, Neal R., "Functions of Repetition in Conversation" *Text* 7 (1987)
245-264.
NORTH, R., "עָשָׁן," *TWAT* VI, 438-441.
NOTH, Martin, *Geschichte Israels,* 7th ed. Göttingen: Vandenhoeck and
Ruprecht, 1969. (1st ed. 1950).
———, *Überlieferungsgeschichte des Pentateuch*. Stuttgart: W. Kohlhammer,
1948.
———, *Überlieferungsgeschichtliche Studien*, I (Schriften der Königsberger
Gelehrten Gesellschaft 18). Halle: Max Niemeyer, 1943. English translation:
The Deuteronomistic History (JSOTSS 15). Sheffield: JSOT Press, 1981.
NÖTSCHER, Friedrich, "Bundesformular und 'Amtsschimmel': Ein kritischer
Überblick," *BZ,* N.F. 9 (1965) 181-214.
La nouvelle rhétorique. The New Rhetoric. Essays en hommage à Chaïm Perelman.
RIP 33 (1979) 1-342.

Ntagwarara, Jean, "Alliance d'Israël au pays de Moab (Dt 28,69-30,20):
Analyse exégétique, histoire rédactionnelle et théologie," Diss. Université
de Sciences Humaines de Strasbourg, 1983. (Director: B. Renaud).

O'Brien, Mark A., *The Deuteronomistic History Hypothesis: A Reassessment*
(OBO 92). Freiburg, Switzerland/Göttingen: Universitätsverlag/Vanden-
hoeck & Ruprecht, 1989.

Olbrechts-Tyteca, Lucie, "Les couples philosophiques: Une nouvelle
approche," *RIP* 33 (1979) 81-98.

Oléron, Pierre, *L'argumentation* (Que sais-je? 2087), 2nd ed. Paris: Presses
Universitaires de France, 1987. (1st ed. 1983).

Oliver, Robert T., *Culture and Communication: The Problem of Penetrating
National and Cultural Boundaries* (American Lecture Series 506).
Springfield, Ill.: Charles C. Tomas, 1962.

Ong, Walter J., *Oralità e scrittura: Le tecnologie della parola.* Translated by
Alessandra Calanchi. Bologna: Il Mulino, 1986.

Ormann, Gustav, "Die Stilmittel im Deuteronomium," *Festschrift für Leo
Baeck.* Berlin: 1938. Pp. 39-53.

Parunak, H. Van Dyke, "Oral Typesetting: Some Uses of Biblical Structure,"
Bib 62 (1981) 153-168.

———, "Some Axioms for Literary Architecture," *Semitics* 8 (1982) 1-16.

———, "Transitional Techniques in the Bible," *JBL* 102 (1983) 525-548.

Patrick, Dale and Scult, Allen, *Rhetoric and Biblical Interpretation* (JSOTSS
82; BLS 26). Sheffield: Almond Press, 1990.

Patte, Daniel, *What Is Structural Exegesis?* (GBS, New Testament Series).
Philadelphia: Fortress, 1976.

Paul, M.J., "Hilkiah and the Law (2 Kings 22) in the 17th and 18th Centuries:
Some Influences on W.M.L. de Wette," *Das Deuteronomium* (ed. N.
Lohfink, 1985). Pp. 9-12.

Peckham, Brian, *The Composition of the Deuteronomistic History* (HSM 35).
Atlanta: Scholars Press, 1985.

Pedersen, Johannes, *Israel: Its Life and Culture.* London: Geoffrey Cumberlege,
Oxford University Press, 1926. (Reprinted 1946). Vols. I-II.

Penna, Angelo, *Deuteronomio* (La Sacra Bibbia). Torino: Marietti, 1976.

Perdue, Leo G., "The Social Character of Paraenesis and Paraenetic
Literature," *Paraenesis: Act and Form, Semeia* 50 (1990), 5-39.

Perelman, Chaïm, *L'empire rhétorique: Rhétorique et argumentation.* Paris:
Librairie philosophique J. Vrin, 1977. English translation: *The Realm of
Rhetoric.* Translated by William Kluback. Notre Dame: University of
Notre Dame Press, 1982.

———, "Logique formelle et logique informelle," *De la métaphysique à la
rhétorique* (ed. Michel Meyer, 1986), pp. 15-21. Unedited text from a
conference given in 1981.

———, "The New Rhetoric: A Theory of Practical Reasoning," *The Great Ideas
Today.* Chicago: Encyclopaedia Britannica, 1970. Pp. 273-312. Reprinted
in: Chaim Perelman, *The New Rhetoric and the Humanities,* pp. 1-42.

———, *The New Rhetoric and the Humanities: Essays on Rhetoric and Its
Applications* (Synthese Library 140). Translated by William Kluback.
Dordrecht: D. Reidel, 1979.

————, "La philosophie du pluralisme et la nouvelle rhétorique," *RIP* 33 (1979) 5-17.

PERELMAN, Chaïm and OLBRECHTS-TYTECA, Lucie, *Traité de l'argumentation: La nouvelle rhétorique,* 5th ed. Bruxelles: Éditions de l'Université de Bruxelles, 1988. (First published in 1958.) English translation: *The New Rhetoric: A Treatise on Argumentation.* Translated by John Wilkinson and Purcell Weaver. Notre Dame/London: University of Notre Dame Press, 1969.

PERLITT, Lothar, *Bundestheologie im Alten Testament* (WMANT 36). Neukirchen: Neukirchener Verlag, 1969.

————, "Deuteronomium," *EKL* I, 823-825.

————, "Deuteronomium 1-3 im Streit der exegetischen Methoden," *Das Deuteronomium* (ed. N. LOHFINK, 1985). Pp. 149-163.

————, "'Ein einzig Volk von Brüdern': Zur deuteronomischen Herkunft der biblischen Bezeichnung 'Bruder,'" *Kirche: Festschrift für Günther Bornkamm* (ed. D. LÜHRMANN and G. STRECKER). Tübingen: J.C.B. Mohr (Paul Siebeck), 1980. Pp. 27-52.

PHILLIPS, Anthony, *Deuteronomy* (The Cambridge Bible Commentary on the New English Bible). Cambridge: The University Press, 1973.

PLATO, *Gorgias* (LCL 166). Greek text with English translation by W.R.M. Lamb. Cambridge, Mass./London: Harvard University Press/William Heinemann Ltd., 1983. (1st ed. 1925.)

————, *Phaedrus* (LCL 36). Greek text with English translation by Harold North Fowler. Cambridge, Mass./London: Harvard University Press/ William Heinemann Ltd., 1982. (1st ed. 1914.)

PLEBE, Armando, *Breve storia della retorica antica.* 2nd ed. (Universale Laterza 715). Bari: Editori Laterza, 1990. 1st edition published in 1968.

PLEBE, Armando and EMANUELE, Pietro, *Manuale di retorica* (Universale Laterza 720). Rome/Bari: Editori Laterza, 1989.

POLAND, Lynn, "The Bible and the Rhetorical Sublime," *The Bible as Rhetoric* (ed. Martin WARNER, 1990), pp. 29-47.

POLK, Timothy, "Paradigms, Parables, and *Měšālîm*: On Reading the *Mašāl* in Scripture," *CBQ* 45 (1983) 564-583.

POLZIN, Robert M., *Biblical Structuralism: Method and Subjectivity in the Study of Ancient Texts* (SBLSS 5). Philadelphia/Missoula: Fortress/Scholars Press, 1977.

————, "Deuteronomy," *The Literary Guide to the Bible* (ed. Robert ALTER and Frank KERMODE). London: Collins, 1987. Pp. 92-101.

————, *Moses and the Deuteronomist: A Literary Study of the Deuteronomic History.* Part One: *Deuteronomy, Joshua, Judges.* New York: Seabury, 1980.

PORTER, J.R., "The Legal Aspects of the Concept of 'Corporate Personality' in the Old Testament," *VT* 15 (1965) 361-380.

POWELL, Mark Allen, *What Is Narrative Criticism?* (GBS, New Testament Series). Minneapolis: Fortress, 1990.

PREMINGER, Alex and GREENSTEIN, Edward L., ed., *The Hebrew Bible in Literary Criticism.* New York: Ungar, 1986.

PREUSS, Horst Dietrich, *Deuteronomium* (Erträge der Forschung 164). Darmstadt: Wissenschaftliche Buchgesellschaft, 1982.

————, *Verspottung fremder Religionen im Alten Testament* (BWANT 92). Stuttgart: W. Kohlhammer, 1971.

————, "גִּלּוּלִים," *TWAT* II, 1-5.

————, "חוה," *TWAT* II, 784-794.

PRITCHARD, James B., ed., *Ancient Near Eastern Texts Relating to the Old Testament*. 3rd ed. with Supplement. Princeton, N.J.: Princeton University Press, 1969.

PSEUDO-LONGINUS, *Del Sublime*. Ed. and translated by Francesco DONADI. Greek text with Italian translation. Milano: Biblioteca Universale Rizzoli, 1991.

QUINTILIAN, *Institutio oratoria*. Latin text with Italian translation by Orazio Frilli. Bologna: Zanichelli 1982-1984. 5 volumes.

RABIN, Chaïm, "Discourse Analysis and the Dating of Deuteronomy," *Interpreting the Hebrew Bible: Essays in Honour of E.I.J. Rosenthal* (ed. J.A. EMERTON and Stefan C. REIF). Cambridge: Cambridge University Press, 1982. Pp. 171-177.

RABINOWITZ, Isaac C., ed. and trans., *The Book of the Honeycomb's Flow: Sēpher Nōpheth Ṣūphîm*. Cf. Judah MESSER LEON.

RADJAWANE, Arnold Nicolaas, "Das deuteronomistische Geschichtswerk: Ein Forschungsbericht," *TRu* 38 (1974) 177-216.

RANKIN, Oliver Shaw, "Alliteration in Hebrew Poetry," *JTS* 31 (1930) 285-291.

RAPHAEL, David D., "Perelman on Justice," *RIP* 33 (1979) 260-276.

RASHI, Cf. ROSENBAUM and SILBERMANN.

RAST, Walter E., *Tradition Hisory and the Old Testament* (GBS, Old Testament Series). Philadelphia: Fortress, 1972.

RAVASI, Gianfranco, "Benedizione e maledizione nell'alleanza: Dt 27-30," *ParSpV* 21 (1990) 47-51.

REBOUL, Olivier, "La figure et l'argument," *De la métaphysique à la rhétorique* (ed. Michel MEYER, 1986), pp. 175-187.

————, *Introduction à la rhétorique: Théorie et pratique* (Collectio premier cycle). Paris: Presses Universitaires de France, 1991.

————, *La rhétorique* (Que sais-je? 2133), 3rd ed. Paris: Presses Universitaires de France, 1984.

REITER, Josef, "Der Bundesschluß im Land Moab: Eine exegetische Studie zu Deuteronomium 29,1-20," Diss. Universität Wien, 1984. (Director: Georg Braulik).

RENAUD, Bernard, *Je suis un Dieu jaloux: Évolution sémantique et signification théologique de* qineʾah (LD 36). Paris: Cerf, 1963.

RENDTORFF, Rolf, "The Future of Pentateuchal Criticism," *Hen* 6 (1984) 1-14.

RENNES, Jean, *Le Deutéronome*. Genève: Labor et Fides, 1967.

"Rhetoric," *The Great Ideas: A Synopticon of Great Books of the Western World* (ed. Mortimer J. ADLER). Vol. 3: *The Great Ideas,* II. Chicago: Encyclopaedia Britannica, 1952. Pp. 645-664.

Rhetorica ad Alexandrum (LCL 317). Greek text with English translation by H. Rackham. Cambridge, Mass./London: Harvard University Press, 1983. First printed in 1937.

Rhetorica ad Herennium (LCL 403). Latin text with English translation by Harry Caplan. Cambridge, Mass: Harvard University Press, 1981.

RICE, Donald and SCHOFER, Peter, "Tropes and Figures: Symbolization and Figuration," *Semiotica* 35 - 1/2 (1981) 93-124.

RICŒUR, Paul, *La métaphore vive* (L'ordre philosophique). Paris: Éditions du Seuil, 1975. English translation: *The Rule of Metaphor: Multi-disciplinary Studies of the Creation of Meaning in Language.* Trans. Robert Czerny. Toronto: University of Toronto Press, 1975.

———, "Rhétorique - poétique - herméneutique," *De la métaphysique à la rhétorique* (ed. Michel MEYER, 1986), pp. 143-155.

RINGGREN, H.,"כֹּל," *TWAT* IV, 145-153.

———, "סָפָה," *TWAT* V, 906-908.

ROBERTSON, David, *The Old Testament and the Literary Critic* (GBS, Old Testament Series). Philadelphia: Fortress, 1977.

ROBINSON, Alan, "Process Analysis Applied to the Book of Deuteronomy," *ZAW* 96 (1984) 185-194.

ROFÉ, Alexander, "The Arrangement of the Laws in Deuteronomy," *ETL* 64 (1988) 265-287.

———, "The Covenant in the Land of Moab (Dt 28,69-30,20): Historico-literary, Comparative, and Formcritical Considerations," *Das Deuteronomium* (ed. N. LOHFINK, 1985). Pp. 310-320.

———, "Ephraimite Versus Deuteronomistic History," *Storia e tradizioni di Israele: Scritti in onore di J. Alberto Soggin* (ed. Daniele GARRONE and Felice ISRAEL). Brescia: Paideia, 1991. Pp. 221-235.

———, "The Monotheistic Argumentation in Deuteronomy IV 32-40: Contents, Composition and Text," *VT* 35 (1985) 434-445.

RÖMER, Thomas, *Israels Väter: Untersuchungen zur Väterthematik im Deuteronomium und in der deuteronomistischen Tradition* (OBO 99). Freiburg, Switzerland/Göttingen: Universitätsverlag/Vandenhoeck & Ruprecht, 1990.

ROSE, Ashley S., "The 'Principles' of Divine Election: Wisdom in 1 Samuel 16," *Rhetorical Criticism* (ed. J.J. JACKSON and M. KESSLER, 1974). Pp. 43-67.

ROSENBAUM, M. and SILBERMANN, A.M., et al., ed., *Pentateuch with Targum Onkelos, Haphtaroth and Rashi's Commentary.* Jerusalem: Feldheim, 1934.

ROSENFIELD, Lawrence W., "The Practical Celebration of Epideictic," *Rhetoric in Transition* (ed. E. WHITE, 1980). Pp. 131-155.

ROSNER, Dov, "The Simile and Its Use in the Old Testament," *Semitics* 4 (1974) 22-36.

ROTH, Wolfgang, "Deuteronomistisches Geschichtswerk/Deuteronomistische Schule," *TRE* 8 (1981) 543-552.

ROWLEY, H.H., "The Prophet Jeremiah and the Book of Deuteronomy," *Studies in Old Testament Prophecy.* Edinburgh: T. & T. Clark, 1950. Pp. 157-174.

SANDMEL, Samuel, "The Haggada within Scripture," *JBL* 80 (1961) 105-122. Reprinted in: *Old Testament Issues.* New York: Harper & Row, 1968. Pp. 94-118.

SASSON, J.M., "Wordplay in the OT," *IDBSup* 968-970.

SAUER, G., "כֹּל," *THAT* I, 828-830.

SAUSSURE, Ferdinand DE, *Cours de linguistique générale.* Paris: 1916. English translation: *Course in General Linguistics* (ed. Charles BALLY, Albert SECHEHAYE, and Albert RIEDLINGER). Translated by Wade Baskin. New York: McGraw Hill, 1959.

SAVAGE, Mary, "Literary Criticism and Biblical Studies: A Rhetorical Analysis of the Joseph Narrative," *Scripture in Context: Essays on the Comparative Method* (PTMS 34; ed. C. EVANS, W. HALLO, and J. WHITE). Pittsburgh: Pickwick Press, 1980. Pp. 79-100.

SCHARBERT, Joseph, " 'Fluchen' und 'Segnen' im Alten Testament," *Bib* 39 (1958) 1-26.

————, "אָלָה," *TWAT* I, 279-285.

SCHENKER, Adrian, "Unwiderrufliche Umkehr und neuer Bund: Vergleich zwischen der Wiederherstellung Israels in Dt 4,25-31; 30,1-14 und dem neuen Bund in Jer 31,31-34," *FZPhTh* 27 (1980) 93-106.

SCHLEY, Donald G., "Yahweh Will Cause You to Return to Egypt in Ships (Deuteronomy XXVIII 68)," *VT* 35 (1985) 369-372.

SCHMID, Hans Heinrich, "Ich will euer Gott sein, und ihr sollt mein Volk sein: Die sogenannte Bundesformel und die Frage nach der Mitte des Alten Testamentes," *Kirche: Festschrift für Günther Bornkamm* (ed. D. LÜHRMANN and G. STRECKER). Tübingen: J.C.B. Mohr (Paul Siebeck), 1980. Pp. 1-25.

SCHOFIELD, J.N., " 'All Israel' in the Deuteronomic Writers," *Essays and Studies Presented to Stanley Arthur Cook* (ed. D. Winton THOMAS). London: Taylor's Foreign Press, 1950. Pp. 25-34.

SCHOTTROFF, W., "זכר," *THAT* I, 507-518.

SCHÜSSLER FIORENZA, Elisabeth, "The Ethics of Biblical Interpretation: Decentering Biblical Scholarship," *JBL* 107 (1988) 3-17.

SCOTT, Robert L., "Intentionality in the Rhetorical Process," *Rhetoric in Transition* (ed. E. WHITE, 1980). Pp. 39-60.

SEITZ, Gottfried, *Redaktionsgeschichtliche Studien zum Deuteronomium* (BWANT 93). Stuttgart/Berlin/Köln/Mainz: W. Kohlhammer, 1971.

SIEGERT, Folker, *Argumentation bei Paulus gezeigt an Röm 9-11* (WUNT 34). Tübingen: J.C.B. Mohr (Paul Siebeck), 1985.

SILBERMAN, Lou H., "Listening to the Text," *JBL* 102 (1983) 3-26.

SIMONS, Herbert W., "Are Scientists Rhetors in Disguise? An Analysis of Discursive Processes Within Scientific Communities," *Rhetoric in Transition* (ed. E. WHITE, 1980). Pp. 115-130.

SIMPSON, D.P., *Cassell's New Latin Dictionary*. New York: Funk and Wagnalls, 1959.

SKWERES, Dieter Edward, "Das Motiv der Strafgrunderfragung in biblischen und neuassyrischen Texten," *BZ*, N.F. 14 (1970) 181-197.

————, *Die Rückverweise im Buch Deuteronomium* (AnBib 79). Rome: Biblical Institute Press, 1979.

SLOAN, Thomas and PERELMAN, Chaïm, "Rhetoric," *Encyclopaedia Britannica*, 15th ed. (1977) XV, 798-805.

SMEND, Rudolf, *Die Bundesformel* (Theologische Studien 68). Zürich: EVZ-Verlag, 1963.

————, "Deuteronomistisches Geschichtswerk," *EKL* I, 821-823.

————, *Die Entstehung des Alten Testaments*. Stuttgart: Kohlhammer, 1978.

————, "Das Gesetz und die Völker: Ein Beitrag zur deuteronomistischen Redaktionsgeschichte," *Probleme biblischer Theologie* (FS. Gerhard von Rad; ed H.W. WOLFF). München: Chr. Kaiser Verlag, 1971. Pp. 494-509.

————, "Questions about the Importance of the Canon in an Old Testament Introduction," *JSOT* 16 (1980) 45-51.

SMITH, George A., *The Legacy of Israel,* ed. Edwyn R. BEVAN and Charles SINGER. Oxford: Clarendon, 1927.

SNYMAN, Andreas H., "On Studying the Figures (*schēmata*) in the New Testament," *Bib* 69 (1988) 93-107.

SOARES-PRABHU, George, "The Historical Critical Method: Reflections on its Relevance for the Study of the Gospels in India Today," *Theologizing in India* (ed. M. AMALADOSS, T.K. JOHN, and G. GISPERT-SAUCH). Bangalore: Theological Publications in India, 1981. Pp. 314-367.

SOGGIN, J. Alberto, *Introduzione all'Antico Testamento: Dalle origini alla chiusura del Canone alessandrino,* 4th ed. (Biblioteca di cultura religiosa 14). Brescia: Paideia 1987.

————, "Kultätiologische Sagen und Katechese im Hexateuch," *VT* 10 (1960) 341-347.

————, *Storia d'Israele: Dalle origini a Bar Kochbà* (Biblioteca di Cultura Religiosa 44). Brescia: Paideia, 1984.

SPERBER, Alexander, *A Historical Grammar of Biblical Hebrew: A Presentation of Problems with Suggestions to their Solution.* Leiden: E.J. Brill, 1966.

SPIECKERMANN, Hermann, *Juda unter Assur in der Sargonidenzeit* (FRLANT 129). Göttingen: Vandenhoeck & Ruprecht, 1982.

SPIVEY, Robert A., "Structuralism and Biblical Studies: The Uninvited Guest," *Int* 28 (1974) 133-145.

STACHOWIAK, Lech, "Auf den Spuren der Paränese im Alten Testament," *ColT* 46 (1976; fasc. specialis) 59-80.

STÄHLI, H.-P., "חוה," *THAT* I, 530-533.

STEINMETZ, David C., "The Superiority of Pre-critical Exegesis," *TToday* 37 (1980) 27-38. Reprinted in: *A Guide to Contemporary Hermeneutics* (ed. D. McKIM, 1986). Pp. 65-77.

STOCK, Augustine, "Chiastic Awareness and Education in Antiquity," *BTB* 14 (1984) 23-27.

————, "The Limits of Historical-Critical Exegesis, *BTB* 13 (1983) 28-31.

STOCKER, Margarita, "Biblical Story and the Heroine," *The Bible as Rhetoric* (ed. Martin WARNER, 1990). Pp. 81-102.

STOLZ, F., "לב," *THAT* I, 861-867.

SUHAMY, Henri, *Les figures du style* (Que sais-je? 1889), 3rd ed. Paris: Presses Universitaires de France, 1988 (1st ed. 1981).

SUTHERLAND, Stewart, "History, Truth, and Narrative," *The Bible as Rhetoric* (ed. Martin WARNER, 1990). Pp. 105-116.

TALBERT, Charles H., "Artistry and Theology: An Analysis of the Architecture of Jn. 1,19-5,47," *CBQ* 32 (1970) 341-366.

TANNEN, Deborah, "Repetition in Conversation as Spontaneous Formulaicity," *Text* 7 (1987) 215-243.

TARELLO, Giovanni, "La nouvelle rhétorique et le droit: L'argument 'a cohaerentia' et l'analyse de la pratique des organes judiciaires," *RIP* 33 (1979) 294-302.

THOMPSON, J.A., *Deuteronomy: An Introduction and Commentary* (The Tyndale Old Testament Commentaries). Leicester/Downers Grove: Inter-Varsity Press, 1974.

Todorov, Tzvetan, "The Place of Style in the Structure of the Text," *Literary Style: A Symposium* (ed. S. Chatman, 1971). Pp. 29-39.

――――, "Synecdoques," *Sémantique de la poésie* (Points 103; ed. G. Genette and T. Todorov). Paris: Éditions de Seuil, 1979. Pp. 7-26.

Tournay, Raymond Jacques, *Voir et entendre Dieu avec les Psaumes; ou la liturgie prophétique du Second Temple à Jerusalem* (Cahiers de la revue biblique 24). Paris: J. Gabalda et Cie., 1988.

Trigg, Roger, " 'Tales Artfully Spun,' " *The Bible as Rhetoric* (ed. Martin Warner, 1990). Pp. 117-132.

Tucker, Gene M., *Form Criticism of the Old Testament* (GBS, Old Testament Series). Philadelphia: Fortress, 1971.

Ueding, Gert and Steinbrink, Bernd, *Grundriß der Rhetorik: Geschichte-Technik-Methode.* Stuttgart: J.B. Metzler, 1986.

Ullmann, Stephen, "Stylistics and Semantics," *Literary Style: A Symposium* (ed. S. Chatman, 1971). Pp. 133-152.

Valesio, Paolo, *Novantiqua: Rhetorics as a Contemporary Theory.* Bloomington: Indiana University Press, 1980.

Van Der Ploeg, J., "Les *šoṭerim* d'Israël," *OTS* 10 (1954) 185-196.

Van Goudoever, Jan, "The Liturgical Significance of the Date in Dt 1,3," *Das Deuteronomium* (ed. N. Lohfink, 1985). Pp. 145-148.

Van Leeuwen, Raymond C., "What Comes out of God's Mouth: Theological Wordplay in Deuteronomy 8," *CBQ* 47 (1985) 55-57.

Van Noorden, Sally, "Rhetorical Arguments in Aristotle and Perelman," *RIP* 33 (1979) 178-187.

Vanoni, Gottfried, "Der Geist und der Buchstabe. Überlegungen zum Verhältnis der Testamente und Beobachtungen zu Dtn 30,1-10," *BN* 14 (1981) 65-98.

Van Rooy, H.F., "Deuteronomy 28,69 - Superscript or Subscript?" *JNWS* 14 (1988) 215-222.

Van Seters, John, "Recent Studies on the Pentateuch: A Crisis in Method," *JAOS* 99 (1979) 663-672.

Vasoli, Cesare, "Topica, retorica e argomentazione nella 'prima filosofia' del Vico," *RIP* 33 (1979) 188-201.

Vermeylen, Jacques, "Les sections narratives de Deut 5-11 et leur relation à Ex 19-34," *Das Deuteronomium* (ed. N. Lohfink, 1985). Pp. 174-207.

Vickers, Brian, *In Defence of Rhetoric.* Oxford: Clarendon Press, 1988.

Vogels, Walter, "The Literary Form of 'The Question of the Nations,' " *EgT* 11 (1980) 159-176.

Von Rad, Gerhard, *Deuteronomium-Studien,* 2nd ed. (FRLANT 58). Göttingen: Vandenhoeck & Ruprecht, 1948. Reprinted in *Gesammelte Studien zum Alten Testament,* II (TBü 48; 1973). English translation: *Studies in Deuteronomy* (SBT 9). Translated by David Stalker. London: SCM, 1953.

――――, "Deuteronomy," *IDB* I, 831-838. New York: Abingdon Press, 1962.

――――, "Es ist noch eine Ruhe vorhanden dem Volke Gottes (Eine biblische Begriffsuntersuchung)," *Gesammelte Studien zum Alten Testament* I (TBü 8). München: Chr. Kaiser, 1965. First published in *Zwischen den Zeiten* 11 (1933) 104-111. English translation: "There Remains Still a Rest for the People of God: An Investigation of a Biblical Conception," *The Problem of the Hexateuch and Other Essays*. Translated by E.W. Trueman Dicken. Pp. 94-102.

————, "Das formgeschichtliche Problem des Hexateuch," *Gesammelte Studien zum Alten Testament* I, 9-86. First Published in BWANT 26. Stuttgart: W. Kohlhammer, 1938. English translation: "The Form-Critical Problem of the Hexateuch," *The Problem of the Hexateuch and Other Essays*. Translated by E.W. Trueman Dicken. London: SCM, 1966. Pp. 1-78.

————, *Das fünfte Buch Mose: Deuteronomium*, 3rd ed. (Das Alte Testament Deutsch [Neues Göttinger Bibelwerk] 8). Göttingen: Vandenhoeck & Ruprecht, 1978 (1st ed. 1964). English translation: *Deuteronomy: A Commentary* (Old Testament Library). Translated by Dorothea Barton. Philadelphia: Westminster, 1966.

————, *Gesammelte Studien zum Alten Testament* I (TBü 8). München: Chr. Kaiser Verlag, 1965.

————, *Gesammelte Studien zum Alten Testament* II (TBü 48). München: Chr. Kaiser Verlag, 1973.

————, "Josephsgeschichte und ältere Chokma," *Gesammelte Studien zum Alten Testament* I, 272-280. First published in *VTS* 1 (1953) 120-127. English translation: "The Joseph Narrative and Ancient Wisdom," *The Problem of the Hexateuch and Other Essays*, 292-300.

————, "Die levitische Predigt in den Büchern der Chronik," *Gesammelte Studien zum Alten Testament* I, 248-261. First published in *FS. Otto Procksch* (Leipzig: J.C. Hinrichs'sche Buchhandlung, 1934), pp. 113-124. English translation: "The Levitical Sermon in I and II Chronicles," *The Problem of the Hexateuch and Other Essays*, 267-280.

————, *Theologie des Alten Testaments*, 4th ed. Band I: *Die Theologie der geschichtlichen Überlieferungen Israels*. München: Chr. Kaiser, 1962. English translation: *Old Testament Theology*. Vol. I: *The Theology of Israel's Historical Traditions*. Translated by D.M.G. Stalker. London: SCM, 1975.

————, *Weisheit in Israel*. Neukirchen-Vluyn: Neukirchener Verlag, 1970. English translation: *Wisdom in Israel*. Translated by James D. Martin. Nashville/New York: Abingdon, 1972.

WARNER, Martin (ed.), *The Bible as Rhetoric: Studies in Biblical Persuasion and Credibility* (Warwick Studies in Philosophy and Literature). London/New York: Routledge, 1990.

————, "The Fourth Gospel's Art of Rational Persuasion," *The Bible as Rhetoric* (ed. Martin WARNER, 1990). Pp. 153-177.

WATSON, Wilfred G.E., *Classical Hebrew Poetry: A Guide to Its Techniques* (JSOTSS 26), 2nd ed. Sheffield: JSOT Press, 1984, 1986.

WATTS, John D.W., "The Deuteronomic Theology," *RevExp* 74 (1977) 321-336.

WEBSTER, Edwin C., "The Rhetoric of Isaiah 63-65," *JSOT* 47 (1990) 89-102.

WEINFELD, Moshe, "*Be* rît," — Covenant vs. Obligation," *Bib* 56 (1975) 120-128.

————, *Deuteronomy and the Deuteronomic School*. Oxford: Clarendon Press, 1972.

————, *Deuteronomy 1-11: A New Translation with Introduction and Commentary* (AB 5). New York: Doubleday, 1991.

————, "Deuteronomy — The Present State of Inquiry," *JBL* 86 (1967) 249-262.

————, "The Emergence of the Deuteronomic Movement: The Historical Antecedents," *Das Deuteronomium* (ed. N. LOHFINK, 1985). Pp. 76-98.

————, "Judge and Officer in Ancient Israel and in the Ancient Near East," *IsrOrSt* 7 (1977) 65-88.

————, "Traces of Assyrian Treaty Formulae in Deuteronomy," *Bib* 46 (1965) 417-427.

————, "בְּרִית," *TWAT* I, 781-808.

WELLEK, Rene, *Concepts of Criticism.* New Haven/London: Yale University Press, 1963.

WELLEK, Rene and WARREN, Austin, *Theory of Literature,* 3rd ed. Harmondsworth, Middlesex: Penguin Books, 1963. Reprinted 1985, 1st ed. 1942.

WENHAM, Gordon, "The Date of Deuteronomy: Linch-pin of Old Testament Criticism," *Them* 10 (1985) 15-20.

WENHAM, Gordon and McCONVILLE, J.G., "Drafting Techniques in Some Deuteronomic Laws," *VT* 30 (1980) 248-251.

WHITE, Eugene E., "Rhetoric as Historical Configuration," *Rhetoric in Transition* (ed. E. WHITE, 1980). Pp. 7-20.

————, (ed.) *Rhetoric in Transition: Studies in the Nature and Uses of Rhetoric.* University Park/London: Pennsylvania University Press, 1980.

WHITE, Leland J., "Historical and Literary Criticism: A Theological Response," *BTB* 13 (1983) 32-34.

WIDENGREN, Geo., *Literary and Psychological Aspects of the Hebrew Prophets.* Uppsala: A.-B. Lundequistska, 1948.

WILDER, Amos, "Scholars, Theologians, and Ancient Rhetoric, " *JBL* 75 (1956) 1-11.

WIMSATT, W.K., "The Intentional Fallacy," in *The Verbal Icon.* New York, 1965. Pp. 3-18.

WINK, Walter, *The Bible in Human Transformation: Toward a New Paradigm for Biblical Study.* Philadelphia: Fortress, 1973.

WISEMAN, D.J., *The Vassal Treaties of Esarhaddon, Iraq* 20 (1958) 1-99.

WOLFF, Hans Walter, *Anthropologie des Alten Testaments.* München: Chr. Kaiser Verlag, 1973.

————, "Das Kerygma des deuteronomistischen Geschichtswerks," *ZAW* 73 (1961) 171-186.

WRIGHT, Addison G., "The Literary Genre Midrash," *CBQ* 28 (1966) 105-138, 417-457.

WRIGHT, G. Ernest, *Deuteronomy, IB* II, 311-537. New York: Abingdon Press, 1953.

————, "The Lawsuit of God: A Form-Critical Study of Deuteronomy 32," *Israel's Prophetic Heritage: Essays in Honor of James Muilenburg* (ed. Bernhard W. ANDERSON & W. HARRELSON). New York: Harper & Brothers, 1962. Pp. 26-67.

WUELLNER, Wilhelm, "Greek Rhetoric and Pauline Argumentation," *Early Christian Literature and the Classical Intellectual Tradition: In Honorem Robert M. Grant* (Théologie Historique 53; ed. William R. SCHOEDEL and Robert L. WILKIN). Paris: Éditions Beauchesne, 1979. Pp. 177-188.

————, "Paul as Pastor: The Function of Rhetorical Questions in First Corinthians," *L'Apôtre Paul: Personnalité, style et conception du ministère* (BETL 73; ed. A. VANHOYE). Leuven: University Press, 1986. Pp. 49-77.

————, "Paul's Rhetoric of Argumentation in Romans: An Alternative to the Donfried-Karris Debate over Romans," *The Romans Debate* (ed. Karl P. DONFRIED). Minneapolis: Augsburg, 1977. Pp. 152-174. Originally published in *CBQ* 38 (1976) 330-351.

————, "Where Is Rhetorical Criticism Taking Us?" *CBQ* 49 (1987) 448-463.

ZIMMERLI, Walther, "Erkenntnis Gottes nach dem Buch Ezechiel," *Gottes Offenbarung: Gesammelte Aufsätze zum Alten Testament* (TBü 19). München: Chr. Kaiser, 1963. First published in ATANT 27 (1954).

ZOBEL, H.-J., "יִשְׂרָאֵל," *TWAT* III, 986-1012.

ZOHARY, Michael, *Plants of the Bible*. Cambridge: Cambridge University Press, 1982.

ZORELL, Franciscus et al. (ed.), *Lexicon hebraicum Veteris Testamenti*. Rome: Biblical Institute Press, 1989. First published 1940.

ZYSKIND, Harold, Introduction to *The New Rhetoric and the Humanities: Essays on Rhetoric and Its Applications* (Synthese Library 140), by Chaïm PERELMAN. Dordrecht: D. Reidel, 1979. Pp. ix-xxi.

————, "The New Rhetoric and Formalism," *RIP* 33 (1979) 18-32.

GLOSSARY

The following definitions are largely citations of or adaptations from E. Corbett, *Classical Rhetoric for the Modern Student,* 2nd ed. (New York 1971); R. Lanham, *A Handlist of Rhetorical Terms: A Guide for Students of English Literature* (Berkeley 1968); and Ch. Perelman and L. Olbrechts-Tyteca, *The New Rhetoric: A Treatise on Argumentation* (Notre Dame, Ind. 1969).

Accumulation: Cf. amplification.

Adjunctio: The use of one verb to express two similar ideas at the beginning or end of successive clauses.

Alliteration: Repetition of initial or medial consonants in two or more adjacent words.

Amplification: The collecting or piling up of words, phrases, or longer sections of text with the aim of keeping the subject present in the thoughts of the audience.

Anacoluthon: Ending of a sentence with a different construction from that with which it began.

Anaphora: Repetition of the same word or group of words at the beginnings of successive clauses.

Anastrophe: Inversion of natural or usual word order.

Annomination: König's term for a strong form of alliteration which is built upon etymologically related terms.

Antonym: A word that is the opposite of another in meaning.

Aposiopesis: Cf. ellipsis.

Apostrophe: Breaking off discourse to address directly some person or thing either present or absent.

Apposition: Placing side by side two co-ordinate elements, the second of which serves as an explanation or modification of the first.

Argument a pari: Conceived as an identification, this argument deals with the application to another species of the same genus of what can be asserted about some particular species.

Argument by analogy: One which is based on the resemblance of structures, such as: A is to B as C is to D.

Argument by transitivity: One which makes it possible to infer that because a relation holds between A and B and between B and C, it therefore holds between A and C.

Argument of comparison: One in which several objects are considered in order to evaluate them through their relations to each other. The idea of measure underlies these arguments.

Argument of direction: One which guards against the use of the device of stages: if you give in this time, you will have to give in a little more next time, and heaven knows where you will stop. It answers the question: What are you driving at?

Argument of division: One based on the notion that a whole is the sum of its parts.

Argument of reciprocity: One which aims at giving the same treatment to two situations which are counterparts of each other. It requires using the concept of symmetry.

Argument of unlimited development: One which insists on the possibility of always going further in a certain direction without being able to foresee a limit to this direction, and this progress is accompanied by a continuous increase of value.

Argument of waste: One which consists in saying that, as one has already begun a task and made sacrifices which would be wasted if the enterprise were given up, one should continue in the same direction.

Argument, pragmatic: One which permits the evaluation of an act or an event in terms of its favorable or unfavorable consequences.

Arguments based on the structure of reality: These arguments make use of reality to establish a relationship between accepted judgments and those one wishes to promote. Most arguments of this type appeal either to relations of *succession* (cause and effect, pragmatic arguments, direction, and development) or of *coexistence* (which unite a person to his or her actions, a group to its members, or an essence to its manifestations, arguments by authority).

Arguments which establish the structure of reality: These arguments normally establish relations through particular cases (example, illustration, model) or through reasoning by analogy or metaphor.

Arrangement: *Dispositio* or τάξις. That part of rhetoric concerned with the effective and orderly organization of a written or spoken discourse.

Association, argumentation by: Processes which bring separate elements together and establish some kind of unity among them. For Perelman and Olbrechts-Tyteca there are three general kinds of arguments which establish such liaisons: quasi-logical arguments, arguments that are based on the structure of reality, and arguments which establish the structure of reality.

Assonance: The repetition of similar vowel sounds.

Asyndeton: Deliberate omission of conjunctions between a series of related words or clauses.

Auxesis (also *climax* or *incrementum*): Words or clauses placed in an order of increasing importance.

Brachyology: Brevity in speech or writing; an abbreviated construction.

Chiasm: Inverted parallelism — a passage in which the second part is inverted and balanced against the first. It can refer to the reversal of grammatical structures, sounds, or words in successive phrases or clauses. Some consider a pattern of A B C / C'B'A' to be chiastic, although others insist that a pivotal theme or crossing point is necessary to make a true chiasm (A B C X C'B'A').

Climax: Cf. **auxesis**.

Commoratio: Emphasizing a strong point by repeating it several times in different words.

Conclusion: Cf. **peroration**.

Conduplicatio: Repetition of a word or words in succeeding clauses.

Confirmation (*amplificatio*): The fifth part of the seven-part classical oration. This was the main part of the speech, the one in which the pros and cons of the argument were brought out; that is, this was the proof.

Confutation: Cf. **refutation**.

Congeries: Word heaps; accumulation.

Deductive Reasoning: Logical argumentation which begins with general premises, from which it draws specific conclusions.

Deliberative genre: Also known as *political, hortatory,* and *symbouleutic* rhetoric. For the ancient Greeks this was the rhetorical genre in which one deliberated about public affairs and politics. More generally, it is that in which we seek to persuade someone to do something or to accept our point of view.

Demonstratio (also *descriptio, hypotyposis,* and ἐνάργεια): Vivid description.

Descriptio: Cf. **demonstratio**.

Dialogism: Fictitious attribution of words to a group of persons engaged in dialogue.

Dispositio: Cf. **arrangement**.

Dissociation, argumentation by: Processes of argumentation which bring about a separation.

Divisio: Division into kinds or classes.

Double hierarchy argument: One in which hierarchies are presented so closely that one serves as the criterion or definition of the other.

Ellipsis: Deliberate omission of a word or words which are readily implied by the context.

Elocutio: The third part of rhetoric, it concerns style. For the ancients *elocutio* was the linguistic expression of the ideas "found" in *inventio*.

Enallage: Substitution of one case, person, gender, number, tense, mood, or part of speech for another.

Enthymeme: A syllogism with one premise (usually the major) omitted; a statement with a supporting reason.

Epanalepsis: Repetition at the end of a clause of the word or group of words that occurred at the beginning of the clause.

Epideictic genre: Also known as *demonstrative, declamatory, panegyrical,* or *ceremonial* oratory. It is the oratory of display, or praise and blame. It is concerned with the reinforcement of values.

Epiphora: Cf. **epistrophe**.

Epistrophe: Repetition of the same word or group of words at the ends of successive clauses.

Ethos: That mode of argumentation concerned with the credibility or moral character of the speaker or writer.

Exordium: The first part of the seven-part classical oration. It caught the audience's attention while introducing the subject.

Exposition (*definitio* or *explicatio*): The third part of the seven-part classical oration. It defines terms and opens issues to be proved.

Figure: Any device or pattern of language in which meaning is changed or enhanced.

Figure of choice: A rhetorical device which imposes or suggests that a choice or a judgment must be made.

Figure of communion: A rhetorical device which increases a sense of solidarity (communion) with the audience.

Figure of presence: A rhetorical device which makes an object present in the mind.

Forensic genre: Also known as *legal* or *judicial* oratory. This was the oratory of lawyers in the courtroom, but it can also refer to any kind of discourse in which a person seeks to defend or condemn someone's actions.

Homoioptoton: The use of various words in a sentence or verse with similar case endings.

Homoioteleuton: The use of similar endings in a clause.

Hyperbaton: A pronounced distortion of syntax for purposes of emphasis.

Hyperbole: The use of exaggerated terms for the purpose of emphasis or heightened effect.

Hypotyposis: Cf. **demonstratio**.

Illustratio: Vivid representation or description.

Illustration: Whereas an example is designed to establish a rule, the role of illustration is to strengthen adherence to a known and accepted rule.

Inclusion (*inclusio*): A three-membered (A B A') chiasm whose outer members are short, compared with the center member.

Incompatibility: A state in which two assertions exist, between which a choice must be made.

Incrementum: Cf. **auxesis**.

Inductive reasoning: Logical argumentation which uses a series of particular examples to draw a general conclusion.

Interpretatio: A repetition or amplification in other words.

Invention: *Inventio* or εὕρεσις. That part of rhetoric concerned with finding arguments. It has to do with the planning of a discourse.

Isocolon: Similarity not only of structure but also of length.

Logos: That mode of argumentation concerned with rational appeal.

Maxim: A short pithy statement of a general truth.

Merismus: A figure which reduces a complete series to (usually) two of its constituent elements. Thus it represents a whole or totality through the detailing of some of its parts. When two named species exhaust the whole genus, the merismus assumes the form of a *polar expression*.

Metaphor: Implied comparison between two things of unlike nature.

Metonymy: Substitution of some attributive or suggestive word for what is actually meant. This often associates causes and effects, the abstract and the concrete, and moral qualities with the physical.

Narration (*narratio* or *praecognitio*): The second part of the seven-part classical oration. It sets forth the facts or gives the history of the problem.

Palindrome: A word, sentence, or verse that is the same read forward or backward.

Parenthesis: A word, phrase, or sentence inserted as an aside in a sentence that is complete in itself.

Paronomasia: Punning, that is, the use of words alike in sound but different in meaning; playing on the sounds and meanings of words.

Partitio: Cf. **proposition**.

Pathos: That mode of argumentation concerned with emotional appeal.

Peristasis: Amplifying by describing attendant circumstances.

Peroration (*peroratio* or *epilogus*): The last part (conclusion) of the seven-part classical oration. This was often an *impassioned* summary, not simply a review of previous arguments.

Personification: An animal or inanimate object is represented as having human attributes or is addressed as if it were human.

Polyptoton: Repetition of words derived from the same root.

Polysyndeton: Deliberate use of many conjunctions.

Prooemium: Cf. **exordium**.

Proof: The presentation of evidence and arguments in a causal chain intended to pull the mind toward belief.

Proposition (*partitio*): The fourth part of the seven-part classical oration. It briefly states the proposition to be proved or the problem to be solved.

Prosopopoeia: Cf. **personification**.

Quasi-logical arguments: These arguments are similar to the formal reasoning of logic or mathematics. They include those which involve incompatibility, identity, definition, tautology, reciprocity, division, dilemma, weights and measures, probabilities, and comparisons.

Refutation (confutation, *refutatio,* or *reprehensio*): The sixth part of the seven-part classical oration. This part answered the opponent's objections.

Rhetoric: A theory of argumentation whose aim is to elicit or increase the adherence of an audience to theses presented for its consent.

Rhetorical question: Asking a question, not for the purpose of eliciting an answer but for the purpose of indirectly asserting or denying something.

Rule of justice: Identical treatment for beings or situations of the same kind.

Scheme: A deviation from the ordinary pattern or arrangement of words.

Sermocinatio: Fictitious attribution of words to a person.

Simile: Explicit comparison between two things of unlike nature.

Synecdoche: A figure of speech in which a part stands for the whole.

Synonym: A word having the same or almost the same meaning as some other word.

Tautology: Repetition of the same idea in different words.

Tautology, apparent: A formal identity between two terms which cannot be identical if the statement is to be of any interest. Statements such as "business is business" or "boys will be boys" are examples of apparent tautologies.

Topics (*Loci* or τόποι): Tested and approved ways of investigating a subject and conducting an argument. They are both the stuff of which arguments are made and the form of those arguments.

Trope: A rhetorical device which involves a deviation from the ordinary and principal meaning of a word.

INDEX OF BIBLICAL REFERENCES

AUTHOR INDEX

Achtemeier, E. 8
Aharoni, Y. 17
Albright, W. 30
Alonso Schökel, L. 18, 40, 109, 154, 220
Alter, R. 18, 40, 75, 131
Amsler, S. 17, 114
Andersen, F. 165
Anderson, B. 18, 40, 42, 160
Andrews, J. 74
Aristotle 19, 45, 49, 50, 53-55, 57-59, 64,
   68, 69, 73-74, 83, 84, 111, 122, 126, 128,
   146, 151, 164, 206
Arnold, C. 46, 48, 51, 52, 57-59, 83, 84
Augustine 45, 68, 74, 129

Ball, I. 43
Baltzer, K. 21, 34
Bar-Efrat, S. 173, 175
Barilli, R. 48,75
Barr, J. 40
Barthélemy, D. 94
Barthes, R. 50, 61, 64, 69, 126, 209
Barton, J. 40, 41, 109
Beaujour, M. 51, 72
Bee, R. 13, 14, 20, 29, 33
Begg, C. 13-15, 35, 36, 94
Bertholet, A. 14
Besters, A. 86
Beyerlin, W. 16, 24
Bitzer, L. 73, 109-111
Black, C.C. 43, 45, 51, 65, 74
Black, E. 46, 48, 50, 57, 59, 60, 67, 74, 76,
   109
Blair, E. 3, 9, 10, 20, 28
Blau, J. 149
Blenkinsopp, J. 40
Boccaccio, P. 160
Boorer, S. 41
Booth, W. 43, 46, 47, 59, 83, 84, 87, 111,
   120, 146, 210
Boston, J. 25
Brandt, W. 48, 50, 51, 56, 57, 59-61, 64,
   70-72, 83, 84, 131, 146, 147, 221, 236

Braulik, G. 7, 8, 13, 14, 16, 19, 21, 22, 24,
   28, 36, 43, 81, 85, 88, 102, 219
Breck, J. 175
Breit, H. 3, 7, 8, 13, 15, 16, 18, 32, 102, 144

Brekelmans, C. 3, 20, 26
Brinton, A. 109, 111
Brongers; H.A. 131, 228
Brown, S. 40
Brown, F.; Driver, S.R.; &Briggs, C. 96, 141
Brown, R. 48, 49, 87
Bryant, D. 47
Buchholz, J. 28, 96
Bühlmann, W. 221
Buis, P. 2-7, 10, 12-16, 20, 27, 28, 32, 35,
   36, 41, 86, 87, 94, 103, 114, 127, 128,
   131, 141, 149, 151, 152, 154, 166, 172,
   175, 192, 205, 237, 238, 240
Bullinger, E. 74, 221
Burke, K. 49, 50, 55, 68, 72, 73, 83, 93,
   109, 122, 129
Buss, M. 109

Carlson, R.A. 152
Casanowicz, I. 222
Cato 48
Cazelles, H. 11, 13, 28, 40, 85, 96, 166
Chaignet, A.-E. 61, 65, 136, 217
Childs, B. 10, 31, 40
Cholewinski, A. 17, 31-36, 113, 150-152,
   157, 172, 174, 175, 178
Christensen, D. 17, 18, 25
Cicero 45, 48, 49, 54-56, 58, 59, 61, 64-70,
   83, 84, 111, 128, 140, 146
Claburn, W. 3, 5, 7, 8, 19
Clements, R.E. 2, 4, 6-8, 13, 27, 28, 85
Clines, D. 43
Coats, G. 40
Cogan, M. 29
Cohen, M. 102
Condon, J. and Yousef, F. 51, 74, 146, 150,
   217
Conroy, C. 219

SUBJECT INDEX

a pari arguments 156, 159, 197
accentuation 130, 139, 145, 200, 201
accumulation 135-139, 186, 193
adjunctio 130
all Israel 13, 21, 85, 86, 88-90, 93, 97, 99, 101, 235, 239
alliteration 222, **223**
amplification 52, 55, 80, 81, 130, **135-139**, 145, 181, 182, 183, 185, 186, 187, 188, 189, 191, 193, 194, 195, 196, 197, 198, 199, 200, 201, 202, 204, 205, 225, 237
anacoluthon 193, 223
analogy 52, 63, 163, 164
anaphora 71, 130, 133, 134, 197, 198, **223-224**
anastrophe **224**
annomination 222
anti-model 164, 190, 191, 204, 221
antonym 138, 142, 194, 212, 215, 221, **224**
aposiopesis 154, 227
apostrophe 12, 71, 130
apparent tautology 158, 167, 182, 188
apposition **225**
arguments
   a pari 156, 159, 197
   based on the structure of reality 156, **160-163**, 181, 240
   by transitivity 156, 157
   of comparison 158, 159
   of division 63, 123, 135, 136, 156, 159, 160, 200, 205
   of reciprocity 156, 157
   of unlimited development 161, 163
   quasi-logical 52, 63, 135, **156-160**, 167, 169, 180, 186, 197
   which establish the structure of reality 156, **163-166**
argumentation 51-53, 57, 60
   modes of **58-61**
arrangement **63-66**, 171, 173, 180, 203
association 62-63, 78
assonance **225**
asyndeton **225-226**

audience 10-12, 28, 45, 47, 57-62, 71, 72, 78, **83-88**, 89-108, 110-111, 126, 127, 128, 129, 140, 157, 180, 181, 183, 185, 186, 187, 192, 195, 196, 201, 203, 204, 205, 206, 217-218, 219, 220, 238-240
aural **16-19**
auxesis 189, **226**
brachyology 222
chiasm 75, 175, 176, 178, 179, 226
climax 71, 226
commonplaces **61-62**
commoratio 216
conduplicatio 130, 226
confirmation 65
confutation 65
copia 136
covenant 7, 9, 19, 20, 27, 33, 36, 87, 102, 107, 112, 113, 123, 124, 137, 148, 152, 157, 158, 159, 162, 167, 180, 181, 185-186, 187, 195, 203, 235, 238-241
convention 120
cult 19-20, 33, 93, 95, 99, 114
deductive reasoning 60
demonstratio 59, 129, 130, 137, 139, 166, 193, 195, 226
descriptio 226
Deuteronomistic 5, 11, 14, 30, 33, 79, 86
diachronic 31, 39, 41, 77, 81
dialogism 12
didacticism **8-10**, 24, 26, 112
direct address **10-12**, 17, 18, 32, 217-218
dispositio 48, 56, 63-66, 75, 171, 180, 203, 206
dissociation 52, 62, 78, 156, 157, **167-168**, 172, 181, 182, 188, 190, 196, 204, 239, 240
divisio 64, 136, 160, 182, 185, 186, 188, 189, **226-227**
division, argument of 63, 123, 135, 136, 156, 159, 160, 200, 205
double discourse 91-92
ellipsis 154
elocutio 48, 56, 67-72, 75, 209-210

Finito di stampare il 23 luglio 1993
Tipografia Poliglotta della Pontificia Università Gregoriana
Piazza della Pilotta, 4 – 00187 Roma